by Arina Tanemura

SAKURA HIME
The Legend of Princess Sakura

2

SAKURA HIME
The Legend of Princess Sakura

CONTENTS

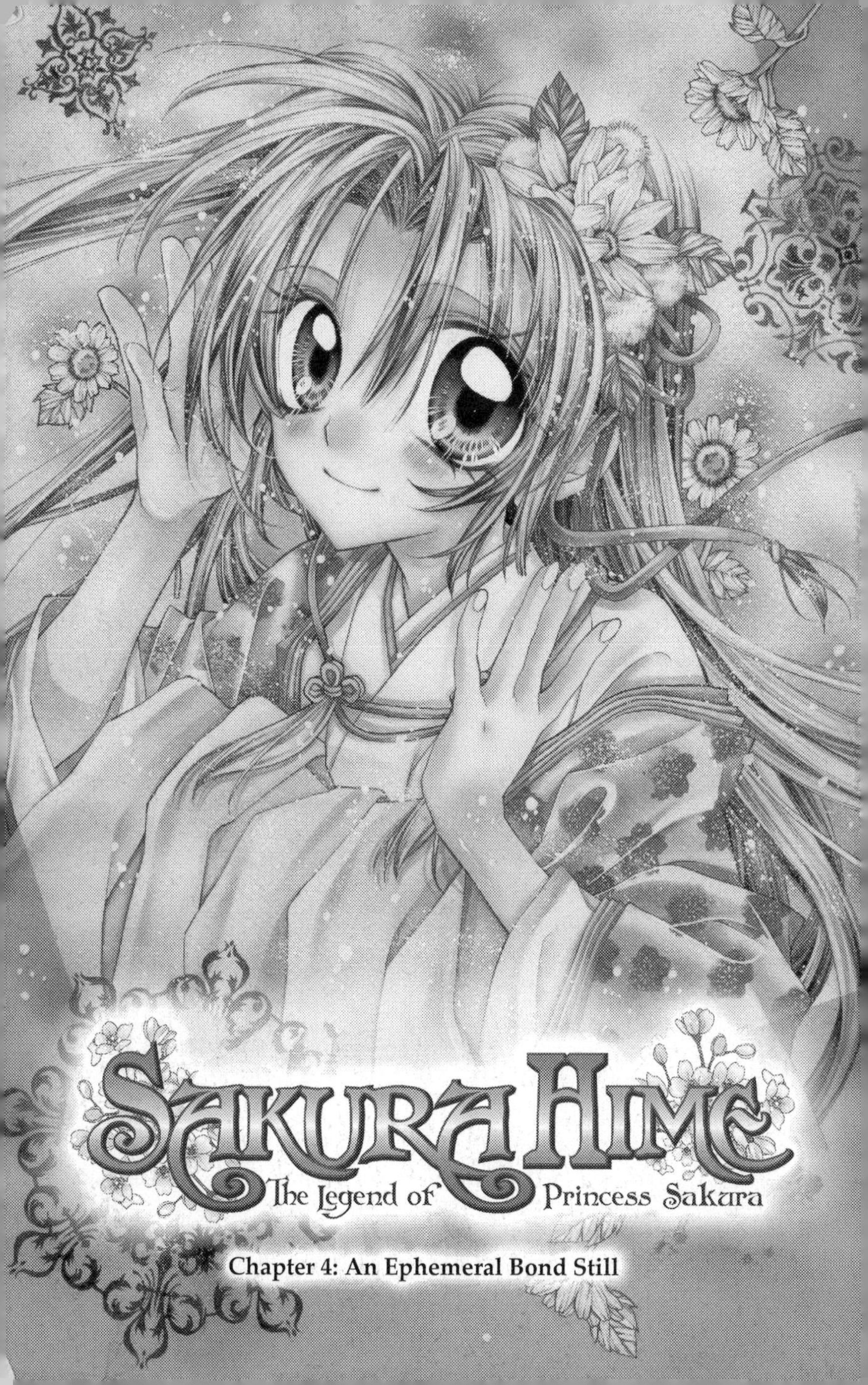
Sakura Hime
The Legend of Princess Sakura
Chapter 4: An Ephemeral Bond Still

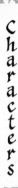

Characters

AOBA

Prince Oura, the emperor's son. He hates Princess Sakura!...?!

PRINCESS SAKURA

Princess Kaguya's granddaughter who has the power to defeat youko. She is Aoba's betrothed.

KOHAKU

A ninja. Klutz.

HAYATE

Kohaku's childhood friend. He used to be human.

ASAGIRI

Princess Sakura's friend.

BYAKUYA

A priestess who knows Princess Sakura's secret.

SAKURA HIME
The Legend of Princess Sakura

Story Thus Far

Heian era. Princess Sakura is 14 years old. She is suddenly ordered by Aoba to leave the countryside where she grew up and come to the capital to prepare for marriage. Determined to choose her own fate, Sakura runs away only to find herself looking up at the full moon, which she had been strictly forbidden to do. As a result, Sakura is attacked by a man-eating youko, or demon, and learns from the priestess Byakuya that she is actually Princess Kaguya's granddaughter and the only person who is able to wield the mystic sword Chizakura that has the power to defeat the youko. And at the same time, she finds out that her soul symbol, the kanji that reveals her fate, is "destroy"...

Aoba finds out about her soul symbol, and he tries to kill her. Heavily wounded, Sakura is saved by the ninja Kohaku. Sakura's wounds heal in just three days and she is tormented by the fact that she may too be a monster like a youko.

After seeing Kohaku fight against the youko, Sakura is inspired to become a princess who can protect her country. She heads for the ninja village in pursuit of a youko, but it is a trap Aoba has set for her. Aoba confronts her and tells her to reveal her true self...?!

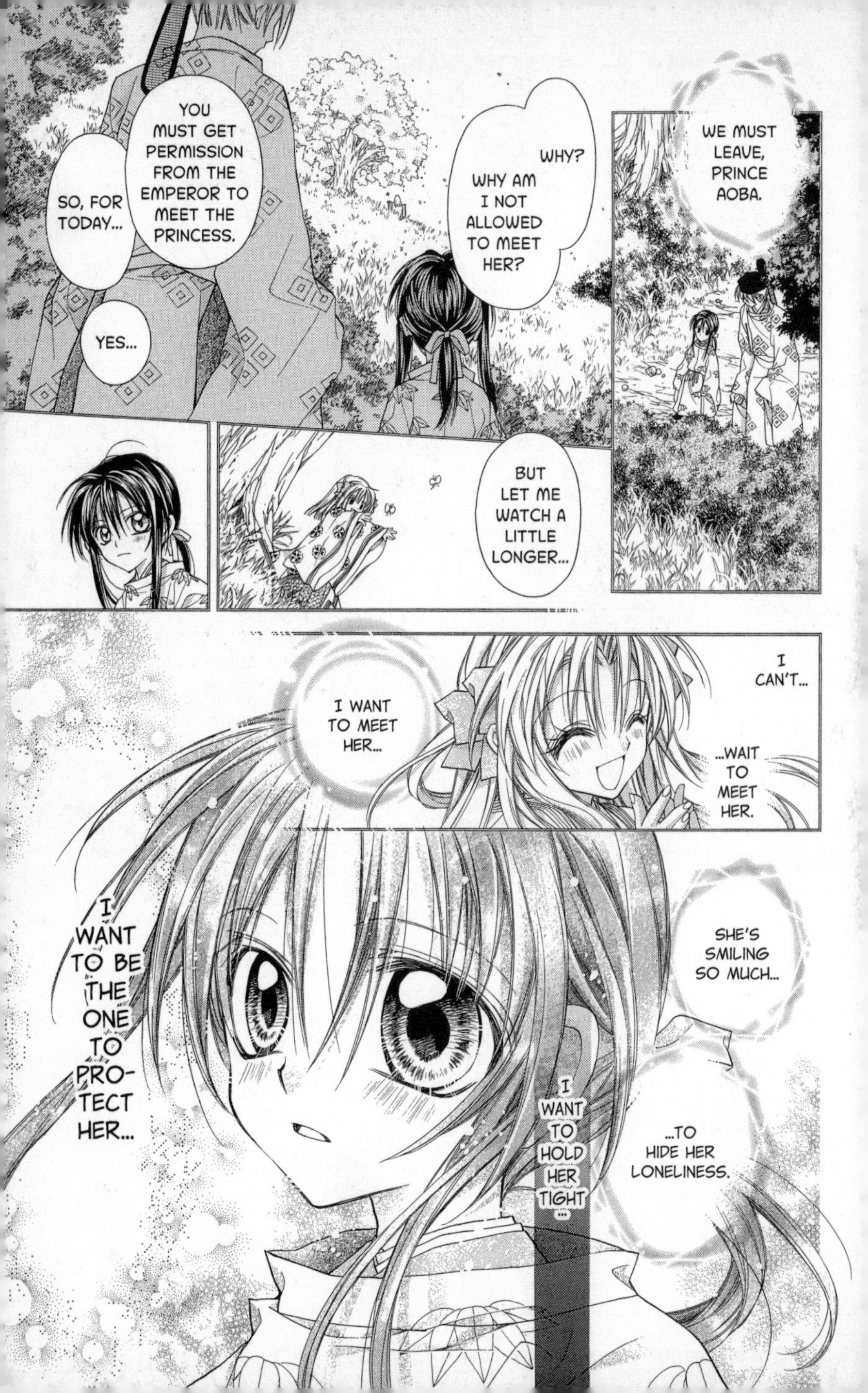
WE MUST LEAVE, PRINCE AOBA.
WHY? WHY AM I NOT ALLOWED TO MEET HER?
YOU MUST GET PERMISSION FROM THE EMPEROR TO MEET THE PRINCESS.
SO, FOR TODAY...
YES...
BUT LET ME WATCH A LITTLE LONGER...
I CAN'T...
...WAIT TO MEET HER.
I WANT TO MEET HER...
SHE'S SMILING SO MUCH...
...TO HIDE HER LONELINESS.
I WANT TO HOLD HER TIGHT...
I WANT TO BE THE ONE TO PROTECT HER...

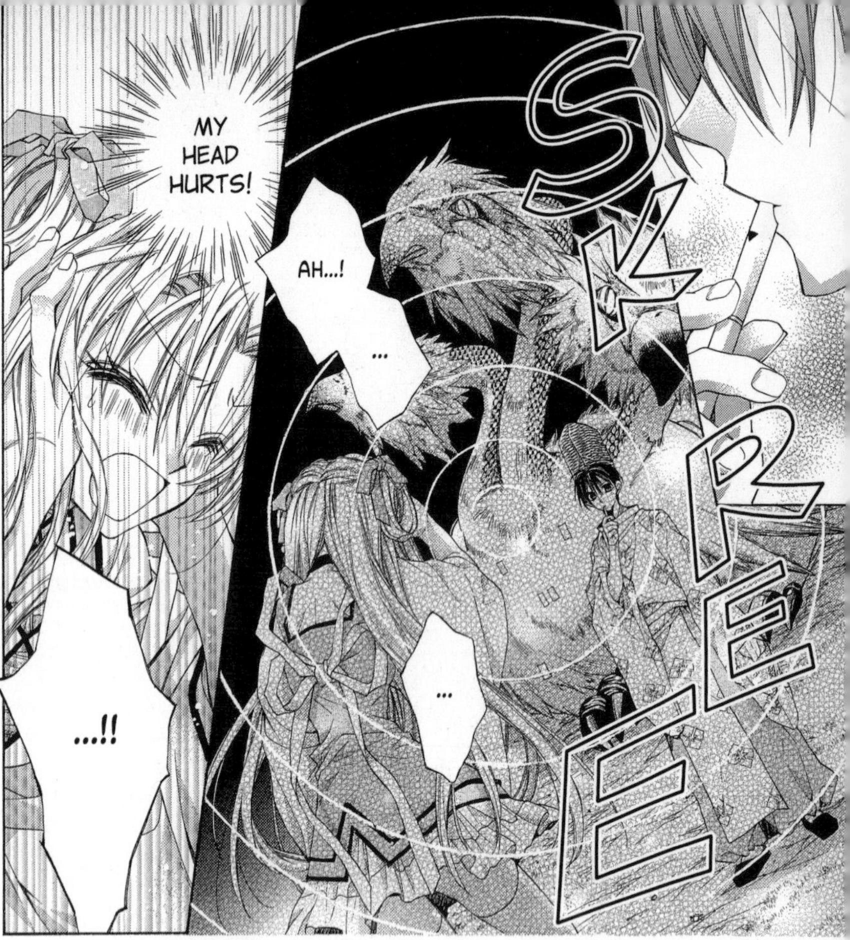
MY HEAD HURTS!
AH...!
...
...
...!!
SKREEE

※ The text in these areas...

Chapter 4: An Ephemeral Bond Still (...gives away the story. Please read it after you read the chapters.)

This is a chapter in which things settle down after Princess Sakura is chased all over the place. The main focus of this chapter is actually Chizakura. The chapter title may seem like it relates to Aoba, but at the same time it's about Sakura's "bond" with Chizakura. I like Aoba in his wolf form, but it isn't very popular with my editor or the readers...

I've started to slow the pace of the story down in this chapter.

Chapter 5: But You'll Get Angry if I Tell You

This was placed in the "New School Term Issue" of *Ribon*, and I was going to add a new twist to the story, so I drew up a summary of the story so far.

(Hayate winking was the big news among my assistants.) I guess this was the chapter in which the characters of Fujimurasaki and Aoba became clear. His Highness Fujimurasaki has a very strange soul symbol. I don't know when I'll be able to show it, but the first time it appears will probably be in a rather unexpected way. Lots of snakes appear in this chapter, so I was drawing them with a picture book in hand, but I started to get tired of it after a while. A lot of animals appear in *Sakura Hime*, but to tell the truth, I've never drawn a lot of animals before. This is pretty much the first time I've drawn horses and wolves, so I'm desperate to do a good job of it... It's okay if I'm creating a single illustration, but in manga, I have to make the artwork look like the animals are moving, so I take a lot of time to draw them. I was very surprised that my assistants liked the Councilor.

HELLO.

Arina Tanemura here.
I bring to you volume 2 of *Sakura Hime: The Legend Of Princess Sakura.*

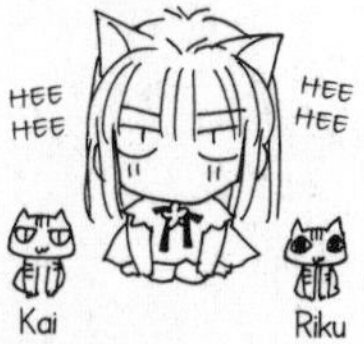
HEE HEE
HEE HEE
Kai
Riku

Recently, I um... I've started to write my own essay-style manga in *Cobalt* magazine! (Published in even-numbered months.)
It's called *Arina's Seed*, I intend to write about many things! (The number of pages will increase to four in the third issue!)
There's a hidden theme behind this essay-style manga: To write what my editor at *Cobalt* wants to learn about me.
I was told, "I want to learn about your days before you made your debut, Tanemura Sensei," so currently I'm writing about before I made my debut as a mangaka. (That will continue for some time.)

I've always loved reading essay-style manga, and I've always wanted to do one myself, but it is a little difficult...?

But I'd like to keep working on it, so please support me on it as well.

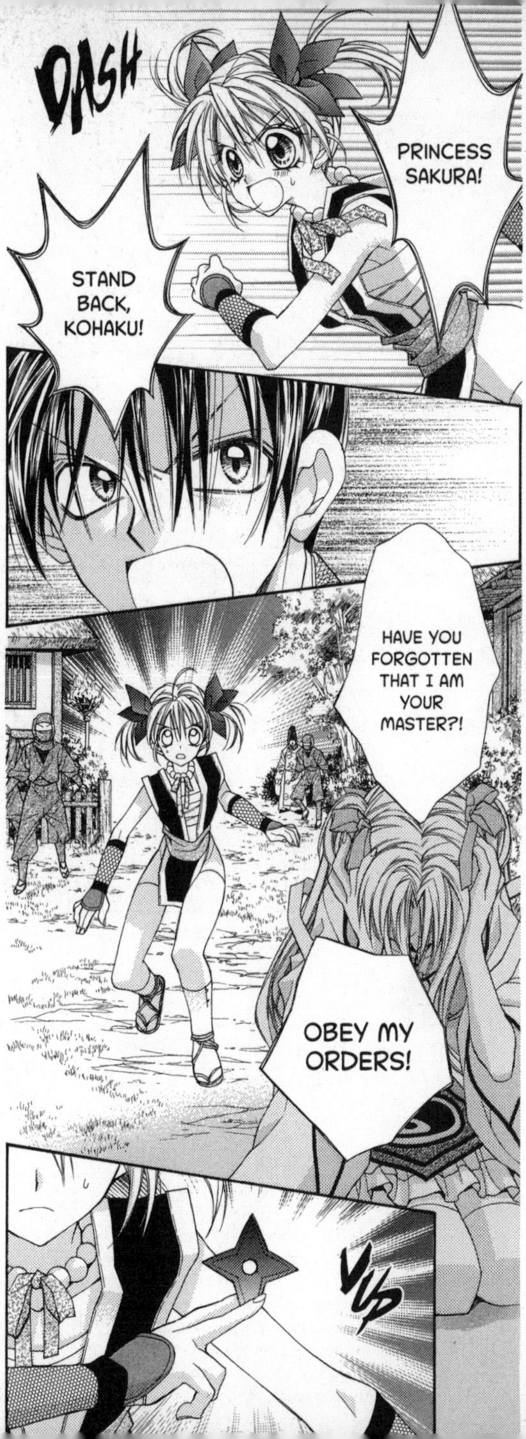
PRINCESS SAKURA!
DASH
STAND BACK, KOHAKU!
HAVE YOU FORGOTTEN THAT I AM YOUR MASTER?!
OBEY MY ORDERS!
VUP

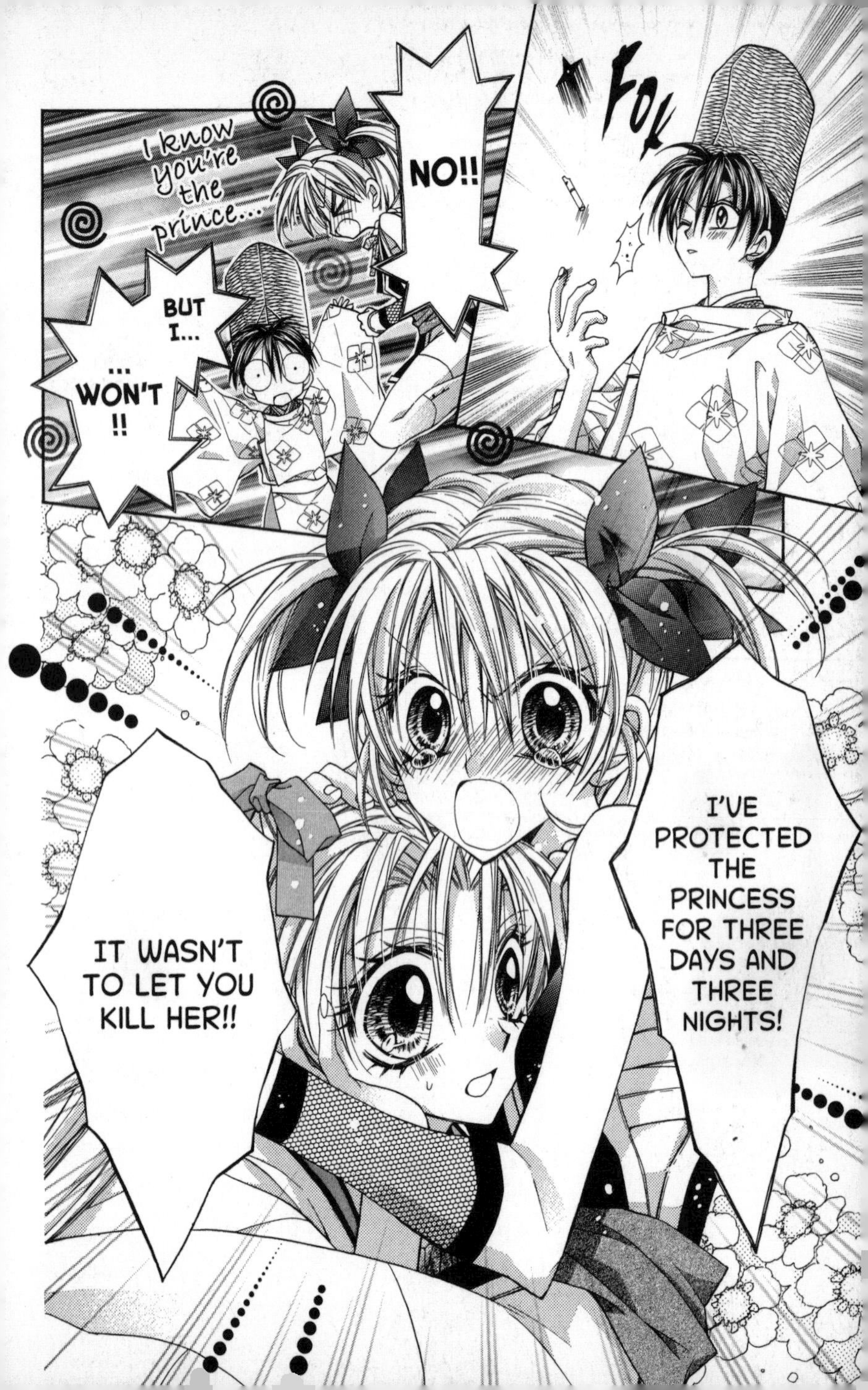
NO!!
I know you're the prince...
BUT I...
... WON'T !!
I'VE PROTECTED THE PRINCESS FOR THREE DAYS AND THREE NIGHTS!
IT WASN'T TO LET YOU KILL HER!!

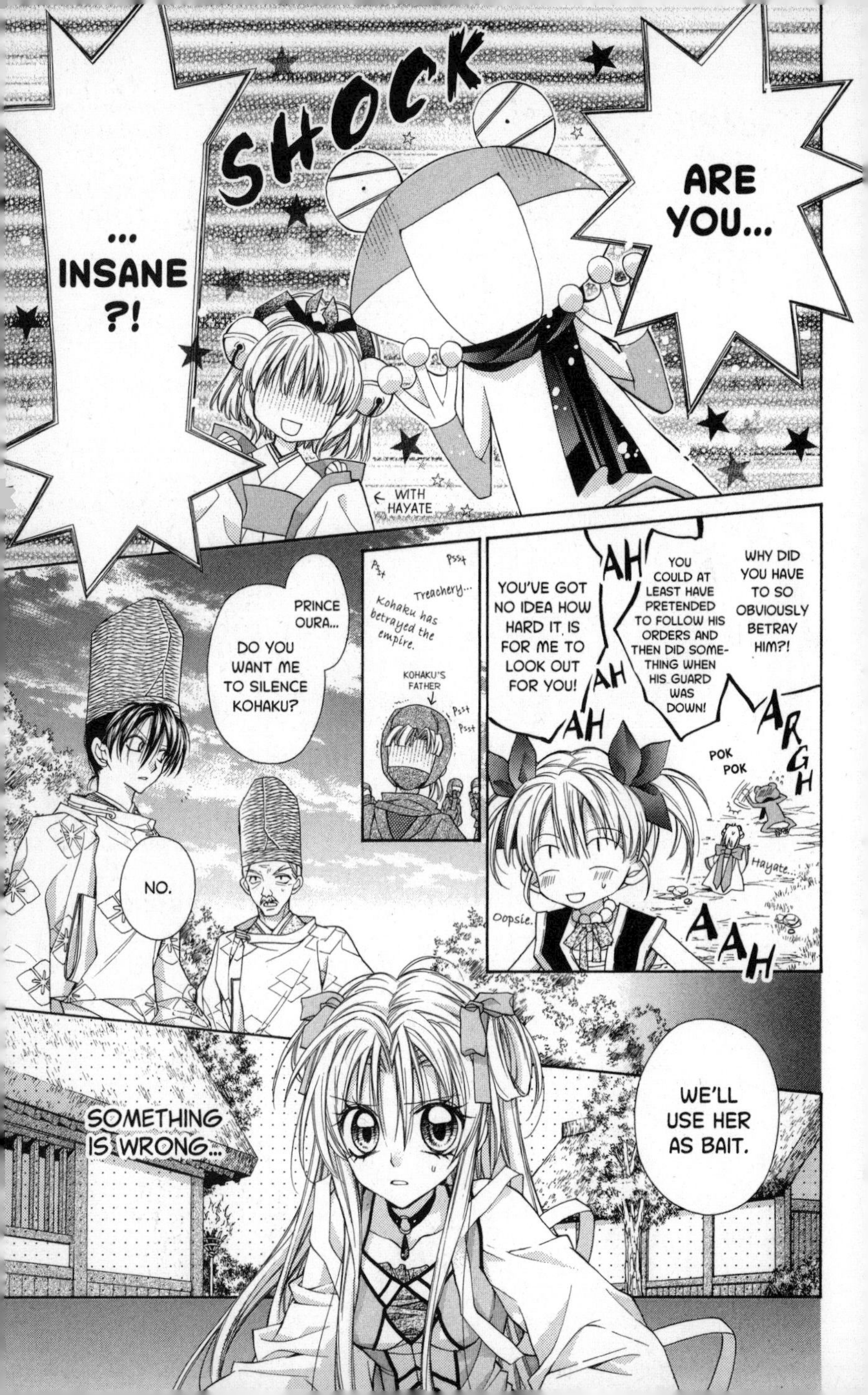
ARE YOU...
SHOCK
... INSANE ?!
← WITH HAYATE
WHY DID YOU HAVE TO SO OBVIOUSLY BETRAY HIM?!
YOU COULD AT LEAST HAVE PRETENDED TO FOLLOW HIS ORDERS AND THEN DID SOMETHING WHEN HIS GUARD WAS DOWN!
YOU'VE GOT NO IDEA HOW HARD IT IS FOR ME TO LOOK OUT FOR YOU!
AH AH AH
ARGH
POK POK
Hayate...
AAAH
Oopsie.
Psst
Psst
Treachery...
Kohaku has betrayed the empire.
KOHAKU'S FATHER
Psst
Psst
PRINCE OURA...
DO YOU WANT ME TO SILENCE KOHAKU?
NO.
WE'LL USE HER AS BAIT.
SOMETHING IS WRONG...

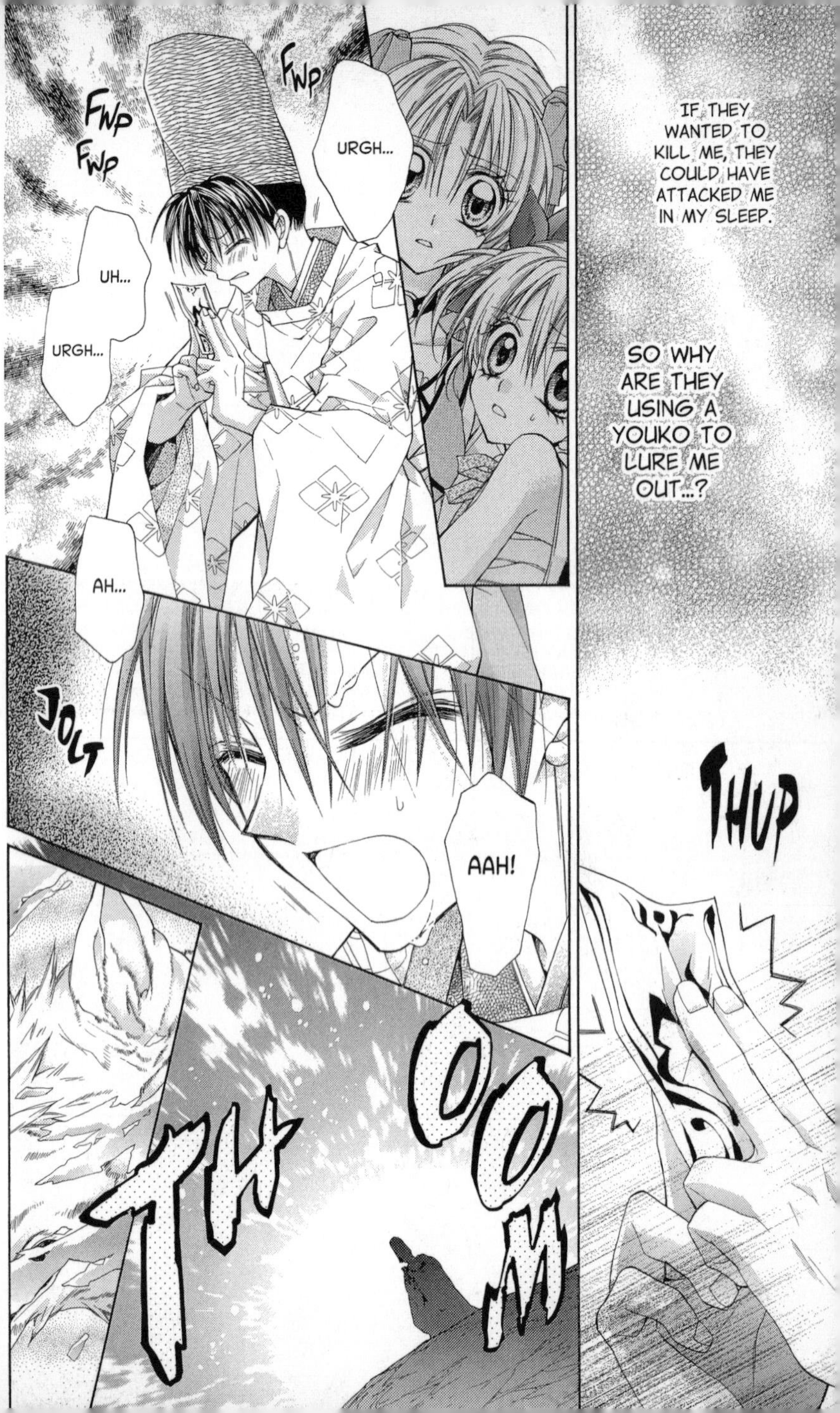
IF THEY WANTED TO KILL ME, THEY COULD HAVE ATTACKED ME IN MY SLEEP.
SO WHY ARE THEY USING A YOUKO TO LURE ME OUT...?
THUP
FWP
URGH...
FWP
FWP
UH...
URGH...
AH...
JOLT
AAH!
THOOOM

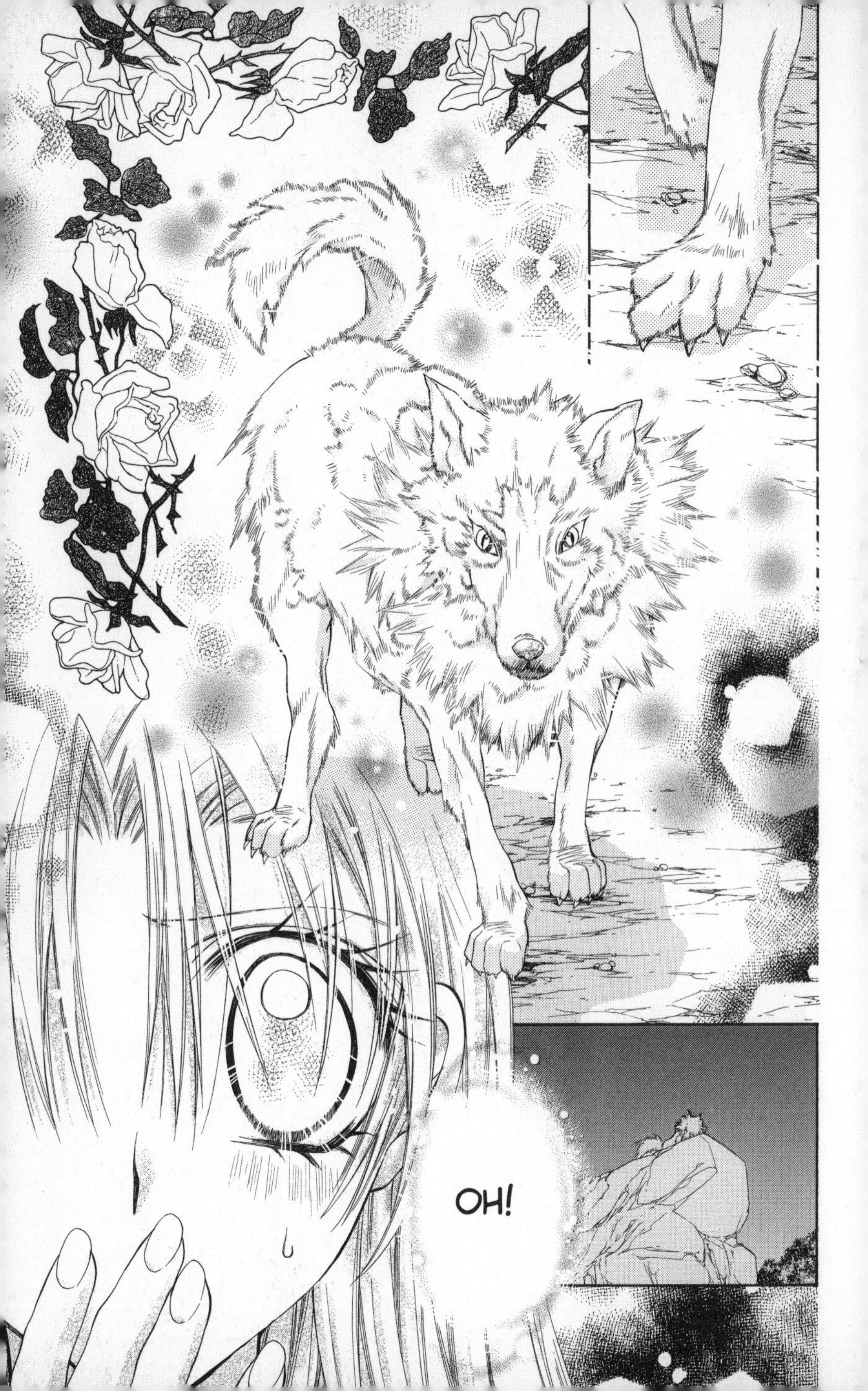
OH!

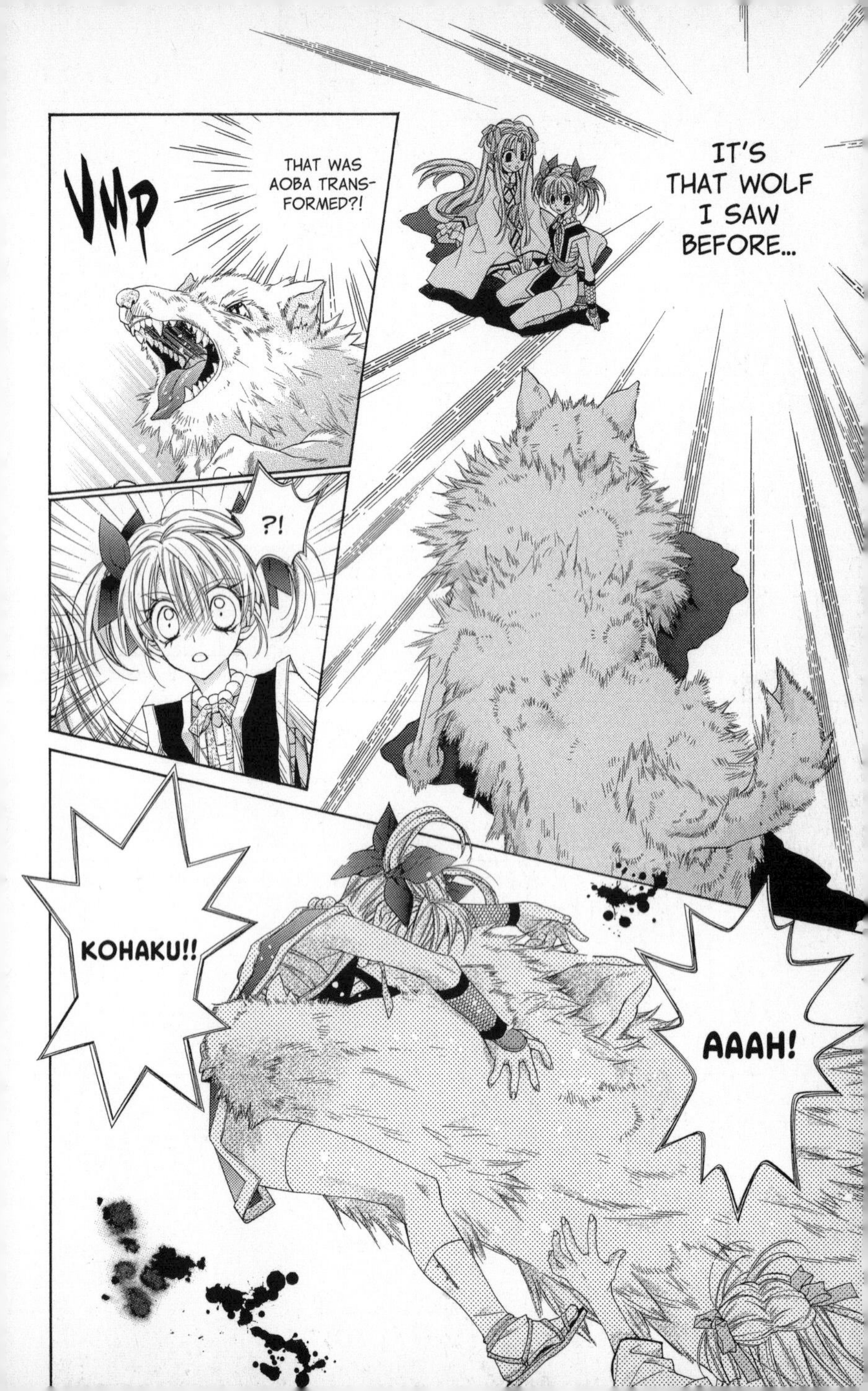
IT'S THAT WOLF I SAW BEFORE...
VMP
THAT WAS AOBA TRANS-FORMED?!
?!
AAAH!
KOHAKU!!

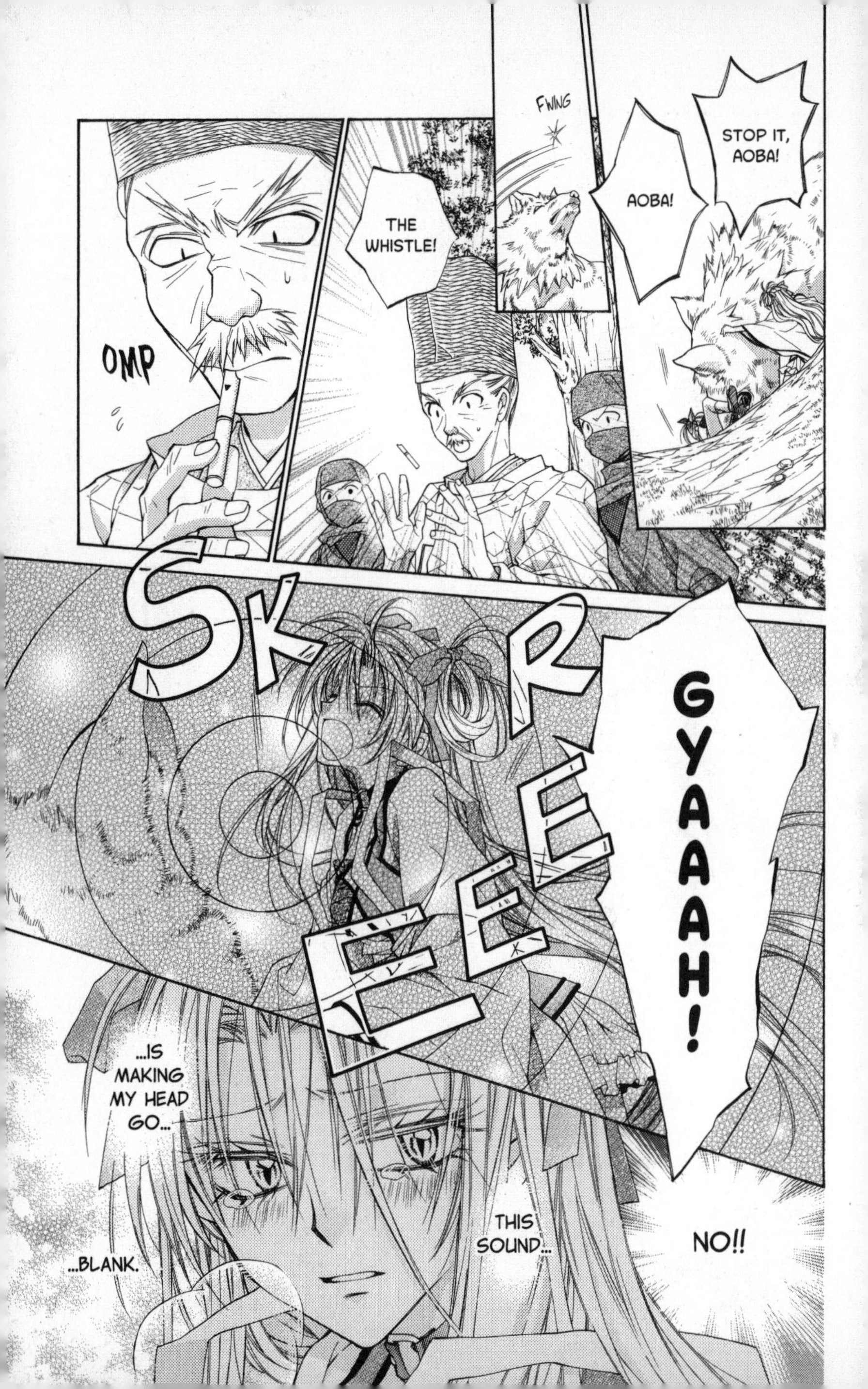
STOP IT, AOBA!
AOBA!
FWING
THE WHISTLE!
OMP
GYAAAH!
SKREEE
NO!!
THIS SOUND...
...IS MAKING MY HEAD GO...
...BLANK.

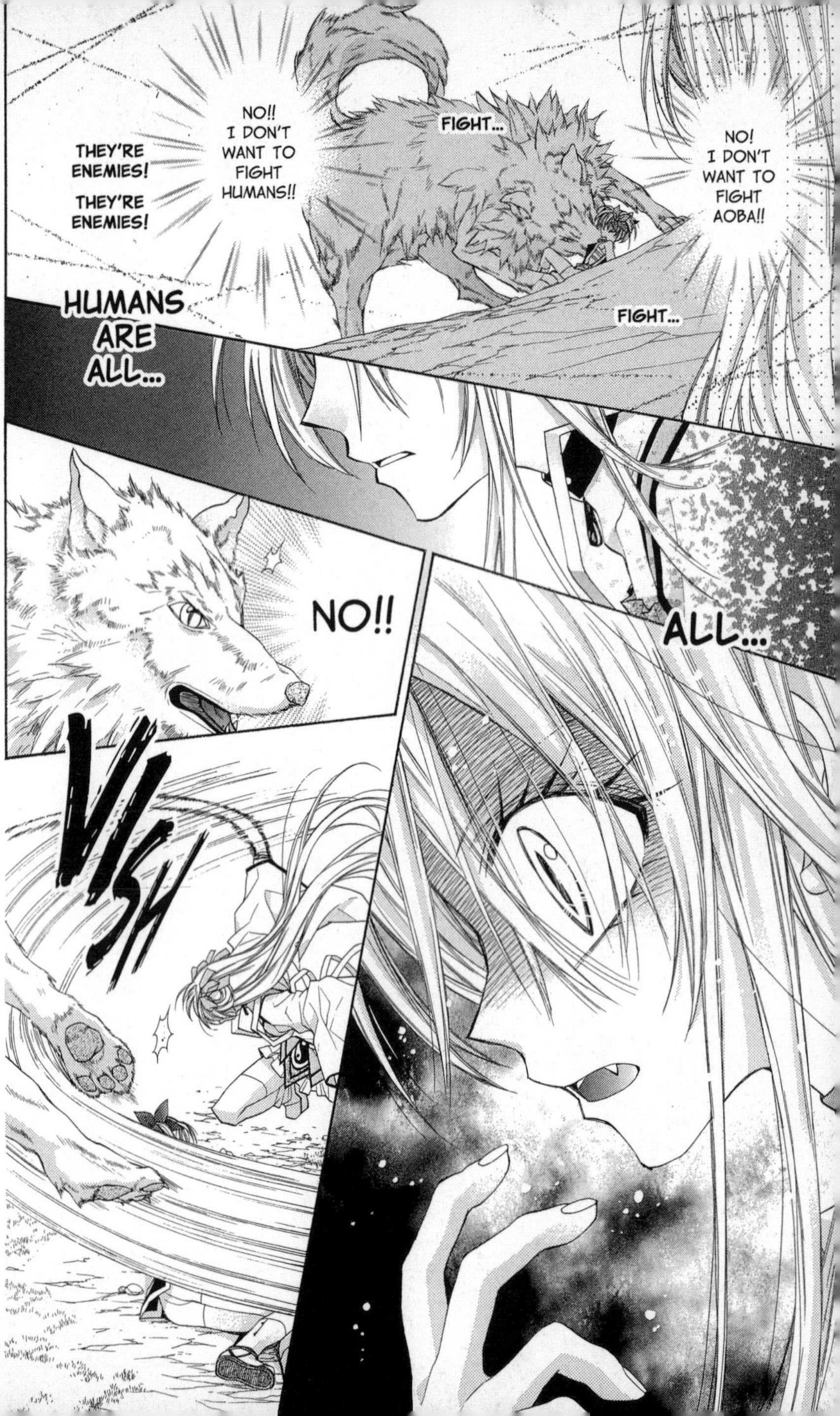
NO! I DON'T WANT TO FIGHT AOBA!!
FIGHT...
NO!! I DON'T WANT TO FIGHT HUMANS!!
THEY'RE ENEMIES!
THEY'RE ENEMIES!
FIGHT...
HUMANS ARE ALL...
ALL...
NO!!
VISH

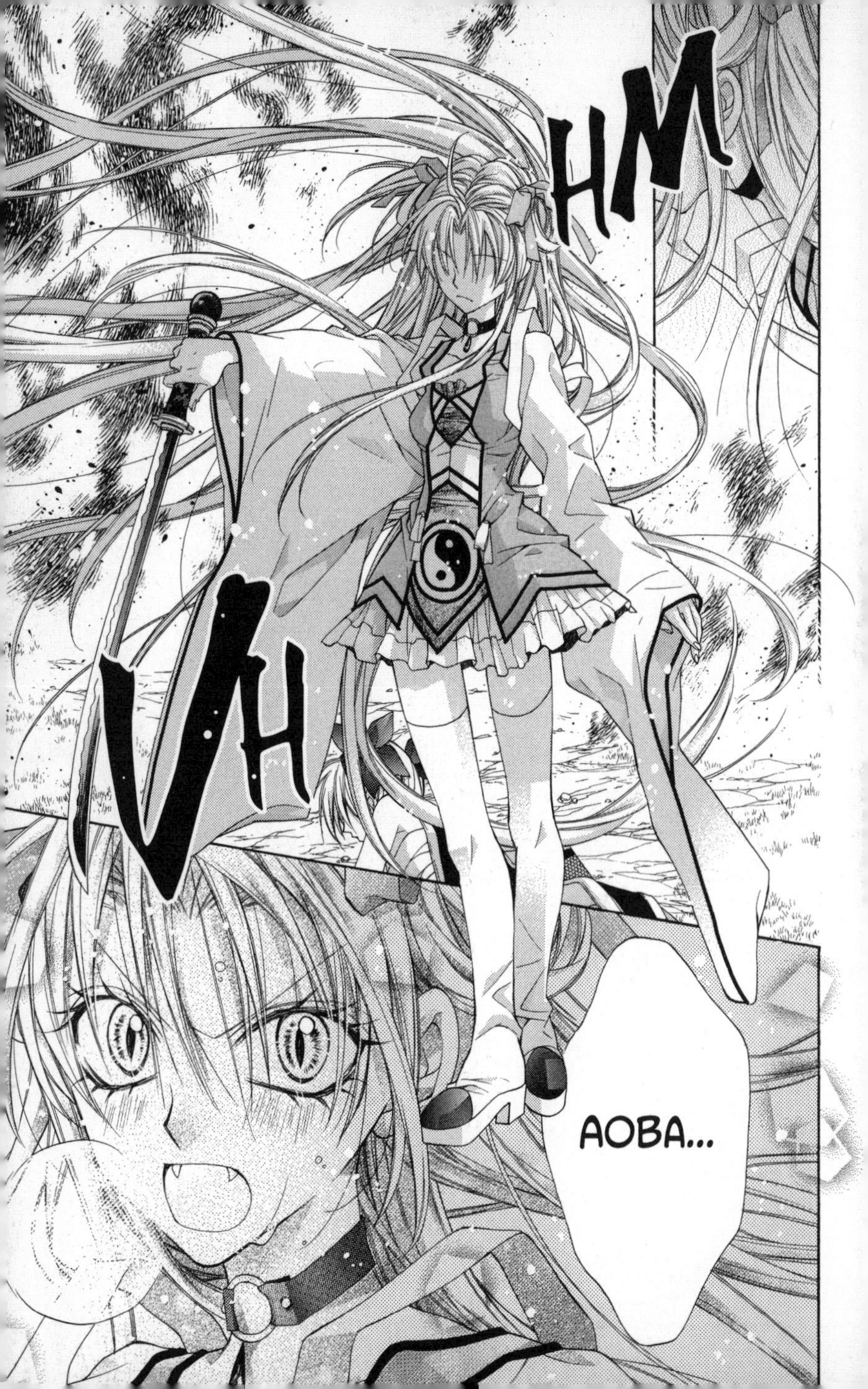
HM
VH
AOBA...

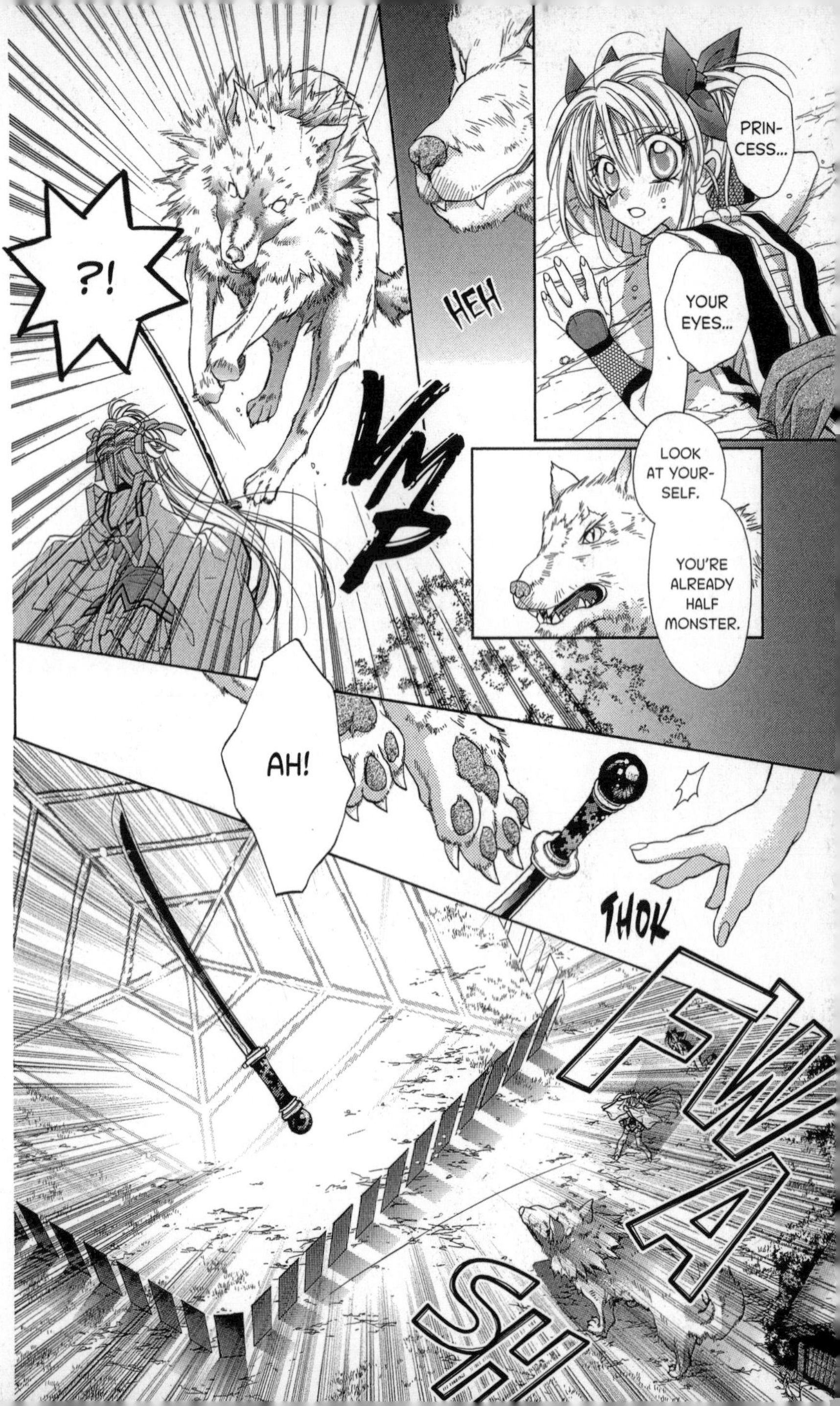
PRIN-CESS...
YOUR EYES...
HEH
LOOK AT YOUR-SELF.
YOU'RE ALREADY HALF MONSTER.
?!
VMP
THOK
AH!
FWASH

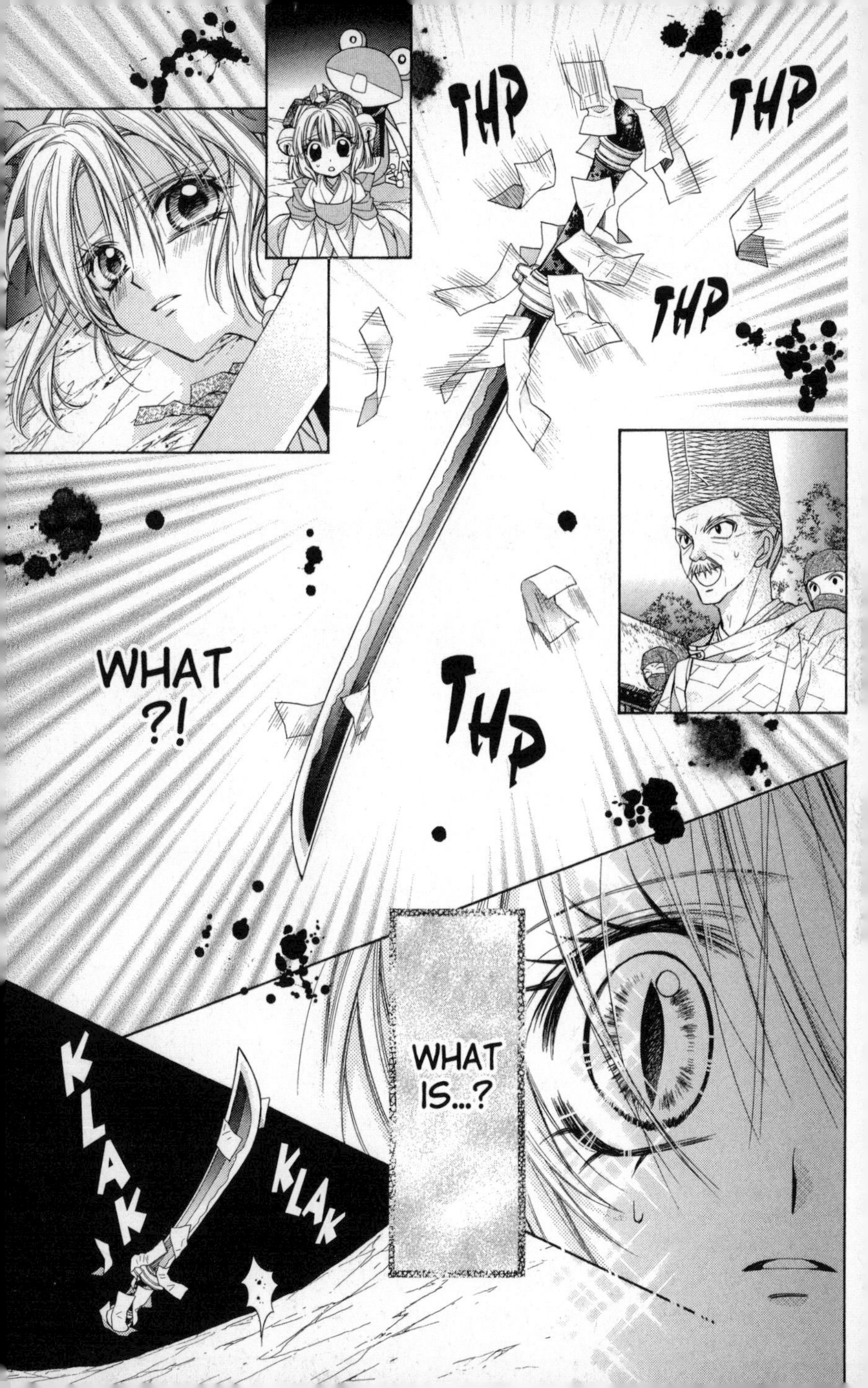
THP
THP
THP
THP
WHAT ?!
WHAT IS...?
KLAK
KLAK

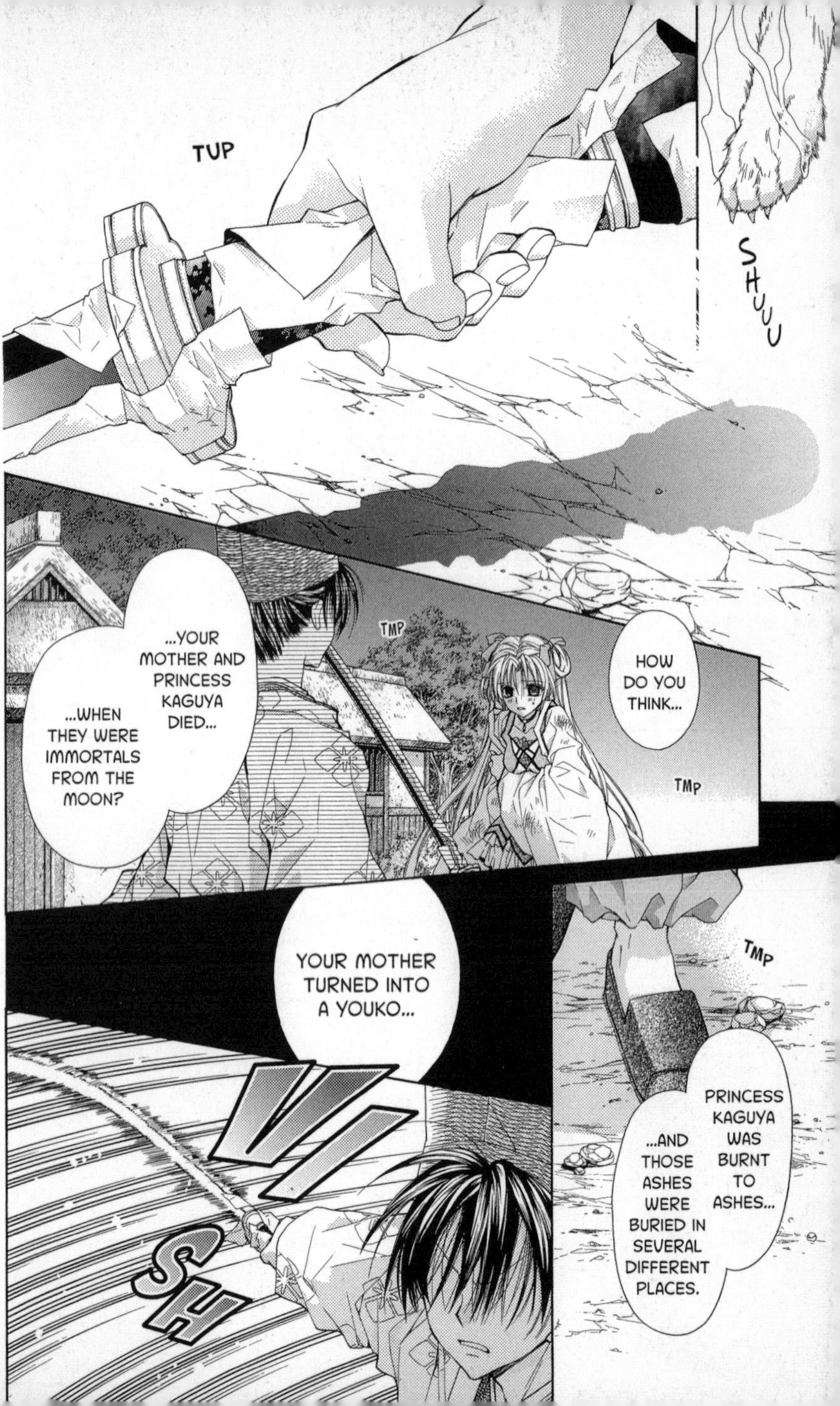
SHUUU
TUP
HOW DO YOU THINK...
TMp
TMP
...YOUR MOTHER AND PRINCESS KAGUYA DIED...
...WHEN THEY WERE IMMORTALS FROM THE MOON?
TMP
PRINCESS KAGUYA WAS BURNT TO ASHES...
...AND THOSE ASHES WERE BURIED IN SEVERAL DIFFERENT PLACES.
YOUR MOTHER TURNED INTO A YOUKO...
SH

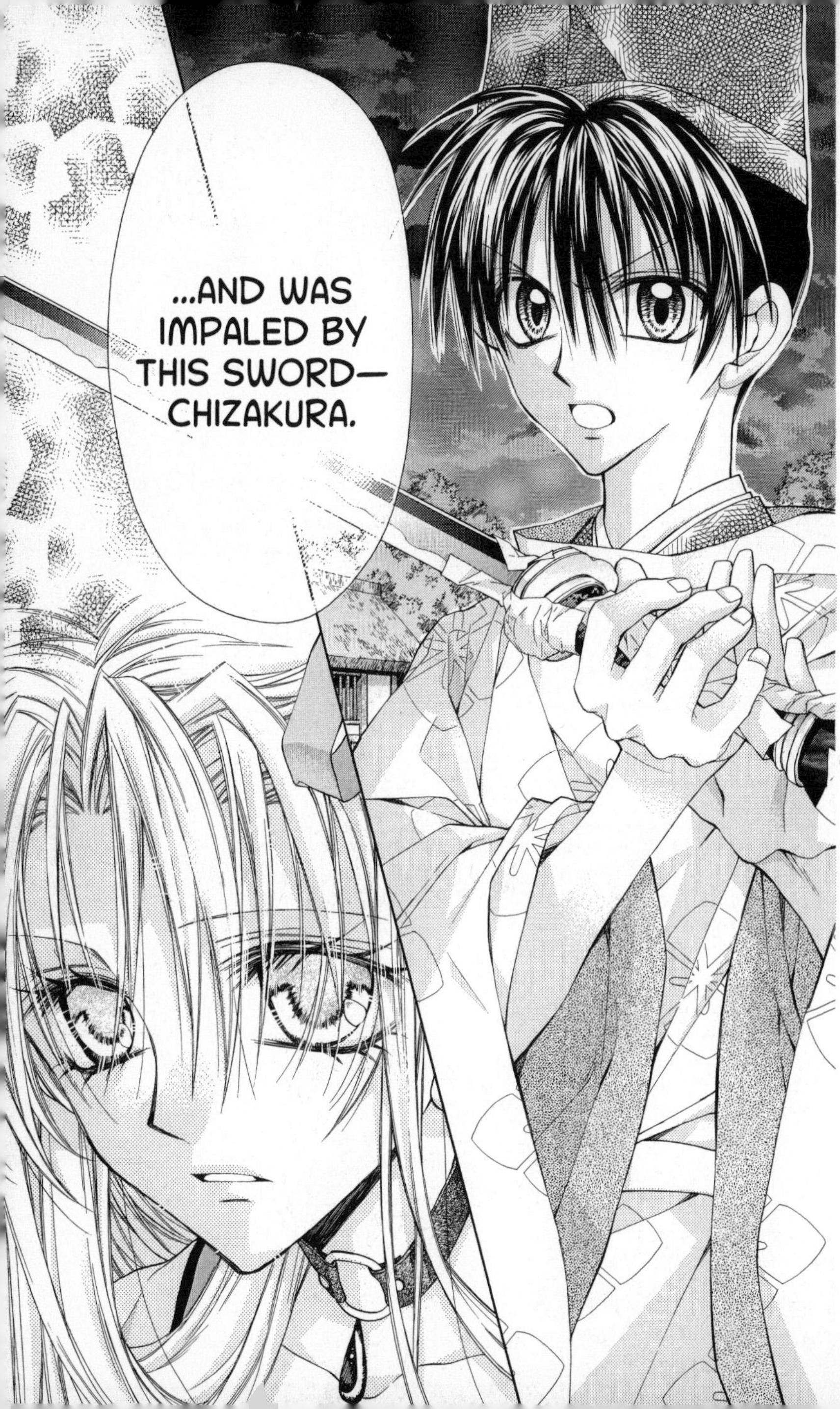
...AND WAS IMPALED BY THIS SWORD—CHIZAKURA.

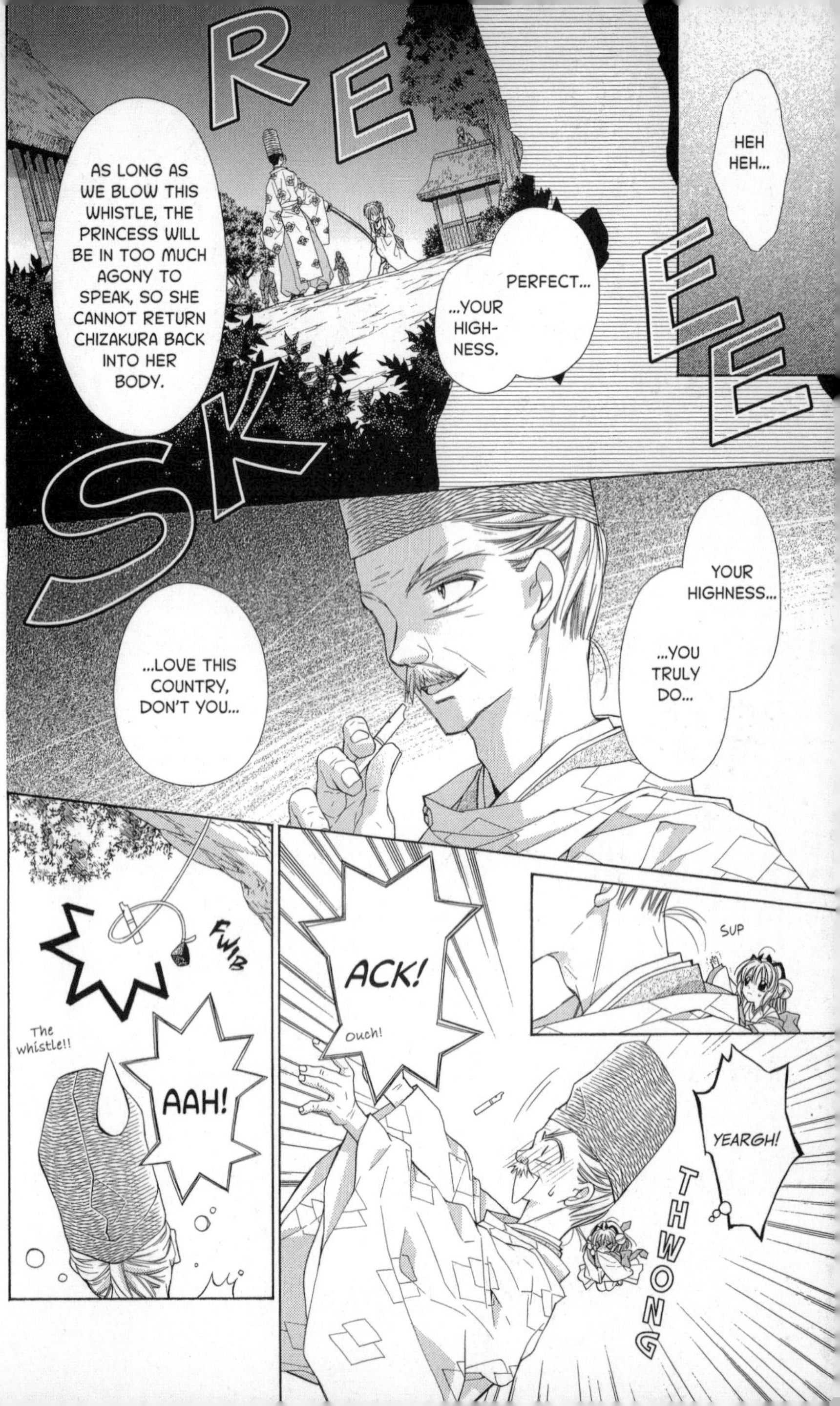
HEH HEH...
PERFECT... ...YOUR HIGHNESS.
AS LONG AS WE BLOW THIS WHISTLE, THE PRINCESS WILL BE IN TOO MUCH AGONY TO SPEAK, SO SHE CANNOT RETURN CHIZAKURA BACK INTO HER BODY.
SKREEEE
YOUR HIGHNESS...
...YOU TRULY DO...
...LOVE THIS COUNTRY, DON'T YOU...
SUP
YEARGH!
THWONG
ACK!
Ouch!
FWIB
AAH!
The whistle!!

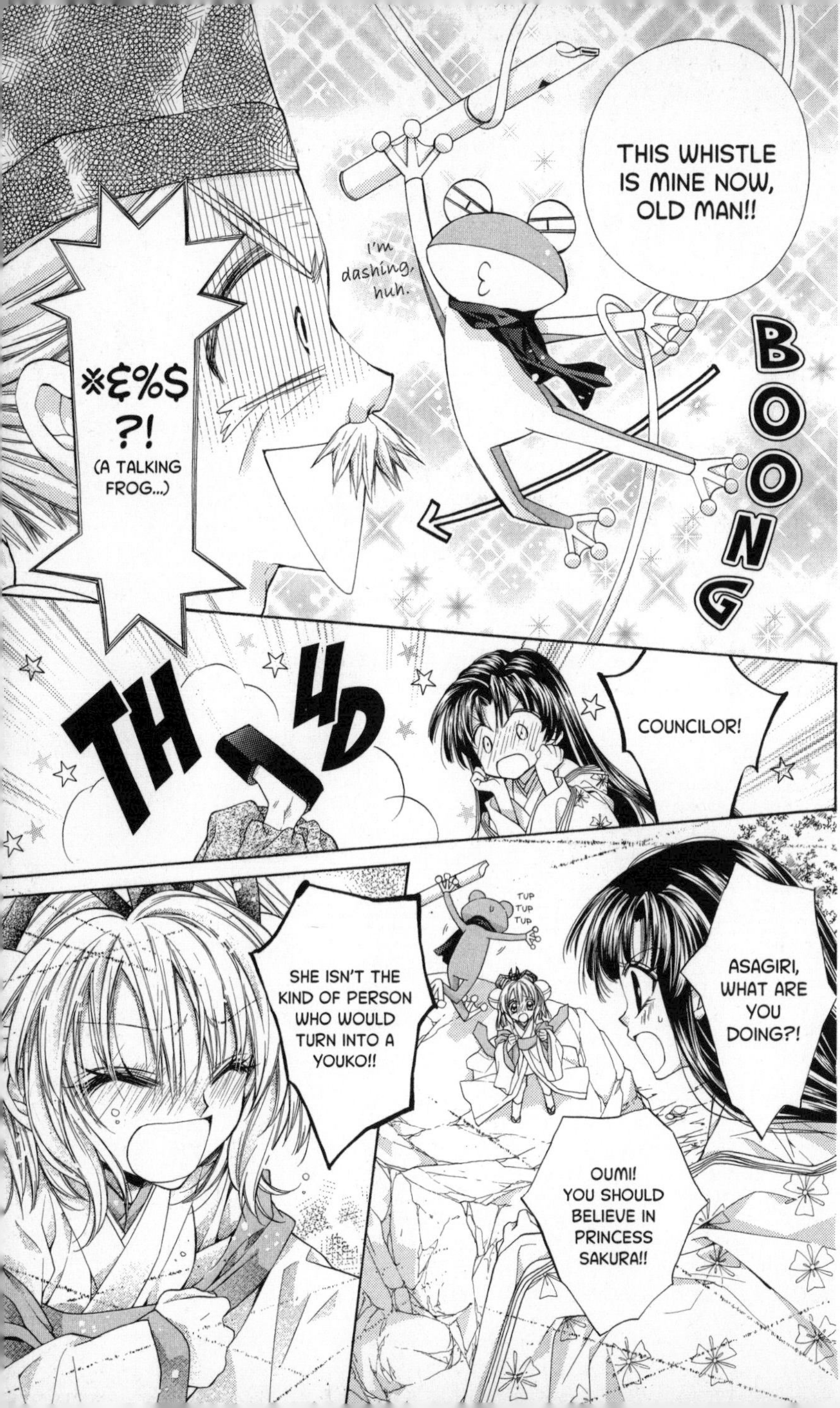
THIS WHISTLE IS MINE NOW, OLD MAN!!
BOONG
I'm dashing, huh.
※€%$?! (A TALKING FROG...)
COUNCILOR!
THUD
ASAGIRI, WHAT ARE YOU DOING?!
OUMI! YOU SHOULD BELIEVE IN PRINCESS SAKURA!!
TUP TUP TUP
SHE ISN'T THE KIND OF PERSON WHO WOULD TURN INTO A YOUKO!!

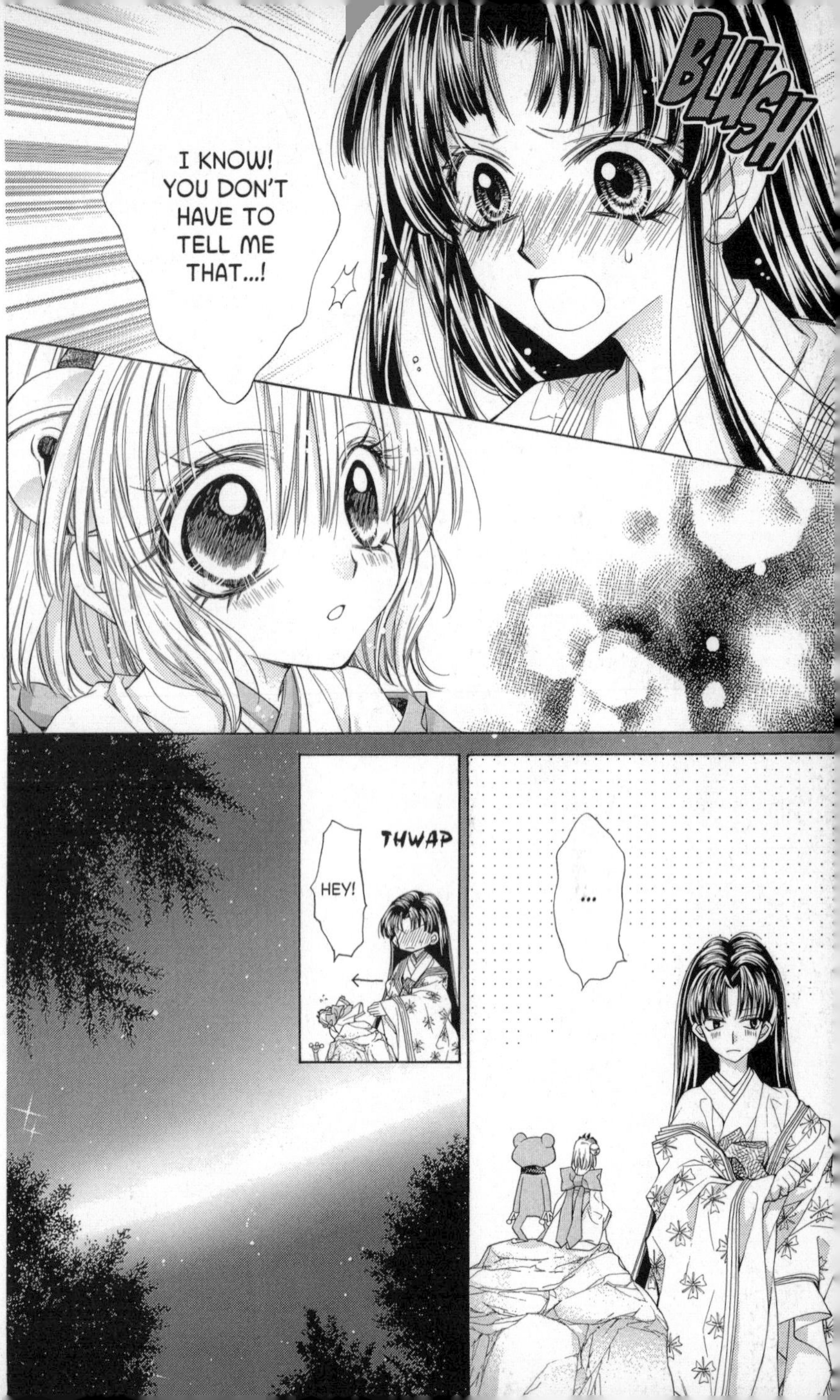
BLUSH
I KNOW! YOU DON'T HAVE TO TELL ME THAT...!
...
THWAP
HEY!

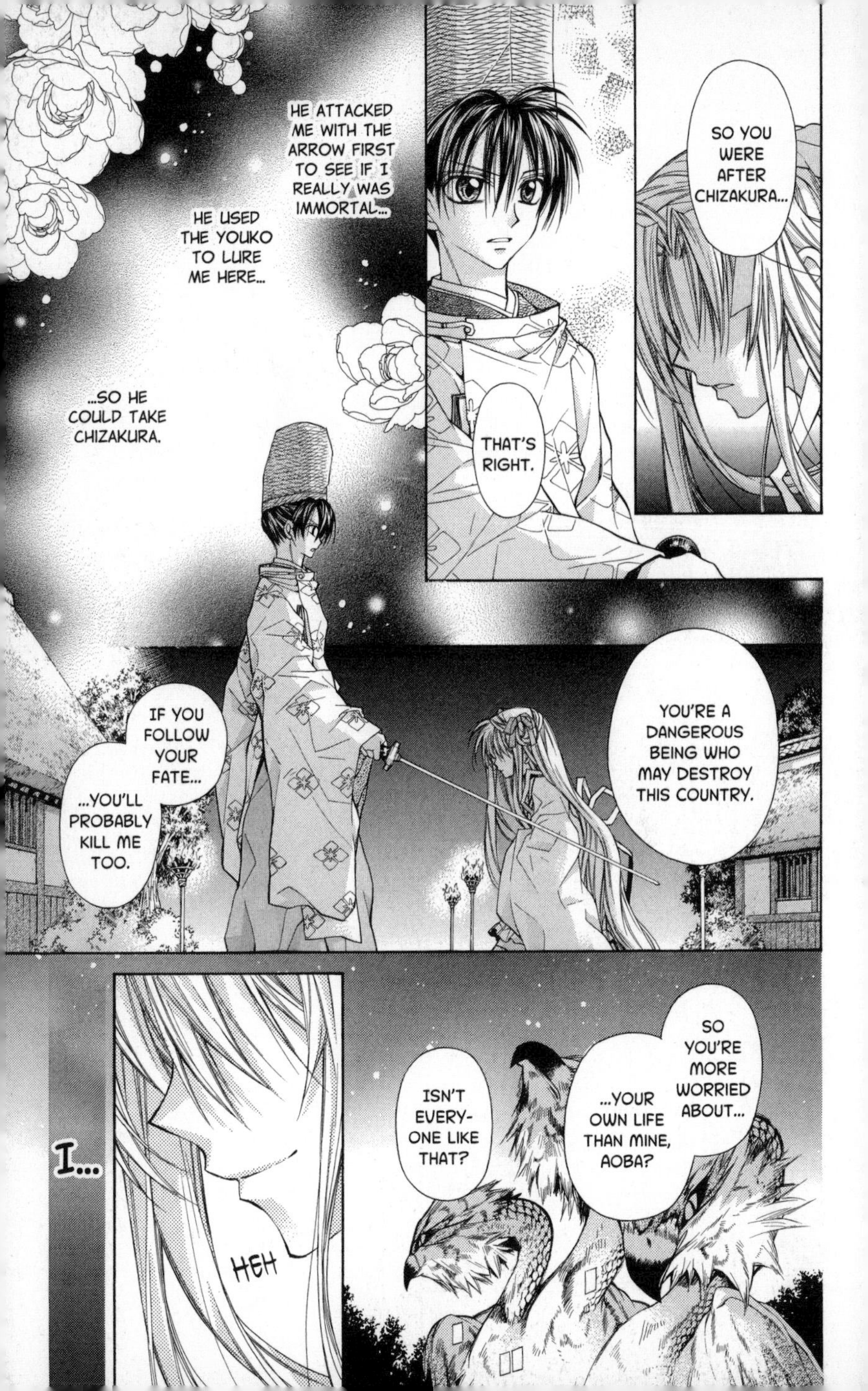
SO YOU WERE AFTER CHIZAKURA...
THAT'S RIGHT.
HE ATTACKED ME WITH THE ARROW FIRST TO SEE IF I REALLY WAS IMMORTAL...
HE USED THE YOUKO TO LURE ME HERE...
...SO HE COULD TAKE CHIZAKURA.
YOU'RE A DANGEROUS BEING WHO MAY DESTROY THIS COUNTRY.
IF YOU FOLLOW YOUR FATE...
...YOU'LL PROBABLY KILL ME TOO.
SO YOU'RE MORE WORRIED ABOUT...
...YOUR OWN LIFE THAN MINE, AOBA?
ISN'T EVERY-ONE LIKE THAT?
HEH
I...

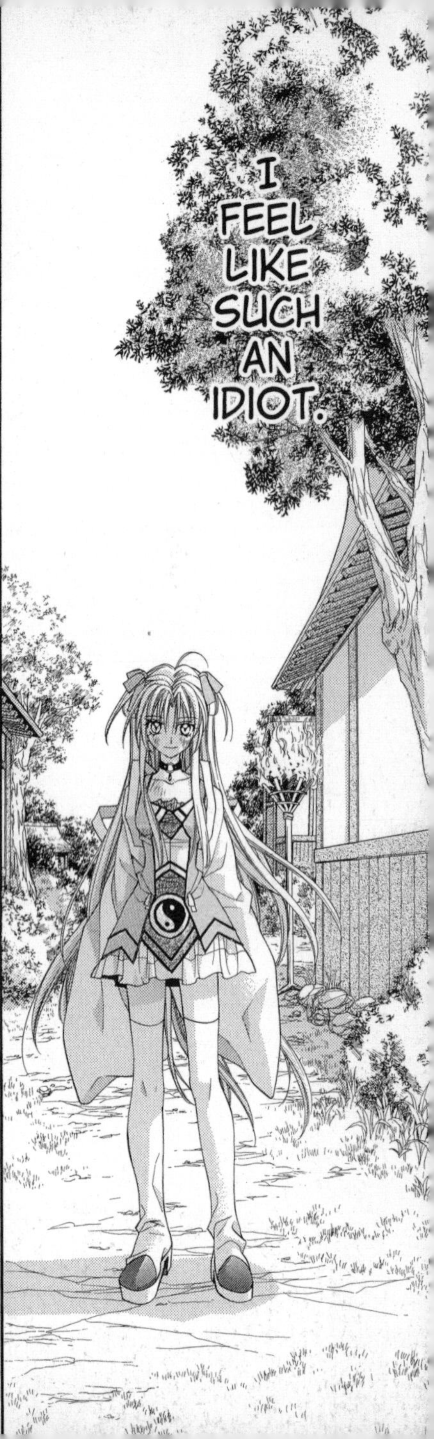
I FEEL LIKE SUCH AN IDIOT.

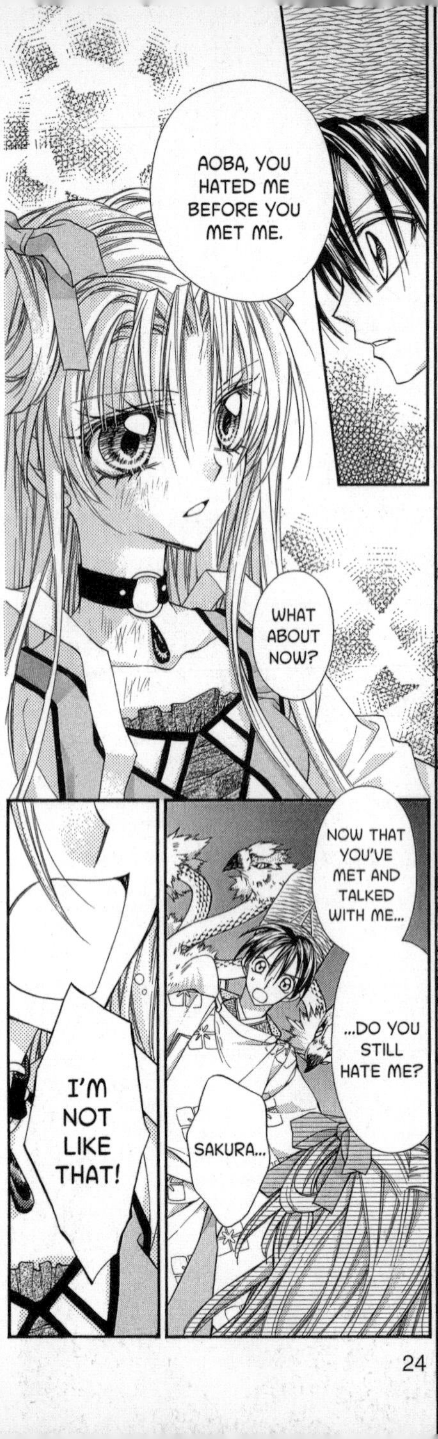
AOBA, YOU HATED ME BEFORE YOU MET ME.
WHAT ABOUT NOW?
NOW THAT YOU'VE MET AND TALKED WITH ME...
...DO YOU STILL HATE ME?
SAKURA...
I'M NOT LIKE THAT!

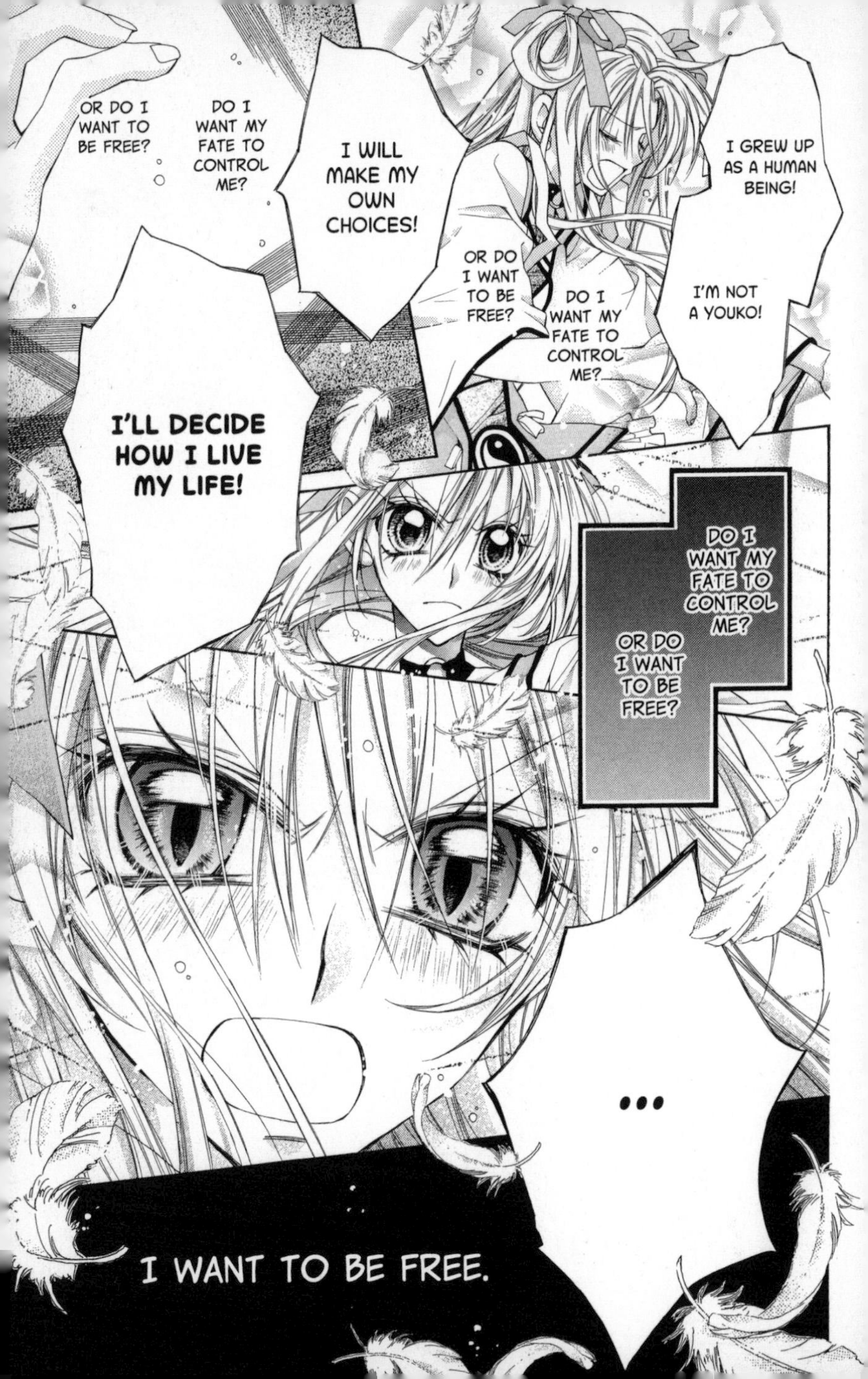
I GREW UP AS A HUMAN BEING!
I'M NOT A YOUKO!
DO I WANT MY FATE TO CONTROL ME?
OR DO I WANT TO BE FREE?
I WILL MAKE MY OWN CHOICES!
DO I WANT MY FATE TO CONTROL ME?
OR DO I WANT TO BE FREE?
I'LL DECIDE HOW I LIVE MY LIFE!
DO I WANT MY FATE TO CONTROL ME?
OR DO I WANT TO BE FREE?
...
I WANT TO BE FREE.

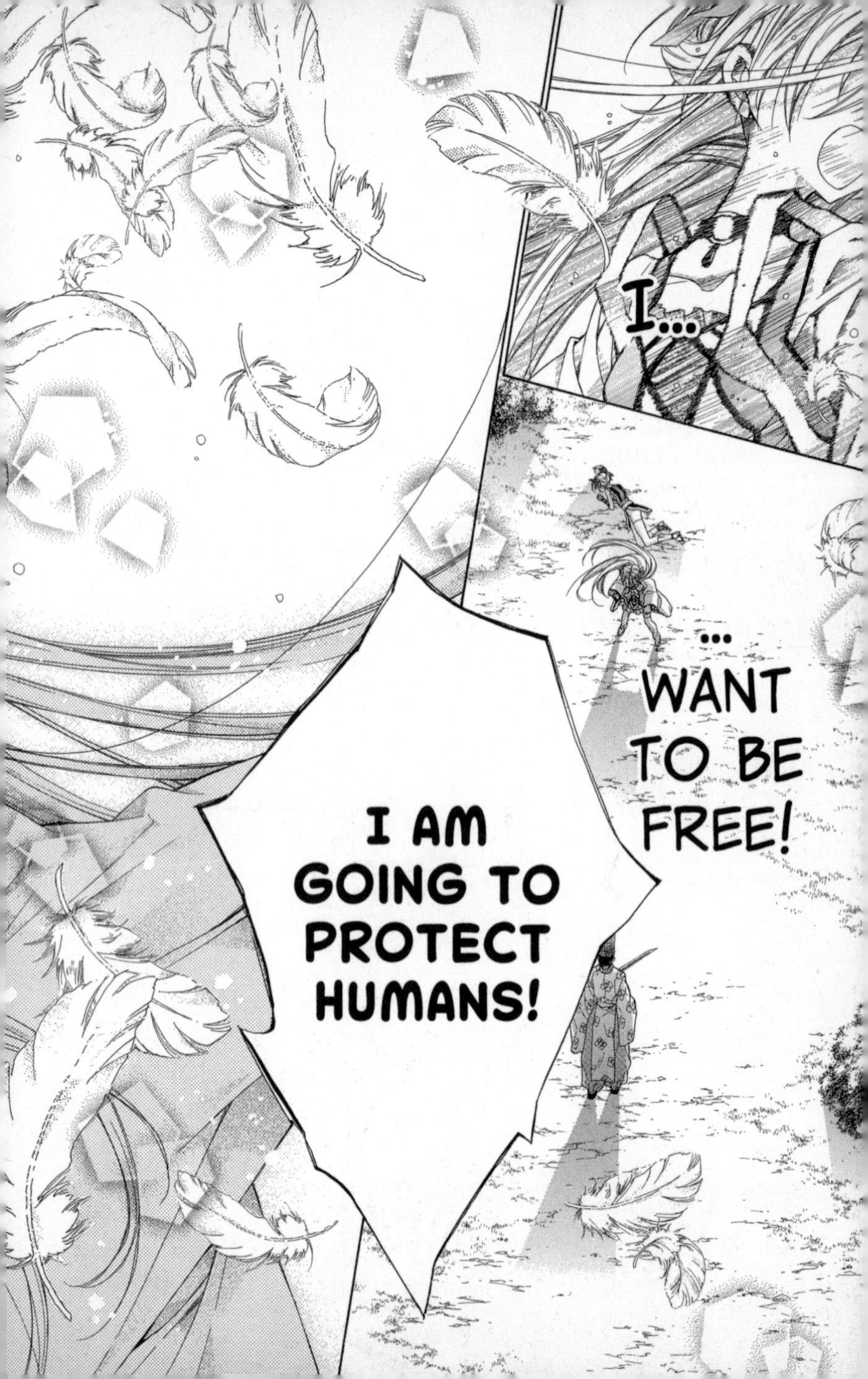
I...
... WANT TO BE FREE!
I AM GOING TO PROTECT HUMANS!

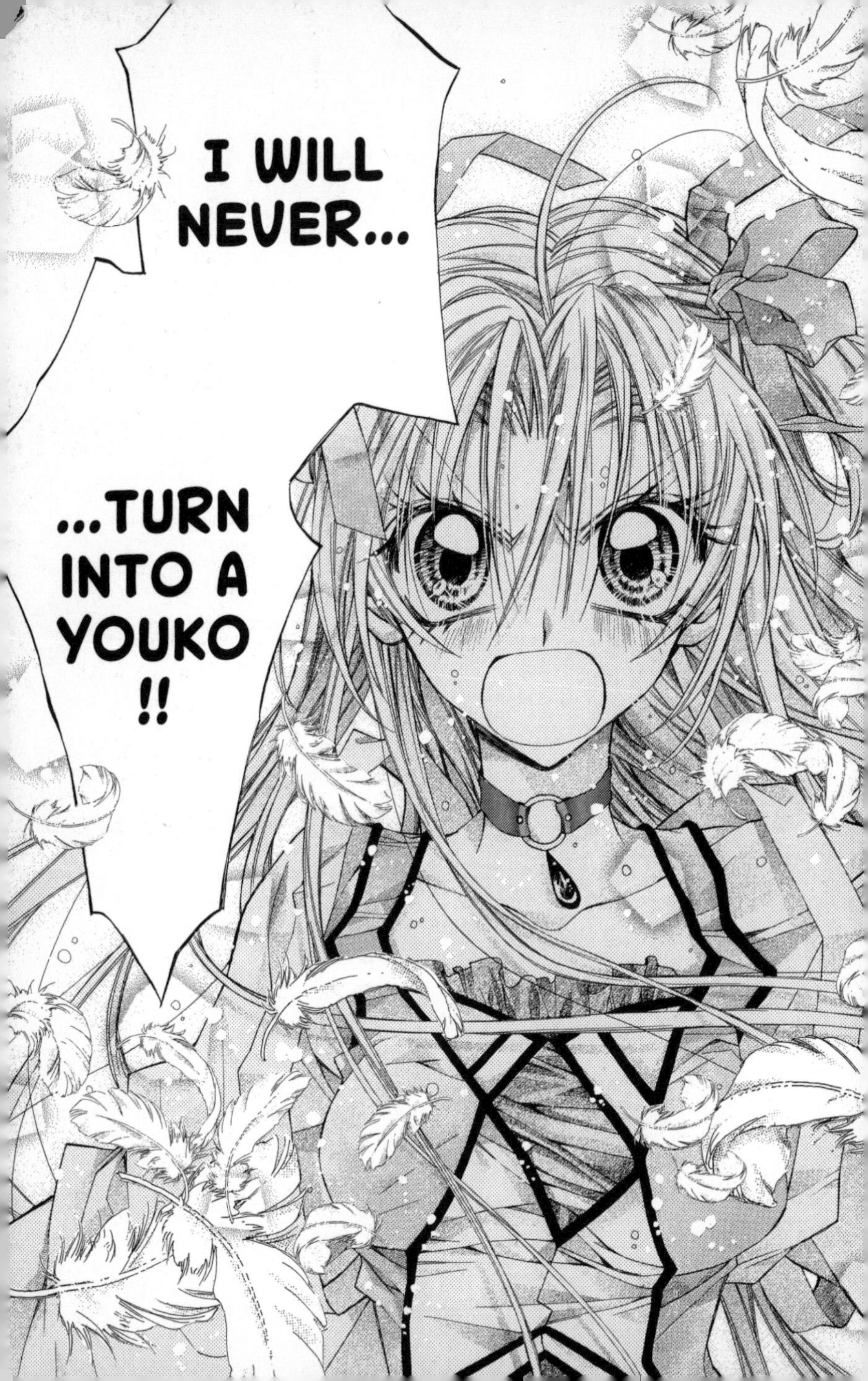
I WILL NEVER...
...TURN INTO A YOUKO !!

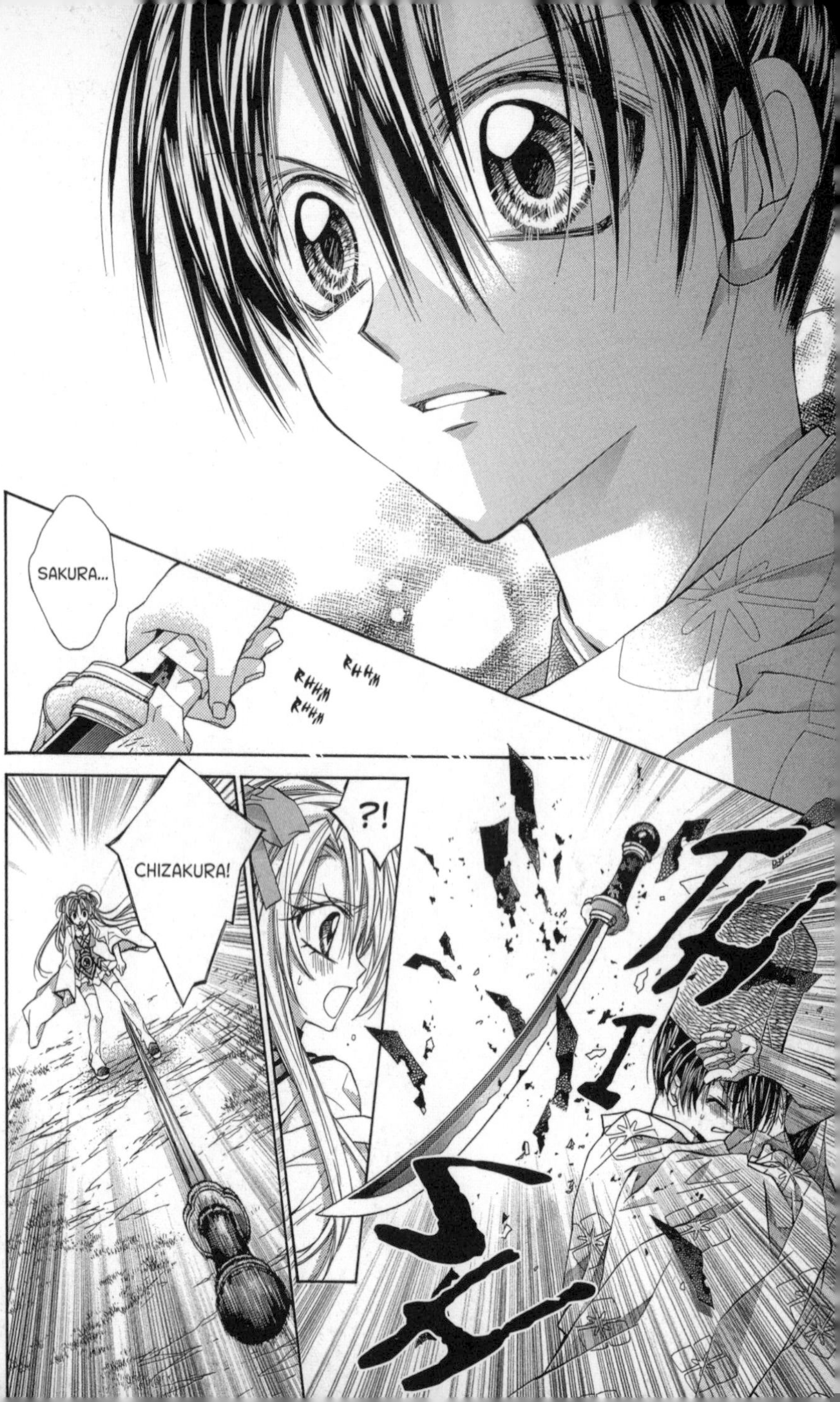
SAKURA...
RHHM
RHHM
RHHM
?!
CHIZAKURA!

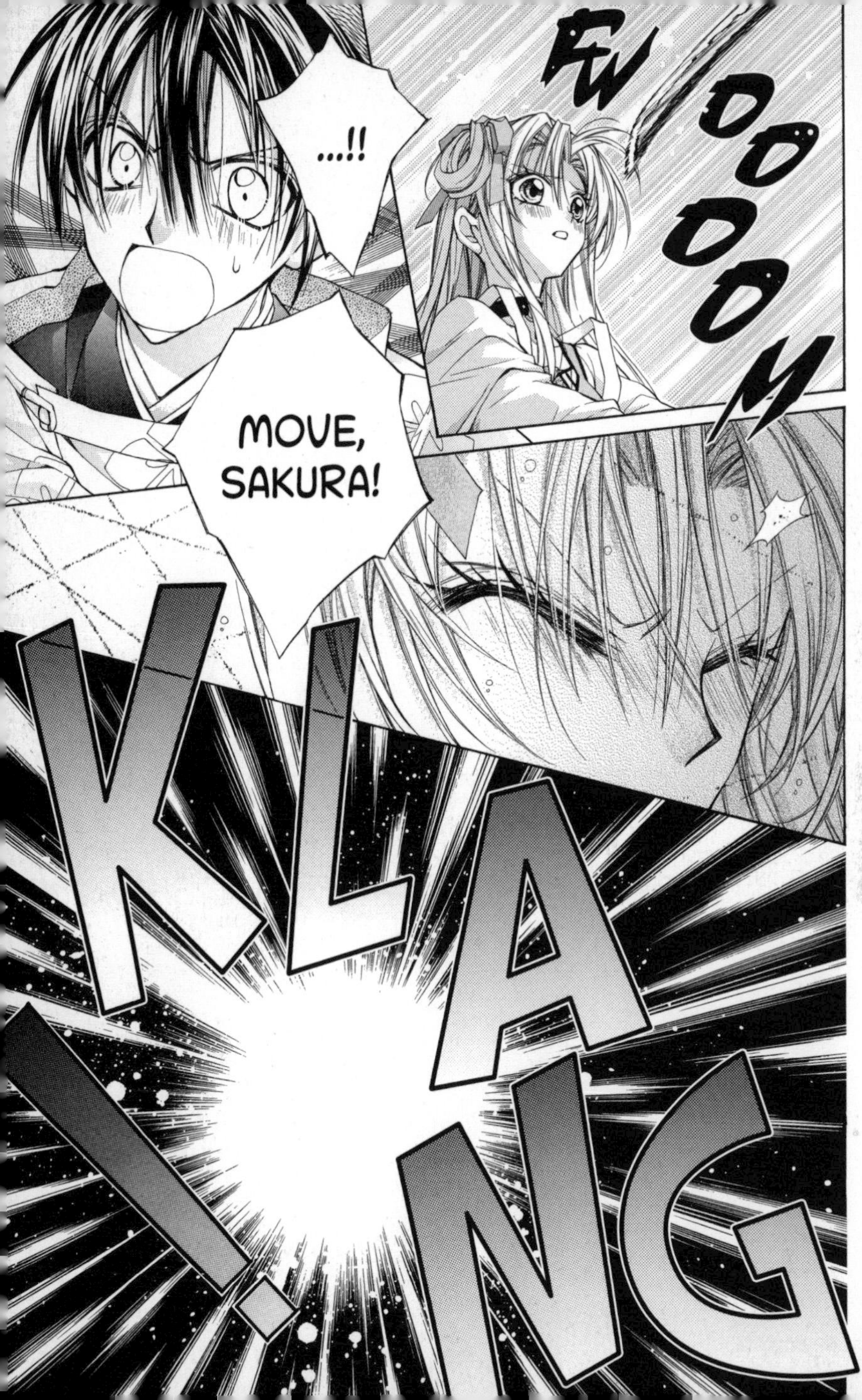
FWOOOOM
...!!
MOVE, SAKURA!
KLANG!

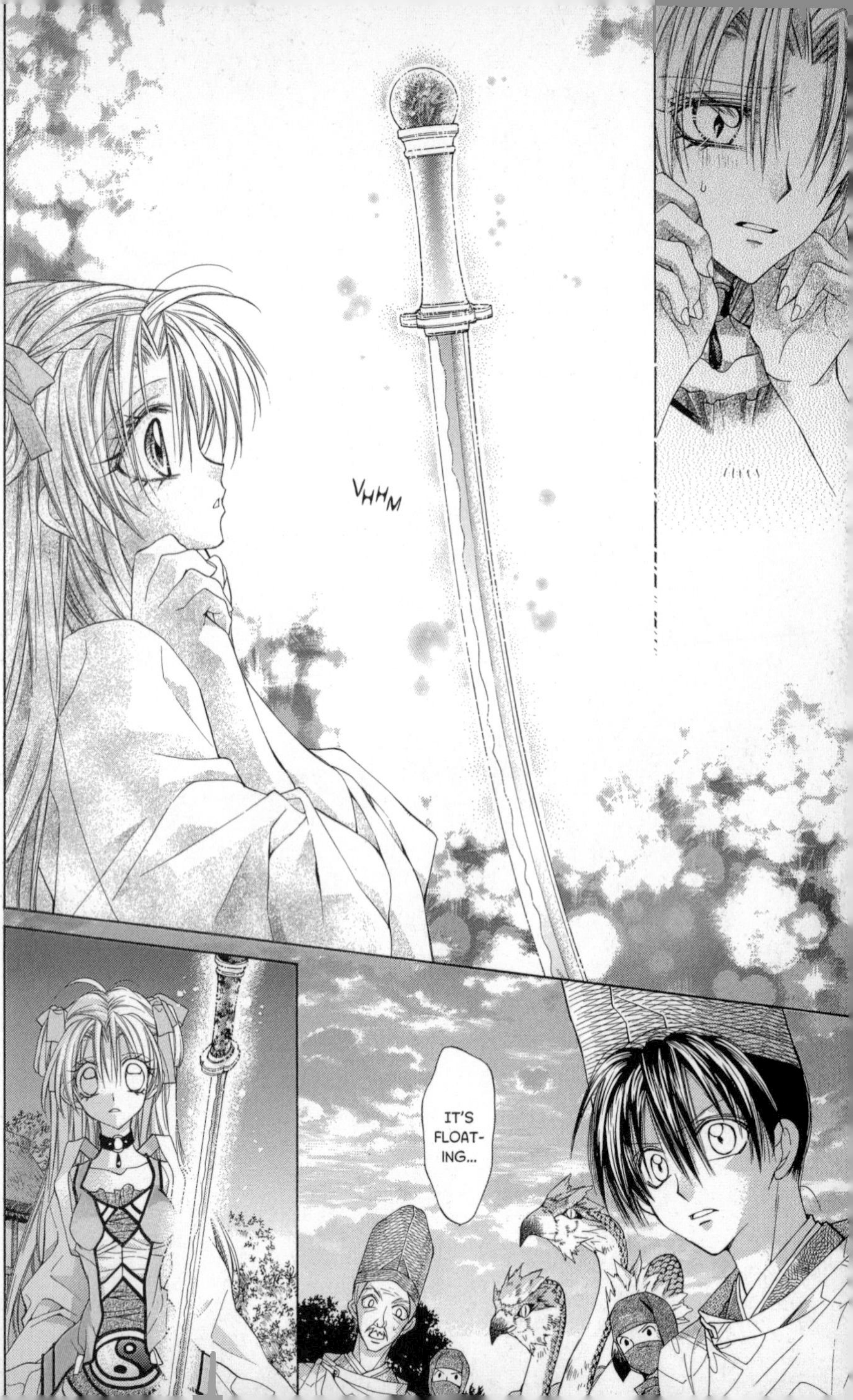
VHHM
IT'S FLOAT-ING...

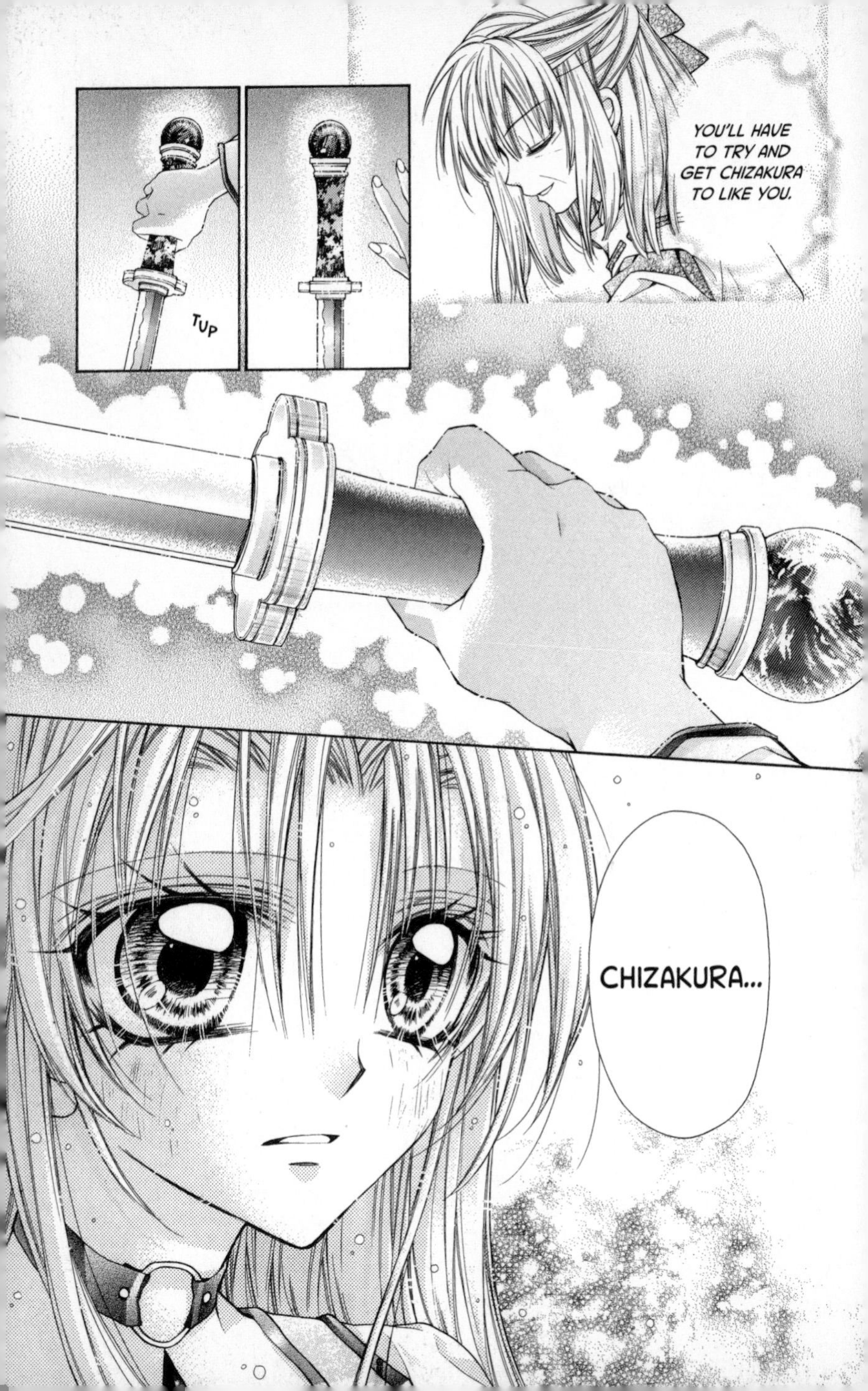
YOU'LL HAVE TO TRY AND GET CHIZAKURA TO LIKE YOU.
TUP
CHIZAKURA...

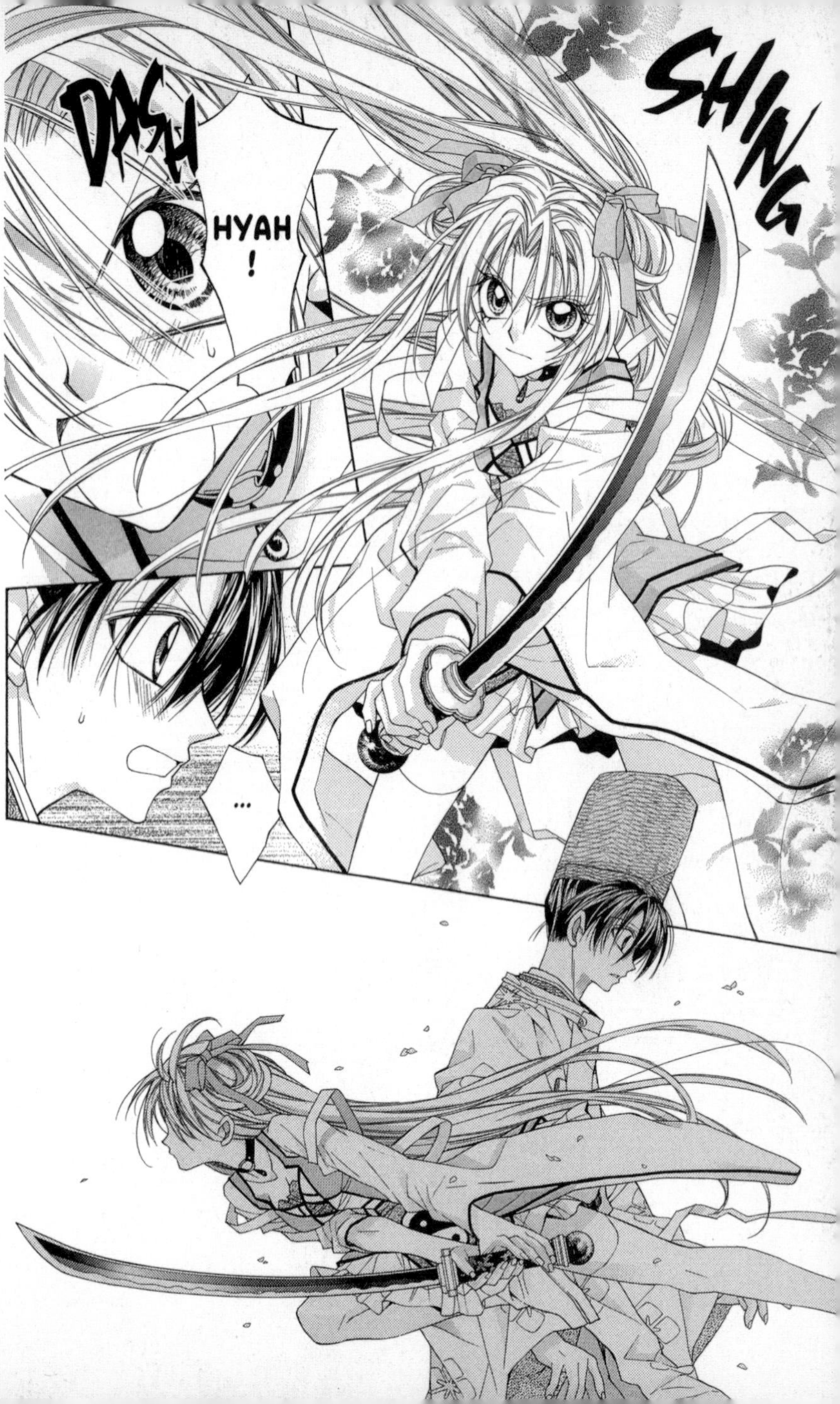
SHING
DASH
HYAH!
...

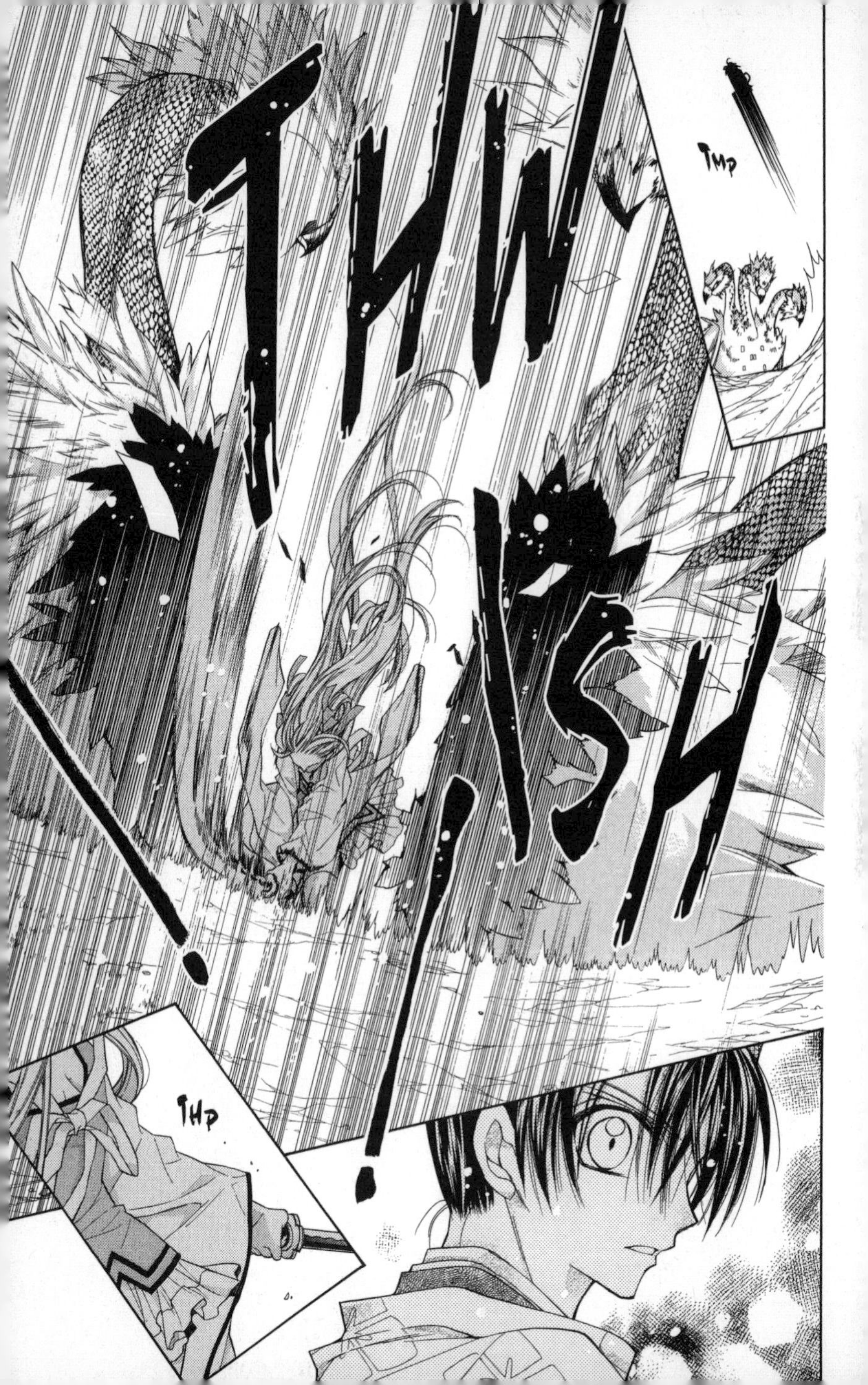
TMP
THWASH!!
THP

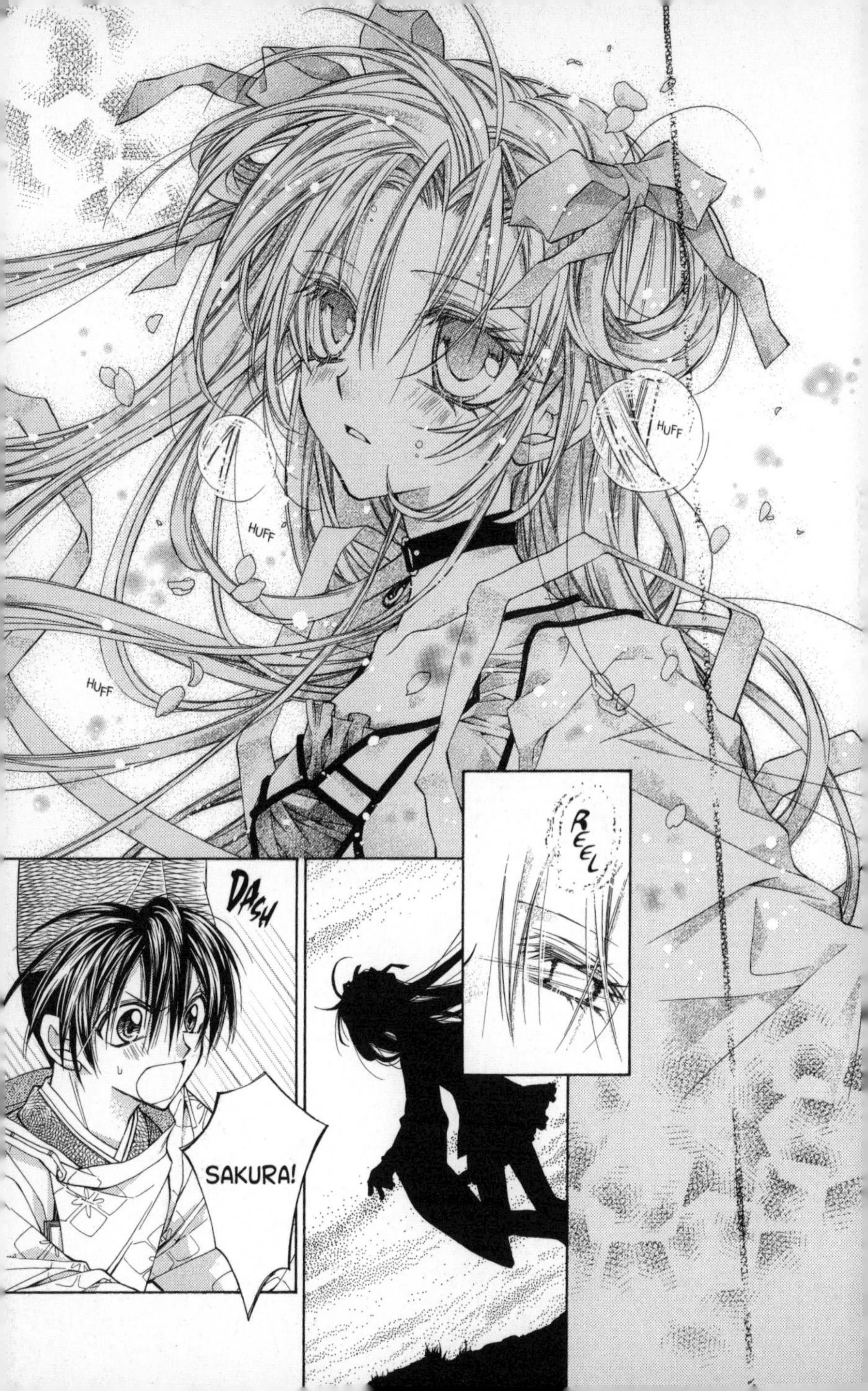
HUFF
HUFF
HUFF
REEL
DASH
SAKURA!

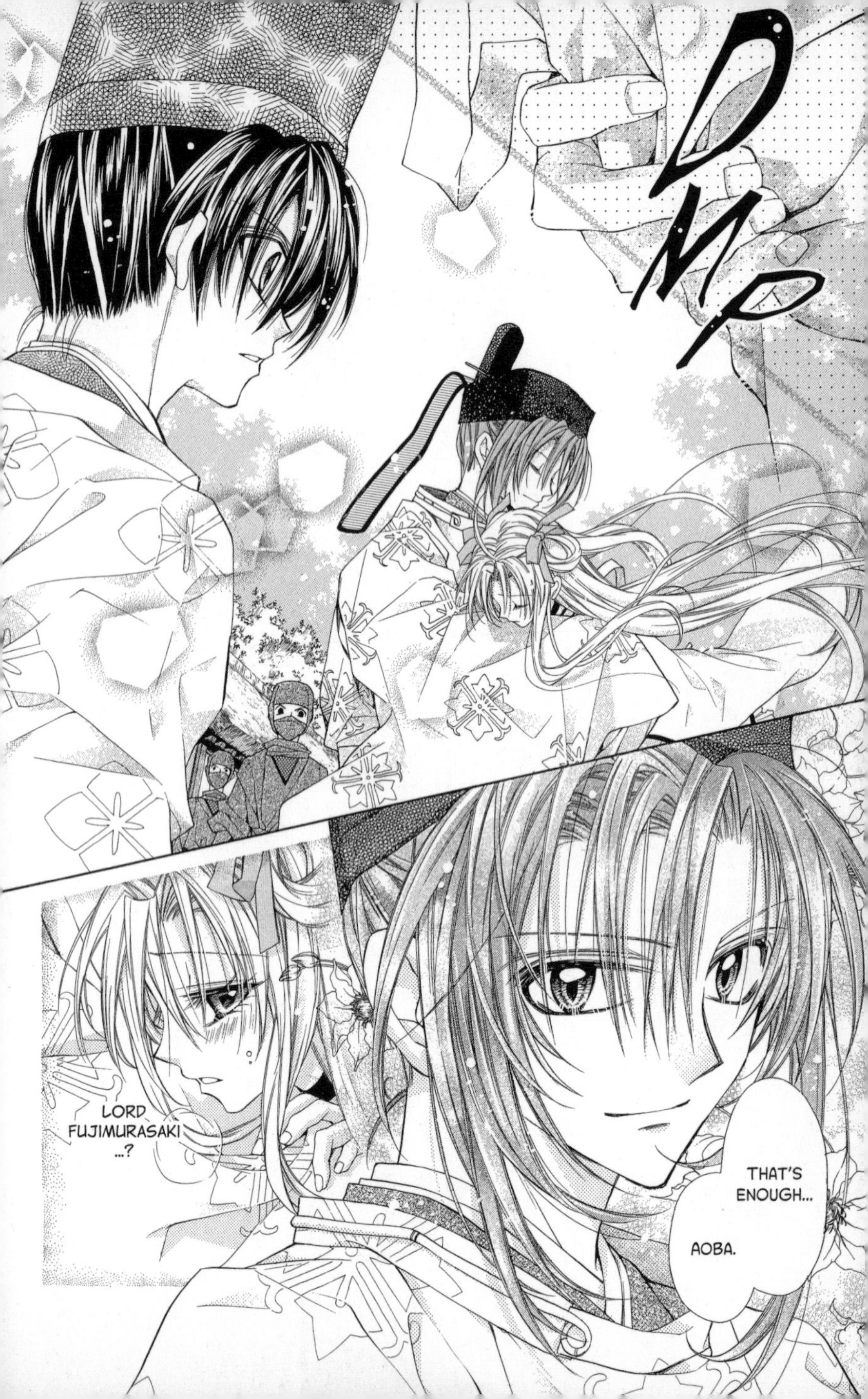
DUMP
THAT'S ENOUGH...
AOBA.
LORD FUJIMURASAKI ...?

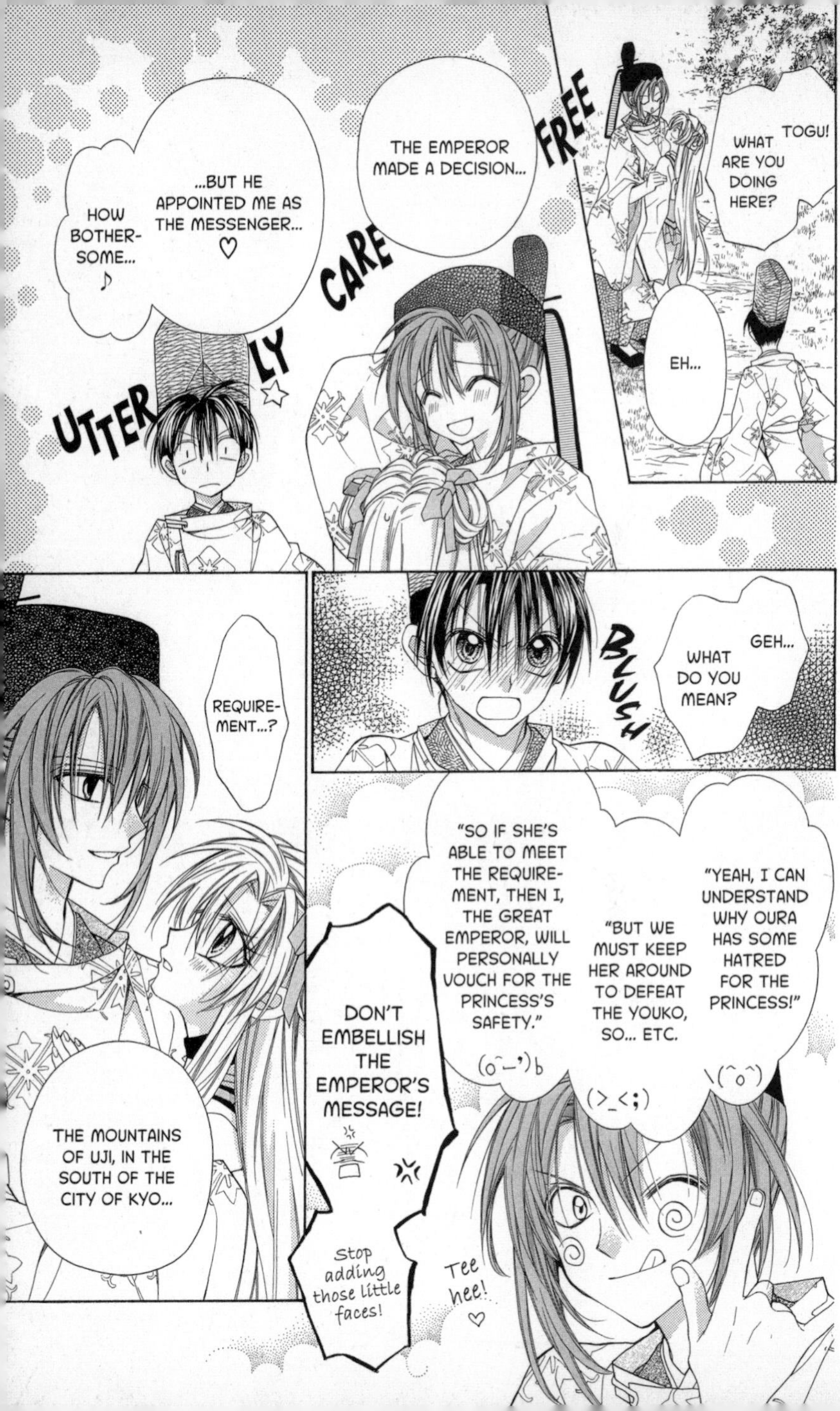
TOGU!
WHAT ARE YOU DOING HERE?
EH...
THE EMPEROR MADE A DECISION...
...BUT HE APPOINTED ME AS THE MESSENGER... ♡
HOW BOTHER-SOME... ♪
UTTERLY CAREFREE ☆
GEH...
WHAT DO YOU MEAN?
BLUSH
"YEAH, I CAN UNDERSTAND WHY OURA HAS SOME HATRED FOR THE PRINCESS!"
\(^o^)
"BUT WE MUST KEEP HER AROUND TO DEFEAT THE YOUKO, SO... ETC.
(>_<;)
"SO IF SHE'S ABLE TO MEET THE REQUIRE-MENT, THEN I, THE GREAT EMPEROR, WILL PERSONALLY VOUCH FOR THE PRINCESS'S SAFETY."
(o^_')b
DON'T EMBELLISH THE EMPEROR'S MESSAGE!
Stop adding those little faces!
Tee hee! ♡
REQUIRE-MENT...?
THE MOUNTAINS OF UJI, IN THE SOUTH OF THE CITY OF KYO...

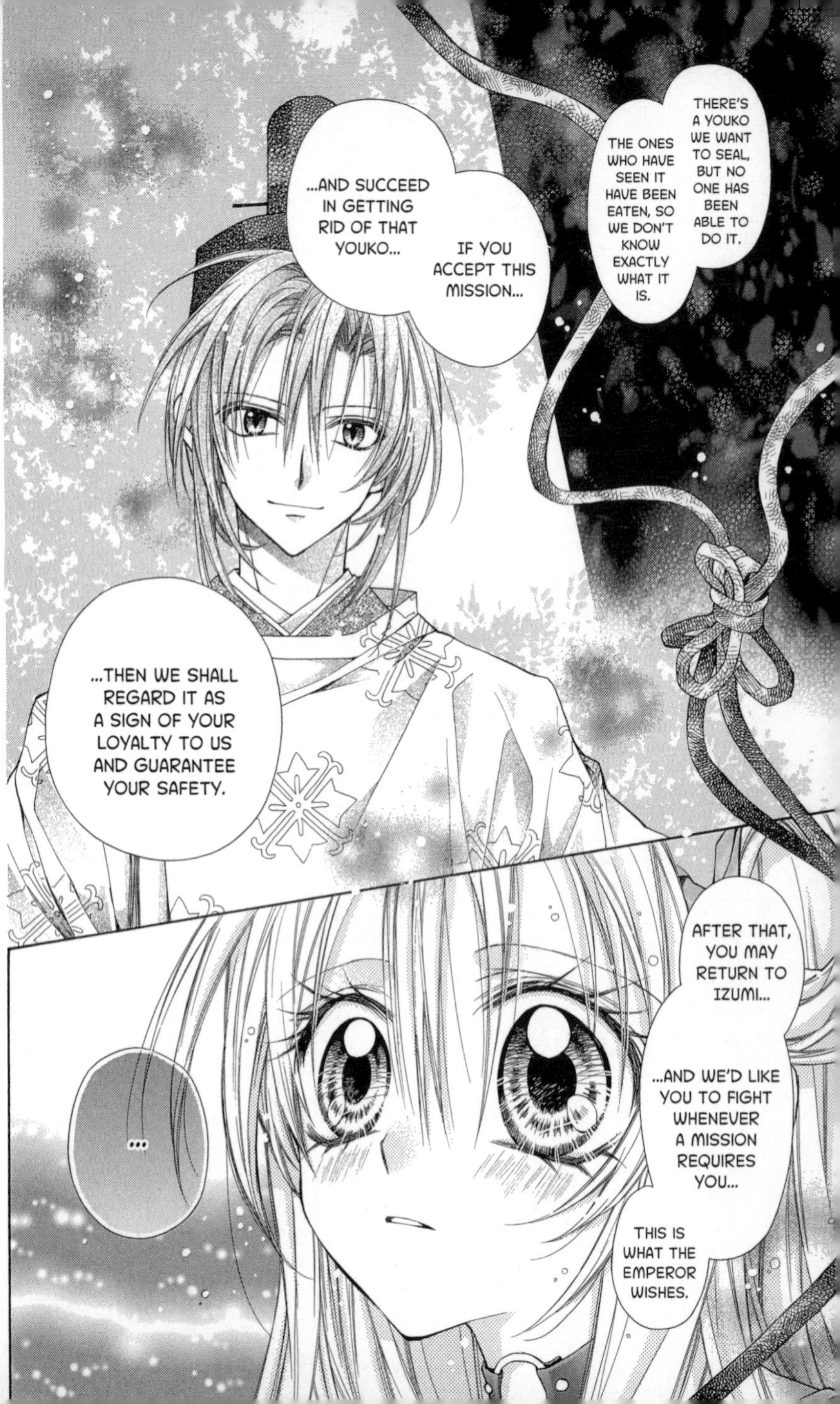
THERE'S A YOUKO WE WANT TO SEAL, BUT NO ONE HAS BEEN ABLE TO DO IT.
THE ONES WHO HAVE SEEN IT HAVE BEEN EATEN, SO WE DON'T KNOW EXACTLY WHAT IT IS.
IF YOU ACCEPT THIS MISSION...
...AND SUCCEED IN GETTING RID OF THAT YOUKO...
...THEN WE SHALL REGARD IT AS A SIGN OF YOUR LOYALTY TO US AND GUARANTEE YOUR SAFETY.
AFTER THAT, YOU MAY RETURN TO IZUMI...
...AND WE'D LIKE YOU TO FIGHT WHENEVER A MISSION REQUIRES YOU...
THIS IS WHAT THE EMPEROR WISHES.
...

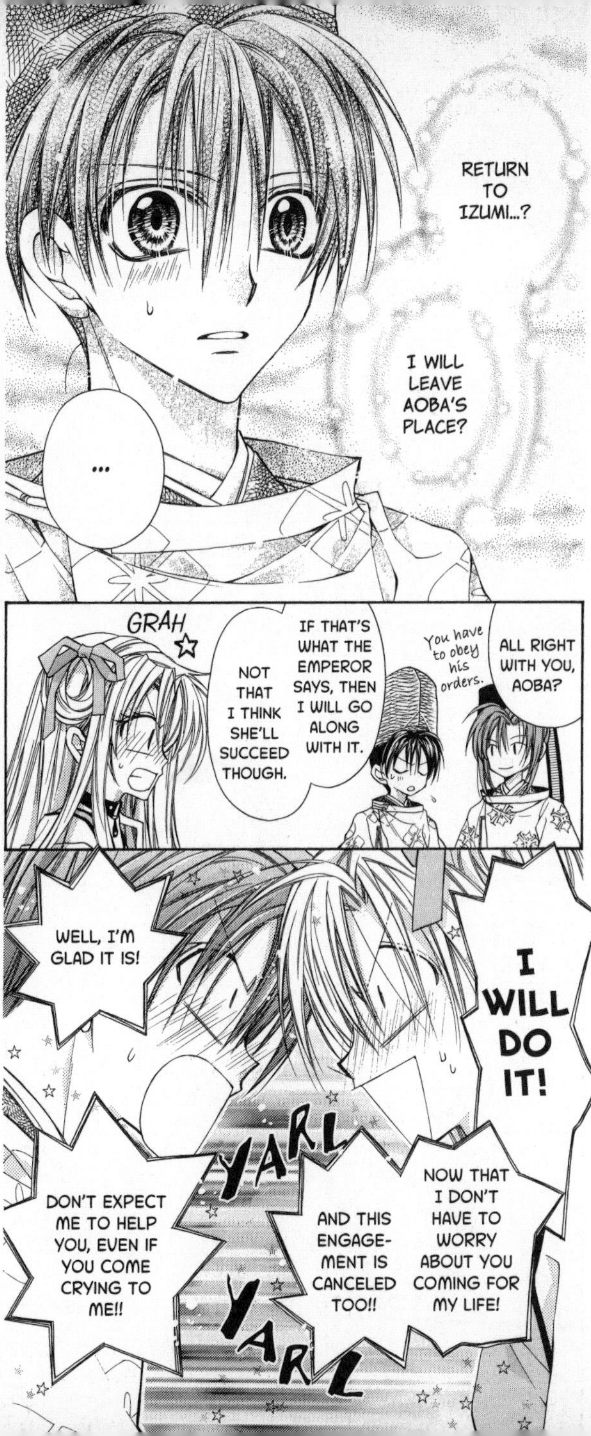
RETURN TO IZUMI...?
I WILL LEAVE AOBA'S PLACE?
...
ALL RIGHT WITH YOU, AOBA?
You have to obey his orders.
IF THAT'S WHAT THE EMPEROR SAYS, THEN I WILL GO ALONG WITH IT.
NOT THAT I THINK SHE'LL SUCCEED THOUGH.
GRAH
I WILL DO IT!
WELL, I'M GLAD IT IS!
NOW THAT I DON'T HAVE TO WORRY ABOUT YOU COMING FOR MY LIFE!
AND THIS ENGAGEMENT IS CANCELED TOO!!
YARL
YARL
DON'T EXPECT ME TO HELP YOU, EVEN IF YOU COME CRYING TO ME!!

The return of?!

PENCHI DE SHAKIN ☆

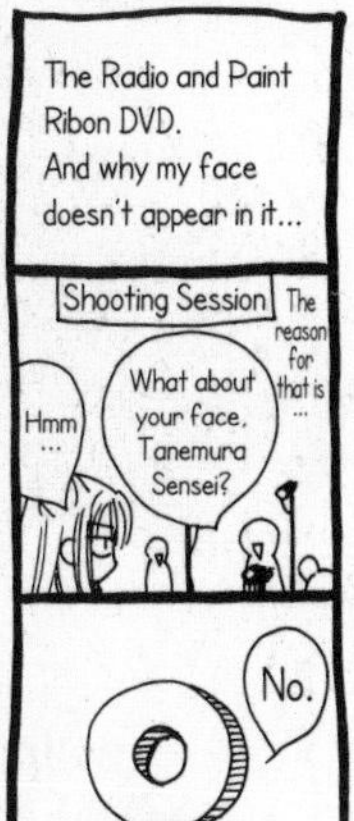
The Radio and Paint Ribon DVD.
And why my face doesn't appear in it...
Shooting Session
The reason for that is...
What about your face, Tanemura Sensei?
Hmm...
No.

It's okay for me to say that, but I'm a selfish person who gets a little annoyed when someone else says it.

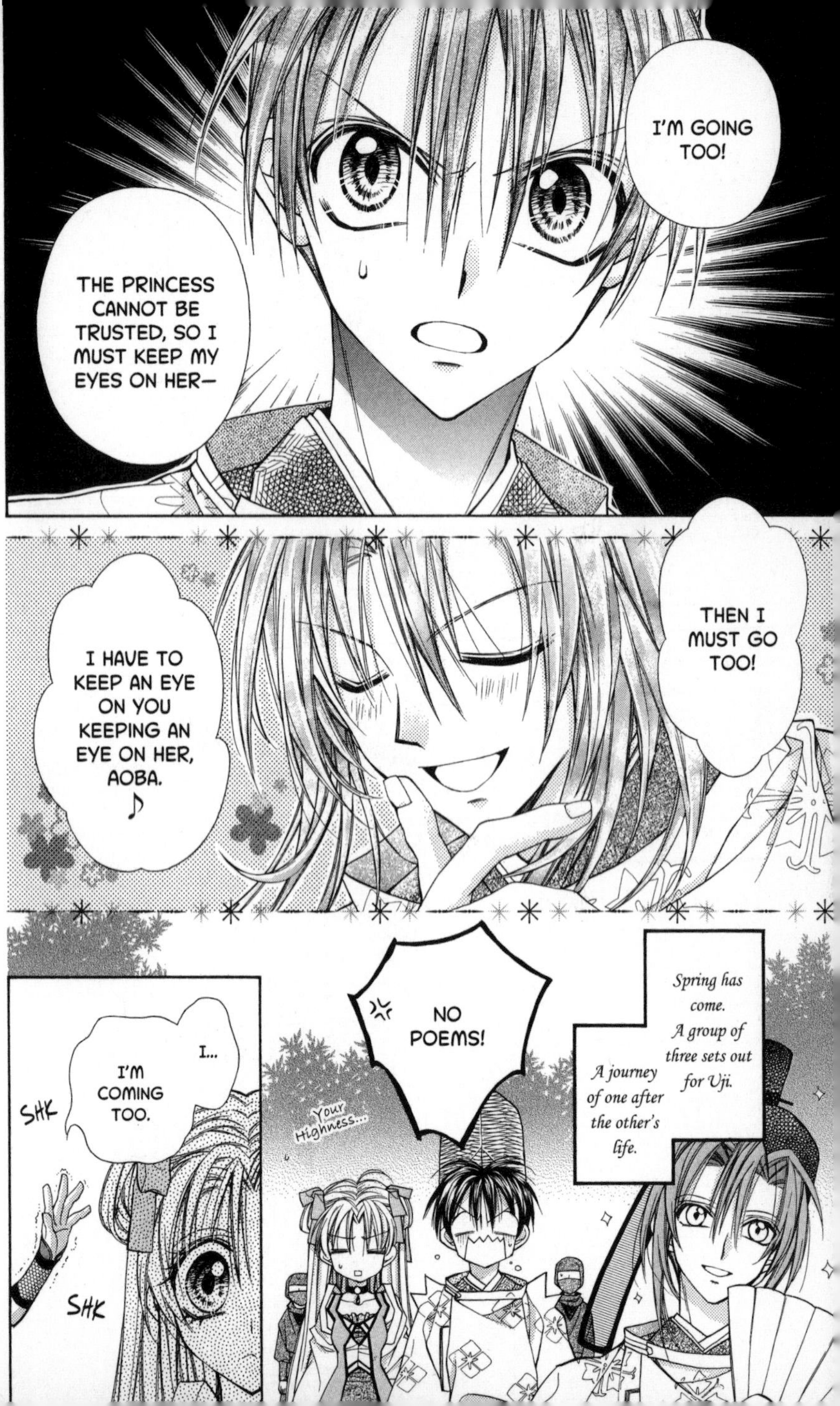
I'M GOING TOO!
THE PRINCESS CANNOT BE TRUSTED, SO I MUST KEEP MY EYES ON HER—
THEN I MUST GO TOO!
I HAVE TO KEEP AN EYE ON YOU KEEPING AN EYE ON HER, AOBA. ♪
Spring has come. A group of three sets out for Uji.
A journey of one after the other's life.
NO POEMS!
Your Highness...
I...
I'M COMING TOO.
SHK
SHK

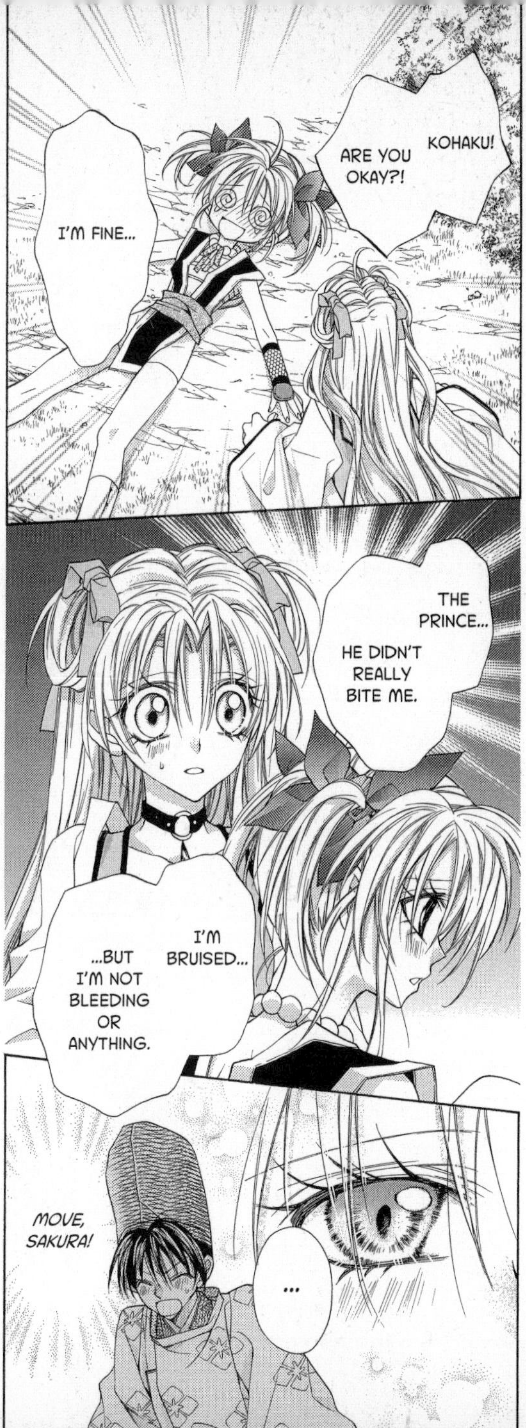
KOHAKU!
ARE YOU OKAY?!
I'M FINE...
THE PRINCE...
HE DIDN'T REALLY BITE ME.
I'M BRUISED...
...BUT I'M NOT BLEEDING OR ANYTHING.
...
MOVE, SAKURA!

AAH, MONSTER HUNTER MEET UP.

Shoko-tan persuaded me, so recently I've started to play *Monster Hunter Freedom Unite.* ≡

I've always loved to level up in role-play games, so I was easily hooked... ≦▽≧✿

I often have Monster Hunter meet ups with the Mitsuki Saiga-san, Meg rock-chan, Ayana Tsubaki-chan, Chiaki Kyan-chan and Chihiro-chan. ♥ (Shoko-tan has been busy, and I still haven't had the opportunity of going hunting with her... ≦_≧;)

Thanks to everybody's help, my Hunter Rank is 9, but I often lose.^;

My favorite monsters are Yian Kut-Ku and Rathalos. ♥
And I'm good at Treasure Hunting in the Jungle area!
(I was able to go up to 40,000 points all alone!!)

I'm a Long Sword user. ♥ (I love the Wailing Cleaver Shin. ♥)

Saiga-san has been introducing me to many people, so every day has been a fresh new day for me these days. ⌒▽⌒ ✿

I'm thinking about having a crêpe party at my place during our Monster Hunter meet up!

✿ Yay! Yay! ✿

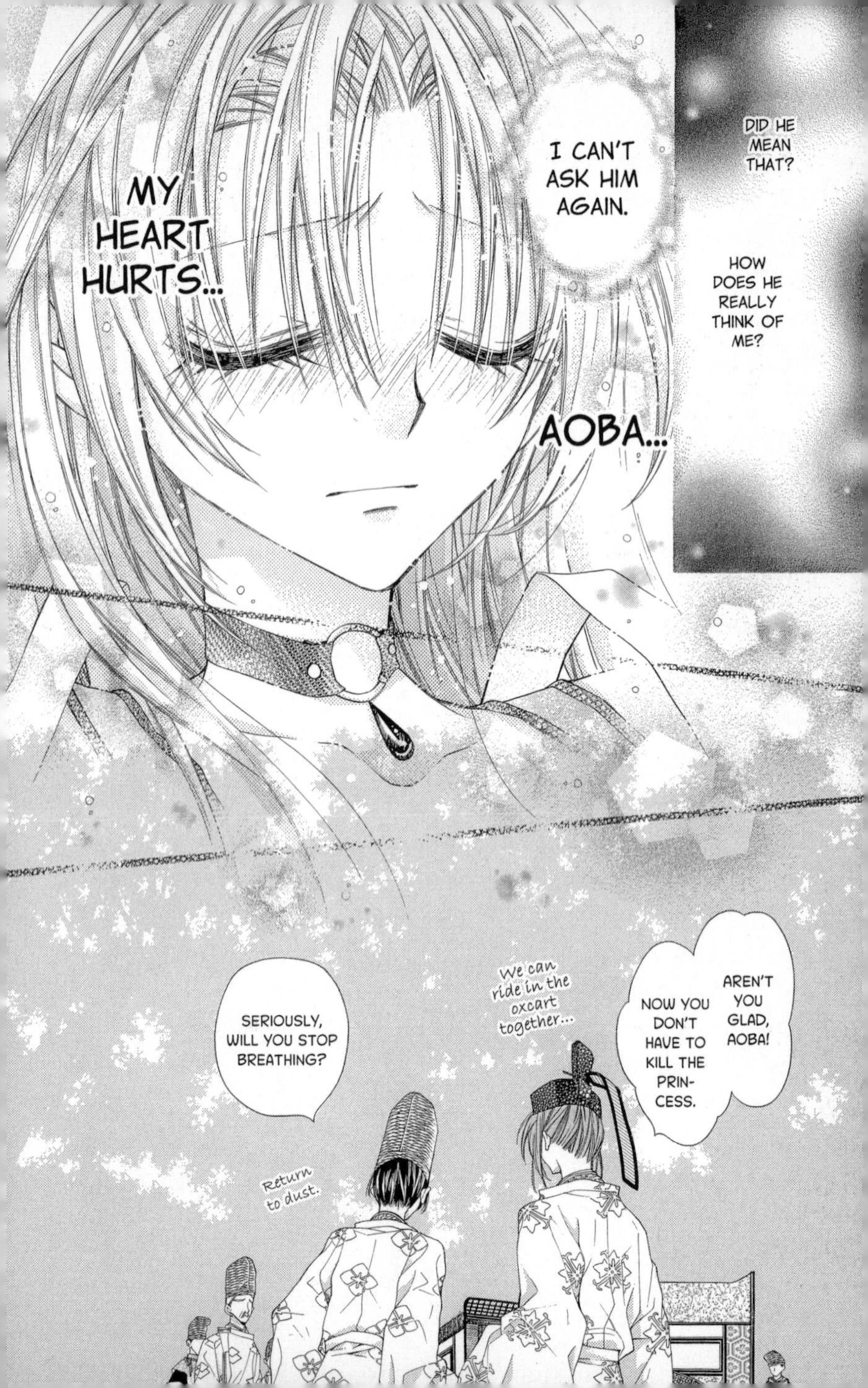
DID HE MEAN THAT?
HOW DOES HE REALLY THINK OF ME?
I CAN'T ASK HIM AGAIN.
MY HEART HURTS...
AOBA...
AREN'T YOU GLAD, AOBA!
NOW YOU DON'T HAVE TO KILL THE PRIN-CESS.
We can ride in the oxcart together...
SERIOUSLY, WILL YOU STOP BREATHING?
Return to dust.

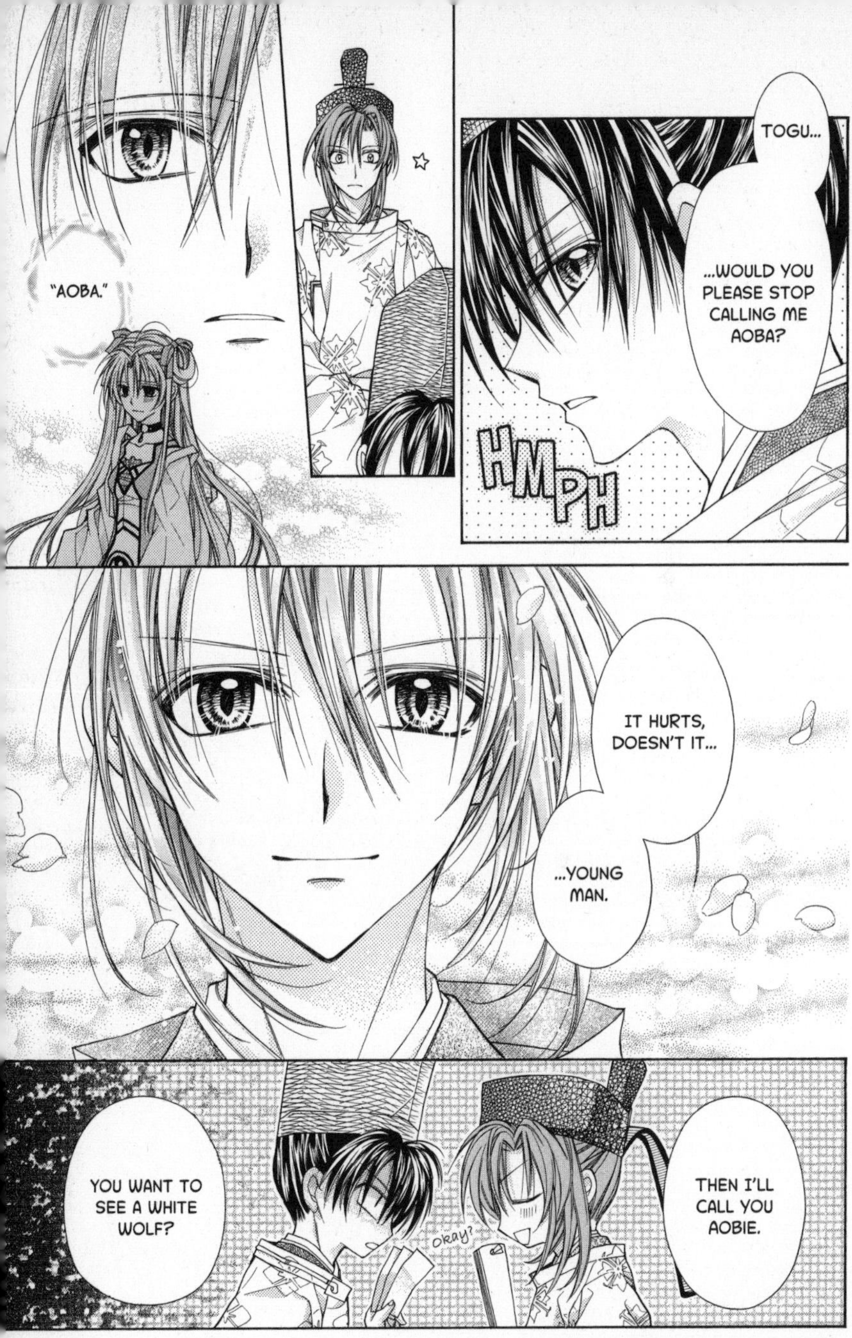
TOGU...
...WOULD YOU PLEASE STOP CALLING ME AOBA?
HMPH
"AOBA."
IT HURTS, DOESN'T IT...
...YOUNG MAN.
THEN I'LL CALL YOU AOBIE.
okay?
YOU WANT TO SEE A WHITE WOLF?

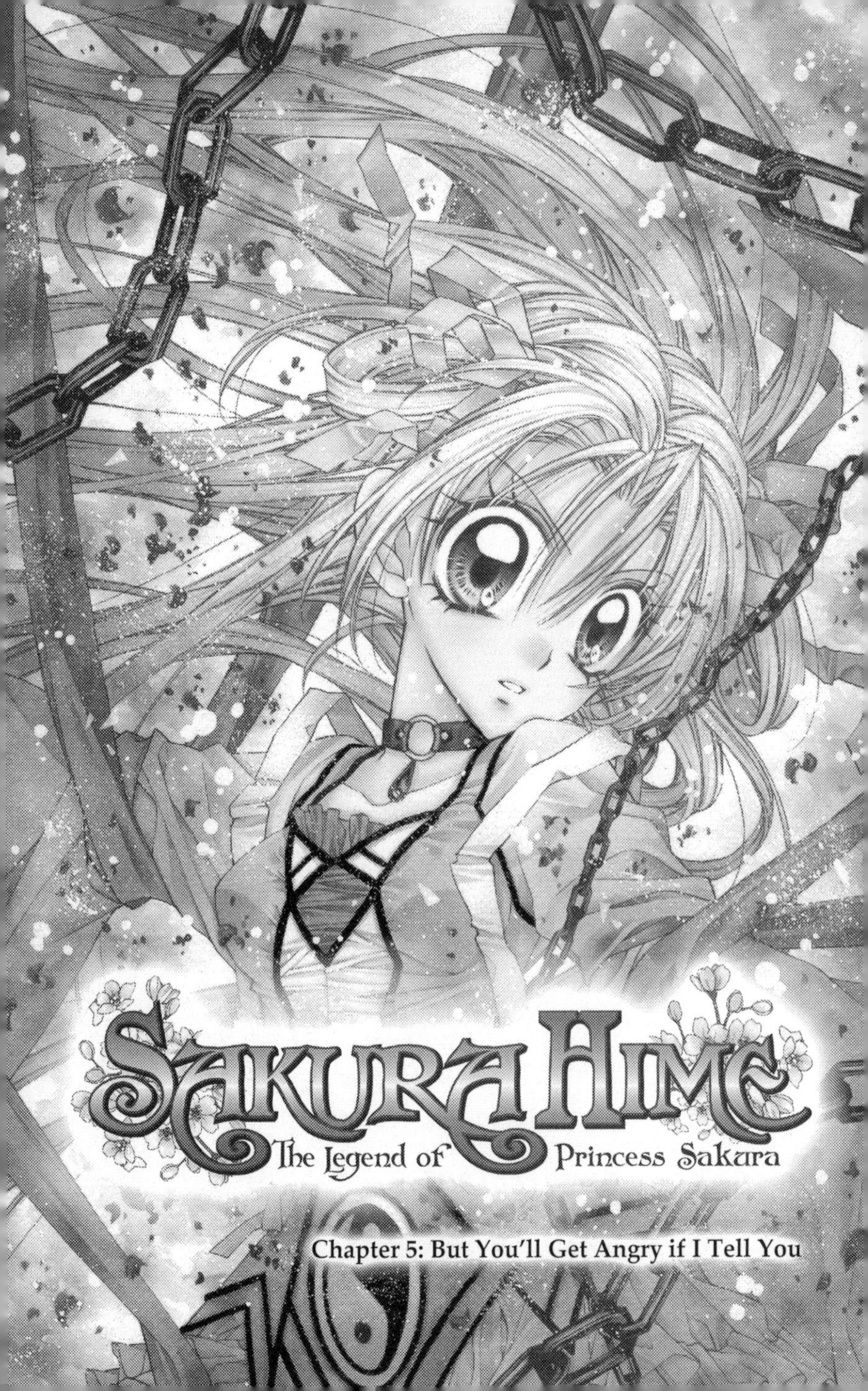
SAKURA HIME
The Legend of Princess Sakura
Chapter 5: But You'll Get Angry if I Tell You

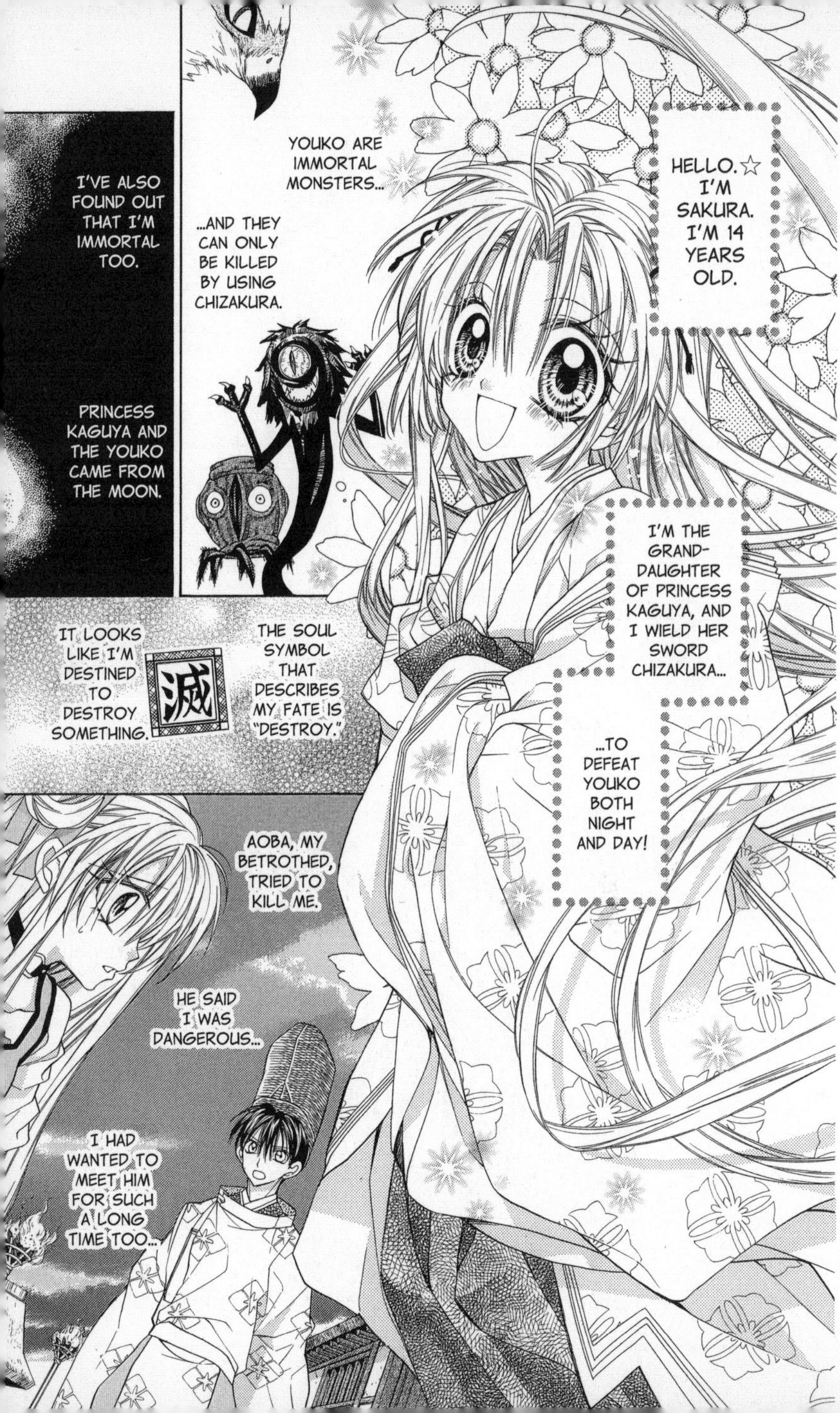
HELLO.☆ I'M SAKURA. I'M 14 YEARS OLD.
I'M THE GRAND-DAUGHTER OF PRINCESS KAGUYA, AND I WIELD HER SWORD CHIZAKURA...
...TO DEFEAT YOUKO BOTH NIGHT AND DAY!
YOUKO ARE IMMORTAL MONSTERS...
...AND THEY CAN ONLY BE KILLED BY USING CHIZAKURA.
I'VE ALSO FOUND OUT THAT I'M IMMORTAL TOO.
PRINCESS KAGUYA AND THE YOUKO CAME FROM THE MOON.
THE SOUL SYMBOL THAT DESCRIBES MY FATE IS "DESTROY."
滅
IT LOOKS LIKE I'M DESTINED TO DESTROY SOMETHING.
AOBA, MY BETROTHED, TRIED TO KILL ME.
HE SAID I WAS DANGEROUS...
I HAD WANTED TO MEET HIM FOR SUCH A LONG TIME TOO...

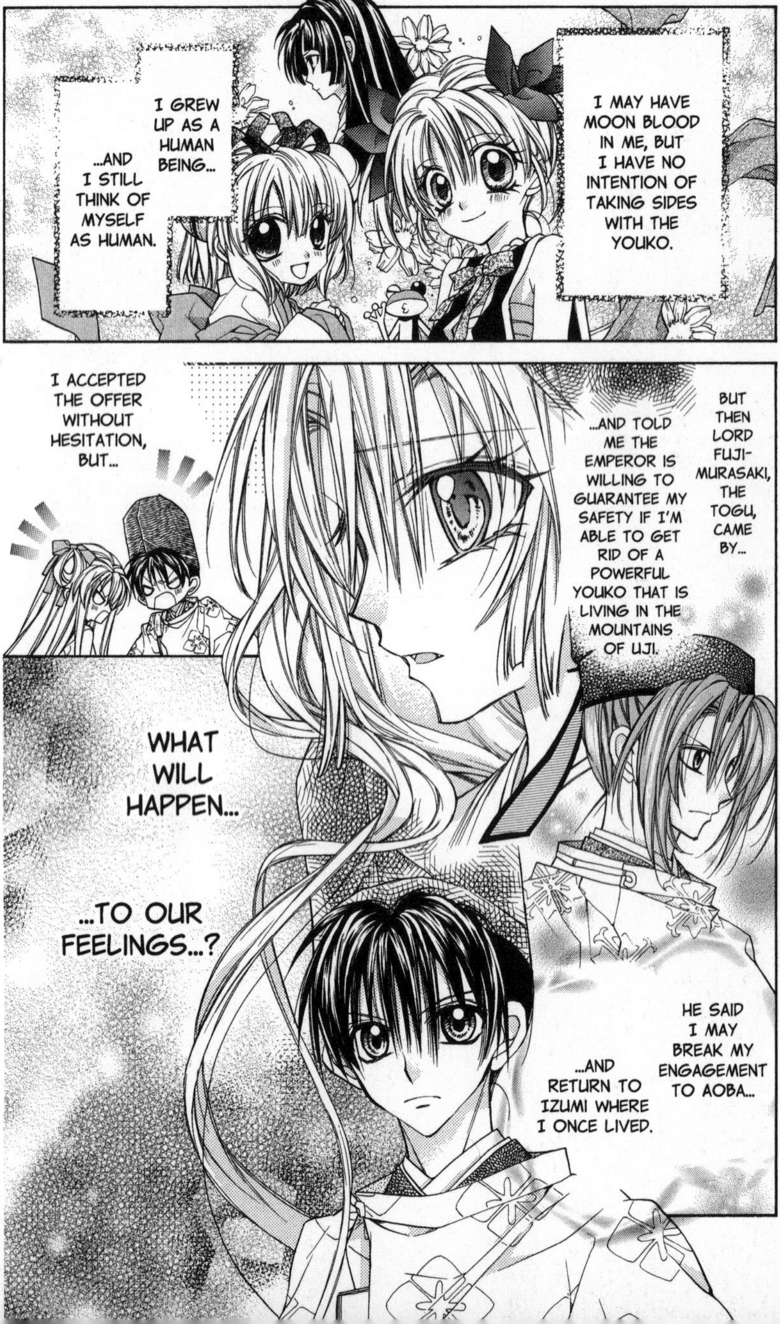

I MAY HAVE MOON BLOOD IN ME, BUT I HAVE NO INTENTION OF TAKING SIDES WITH THE YOUKO.
I GREW UP AS A HUMAN BEING...
...AND I STILL THINK OF MYSELF AS HUMAN.
BUT THEN LORD FUJI-MURASAKI, THE TOGU, CAME BY...
...AND TOLD ME THE EMPEROR IS WILLING TO GUARANTEE MY SAFETY IF I'M ABLE TO GET RID OF A POWERFUL YOUKO THAT IS LIVING IN THE MOUNTAINS OF UJI.
I ACCEPTED THE OFFER WITHOUT HESITATION, BUT...
HE SAID I MAY BREAK MY ENGAGEMENT TO AOBA...
...AND RETURN TO IZUMI WHERE I ONCE LIVED.
WHAT WILL HAPPEN...
...TO OUR FEELINGS...?

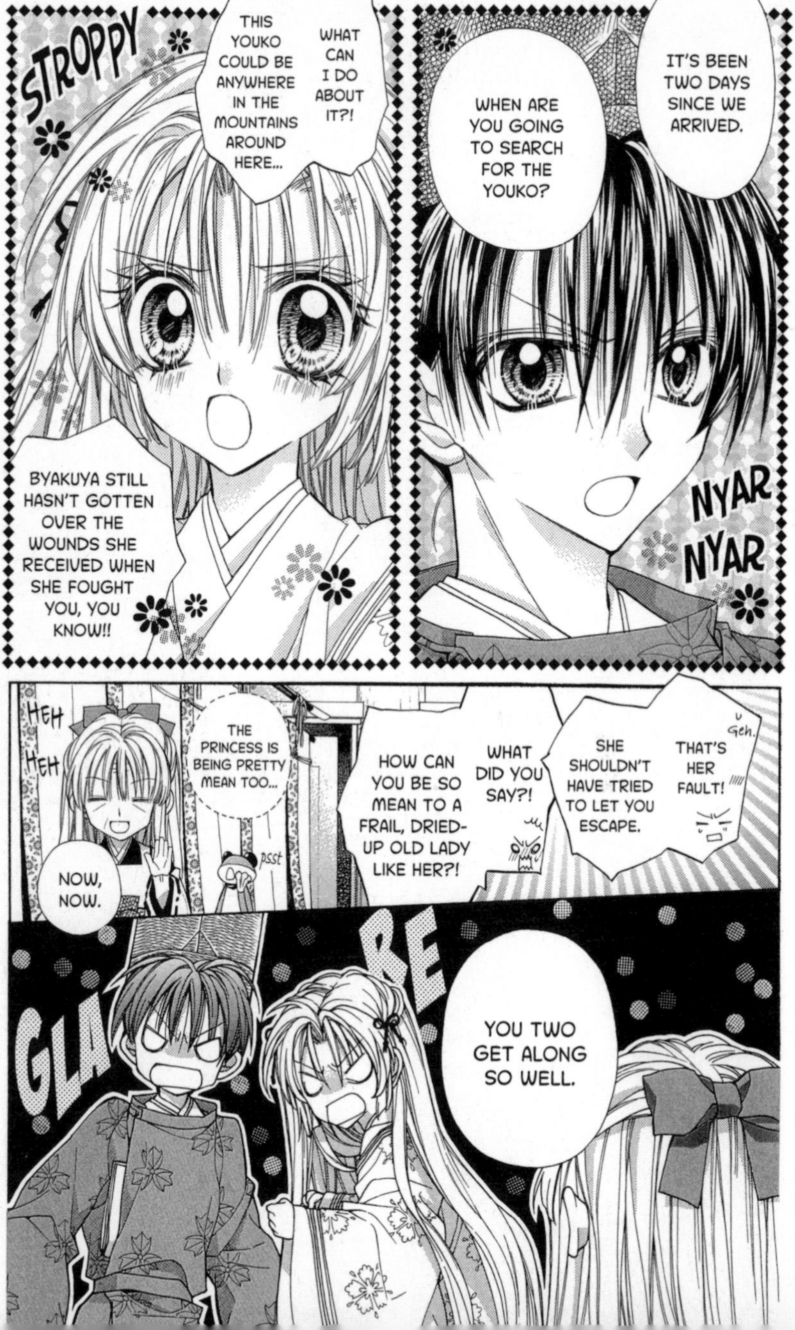
IT'S BEEN TWO DAYS SINCE WE ARRIVED.
WHEN ARE YOU GOING TO SEARCH FOR THE YOUKO?
NYAR NYAR
STROPPY
WHAT CAN I DO ABOUT IT?!
THIS YOUKO COULD BE ANYWHERE IN THE MOUNTAINS AROUND HERE...
BYAKUYA STILL HASN'T GOTTEN OVER THE WOUNDS SHE RECEIVED WHEN SHE FOUGHT YOU, YOU KNOW!!
Geh.
THAT'S HER FAULT!
SHE SHOULDN'T HAVE TRIED TO LET YOU ESCAPE.
WHAT DID YOU SAY?!
HOW CAN YOU BE SO MEAN TO A FRAIL, DRIED-UP OLD LADY LIKE HER?!
THE PRINCESS IS BEING PRETTY MEAN TOO...
psst
HEH HEH
NOW, NOW.
YOU TWO GET ALONG SO WELL.
GLARE

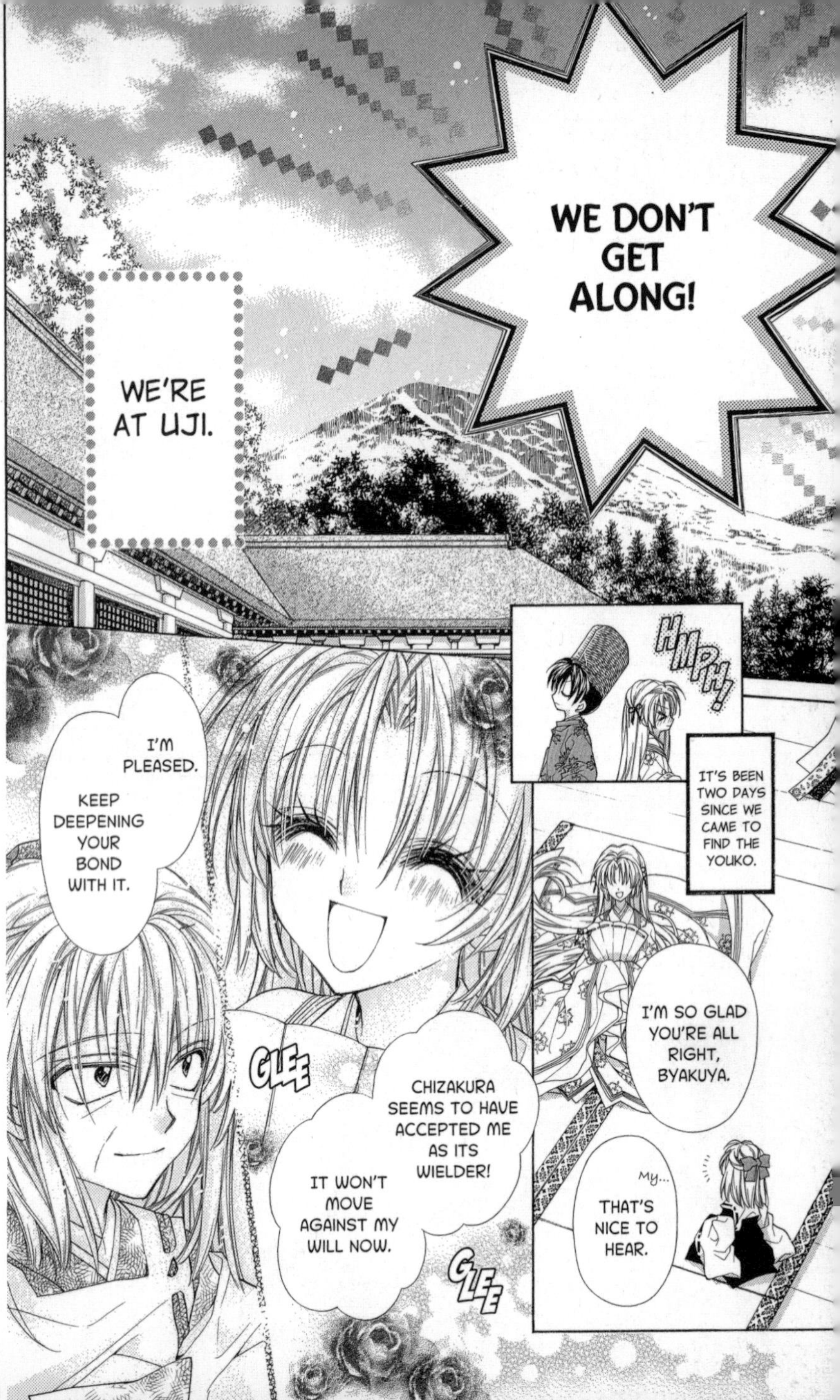
WE DON'T GET ALONG!
WE'RE AT UJI.
HMPH!
IT'S BEEN TWO DAYS SINCE WE CAME TO FIND THE YOUKO.
I'M SO GLAD YOU'RE ALL RIGHT, BYAKUYA.
My...
THAT'S NICE TO HEAR.
CHIZAKURA SEEMS TO HAVE ACCEPTED ME AS ITS WIELDER!
IT WON'T MOVE AGAINST MY WILL NOW.
GLEE
GLEE
I'M PLEASED.
KEEP DEEPENING YOUR BOND WITH IT.

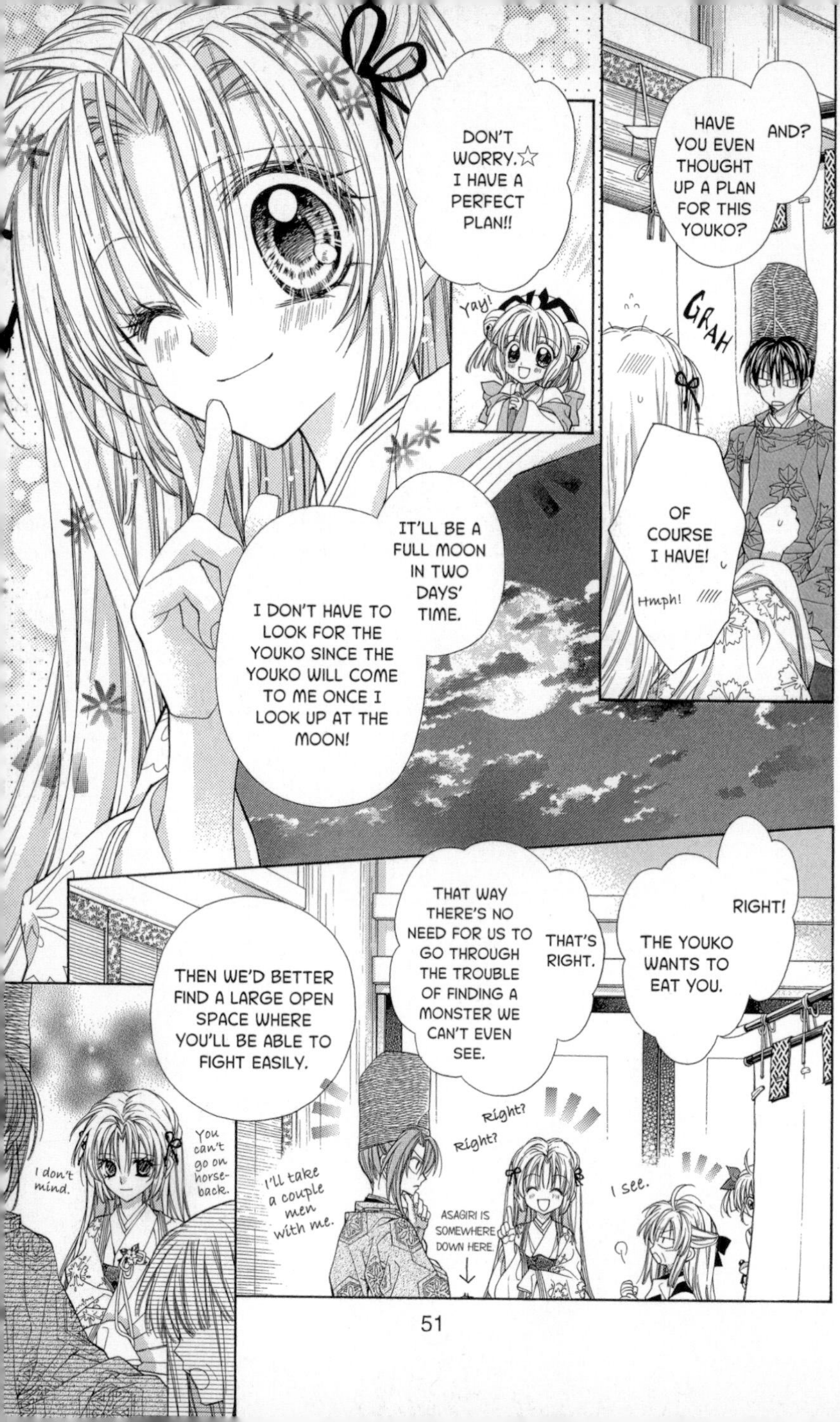
AND?
HAVE YOU EVEN THOUGHT UP A PLAN FOR THIS YOUKO?
GRAH
OF COURSE I HAVE!
Hmph!
DON'T WORRY.☆ I HAVE A PERFECT PLAN!!
Yay!
IT'LL BE A FULL MOON IN TWO DAYS' TIME.
I DON'T HAVE TO LOOK FOR THE YOUKO SINCE THE YOUKO WILL COME TO ME ONCE I LOOK UP AT THE MOON!
RIGHT!
THE YOUKO WANTS TO EAT YOU.
THAT'S RIGHT.
THAT WAY THERE'S NO NEED FOR US TO GO THROUGH THE TROUBLE OF FINDING A MONSTER WE CAN'T EVEN SEE.
Right?
Right?
I see.
ASAGIRI IS SOMEWHERE DOWN HERE.
I'll take a couple men with me.
THEN WE'D BETTER FIND A LARGE OPEN SPACE WHERE YOU'LL BE ABLE TO FIGHT EASILY.
You can't go on horse-back.
I don't mind.

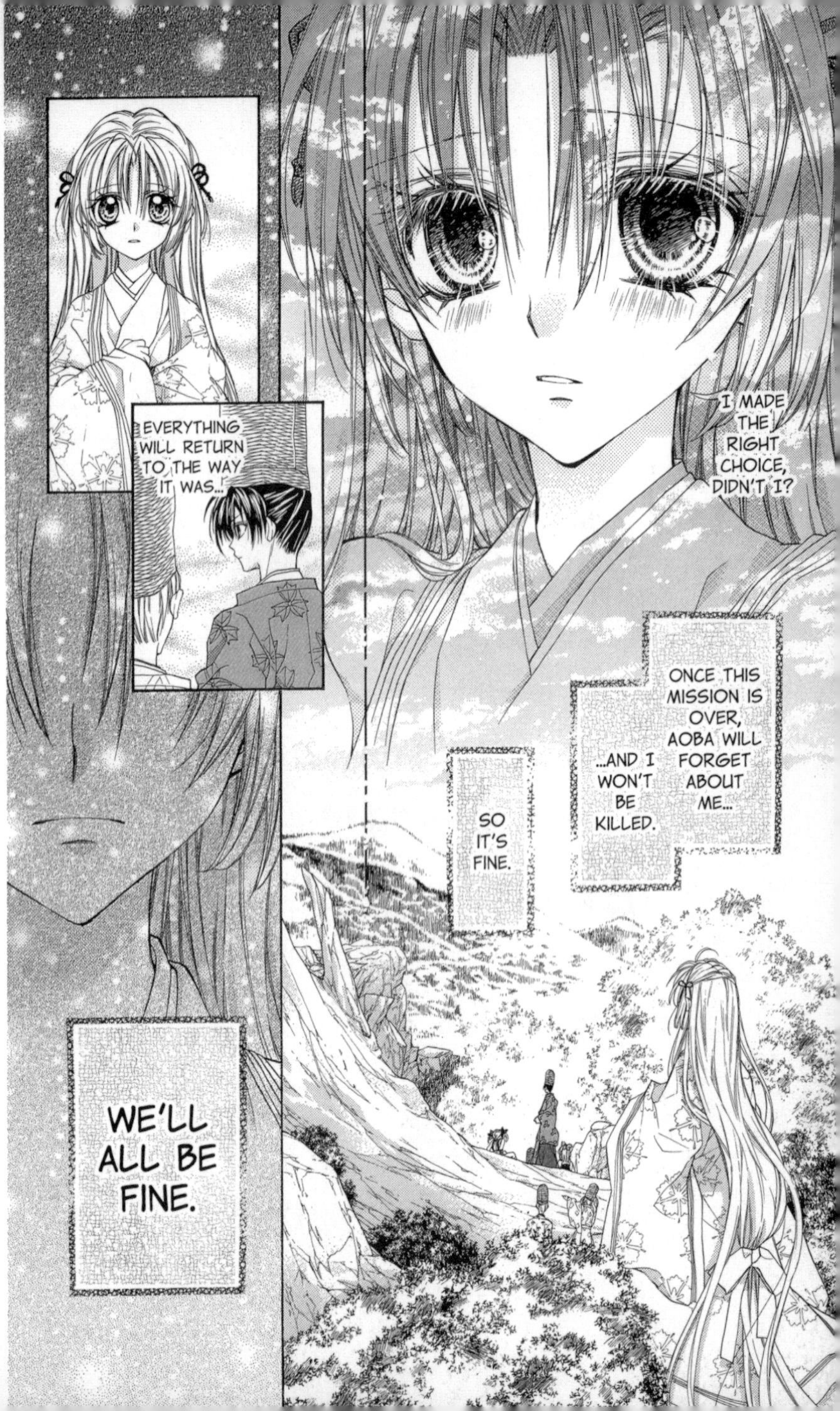
I MADE THE RIGHT CHOICE, DIDN'T I?
ONCE THIS MISSION IS OVER, AOBA WILL FORGET ABOUT ME...
...AND I WON'T BE KILLED.
SO IT'S FINE.
EVERYTHING WILL RETURN TO THE WAY IT WAS...
WE'LL ALL BE FINE.

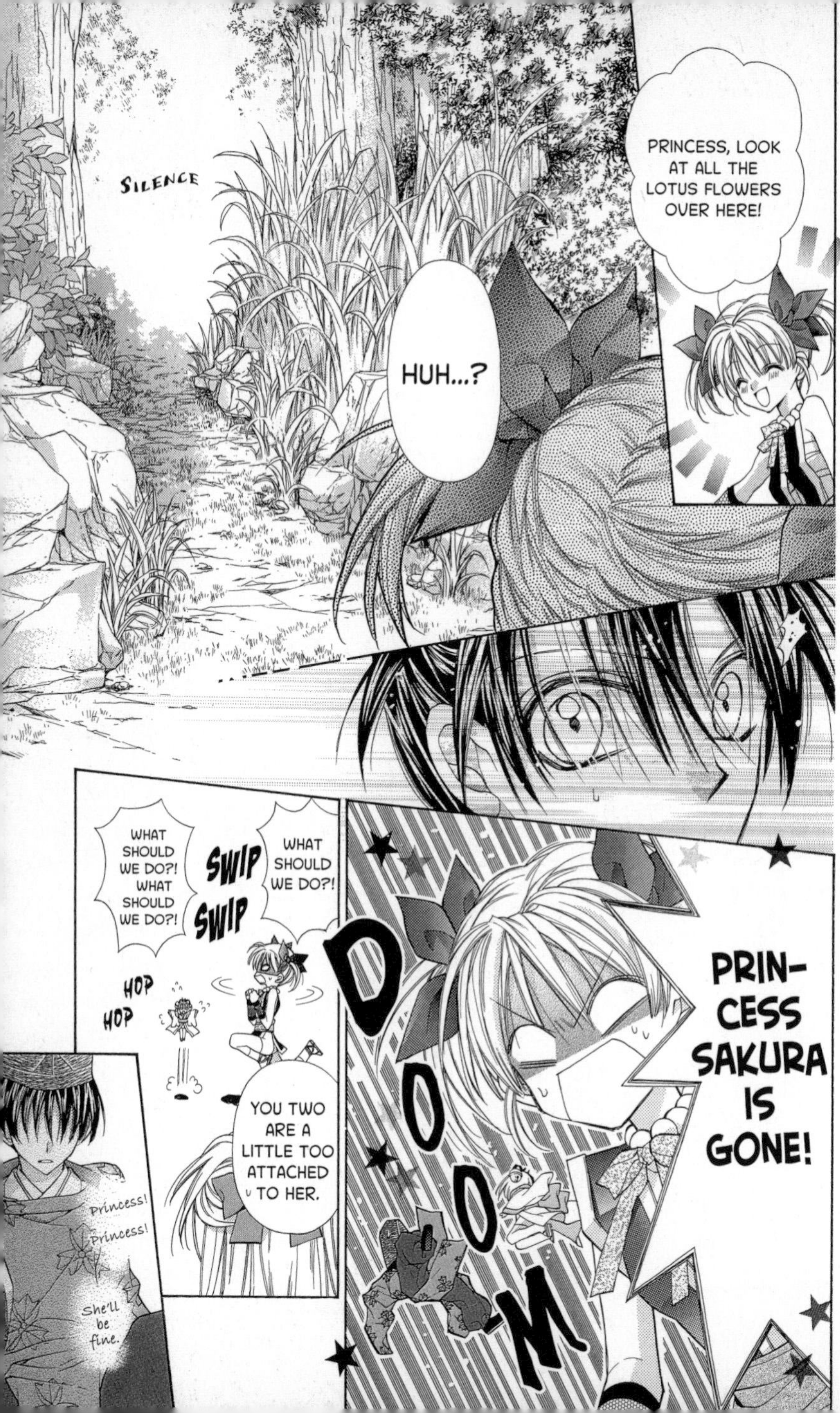
PRINCESS, LOOK AT ALL THE LOTUS FLOWERS OVER HERE!
HUH...?
SILENCE
PRIN-CESS SAKURA IS GONE!
DOOOM
WHAT SHOULD WE DO?!
SWIP SWIP
WHAT SHOULD WE DO?! WHAT SHOULD WE DO?!
HOP HOP
YOU TWO ARE A LITTLE TOO ATTACHED TO HER.
Princess! Princess!
She'll be fine.

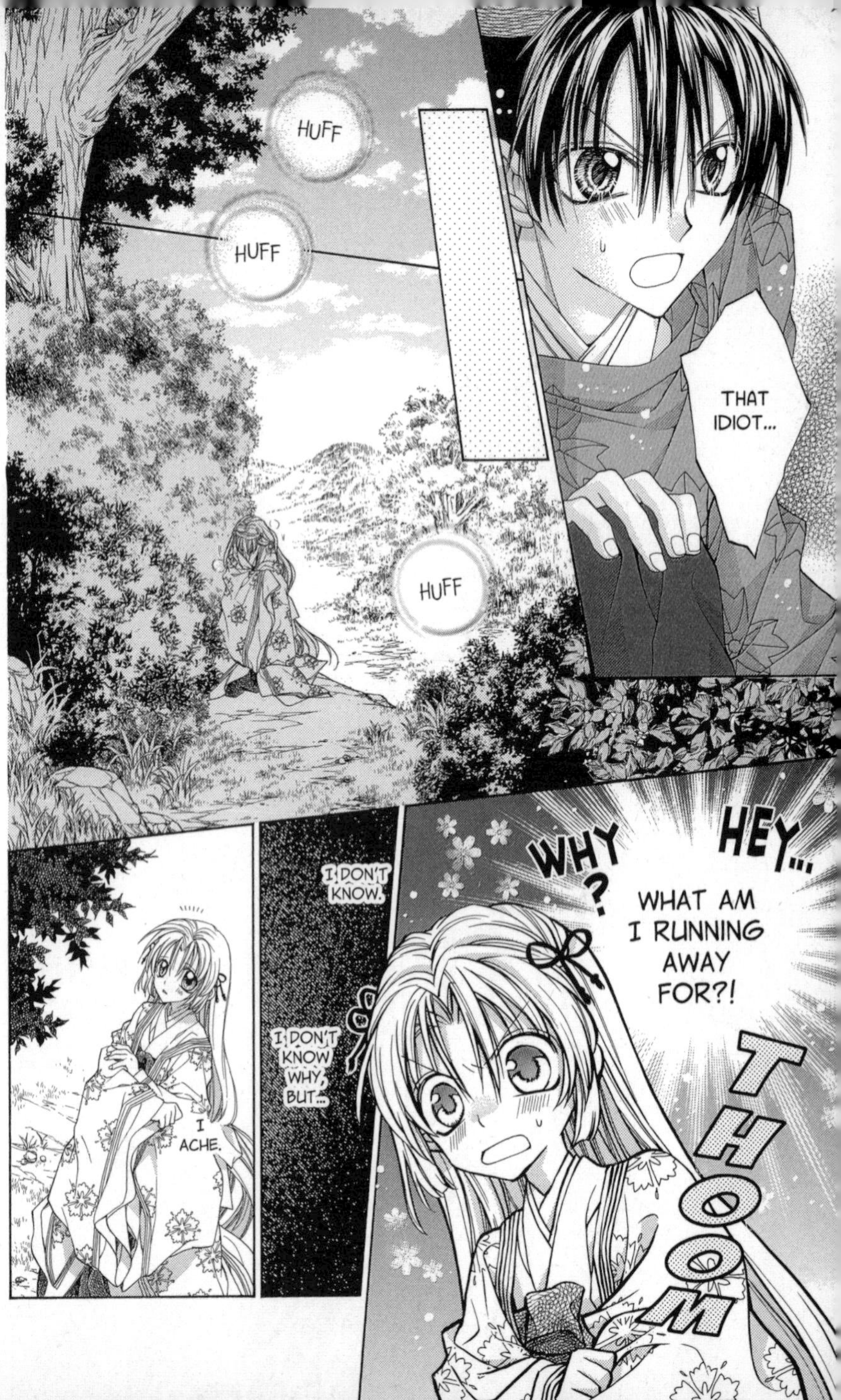
THAT IDIOT...
HUFF
HUFF
HUFF
HEY...
WHAT AM I RUNNING AWAY FOR?!
WHY?
THOOM
I DON'T KNOW.
I DON'T KNOW WHY, BUT...
I ACHE.

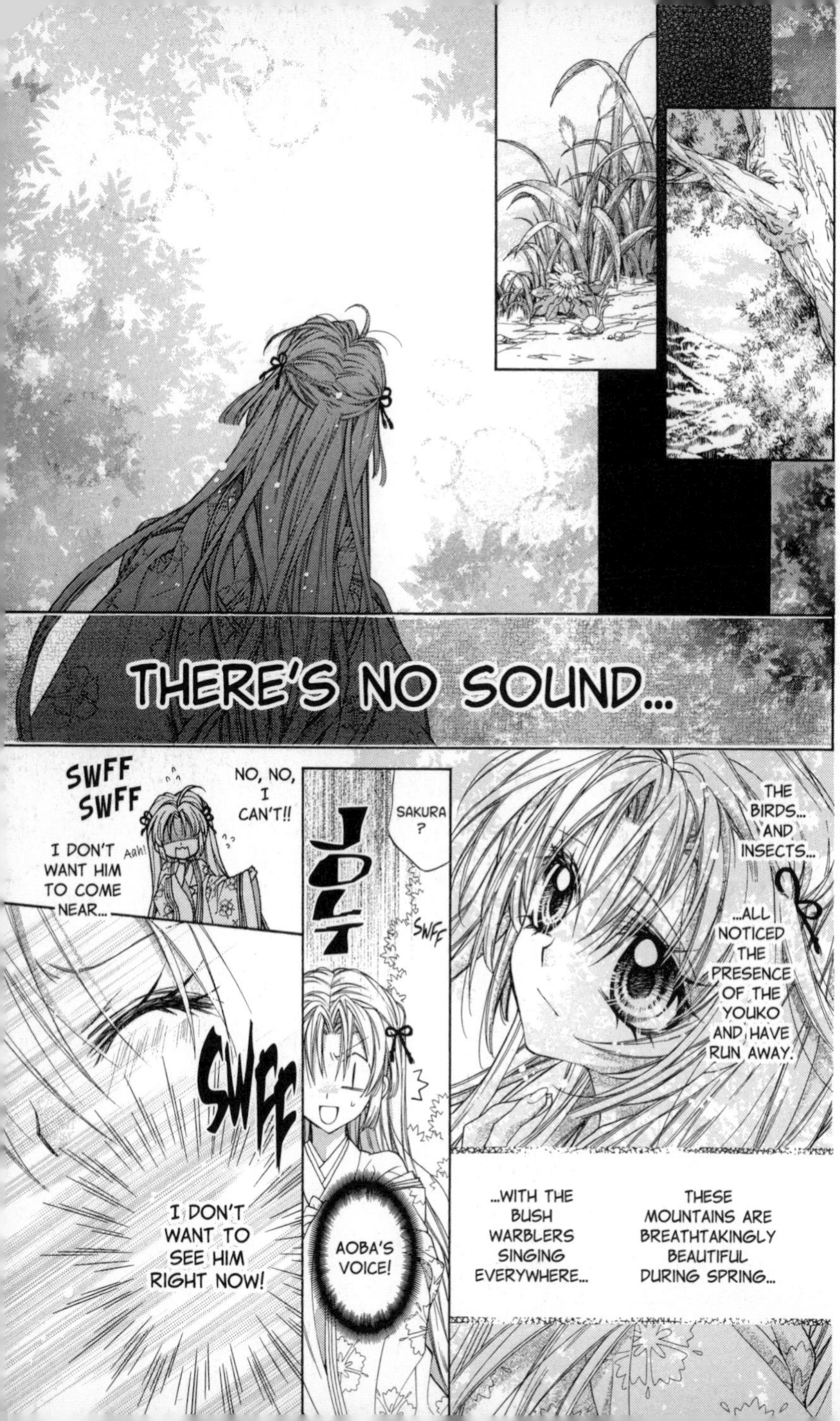
THERE'S NO SOUND...
THE BIRDS... AND INSECTS...
...ALL NOTICED THE PRESENCE OF THE YOUKO AND HAVE RUN AWAY.
THESE MOUNTAINS ARE BREATHTAKINGLY BEAUTIFUL DURING SPRING...
...WITH THE BUSH WARBLERS SINGING EVERYWHERE...
SAKURA?
JOLT
SWFF
AOBA'S VOICE!
SWFF SWFF
NO, NO, I CAN'T!!
Aah!
I DON'T WANT HIM TO COME NEAR...
SWFF
I DON'T WANT TO SEE HIM RIGHT NOW!

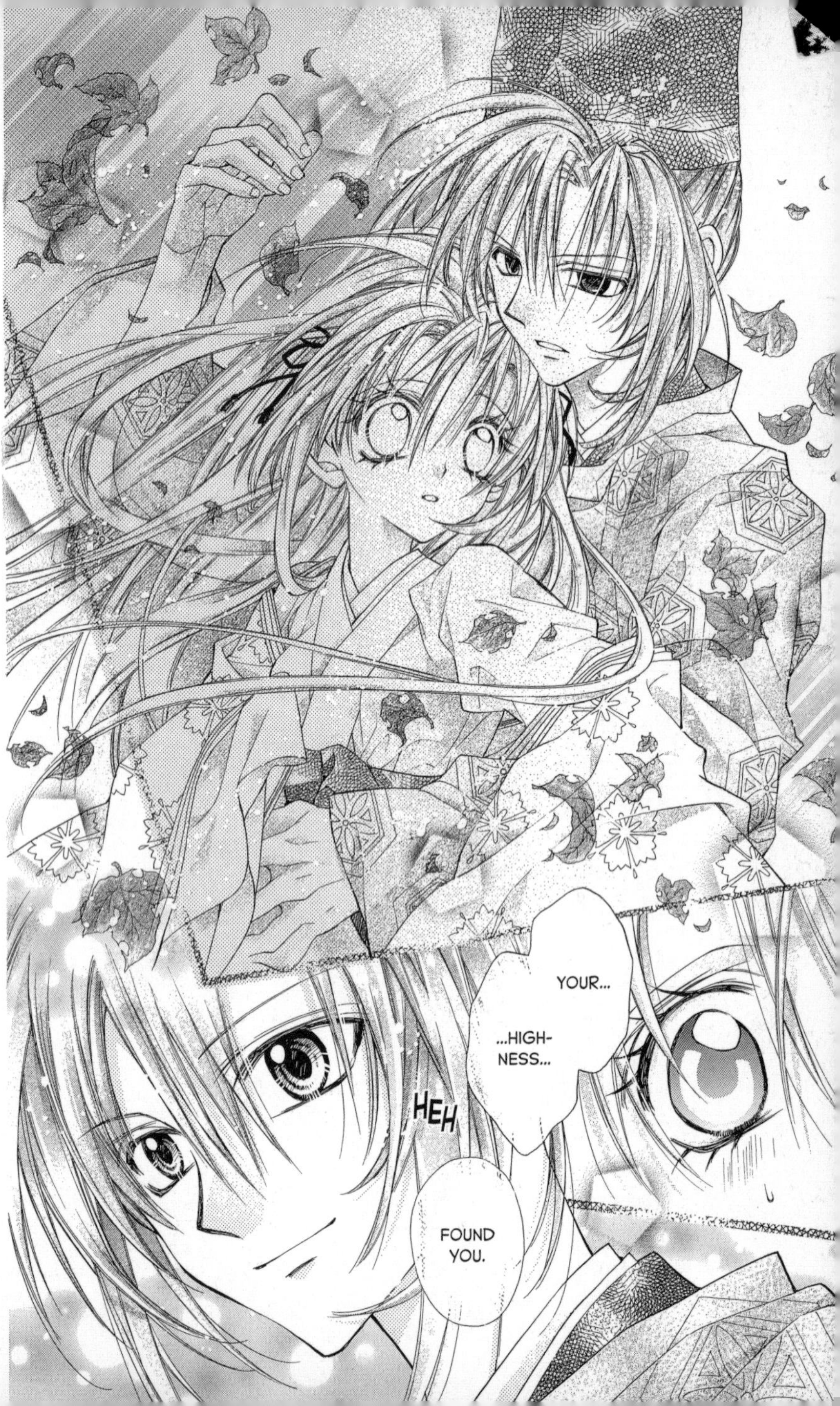
YOUR...
...HIGH-NESS...
HEH
FOUND YOU.

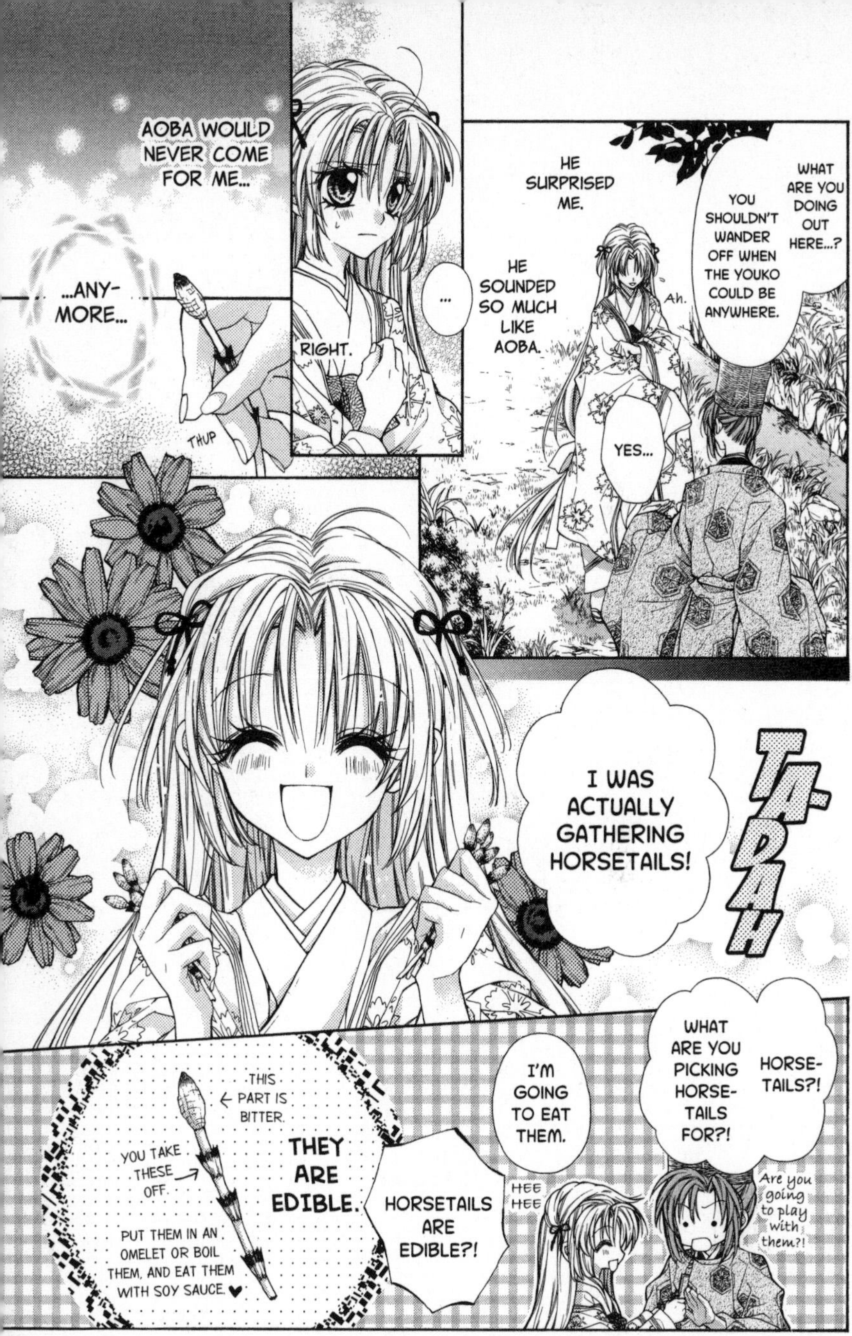
WHAT ARE YOU DOING OUT HERE...?
YOU SHOULDN'T WANDER OFF WHEN THE YOUKO COULD BE ANYWHERE.
Ah.
HE SURPRISED ME.
HE SOUNDED SO MUCH LIKE AOBA.
YES...
...
RIGHT.
AOBA WOULD NEVER COME FOR ME...
...ANY-MORE...
THUP
I WAS ACTUALLY GATHERING HORSETAILS!
TA-DAH
HORSE-TAILS?!
WHAT ARE YOU PICKING HORSE-TAILS FOR?!
I'M GOING TO EAT THEM.
Are you going to play with them?!
HEE HEE
HORSETAILS ARE EDIBLE?!
THEY ARE EDIBLE.
THIS PART IS BITTER.
YOU TAKE THESE OFF.
PUT THEM IN AN OMELET OR BOIL THEM, AND EAT THEM WITH SOY SAUCE. ♥

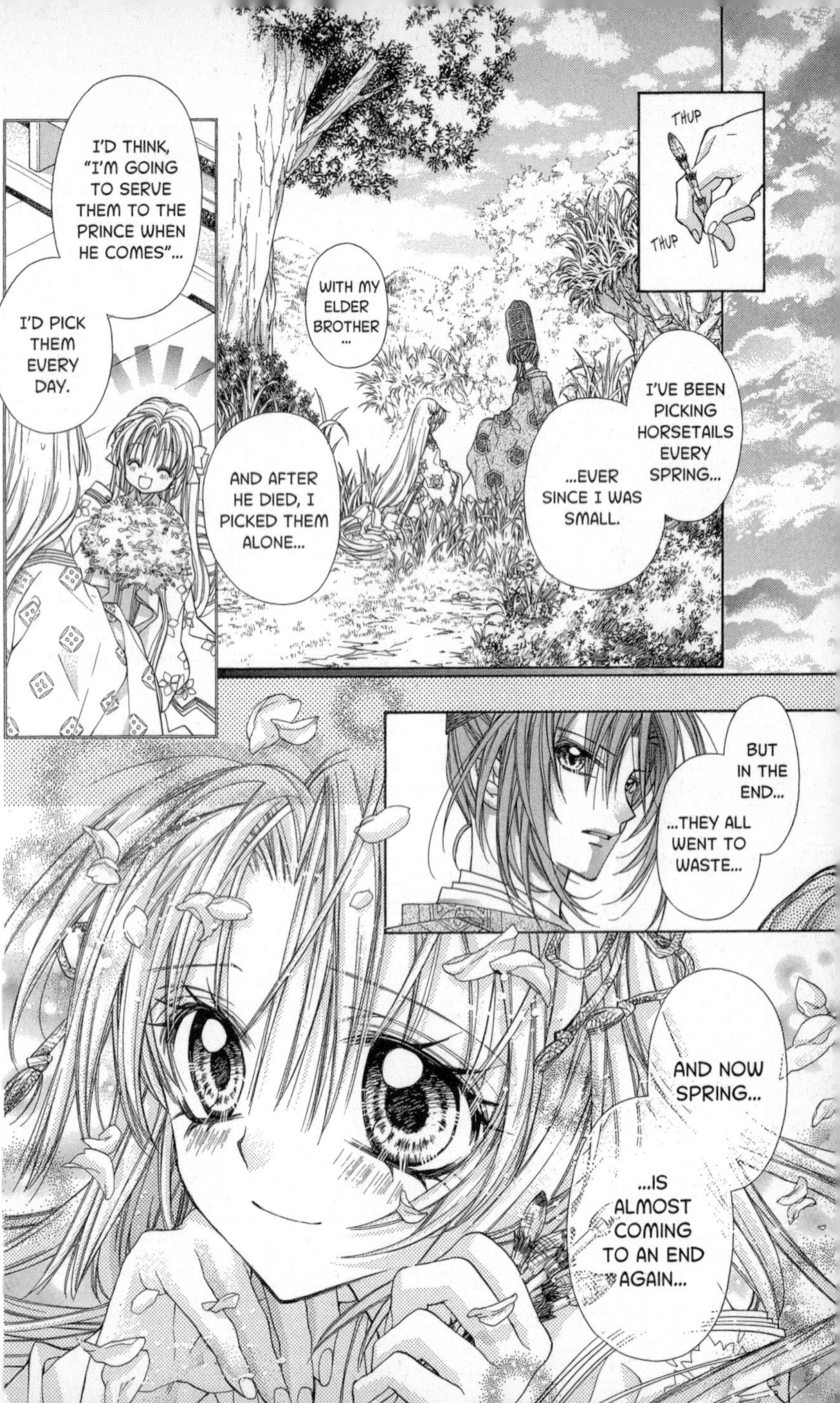
THUP
THUP
I'VE BEEN PICKING HORSETAILS EVERY SPRING...
...EVER SINCE I WAS SMALL.
WITH MY ELDER BROTHER...
AND AFTER HE DIED, I PICKED THEM ALONE...
I'D THINK, "I'M GOING TO SERVE THEM TO THE PRINCE WHEN HE COMES"...
I'D PICK THEM EVERY DAY.
BUT IN THE END...
...THEY ALL WENT TO WASTE...
AND NOW SPRING...
...IS ALMOST COMING TO AN END AGAIN...

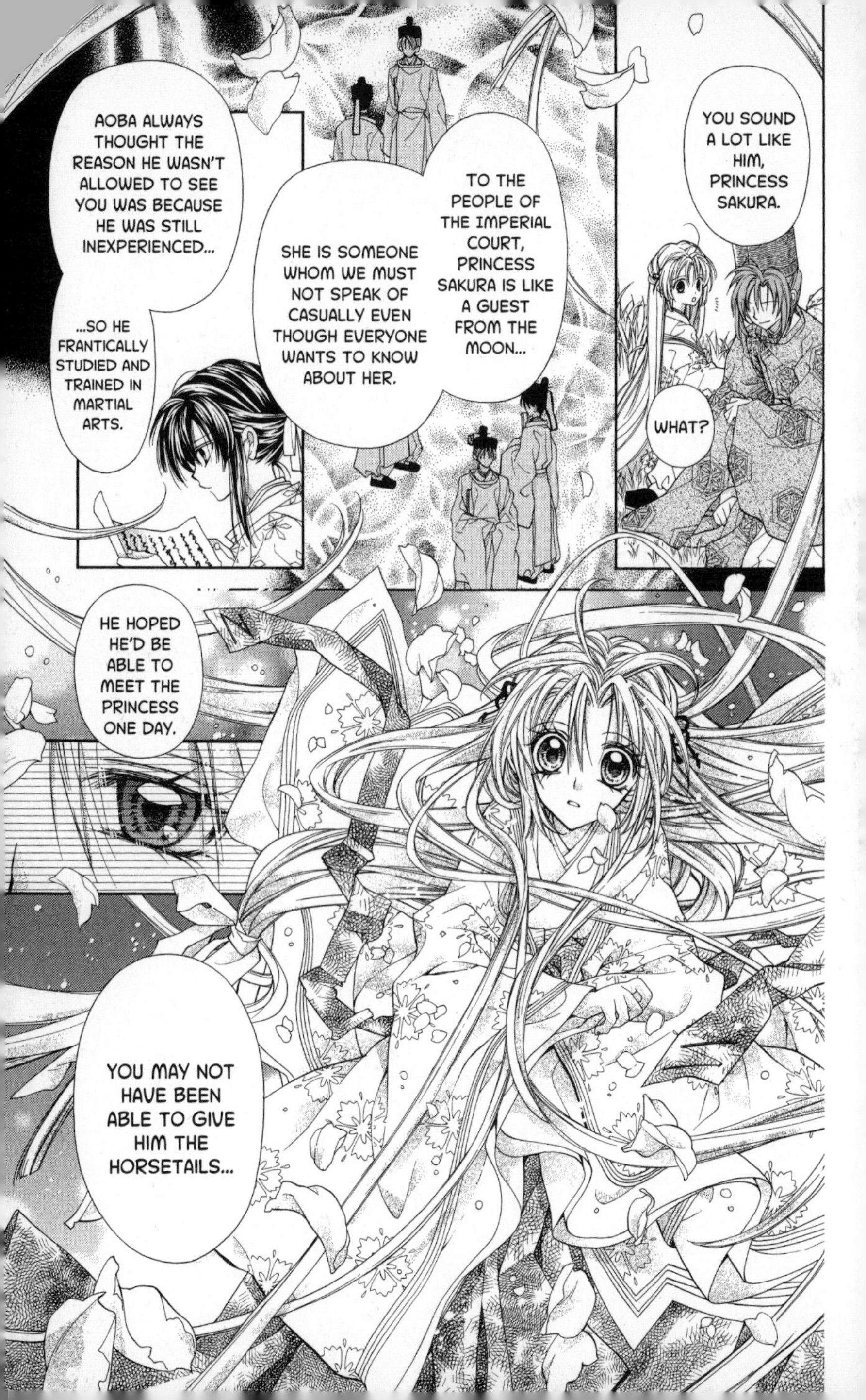
YOU SOUND A LOT LIKE HIM, PRINCESS SAKURA.
WHAT?
TO THE PEOPLE OF THE IMPERIAL COURT, PRINCESS SAKURA IS LIKE A GUEST FROM THE MOON...
SHE IS SOMEONE WHOM WE MUST NOT SPEAK OF CASUALLY EVEN THOUGH EVERYONE WANTS TO KNOW ABOUT HER.
AOBA ALWAYS THOUGHT THE REASON HE WASN'T ALLOWED TO SEE YOU WAS BECAUSE HE WAS STILL INEXPERIENCED...
...SO HE FRANTICALLY STUDIED AND TRAINED IN MARTIAL ARTS.
HE HOPED HE'D BE ABLE TO MEET THE PRINCESS ONE DAY.
YOU MAY NOT HAVE BEEN ABLE TO GIVE HIM THE HORSETAILS...

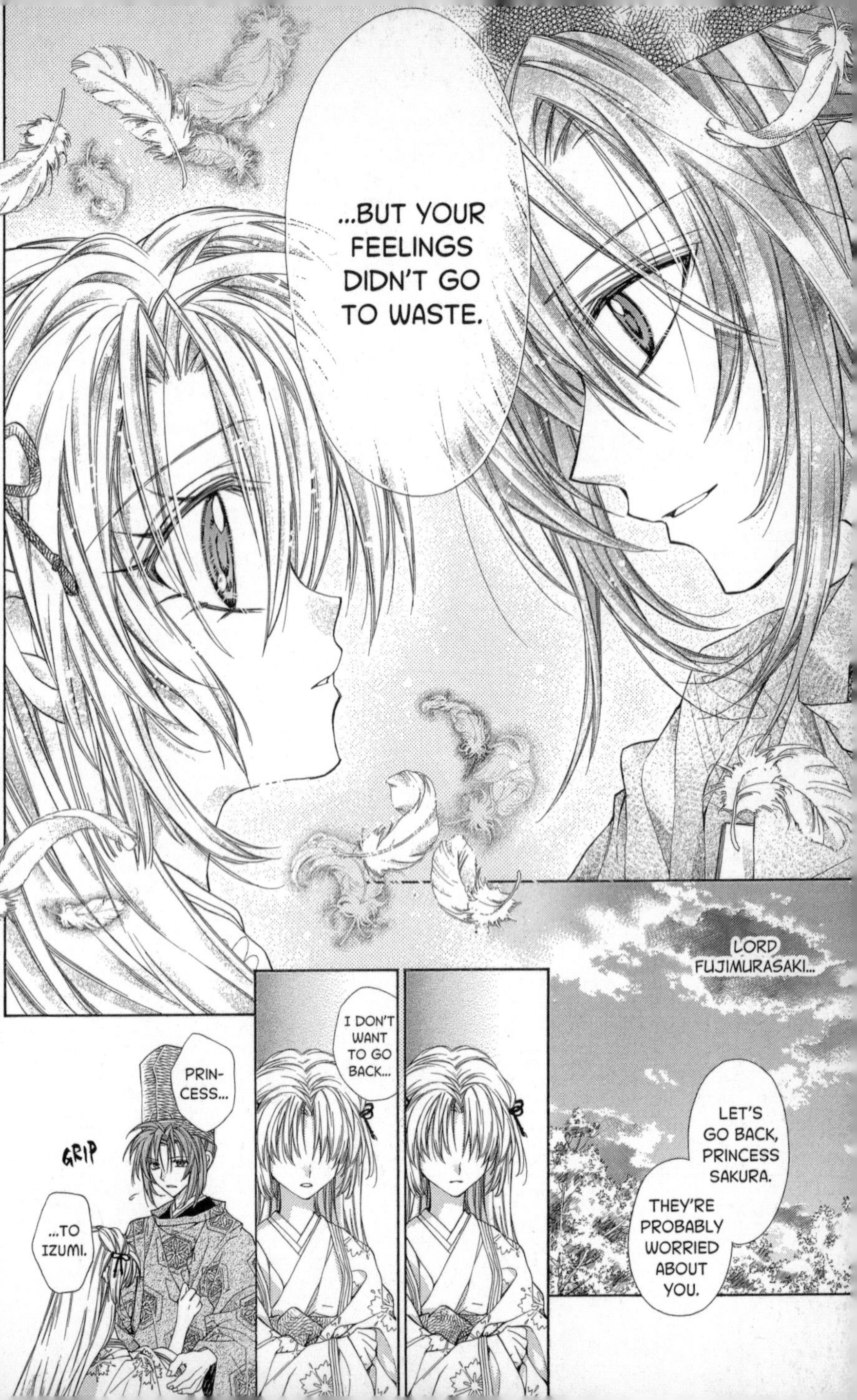
...BUT YOUR FEELINGS DIDN'T GO TO WASTE.
LORD FUJIMURASAKI...
LET'S GO BACK, PRINCESS SAKURA.
THEY'RE PROBABLY WORRIED ABOUT YOU.
I DON'T WANT TO GO BACK...
PRIN-CESS...
GRIP
...TO IZUMI.

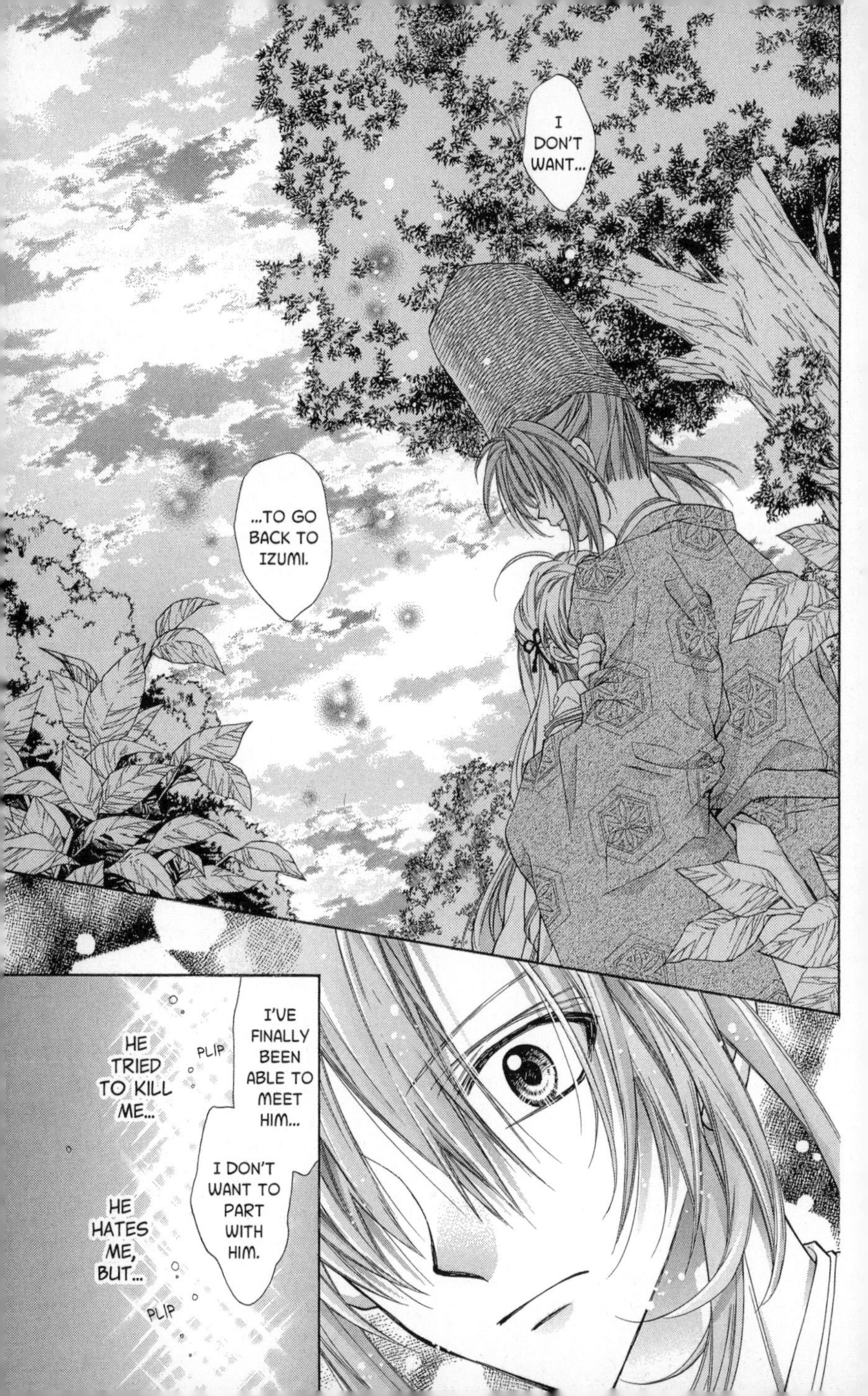
I DON'T WANT...
...TO GO BACK TO IZUMI.
I'VE FINALLY BEEN ABLE TO MEET HIM...
I DON'T WANT TO PART WITH HIM.
PLIP
HE TRIED TO KILL ME...
HE HATES ME, BUT...
PLIP

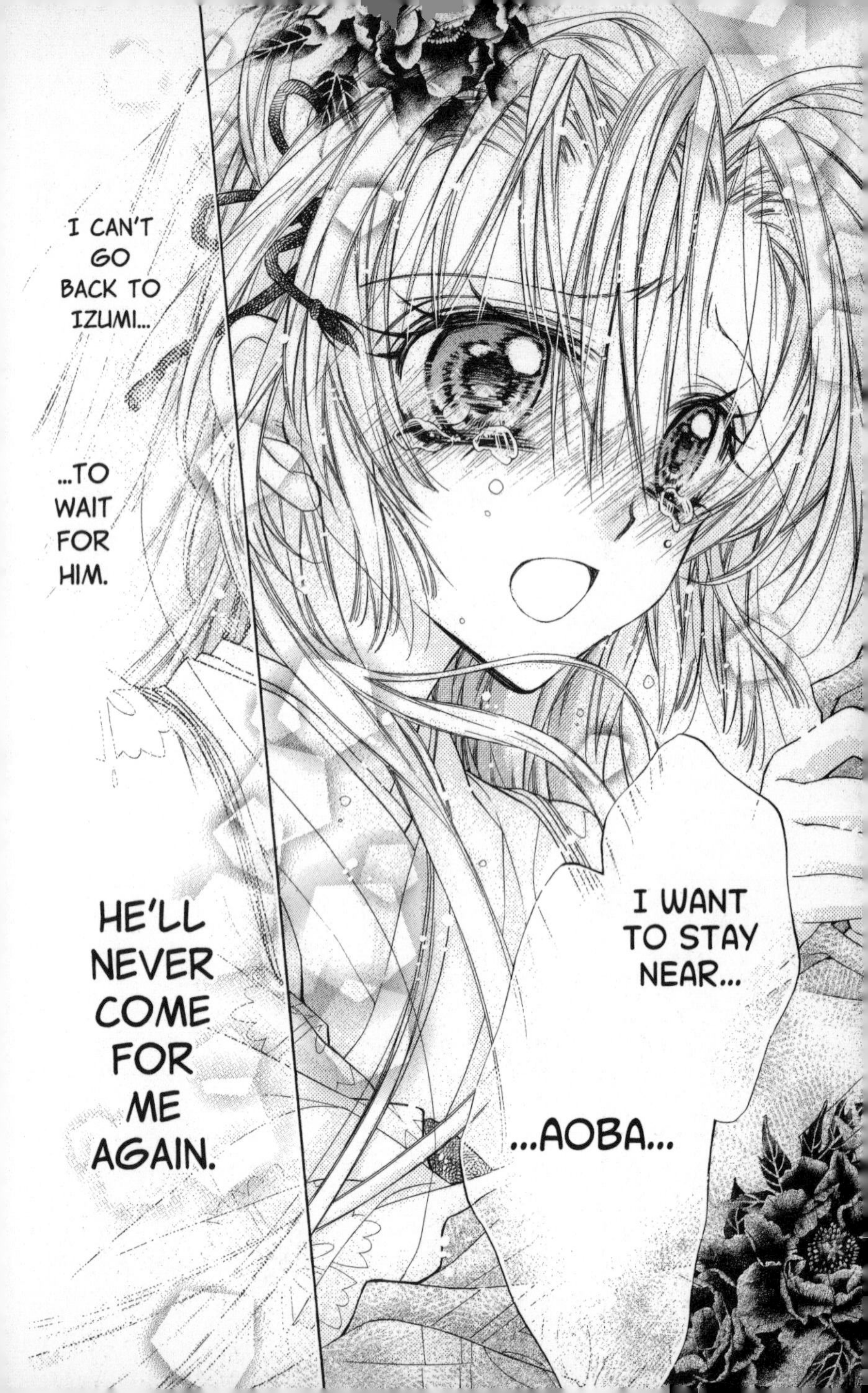
I WANT TO STAY NEAR...
...AOBA...
I CAN'T GO BACK TO IZUMI...
...TO WAIT FOR HIM.
HE'LL NEVER COME FOR ME AGAIN.

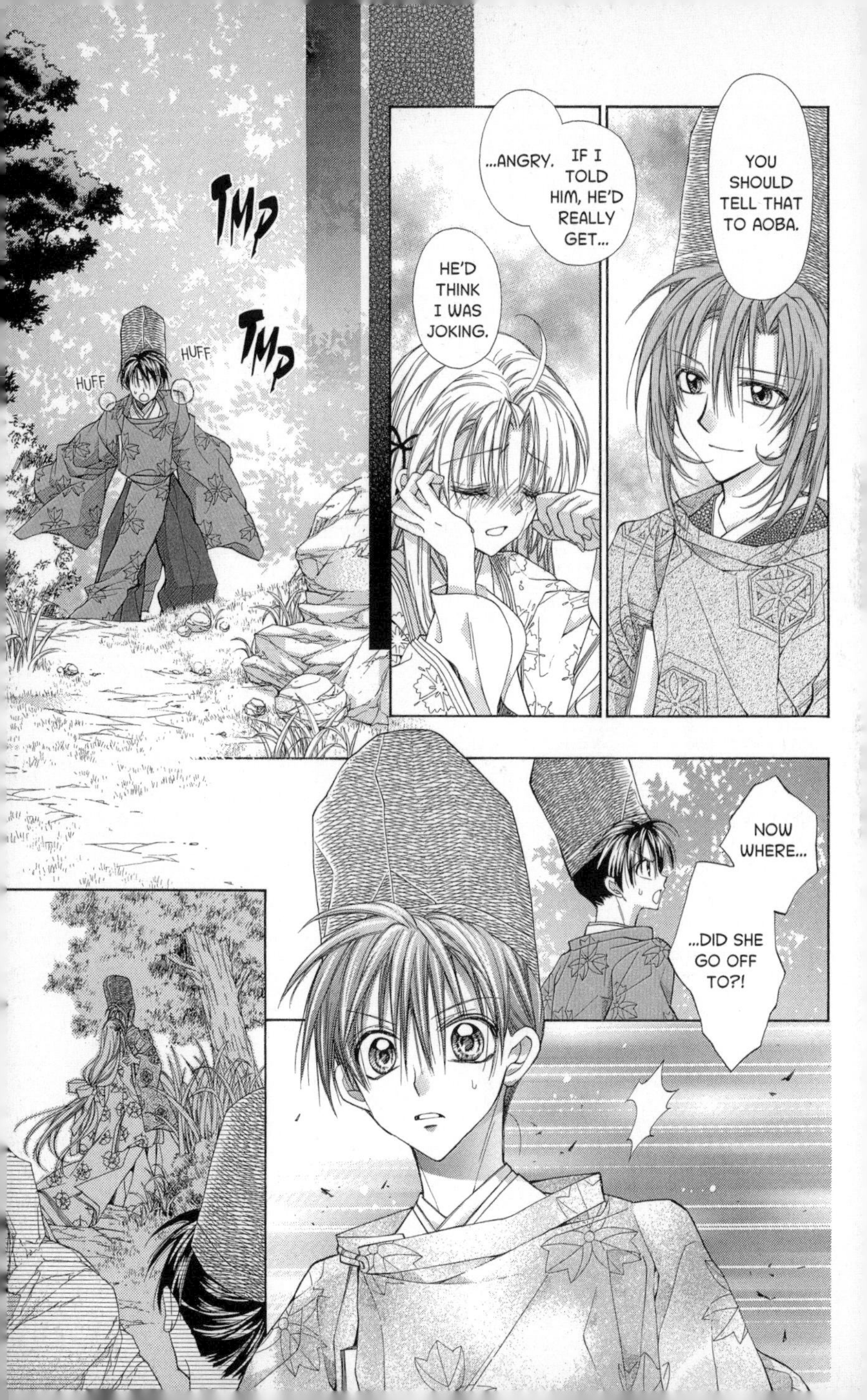
YOU SHOULD TELL THAT TO AOBA.
IF I TOLD HIM, HE'D REALLY GET...
...ANGRY.
HE'D THINK I WAS JOKING.
TMP
TMP
HUFF
HUFF
NOW WHERE...
...DID SHE GO OFF TO?!

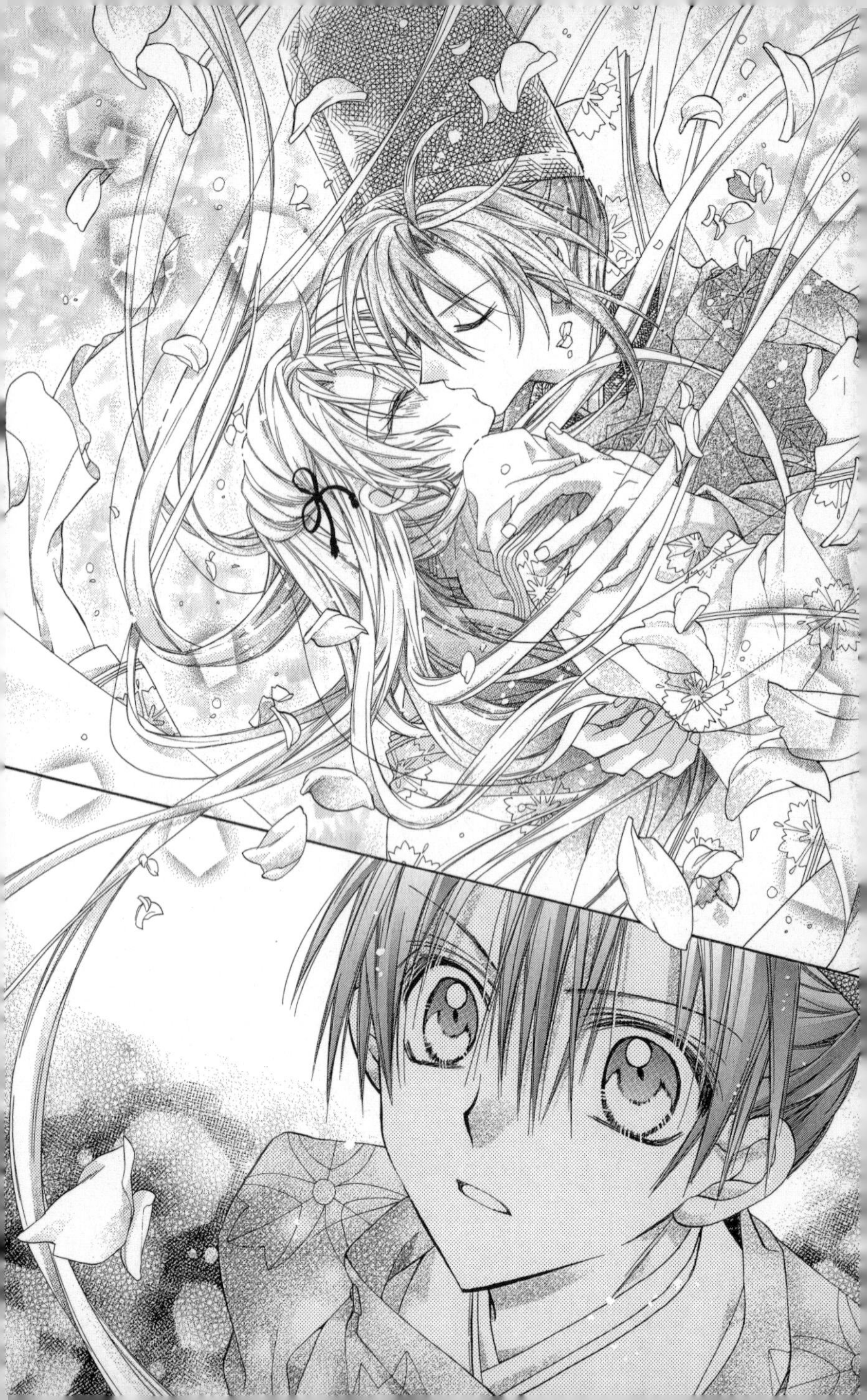

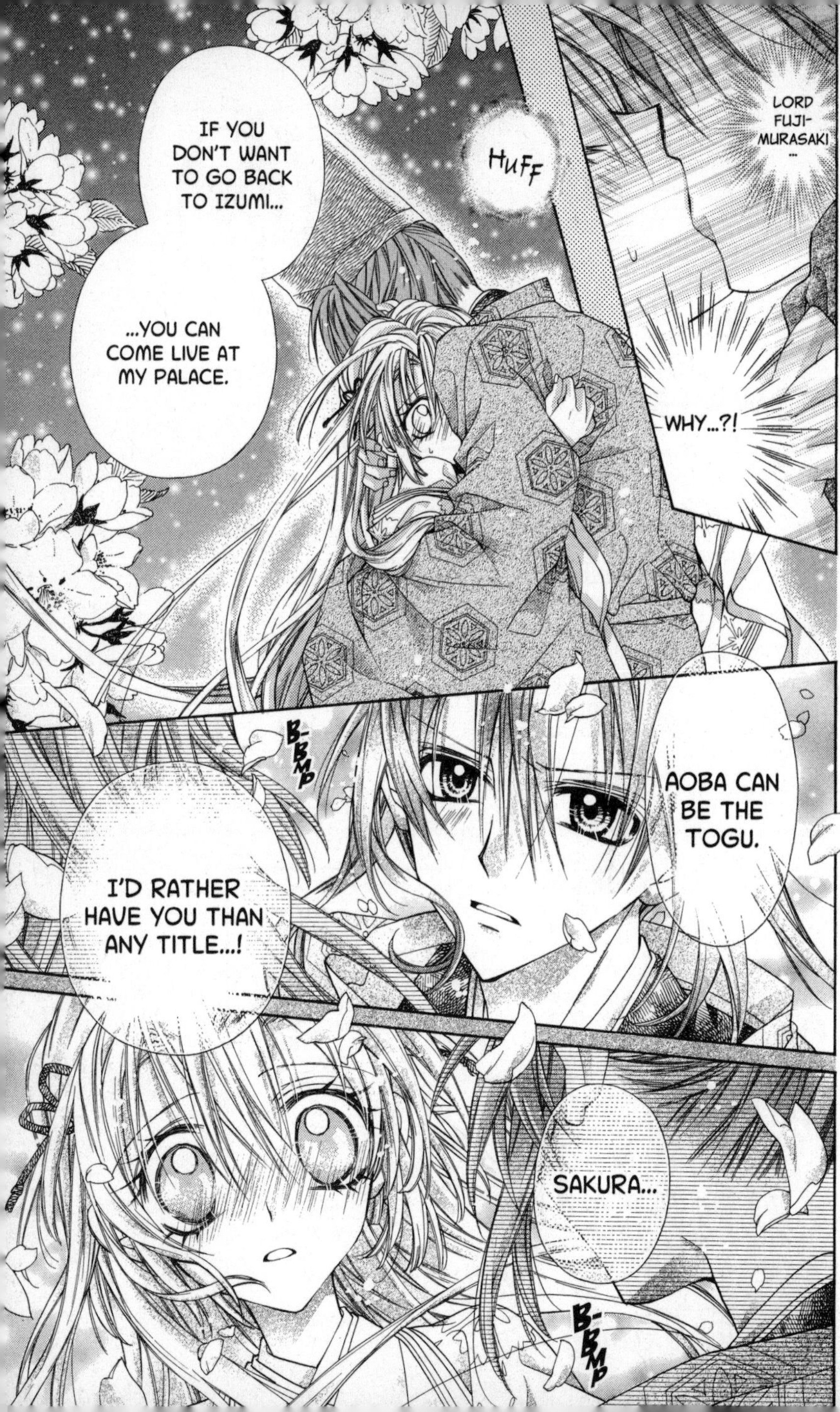

LORD FUJI-MURASAKI...
WHY...?!
HUFF
IF YOU DON'T WANT TO GO BACK TO IZUMI...
...YOU CAN COME LIVE AT MY PALACE.
AOBA CAN BE THE TOGU.
B-BMP
I'D RATHER HAVE YOU THAN ANY TITLE...!
SAKURA...
B-BMP

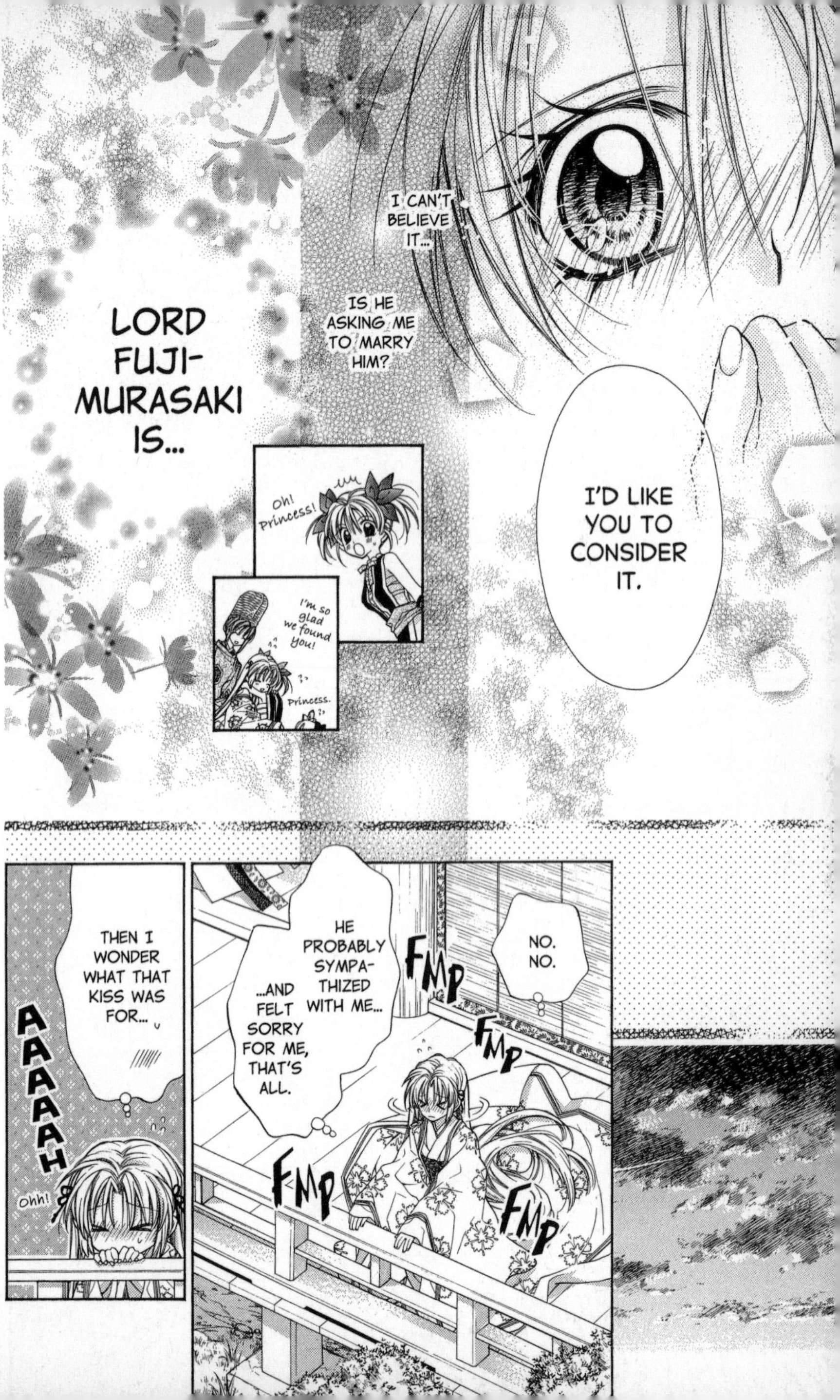
I'D LIKE YOU TO CONSIDER IT.
I CAN'T BELIEVE IT...
IS HE ASKING ME TO MARRY HIM?
Oh! Princess!
I'm so glad we found you!
Princess.
LORD FUJI-MURASAKI IS...
NO. NO.
FMP
FMP
HE PROBABLY SYMPA-THIZED WITH ME...
...AND FELT SORRY FOR ME, THAT'S ALL.
FMP
FMP
THEN I WONDER WHAT THAT KISS WAS FOR...
AAAAAH
Ohh!

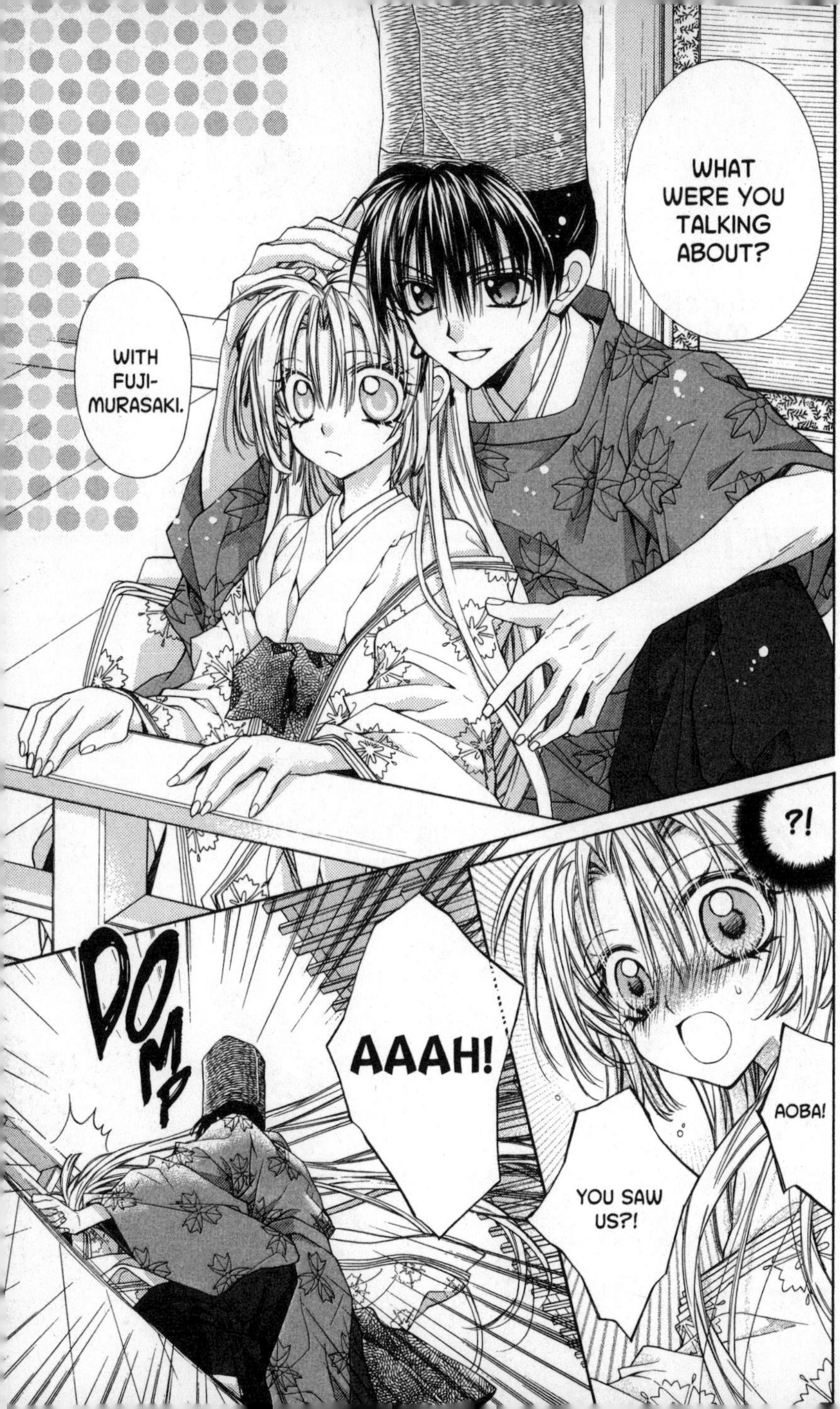
WHAT WERE YOU TALKING ABOUT?
WITH FUJI-MURASAKI.
?!
AOBA!
YOU SAW US?!
DOMP
AAAH!

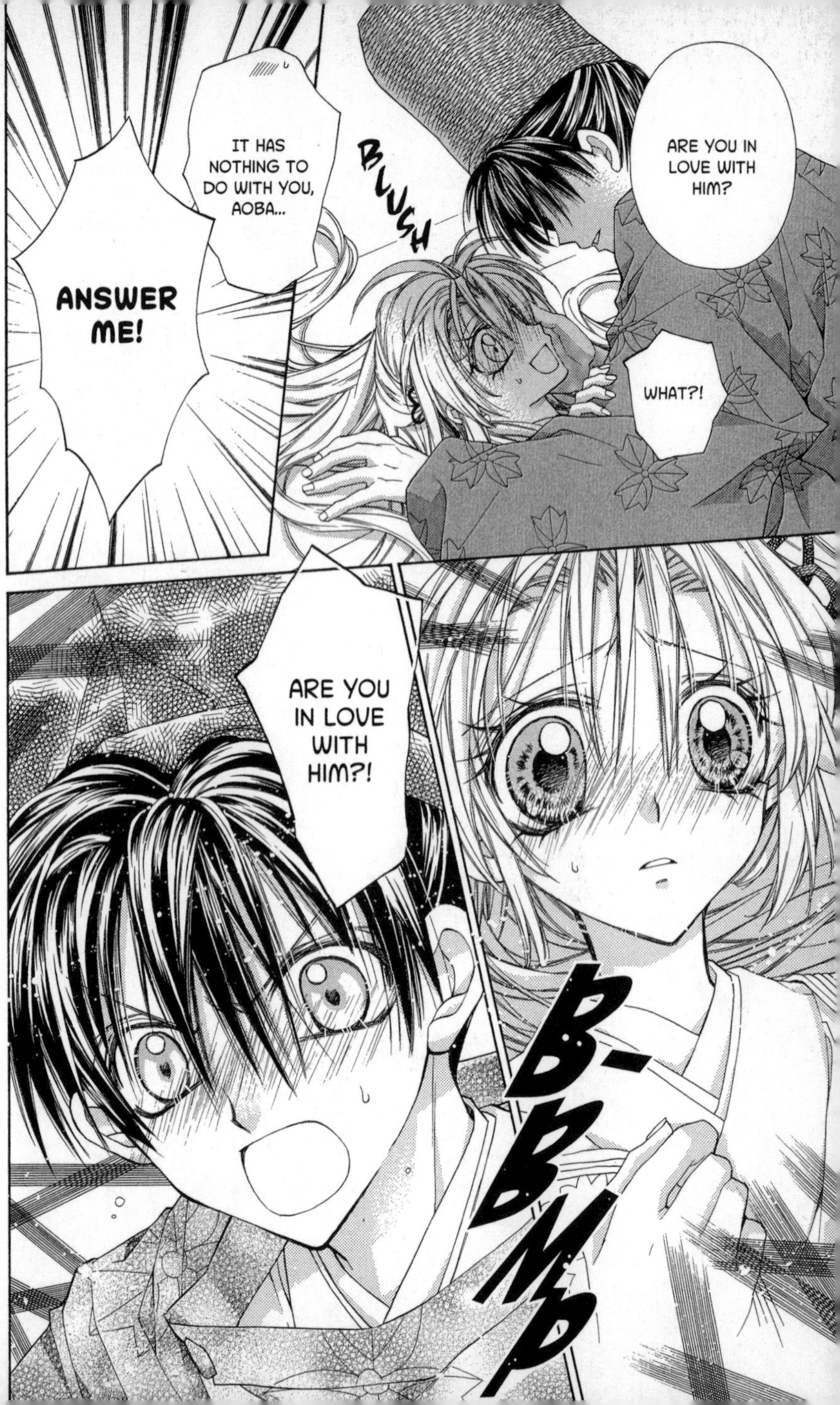
ARE YOU IN LOVE WITH HIM?
WHAT?!
BLUSH
IT HAS NOTHING TO DO WITH YOU, AOBA...
ANSWER ME!
ARE YOU IN LOVE WITH HIM?!
B-BBMP

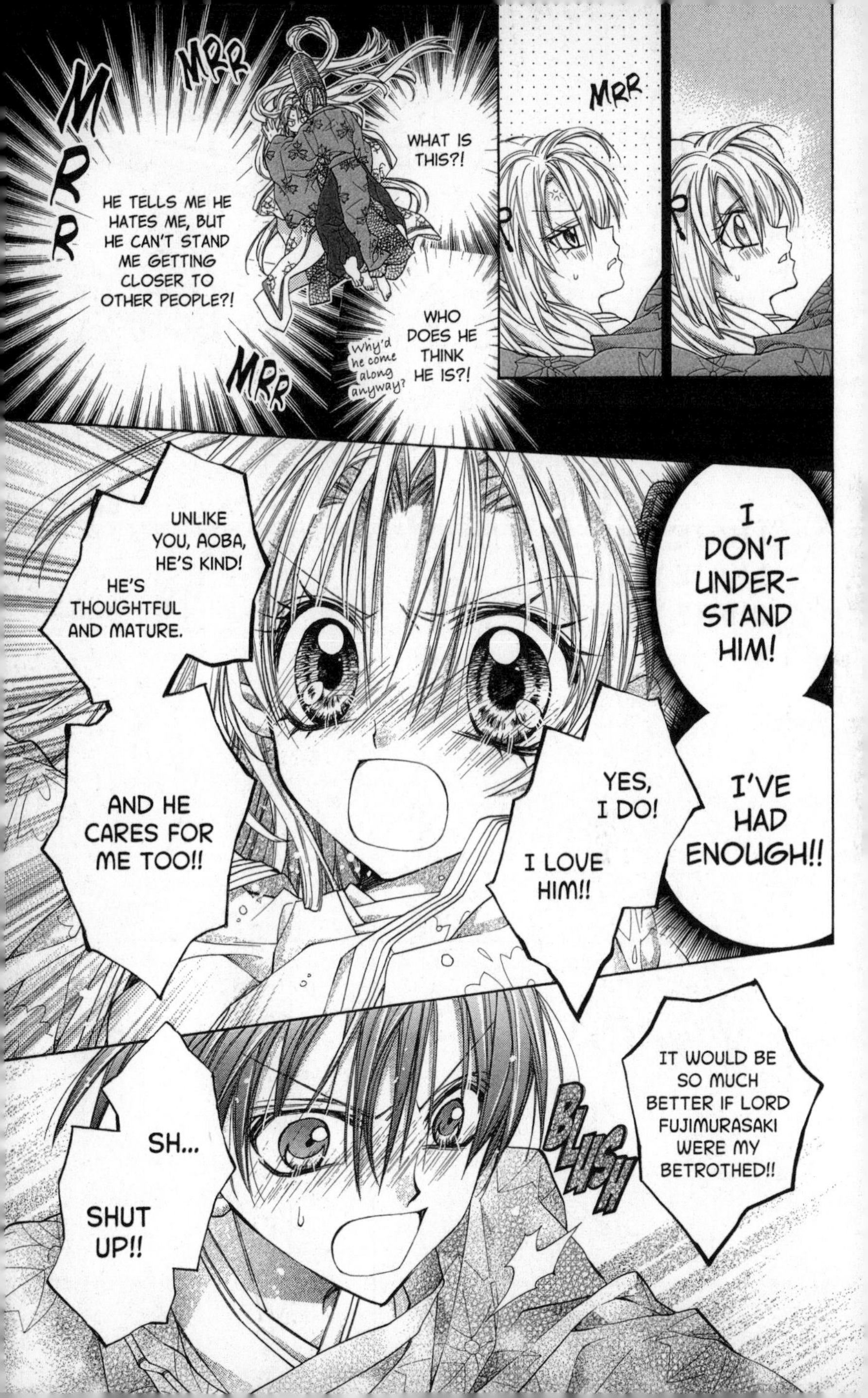
MRR
WHAT IS THIS?!
MRR
MRR
HE TELLS ME HE HATES ME, BUT HE CAN'T STAND ME GETTING CLOSER TO OTHER PEOPLE?!
WHO DOES HE THINK HE IS?!
Why'd he come along anyway?
MRR
I DON'T UNDER-STAND HIM!
I'VE HAD ENOUGH!!
YES, I DO!
I LOVE HIM!!
UNLIKE YOU, AOBA, HE'S KIND!
HE'S THOUGHTFUL AND MATURE.
AND HE CARES FOR ME TOO!!
IT WOULD BE SO MUCH BETTER IF LORD FUJIMURASAKI WERE MY BETROTHED!!
BLUSH
SH...
SHUT UP!!

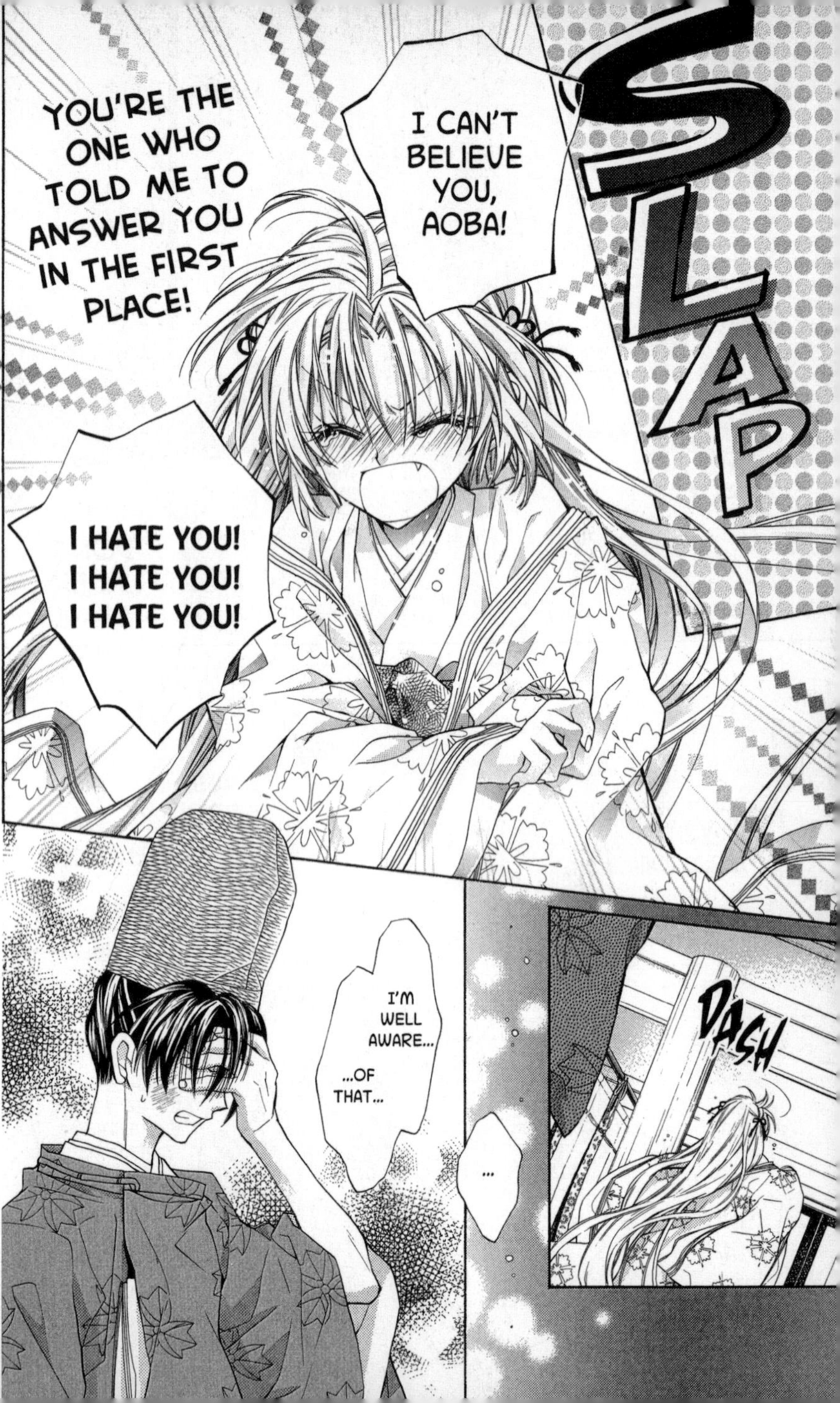
SLAP
I CAN'T BELIEVE YOU, AOBA!
YOU'RE THE ONE WHO TOLD ME TO ANSWER YOU IN THE FIRST PLACE!
I HATE YOU! I HATE YOU! I HATE YOU!
DASH
I'M WELL AWARE...
...OF THAT...
...

RAJIO DE SHAKIN☆ ENDED

Rajio De Shakin☆, which was being distributed on Shueisha's S-Raji Internet Site, has finished.

Mr. Takeda told me, "I'll let you do anything you want to at the last recording session," so I made it an open recording session. (I've always wanted to try that.)

And the guest was Sho-Comi's Ai Minase Sensei. I was very happy to be able to work with such wonderful people.

We held a party at "Zauo" on the first floor of the Shinjuku Washington Hotel!

You have to catch the fish yourself and then the restaurant will cook it for you. The place is huge!! It's like, is this really the first floor of a hotel?! (laugh) I caught around six fish. It was great. ♥

I liked the place so much that I made a reservation for a meal I had with my assistants there three days later.

I'd love to go again.

I want to do another radio program again with the same people too.

↑ The important thing is that I write it here.

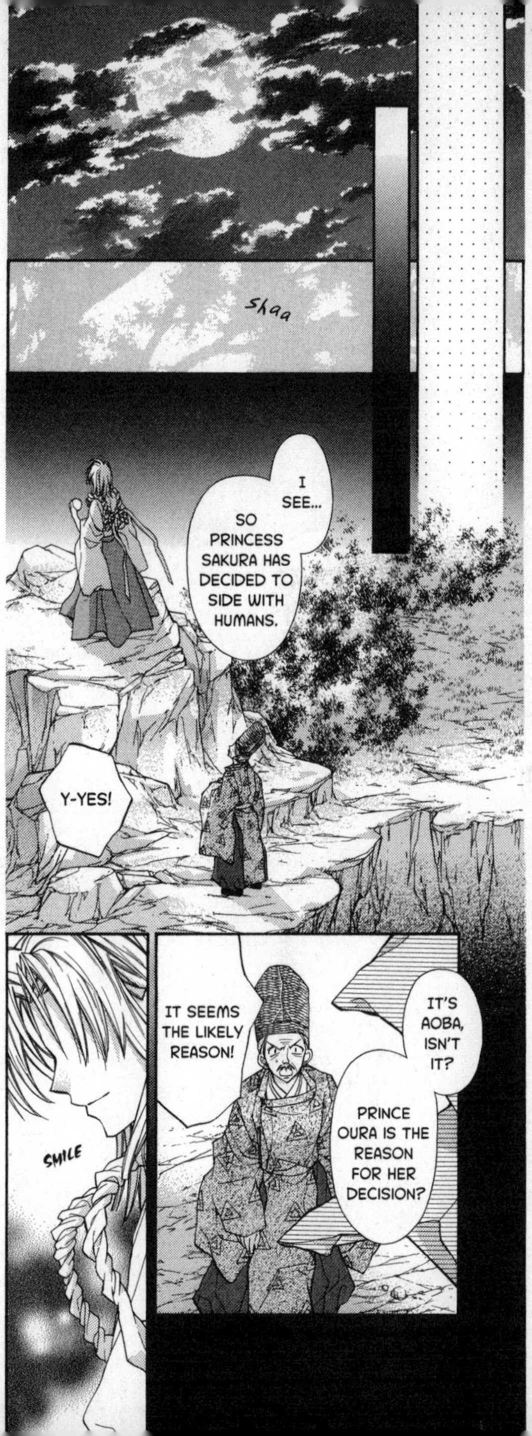
Shaa
I SEE... SO PRINCESS SAKURA HAS DECIDED TO SIDE WITH HUMANS.
Y-YES!
IT'S AOBA, ISN'T IT?
PRINCE OURA IS THE REASON FOR HER DECISION?
IT SEEMS THE LIKELY REASON!
SMILE

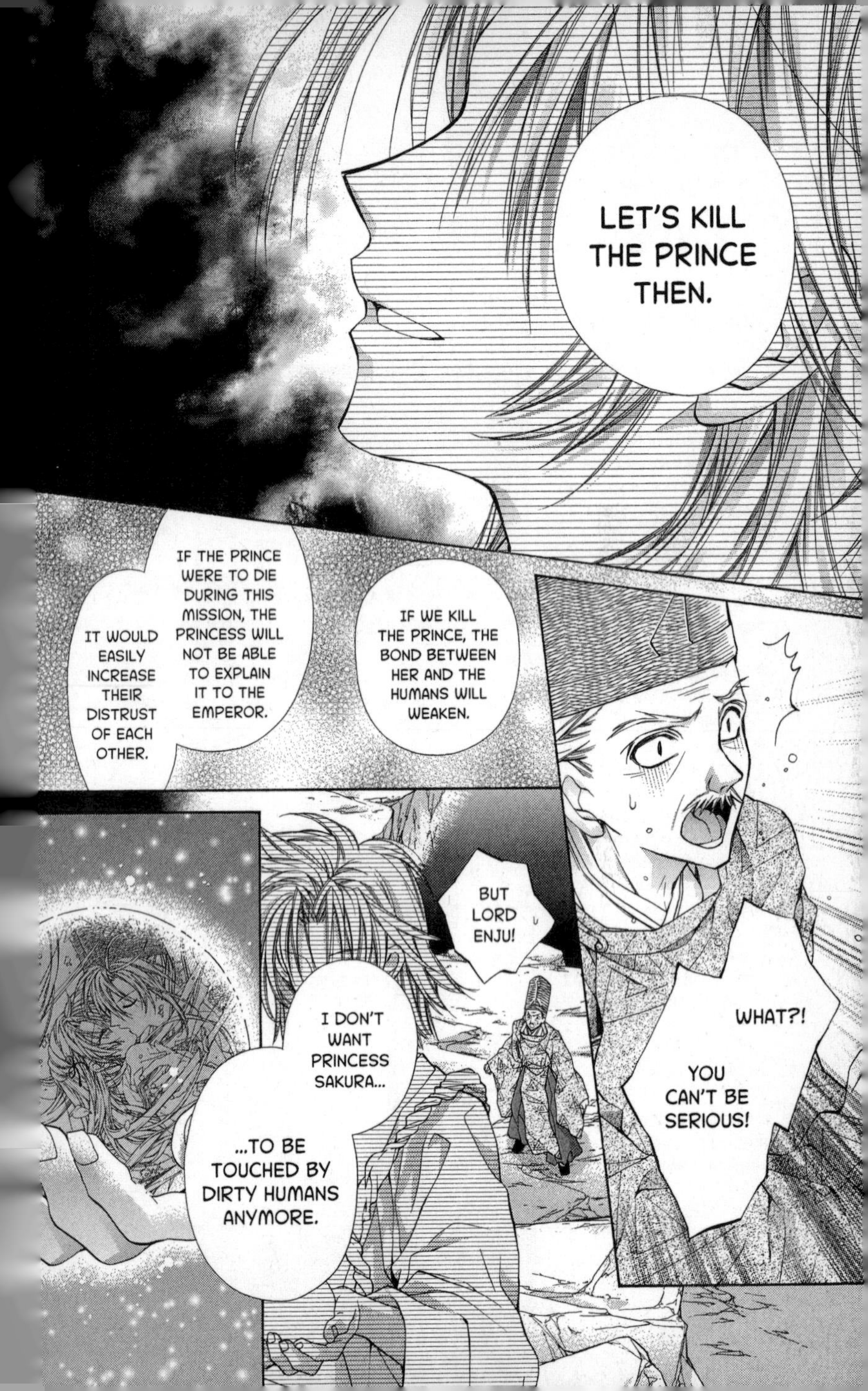
LET'S KILL THE PRINCE THEN.
WHAT?!
YOU CAN'T BE SERIOUS!
IF WE KILL THE PRINCE, THE BOND BETWEEN HER AND THE HUMANS WILL WEAKEN.
IF THE PRINCE WERE TO DIE DURING THIS MISSION, THE PRINCESS WILL NOT BE ABLE TO EXPLAIN IT TO THE EMPEROR.
IT WOULD EASILY INCREASE THEIR DISTRUST OF EACH OTHER.
BUT LORD ENJU!
I DON'T WANT PRINCESS SAKURA...
...TO BE TOUCHED BY DIRTY HUMANS ANYMORE.

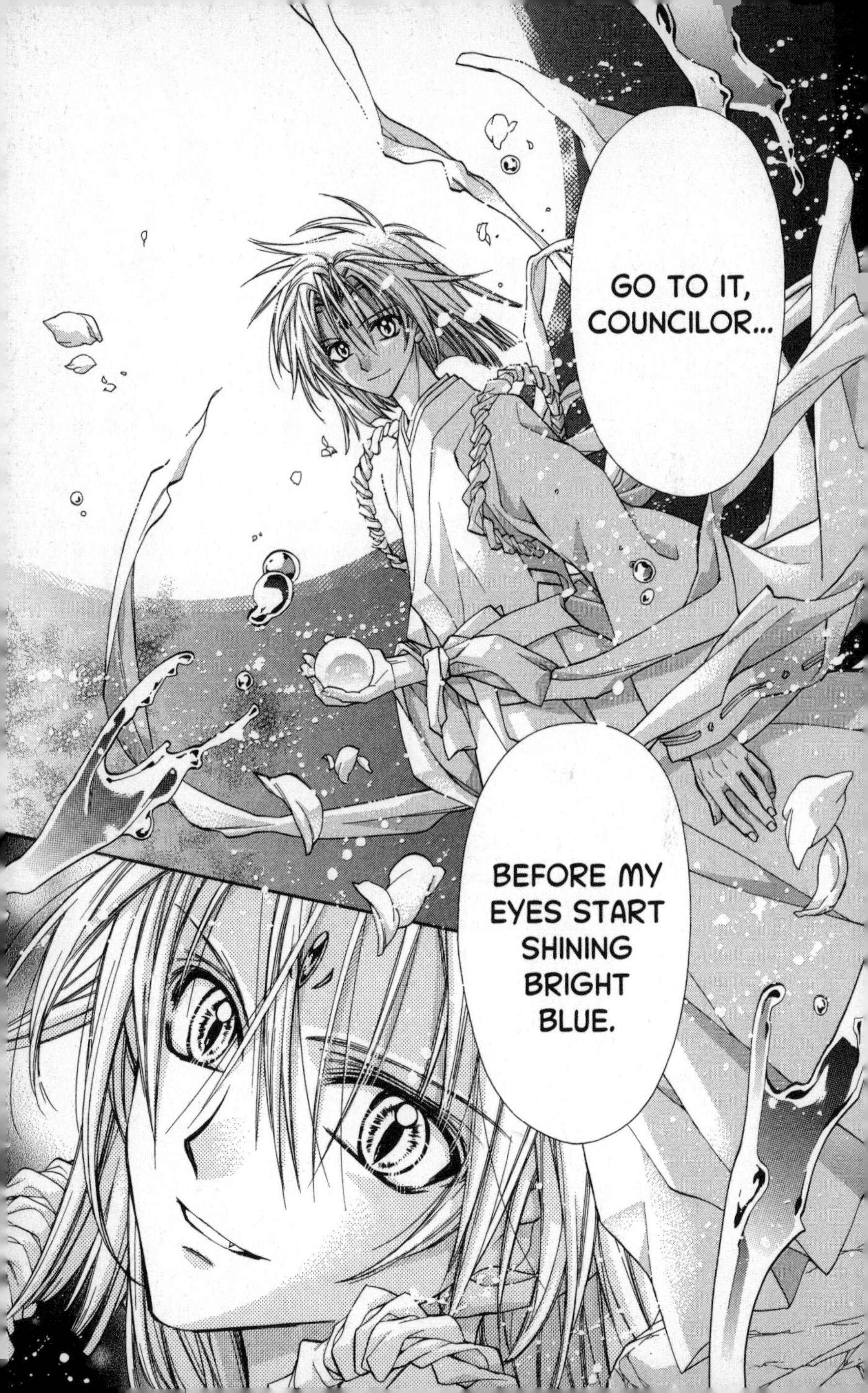
GO TO IT, COUNCILOR...
BEFORE MY EYES START SHINING BRIGHT BLUE.

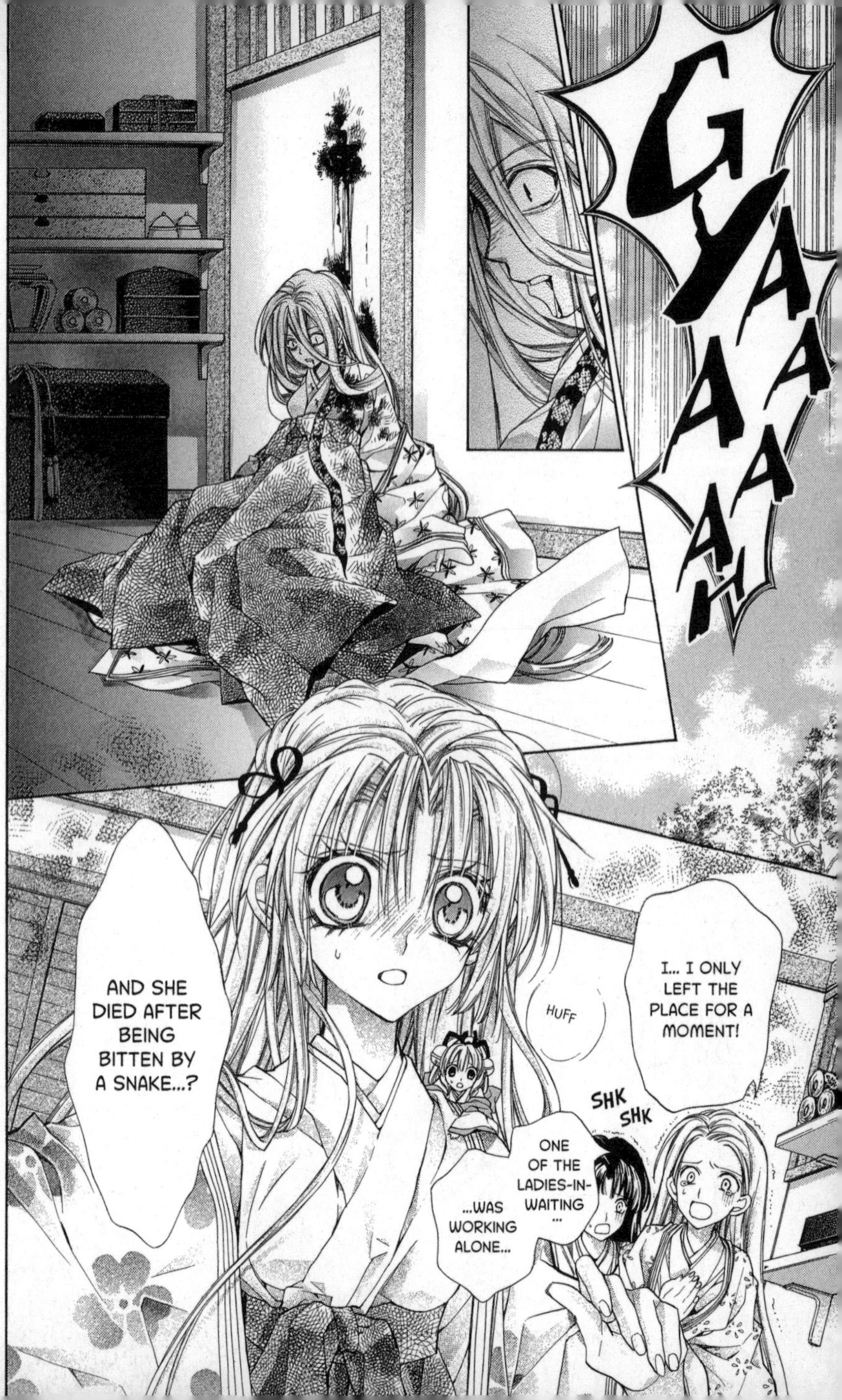
GYAAAAAH
I... I ONLY LEFT THE PLACE FOR A MOMENT!
HUFF
SHK SHK
ONE OF THE LADIES-IN-WAITING ...
...WAS WORKING ALONE...
AND SHE DIED AFTER BEING BITTEN BY A SNAKE...?

ABOUT SAKURA HIME

I wrote so much about *Macross F* in volume 1 that they told me, "Could you write a little more about the Princess Sakura series?" So I'm going to write a little about this series. Hm, but ever since *Full Moon* I've been trying not to talk about the series until it has finished. But I'll write a little bit about it.

I came up with the idea of the soul symbol when I was doing some calligraphy for New Year's with Mizuse-san. We were writing a single kanji that would represent our goals for the upcoming year—along the lines of akashic records, you know? The word "fate" has a strong meaning to it, and I think it's enchanting.

I am the creator of this series so I know what "fate" awaits each of my characters... I thought I'd be able to give each a kanji character that suits him or her.

I'm also thinking about including all the ideas I've always wanted to write about, but most of them are things that I really can't do in *Ribon*.

But the current editor-in-chief (Kunta-san) is the type of person who's like, "It's all okay as long as it's fun!" I'm able to work pretty freely now. (People often say I go out of control and the editorial office is unable to hold me back, but it's the other way around! (laugh) The editorial office keeps pushing me to do more, and I tend to hold back.
(This is something I need to fix. I have to push myself more!)

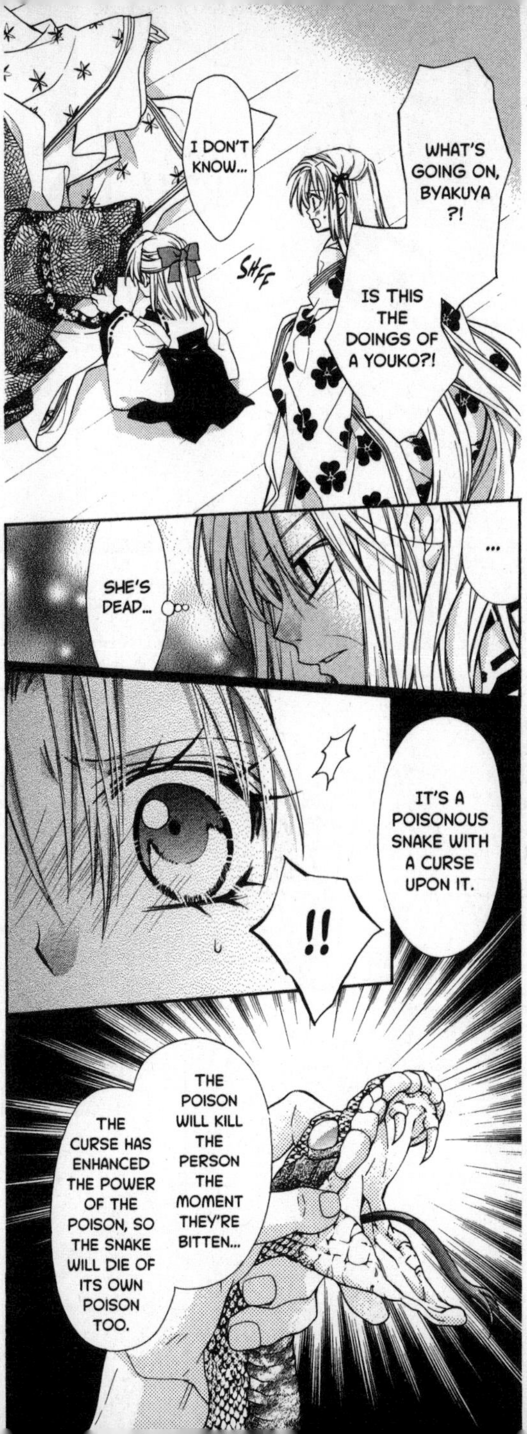
WHAT'S GOING ON, BYAKUYA ?!
IS THIS THE DOINGS OF A YOUKO?!
I DON'T KNOW...
SHFF
...
SHE'S DEAD...
IT'S A POISONOUS SNAKE WITH A CURSE UPON IT.
!!
THE POISON WILL KILL THE PERSON THE MOMENT THEY'RE BITTEN...
THE CURSE HAS ENHANCED THE POWER OF THE POISON, SO THE SNAKE WILL DIE OF ITS OWN POISON TOO.

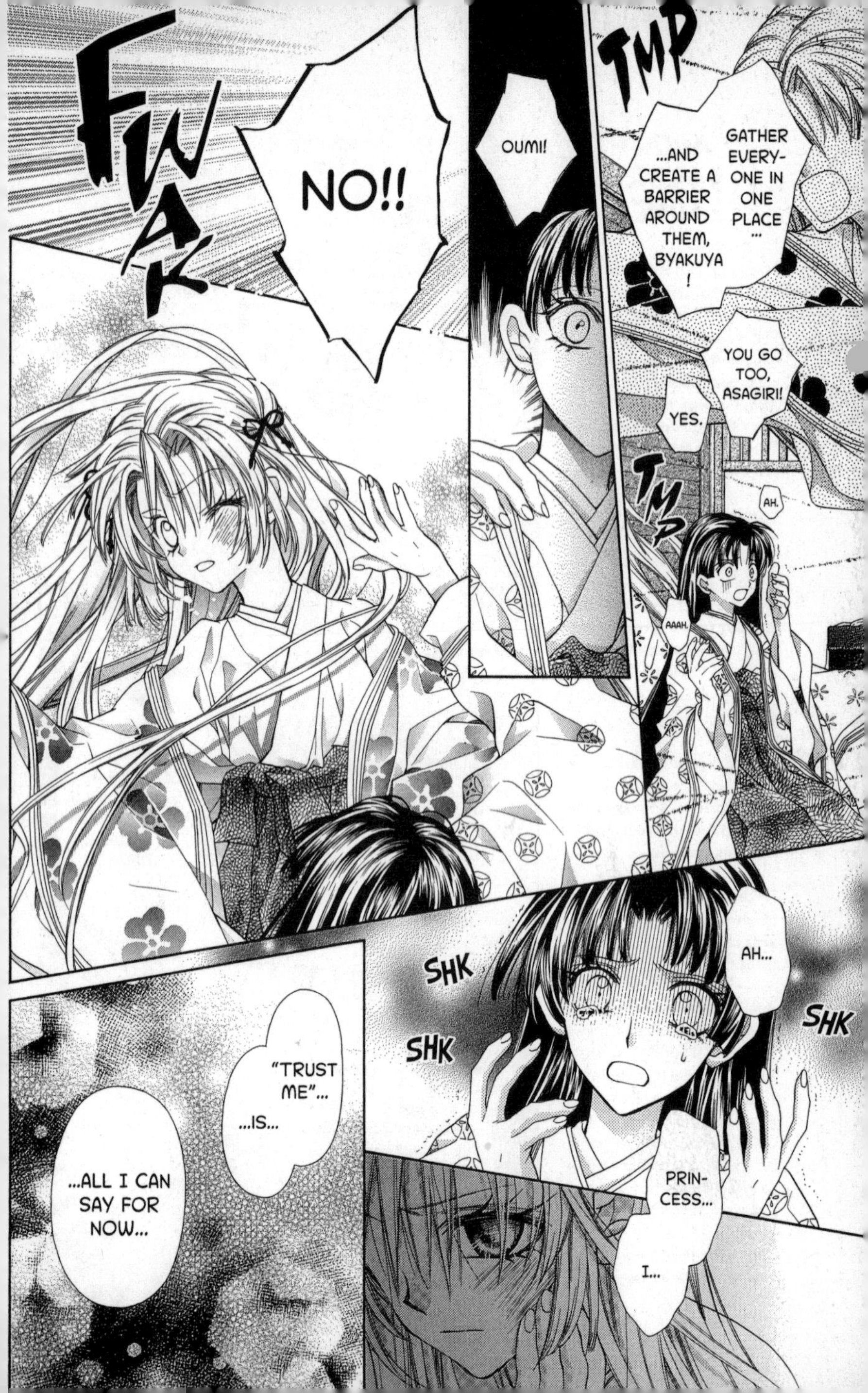
TMP
GATHER EVERYONE IN ONE PLACE...
...AND CREATE A BARRIER AROUND THEM, BYAKUYA!
YOU GO TOO, ASAGIRI!
YES.
TMP
AH.
AAAH.
OUMI!
FWAK
NO!!
SHK
AH...
SHK
SHK
PRINCESS...
I...
"TRUST ME"...
...IS...
...ALL I CAN SAY FOR NOW...

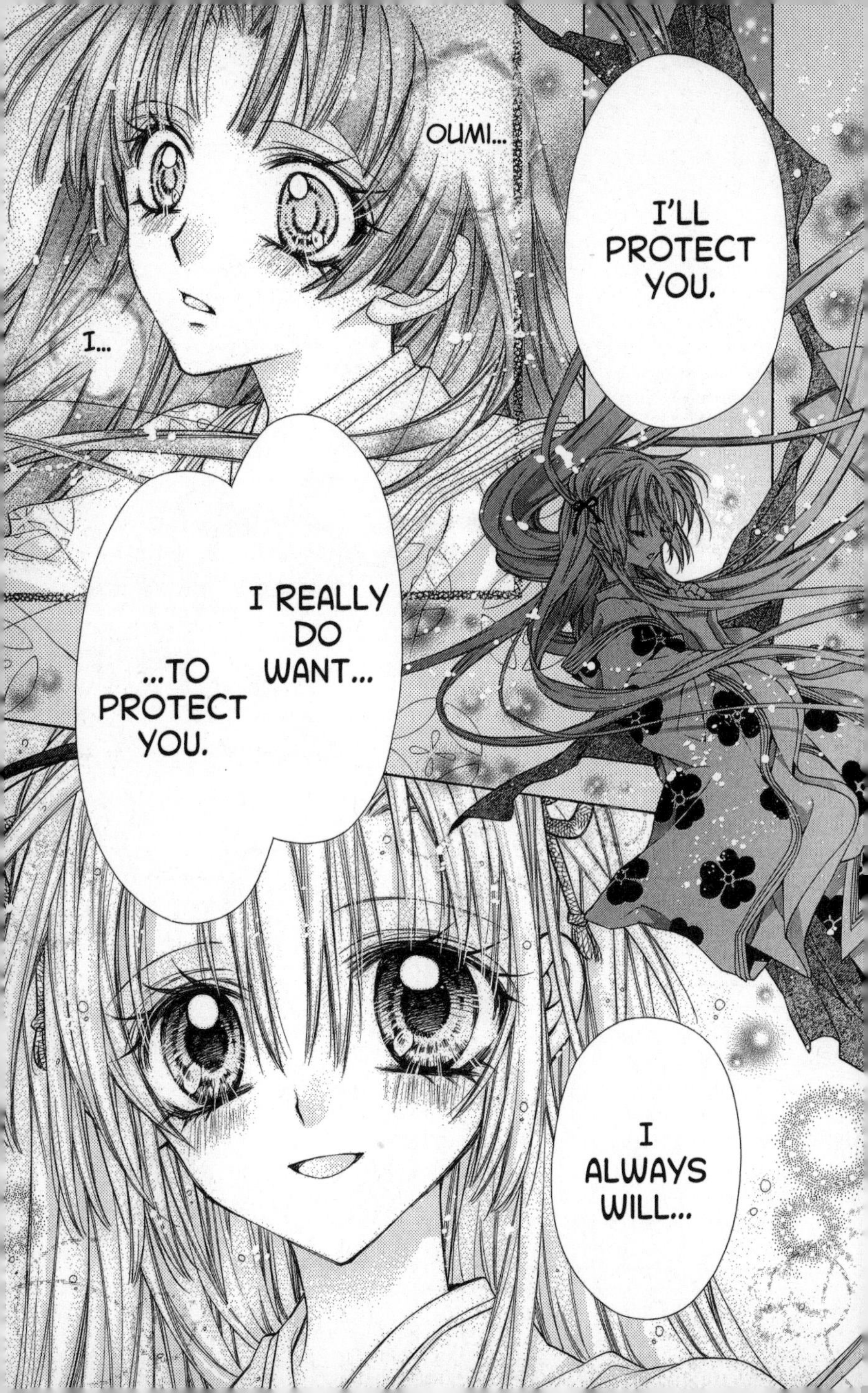
I'LL PROTECT YOU.
OUMI...
I...
I REALLY DO WANT...
...TO PROTECT YOU.
I ALWAYS WILL...

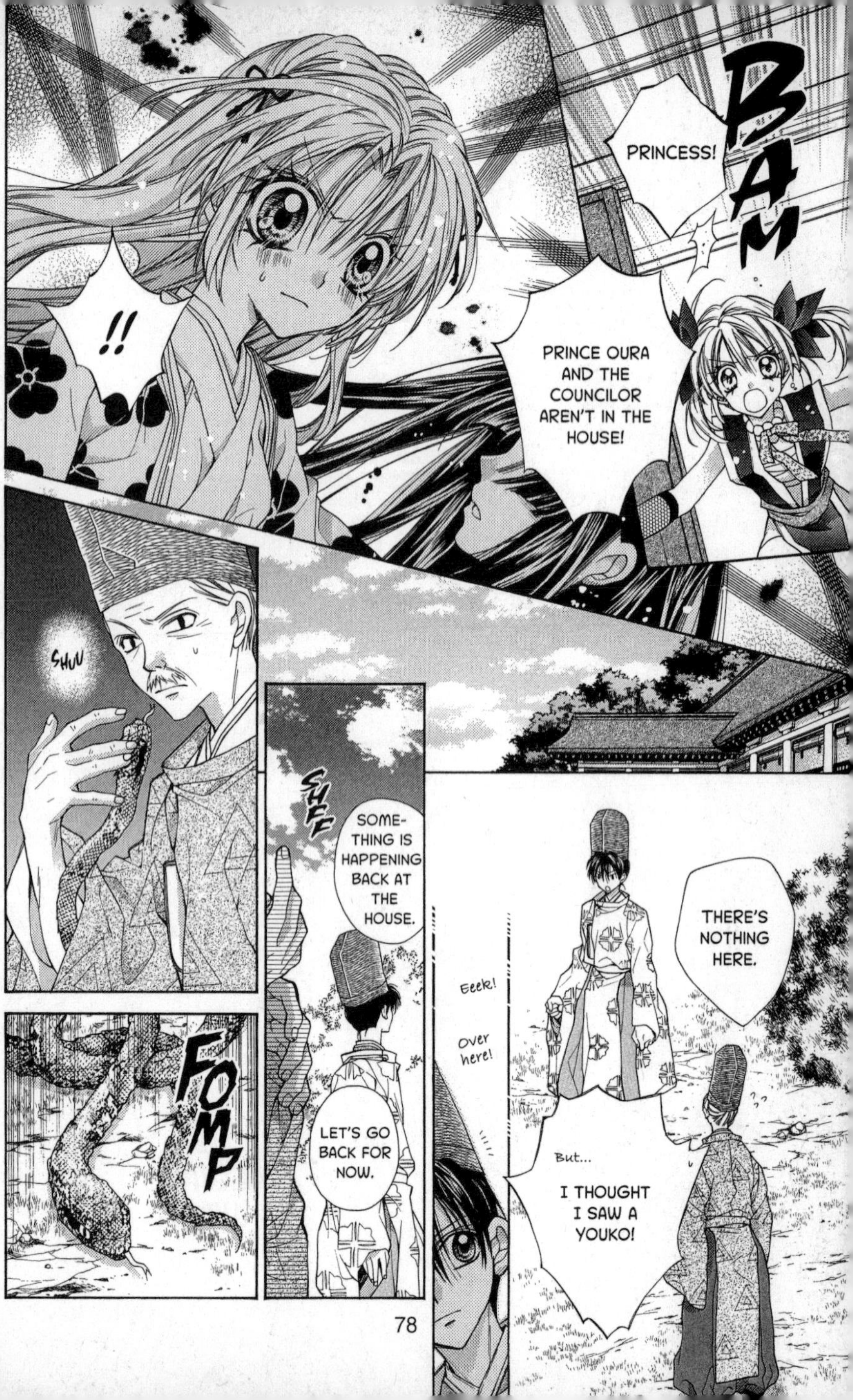
BAM
PRINCESS!
PRINCE OURA AND THE COUNCILOR AREN'T IN THE HOUSE!
!!
SHUU
THERE'S NOTHING HERE.
Eeek!
Over here!
But...
I THOUGHT I SAW A YOUKO!
SHFF
SOME-THING IS HAPPENING BACK AT THE HOUSE.
LET'S GO BACK FOR NOW.
FOMP

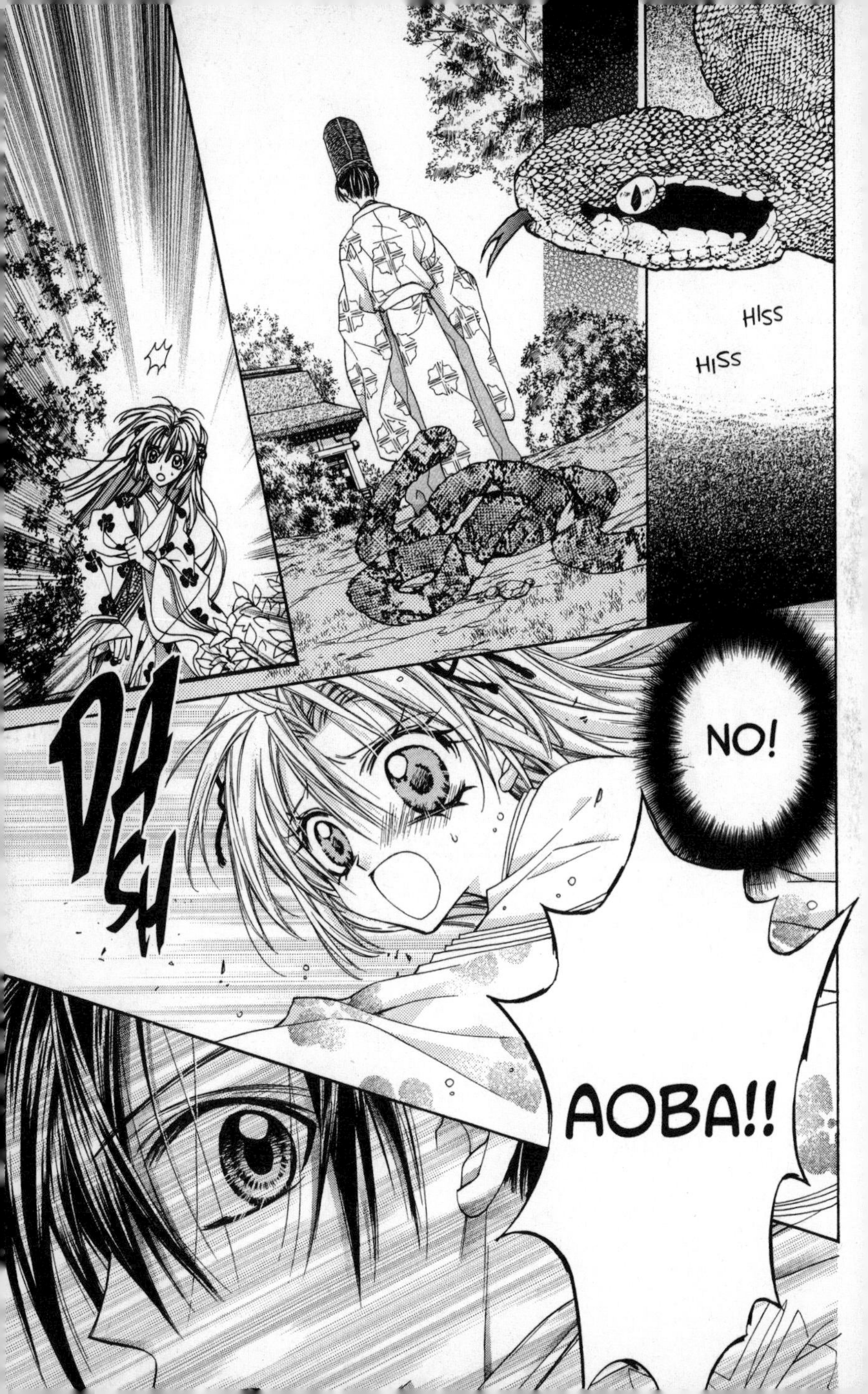
HISS
HISS
NO!
DASH
AOBA!!

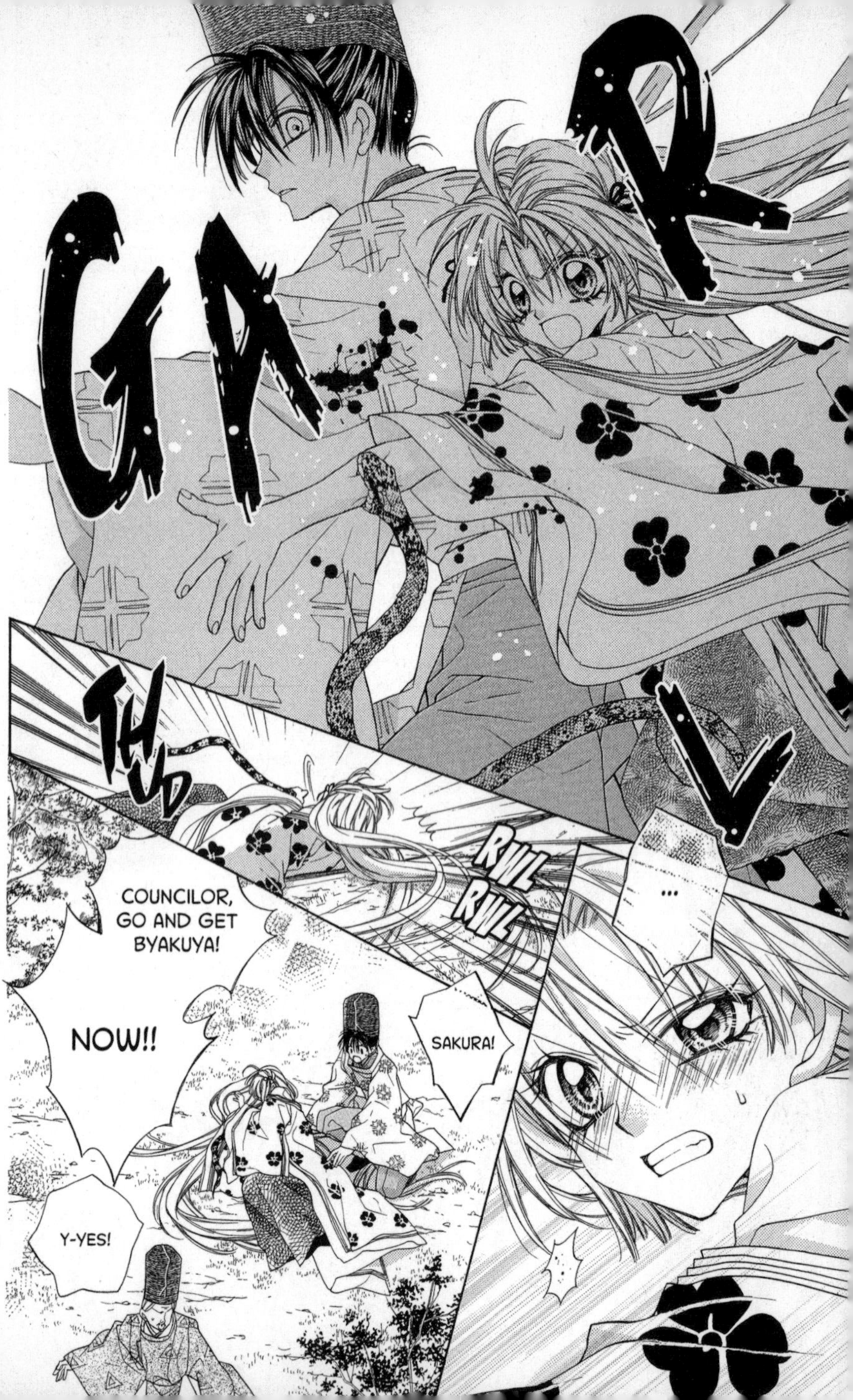
THUD
RWL RWL
...
SAKURA!
COUNCILOR, GO AND GET BYAKUYA!
NOW!!
Y-YES!

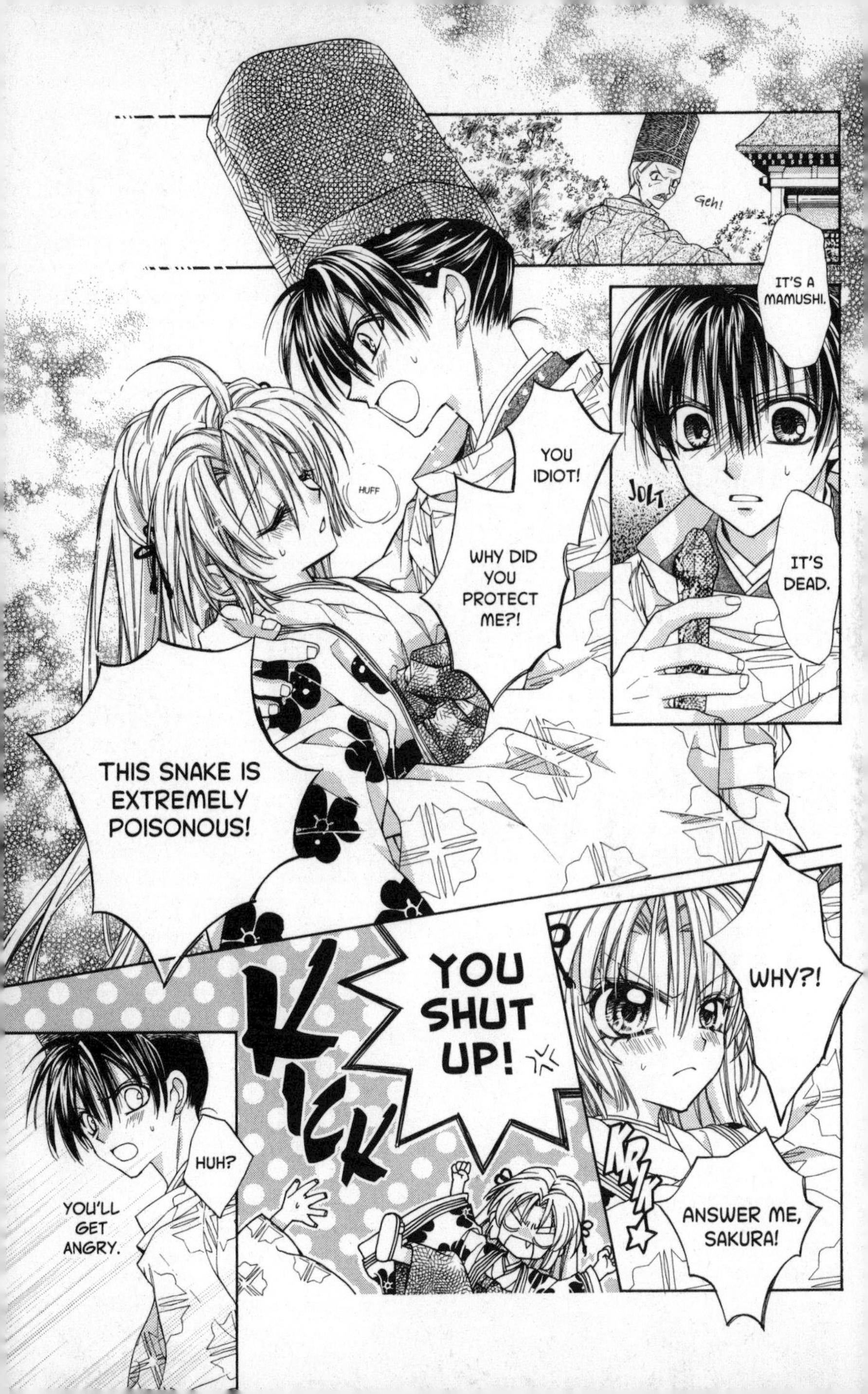
Geh!
IT'S A MAMUSHI.
JOLT
IT'S DEAD.
HUFF
YOU IDIOT!
WHY DID YOU PROTECT ME?!
THIS SNAKE IS EXTREMELY POISONOUS!
WHY?!
KRAK
ANSWER ME, SAKURA!
YOU SHUT UP!
KICK
HUH?
YOU'LL GET ANGRY.

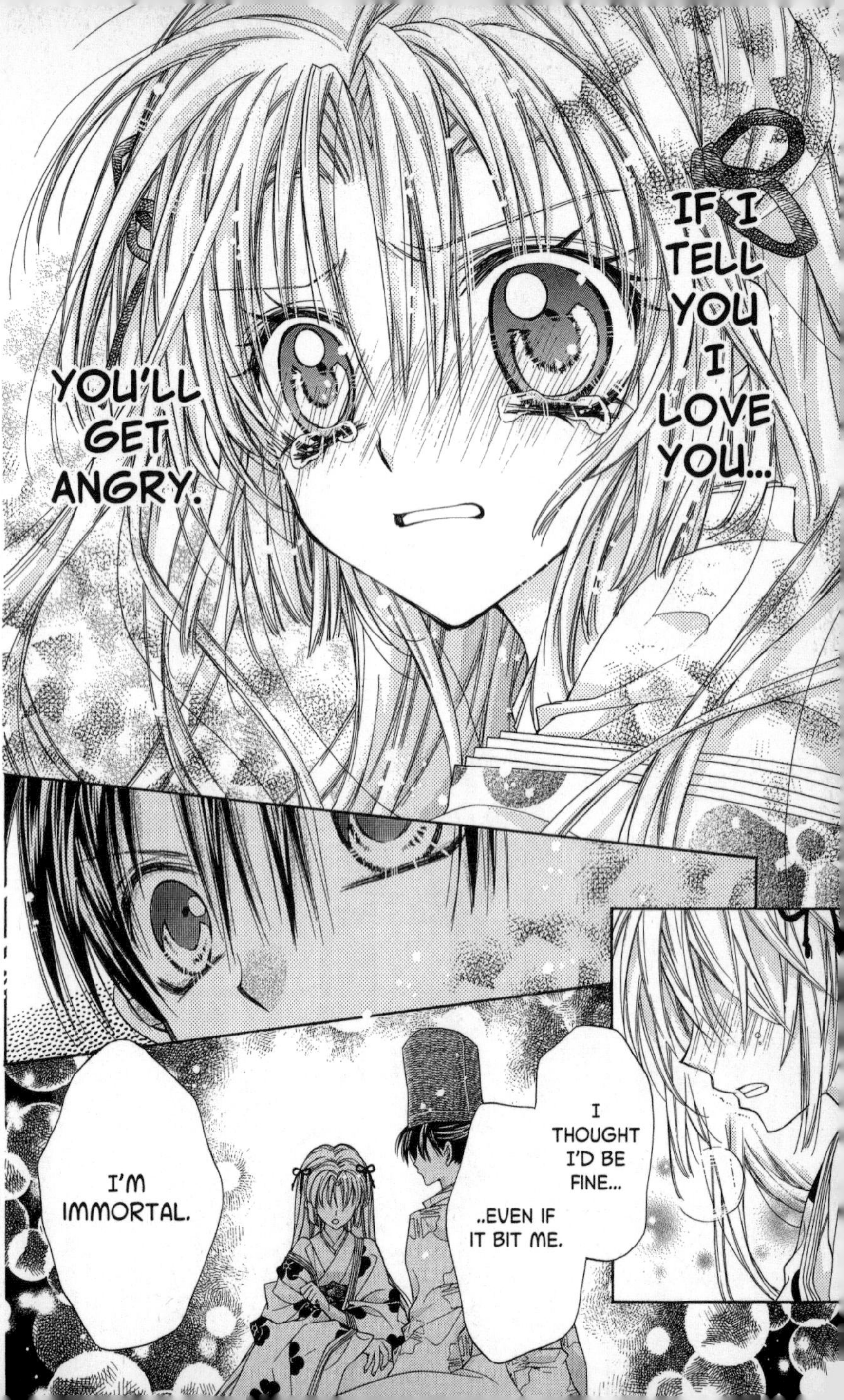
IF I TELL YOU I LOVE YOU...
YOU'LL GET ANGRY.
I THOUGHT I'D BE FINE...
..EVEN IF IT BIT ME.
I'M IMMORTAL.

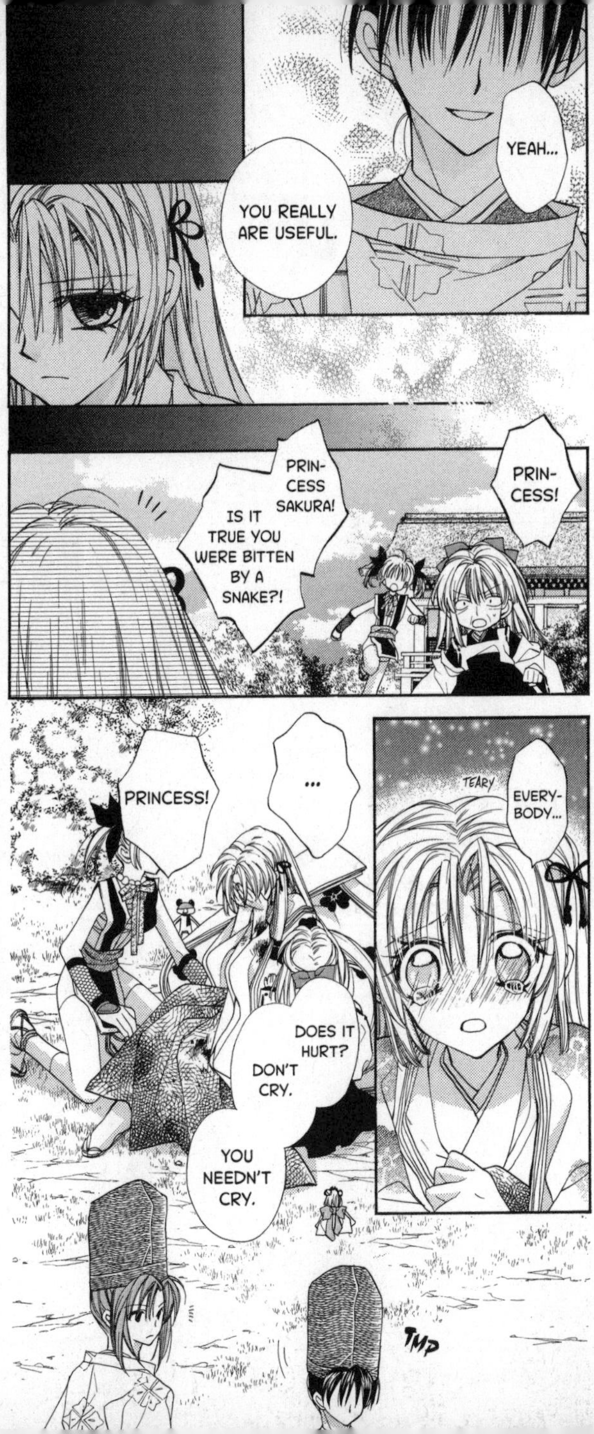
YEAH...
YOU REALLY ARE USEFUL.
PRIN-CESS!
PRIN-CESS SAKURA! IS IT TRUE YOU WERE BITTEN BY A SNAKE?!
TEARY
EVERY-BODY...
...
PRINCESS!
DOES IT HURT? DON'T CRY.
YOU NEEDN'T CRY.
TMP

The return of?!

PENCHI DE SHAKIN☆

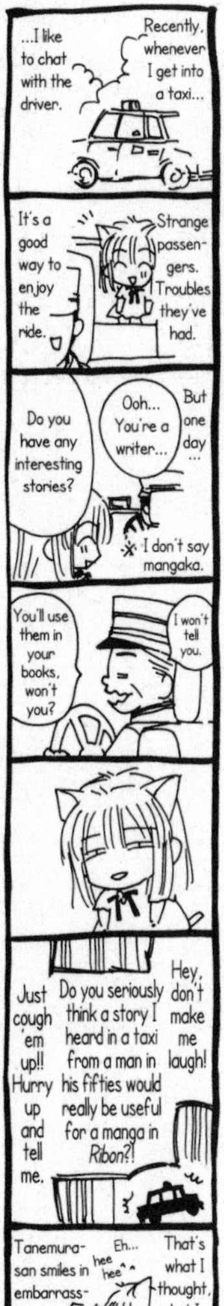
Recently, whenever I get into a taxi...
...I like to chat with the driver.
Strange passengers. Troubles they've had.
It's a good way to enjoy the ride.
But one day...
Ooh... You're a writer...
Do you have any interesting stories?
※I don't say mangaka.
I won't tell you.
You'll use them in your books, won't you?
Hey, don't make me laugh!
Do you seriously think a story I heard in a taxi from a man in his fifties would really be useful for a manga in Ribon?!
Just cough 'em up!! Hurry up and tell me.
That's what I thought, but I just smiled.
Eh...
hee hee
Tanemura-san smiles in embarrass-ment.

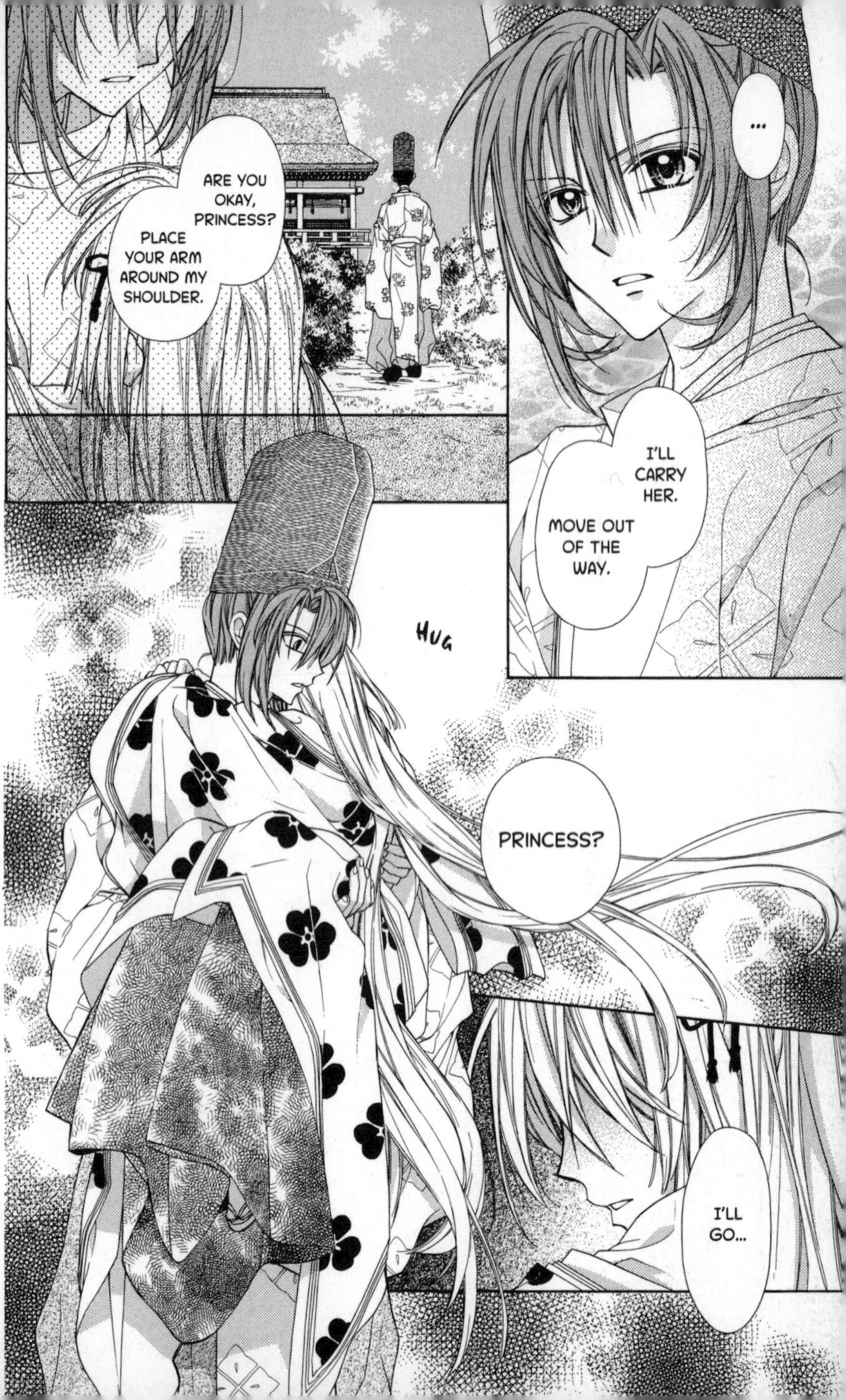
...
I'LL CARRY HER.
MOVE OUT OF THE WAY.
ARE YOU OKAY, PRINCESS?
PLACE YOUR ARM AROUND MY SHOULDER.
HUG
PRINCESS?
I'LL GO...

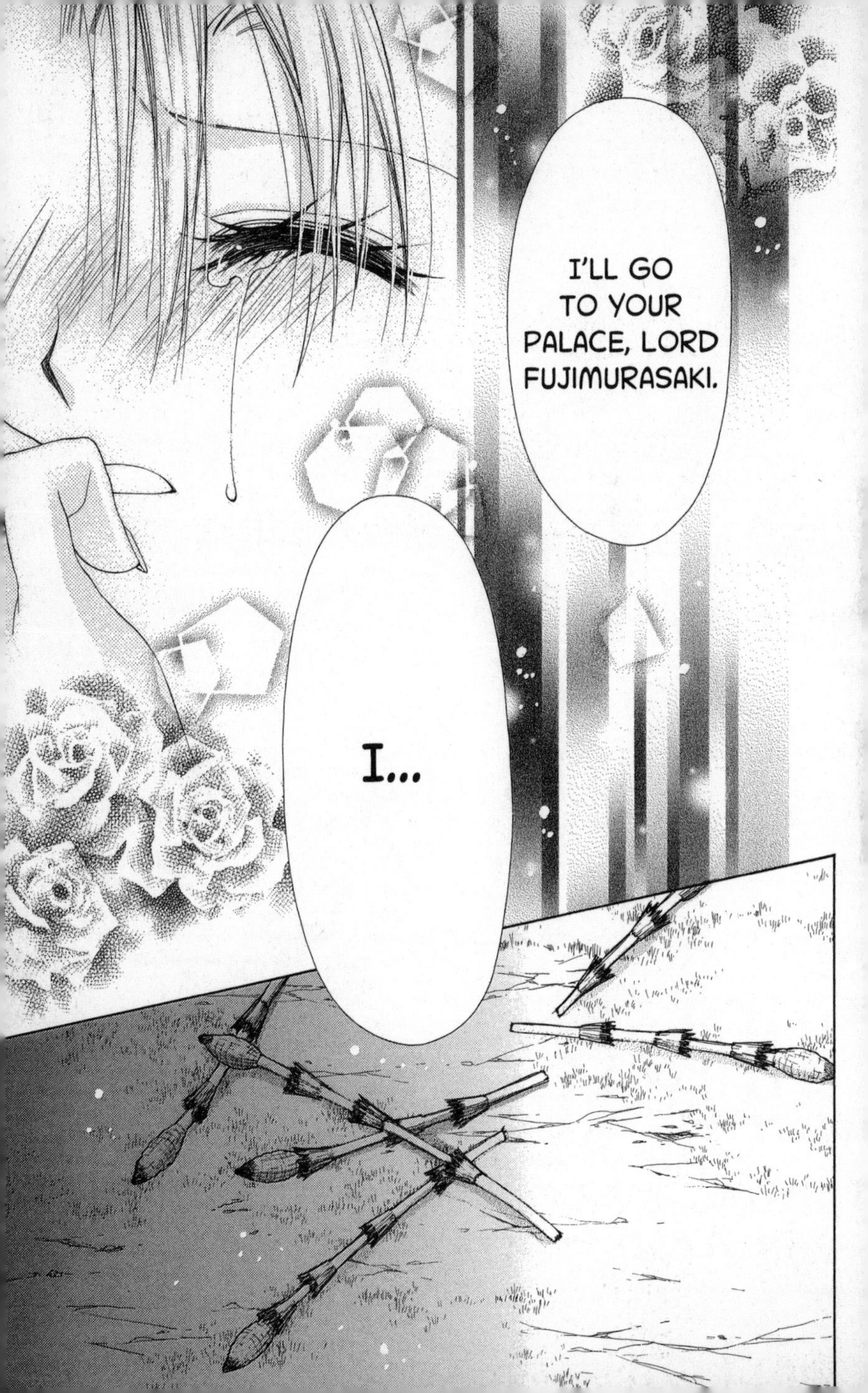
I'LL GO TO YOUR PALACE, LORD FUJIMURASAKI.
I...

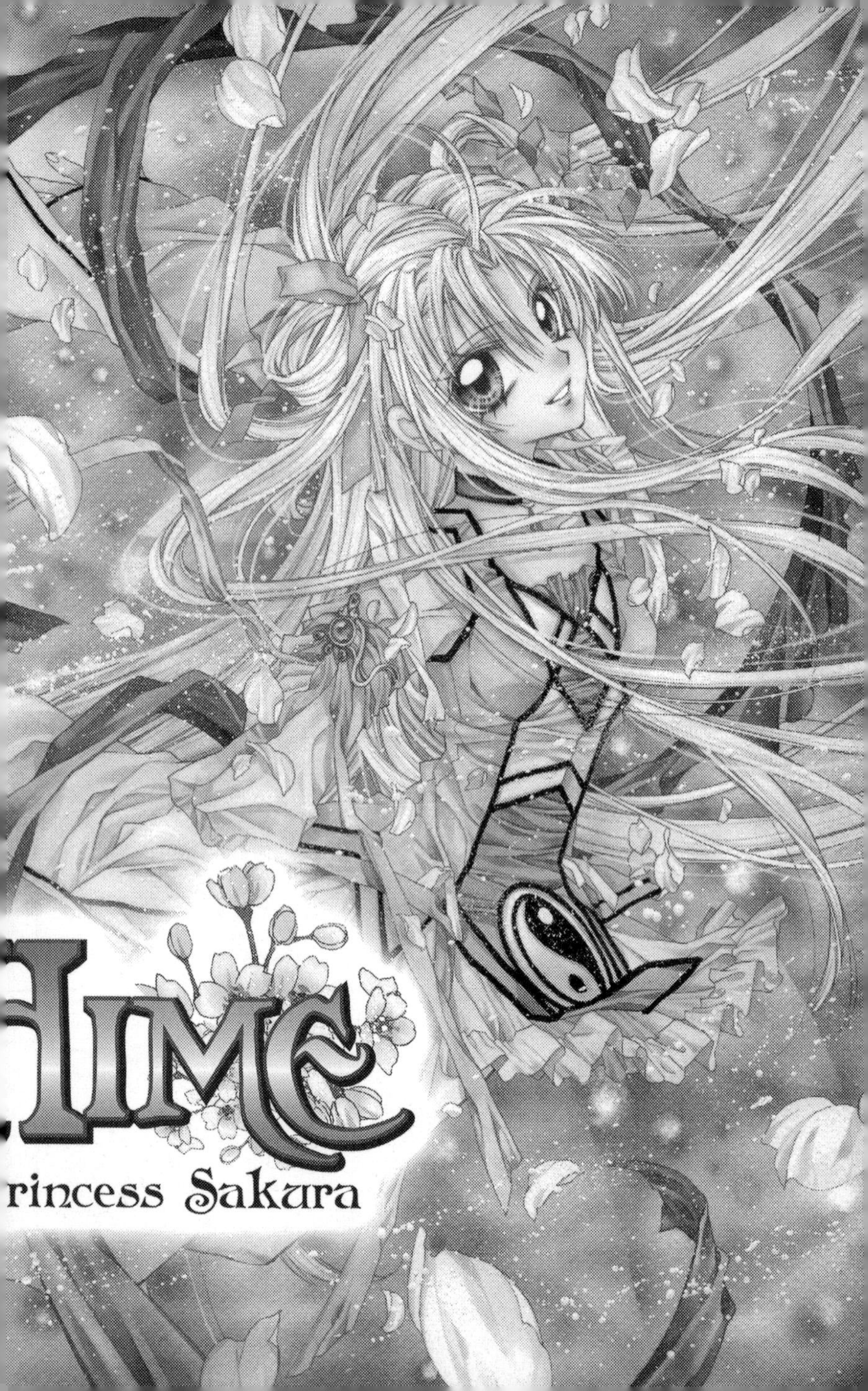
IME
rincess Sakura

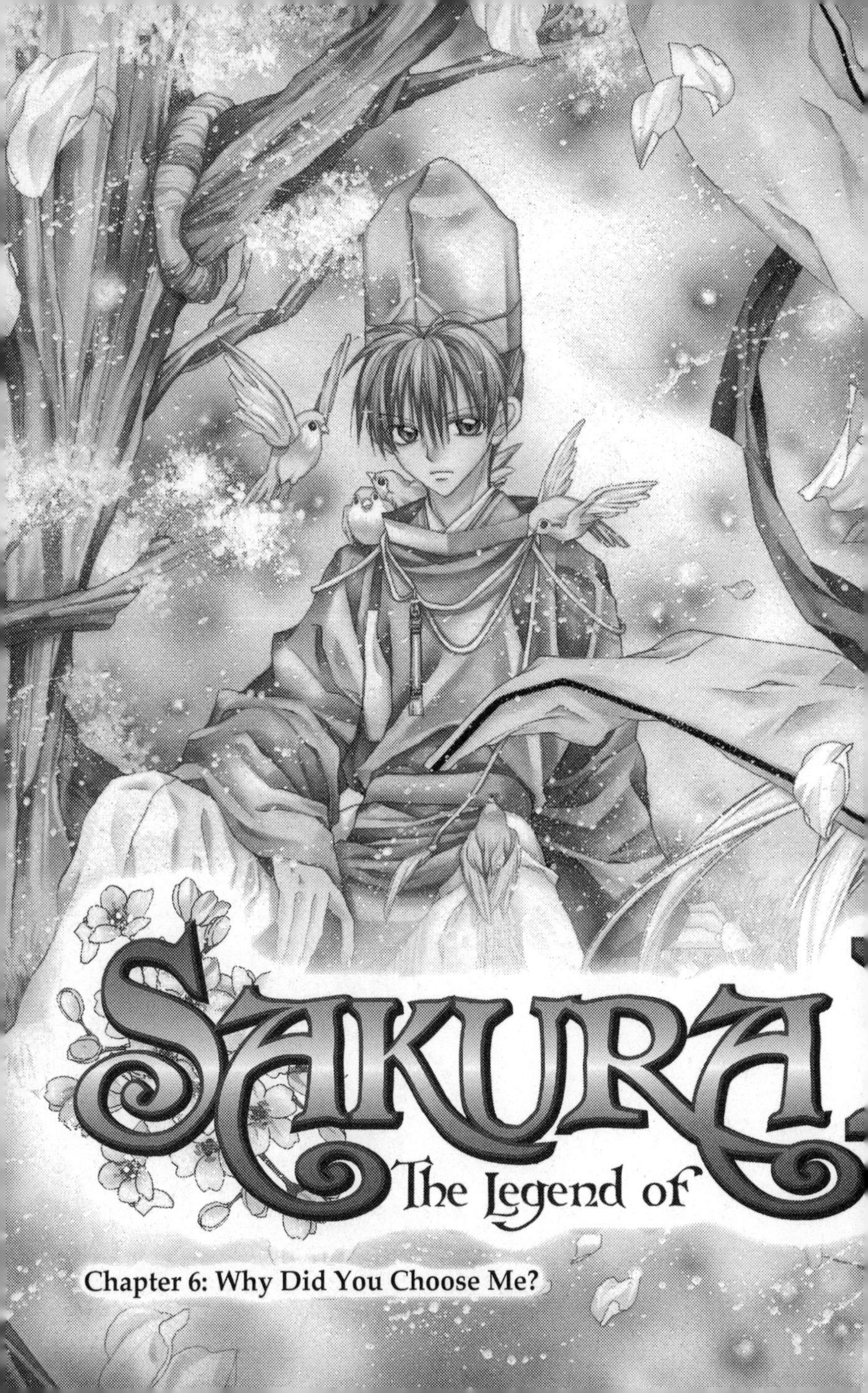
SAKURA
The Legend of
Chapter 6: Why Did You Choose Me?

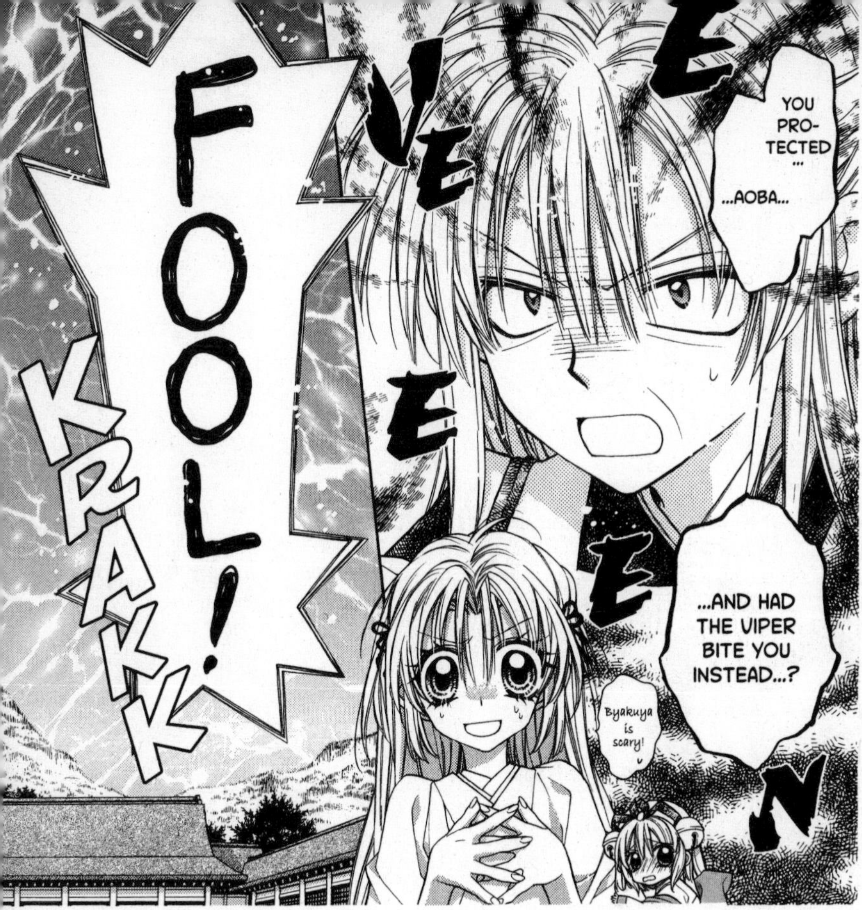
YOU PRO- TECTED ...
...AOBA...
FOOL!
KRAKK
VEEEEN
...AND HAD THE VIPER BITE YOU INSTEAD...?
Byakuya is scary!

※ I'm giving away the story.

Chapter 6: Why Did You Choose Me?

This is a rather restrained chapter for one that was placed in the front of the magazine. But it is my favorite chapter so far.
In the fan letters I receive, I'm often asked, "What is Fujimurasaki thinking about?!" I'll write about that sooner or later. He's a complex guy who is caught between his position as the Togu and his feelings... (Not that it concerns me.)

The title of chapter 5 was in Sakura's words, so this chapter is in Aoba's words. He says this in the scene with Byakuya, but Aoba's popularity rose after this chapter. Tough, isn't it, young man? There is also another reason why Aoba is unable to get himself to have a relationship with Sakura, and I'll write about that sooner or later too. (I'm sorry it's all like this... But this series just started, so I really can't say too much about it yet.)

I can't believe I was thinking about concluding the Aoba story arc in just five chapters...
I think it's going to continue... It looks like we'll be able to publish volume 3 a little faster, so I'd like to settle it in that volume. The reason Sakura falls in love with Aoba is because nobody has really paid any attention to her in her life until now. She strongly believes "things can't be as bad as they were back then." That's how she is able to bear the hardships.

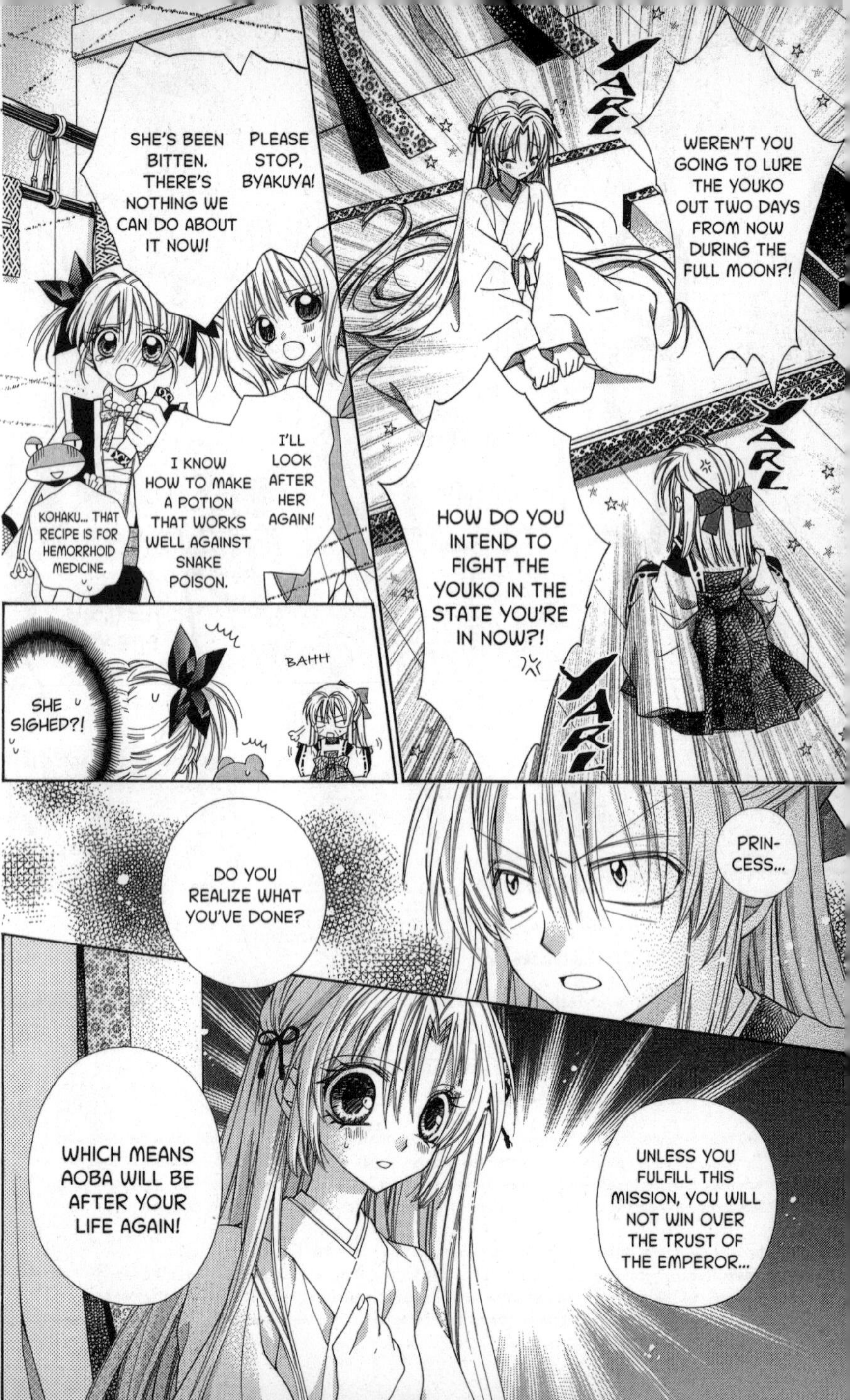
YARL
WEREN'T YOU GOING TO LURE THE YOUKO OUT TWO DAYS FROM NOW DURING THE FULL MOON?!
YARL
HOW DO YOU INTEND TO FIGHT THE YOUKO IN THE STATE YOU'RE IN NOW?!
YARL
PLEASE STOP, BYAKUYA!
SHE'S BEEN BITTEN. THERE'S NOTHING WE CAN DO ABOUT IT NOW!
I'LL LOOK AFTER HER AGAIN!
I KNOW HOW TO MAKE A POTION THAT WORKS WELL AGAINST SNAKE POISON.
KOHAKU... THAT RECIPE IS FOR HEMORRHOID MEDICINE.
BAHH
SHE SIGHED?!
PRIN-CESS...
DO YOU REALIZE WHAT YOU'VE DONE?
UNLESS YOU FULFILL THIS MISSION, YOU WILL NOT WIN OVER THE TRUST OF THE EMPEROR...
WHICH MEANS AOBA WILL BE AFTER YOUR LIFE AGAIN!

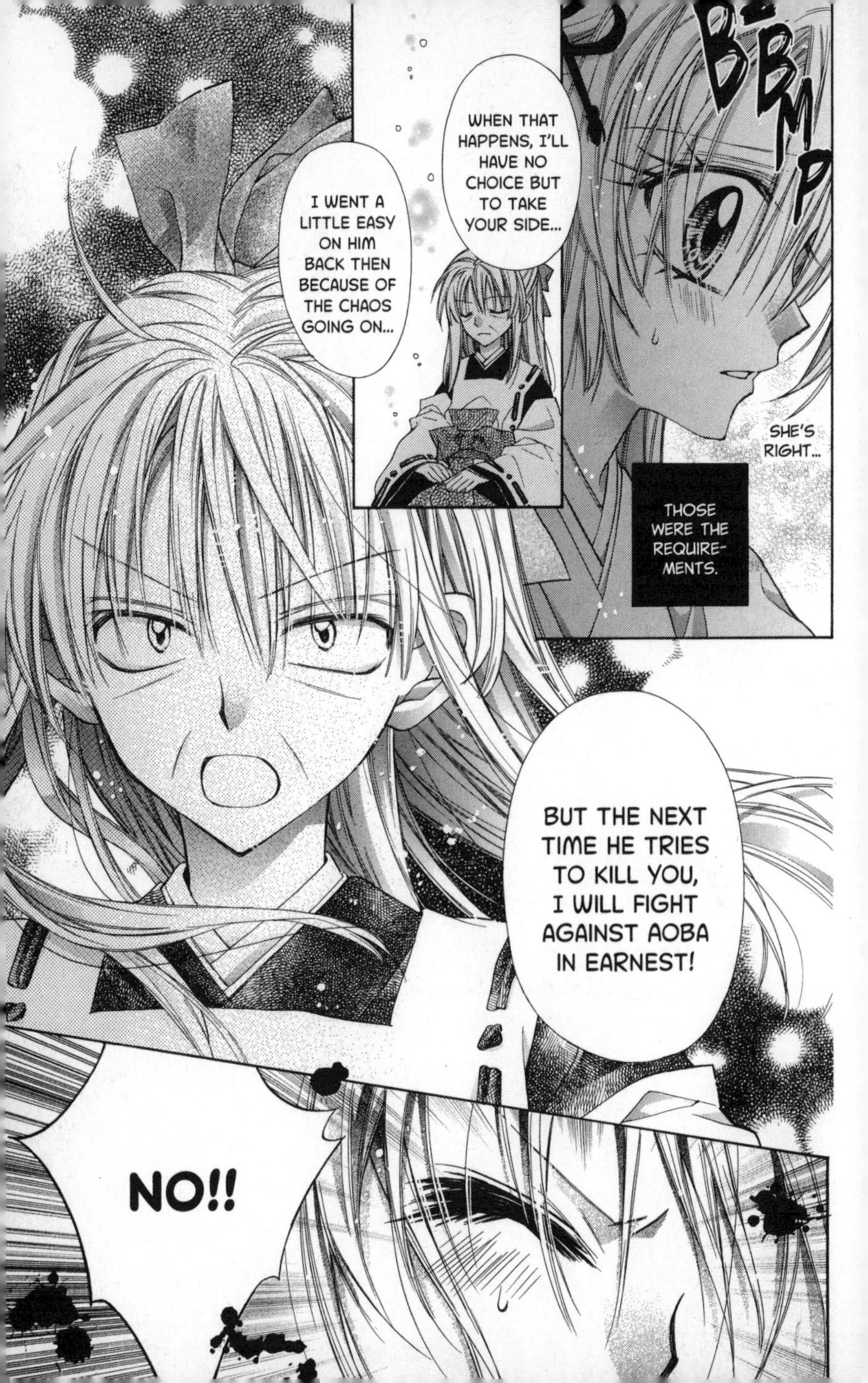
BBMP
SHE'S RIGHT...
THOSE WERE THE REQUIRE-MENTS.
WHEN THAT HAPPENS, I'LL HAVE NO CHOICE BUT TO TAKE YOUR SIDE...
I WENT A LITTLE EASY ON HIM BACK THEN BECAUSE OF THE CHAOS GOING ON...
BUT THE NEXT TIME HE TRIES TO KILL YOU, I WILL FIGHT AGAINST AOBA IN EARNEST!
NO!!

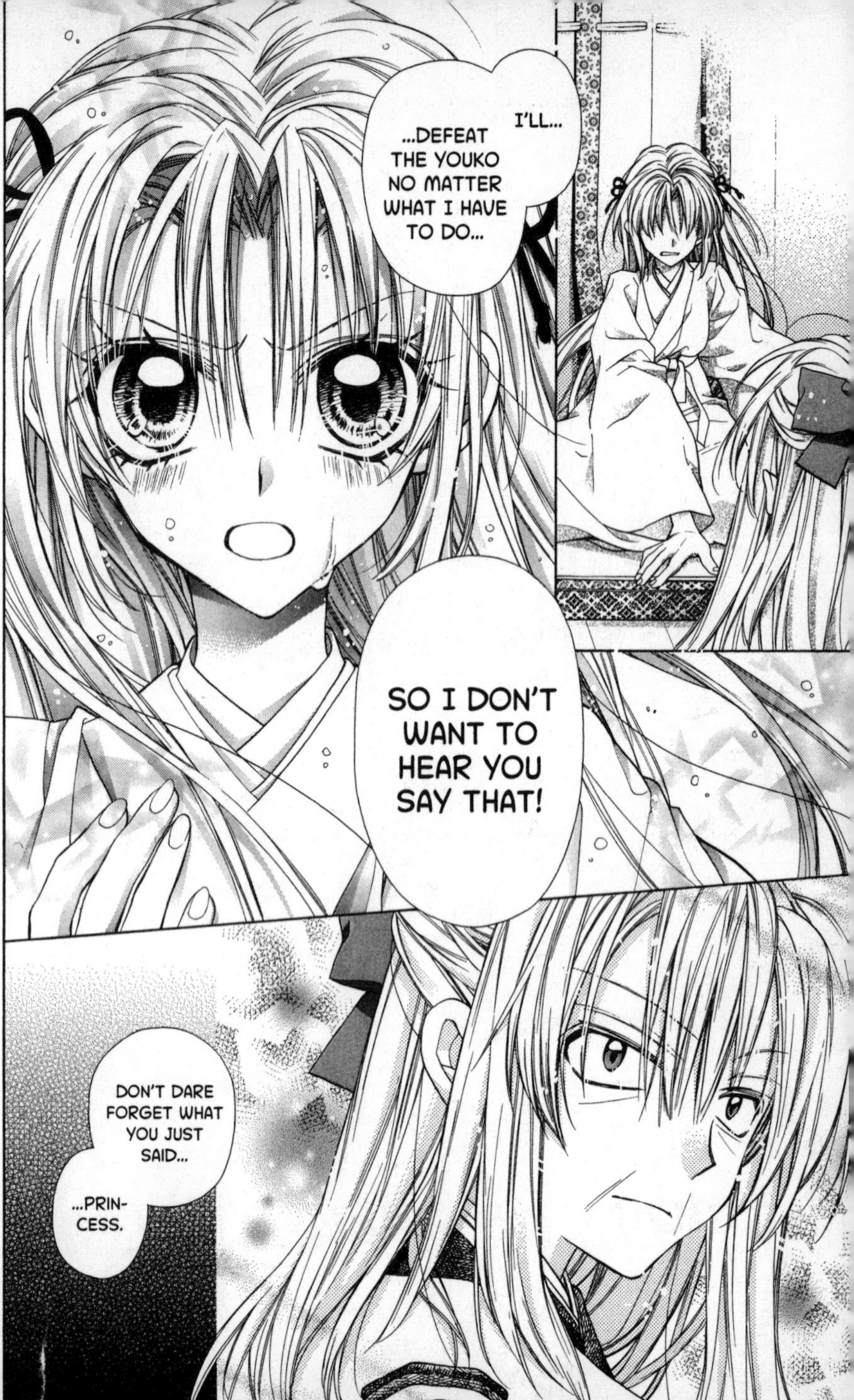
I'LL...
...DEFEAT THE YOUKO NO MATTER WHAT I HAVE TO DO...
SO I DON'T WANT TO HEAR YOU SAY THAT!
DON'T DARE FORGET WHAT YOU JUST SAID...
...PRIN-CESS.

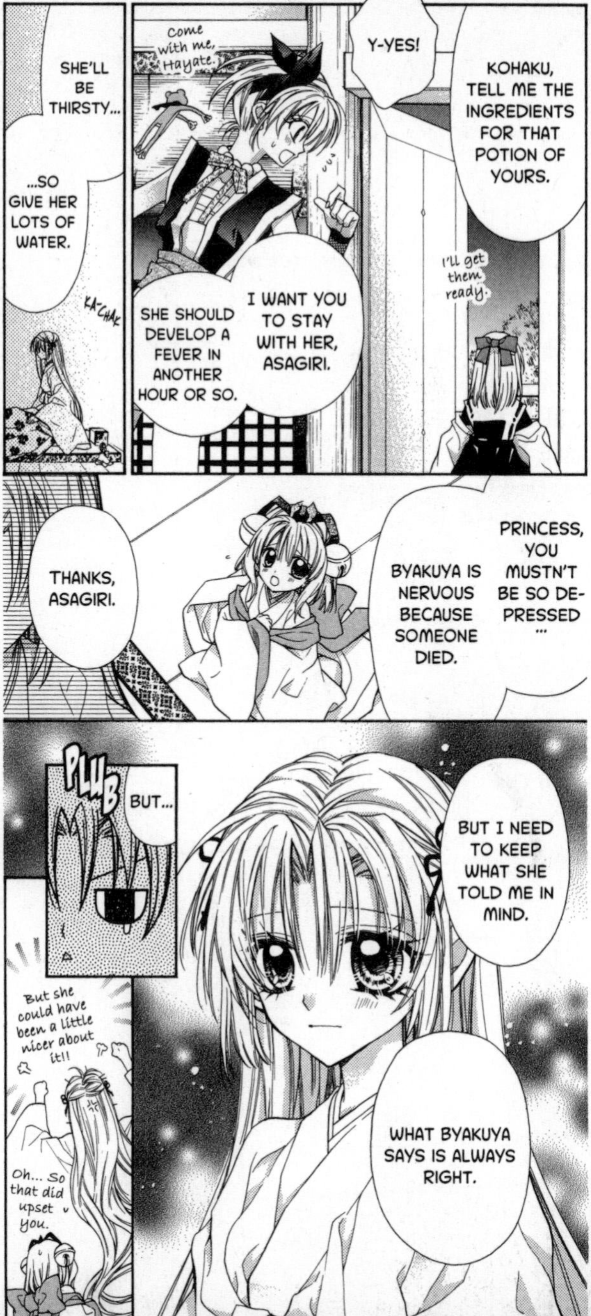
KOHAKU, TELL ME THE INGREDIENTS FOR THAT POTION OF YOURS.
I'll get them ready.
Y-YES!
Come with me, Hayate.
I WANT YOU TO STAY WITH HER, ASAGIRI.
SHE SHOULD DEVELOP A FEVER IN ANOTHER HOUR OR SO.
SHE'LL BE THIRSTY...
...SO GIVE HER LOTS OF WATER.
KA-CHAK
PRINCESS, YOU MUSTN'T BE SO DE-PRESSED...
BYAKUYA IS NERVOUS BECAUSE SOMEONE DIED.
THANKS, ASAGIRI.
BUT I NEED TO KEEP WHAT SHE TOLD ME IN MIND.
WHAT BYAKUYA SAYS IS ALWAYS RIGHT.
PLUB
BUT...
But she could have been a little nicer about it!!
Oh... So that did upset you.

The return of?!

PENCHI DE SHAKIN☆

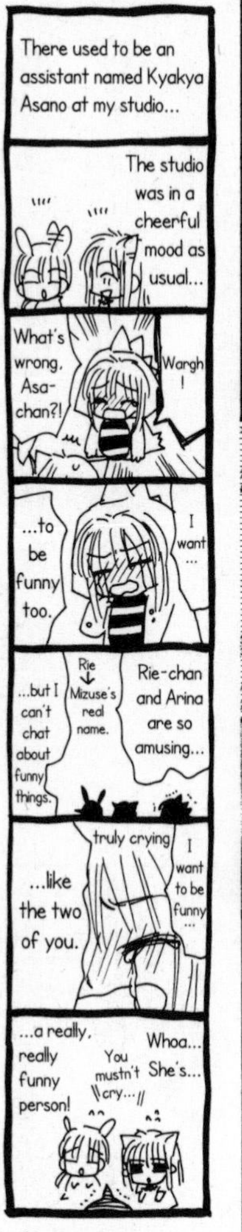
There used to be an assistant named Kyakya Asano at my studio...
The studio was in a cheerful mood as usual...
What's wrong, Asa-chan?!
Wargh!
...to be funny too.
I want...
...but I can't chat about funny things.
Rie-chan and Arina are so amusing...
Rie → Mizuse's real name.
...like the two of you.
truly crying
I want to be funny...
...a really, really funny person!
Whoa... She's...
You mustn't cry...

She's now a fine mother with a child...

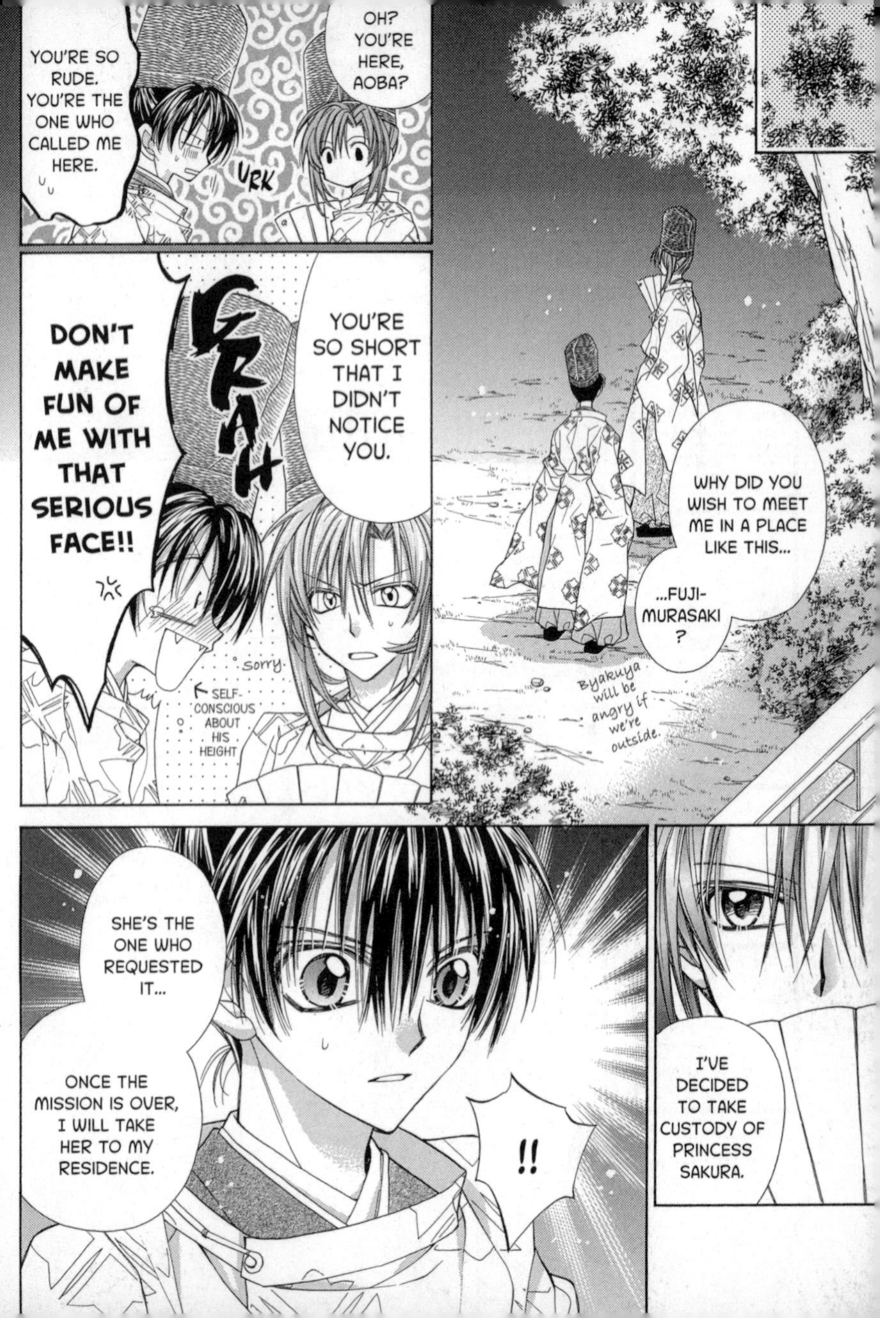
WHY DID YOU WISH TO MEET ME IN A PLACE LIKE THIS...
...FUJI-MURASAKI?
Byakuya will be angry if we're outside.
OH? YOU'RE HERE, AOBA?
YOU'RE SO RUDE. YOU'RE THE ONE WHO CALLED ME HERE.
URK
YOU'RE SO SHORT THAT I DIDN'T NOTICE YOU.
GRAH
DON'T MAKE FUN OF ME WITH THAT SERIOUS FACE!!
Sorry.
SELF-CONSCIOUS ABOUT HIS HEIGHT
I'VE DECIDED TO TAKE CUSTODY OF PRINCESS SAKURA.
SHE'S THE ONE WHO REQUESTED IT...
ONCE THE MISSION IS OVER, I WILL TAKE HER TO MY RESIDENCE.
!!

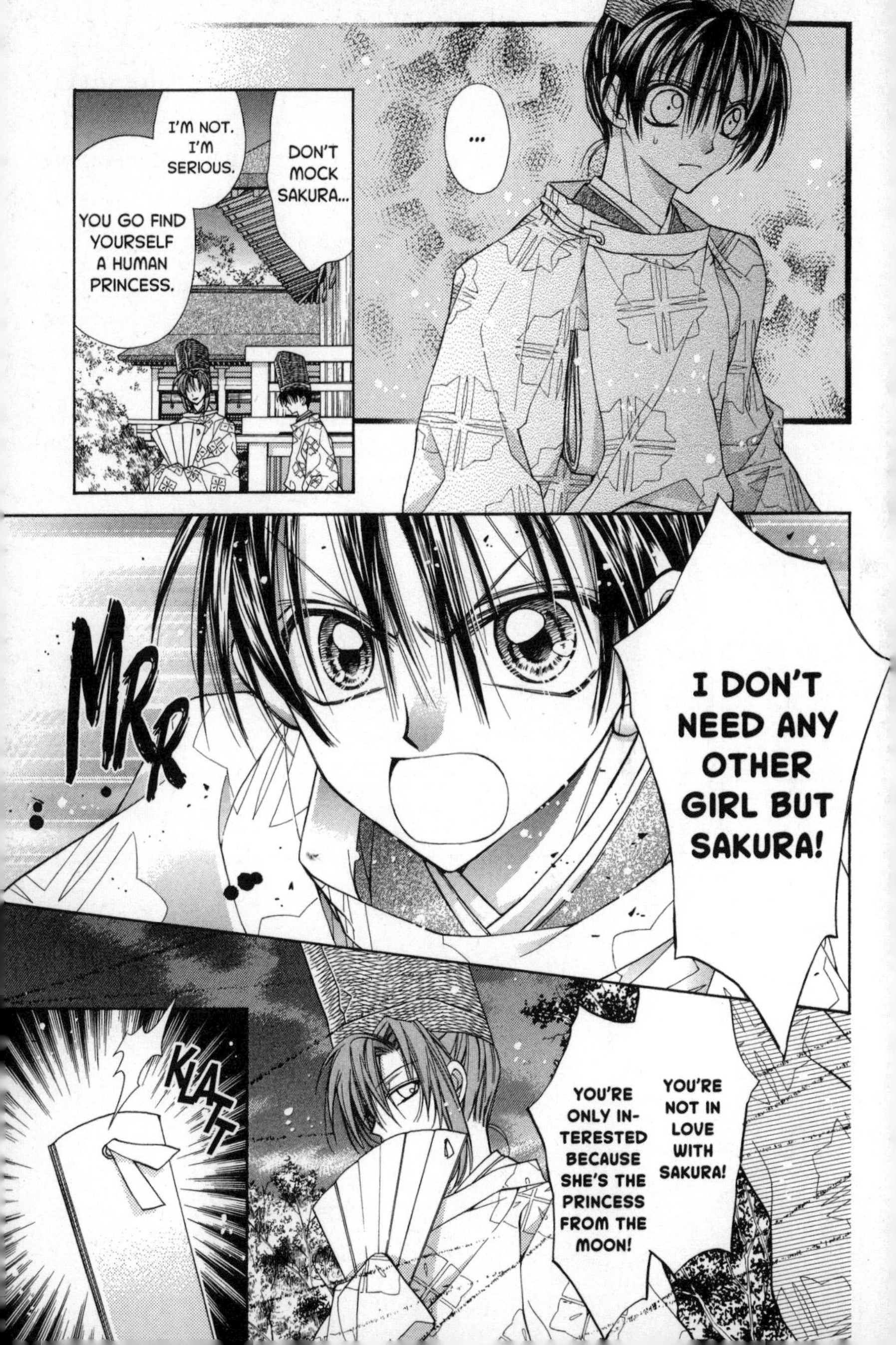
...
DON'T MOCK SAKURA...
I'M NOT. I'M SERIOUS.
YOU GO FIND YOURSELF A HUMAN PRINCESS.
I DON'T NEED ANY OTHER GIRL BUT SAKURA!
MRR
YOU'RE NOT IN LOVE WITH SAKURA!
YOU'RE ONLY IN-TERESTED BECAUSE SHE'S THE PRINCESS FROM THE MOON!
KLATT

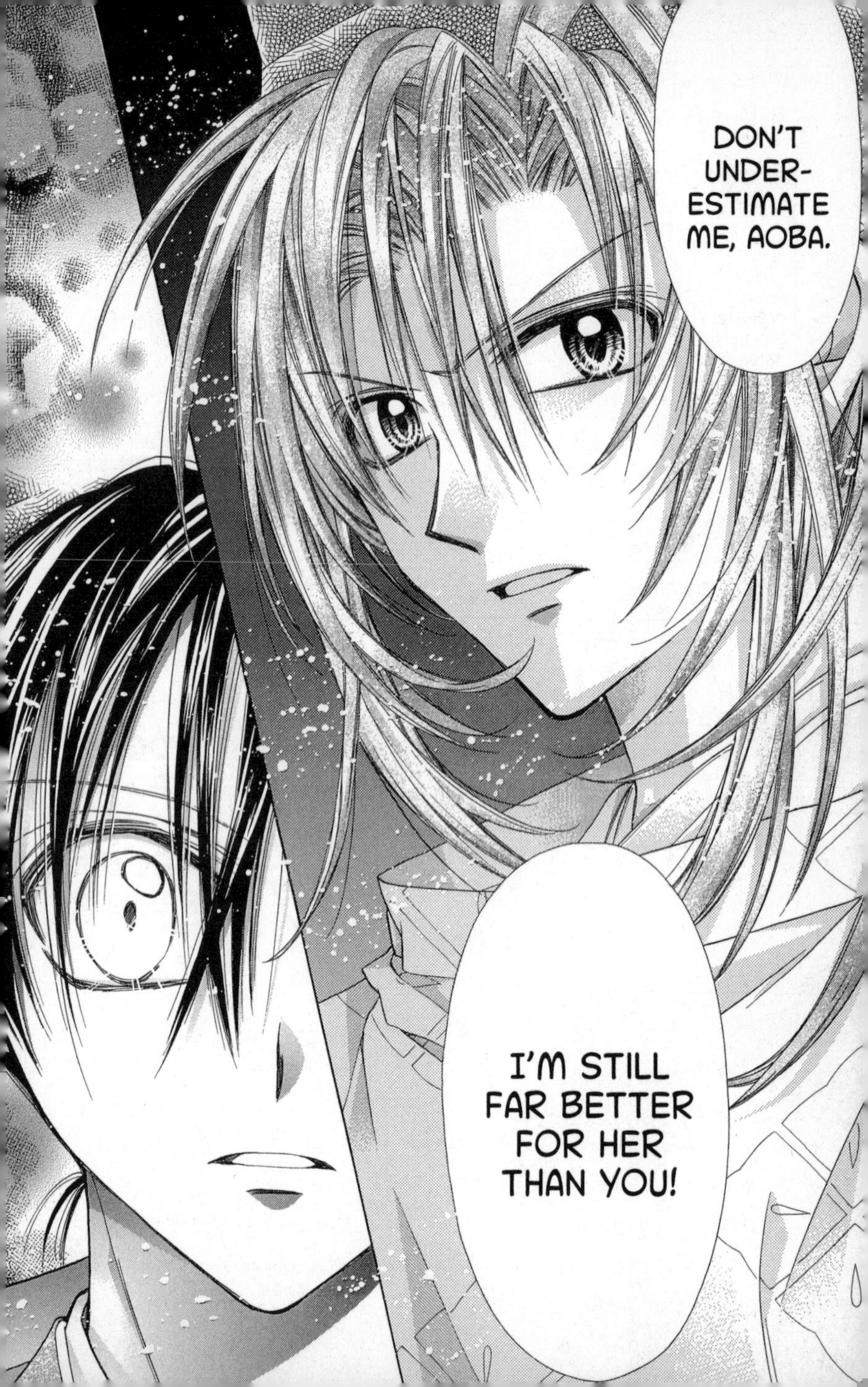
DON'T UNDER-ESTIMATE ME, AOBA.
I'M STILL FAR BETTER FOR HER THAN YOU!

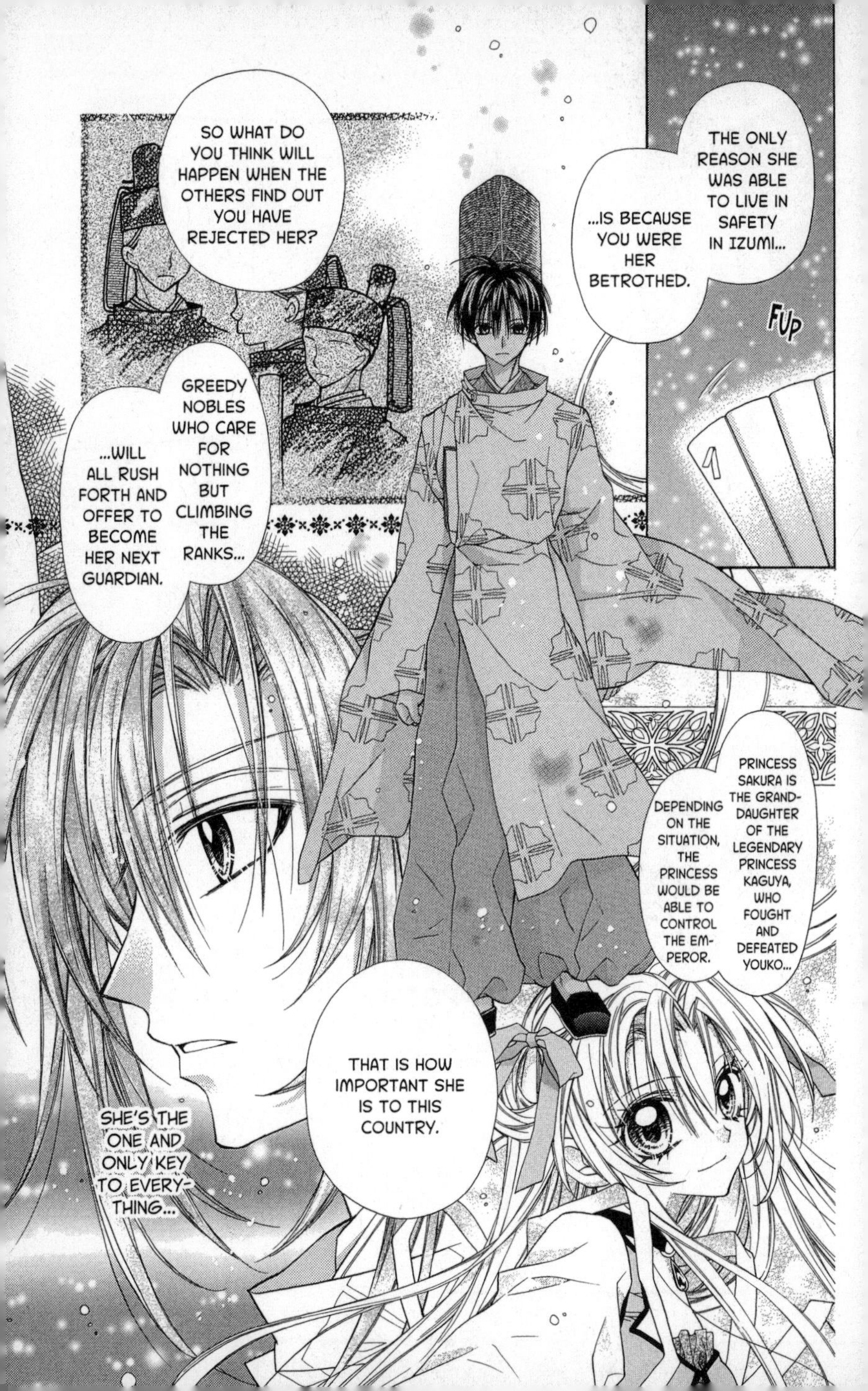
THE ONLY REASON SHE WAS ABLE TO LIVE IN SAFETY IN IZUMI...
...IS BECAUSE YOU WERE HER BETROTHED.
FUP
SO WHAT DO YOU THINK WILL HAPPEN WHEN THE OTHERS FIND OUT YOU HAVE REJECTED HER?
GREEDY NOBLES WHO CARE FOR NOTHING BUT CLIMBING THE RANKS...
...WILL ALL RUSH FORTH AND OFFER TO BECOME HER NEXT GUARDIAN.
PRINCESS SAKURA IS THE GRAND-DAUGHTER OF THE LEGENDARY PRINCESS KAGUYA, WHO FOUGHT AND DEFEATED YOUKO...
DEPENDING ON THE SITUATION, THE PRINCESS WOULD BE ABLE TO CONTROL THE EM-PEROR.
THAT IS HOW IMPORTANT SHE IS TO THIS COUNTRY.
SHE'S THE ONE AND ONLY KEY TO EVERY-THING...

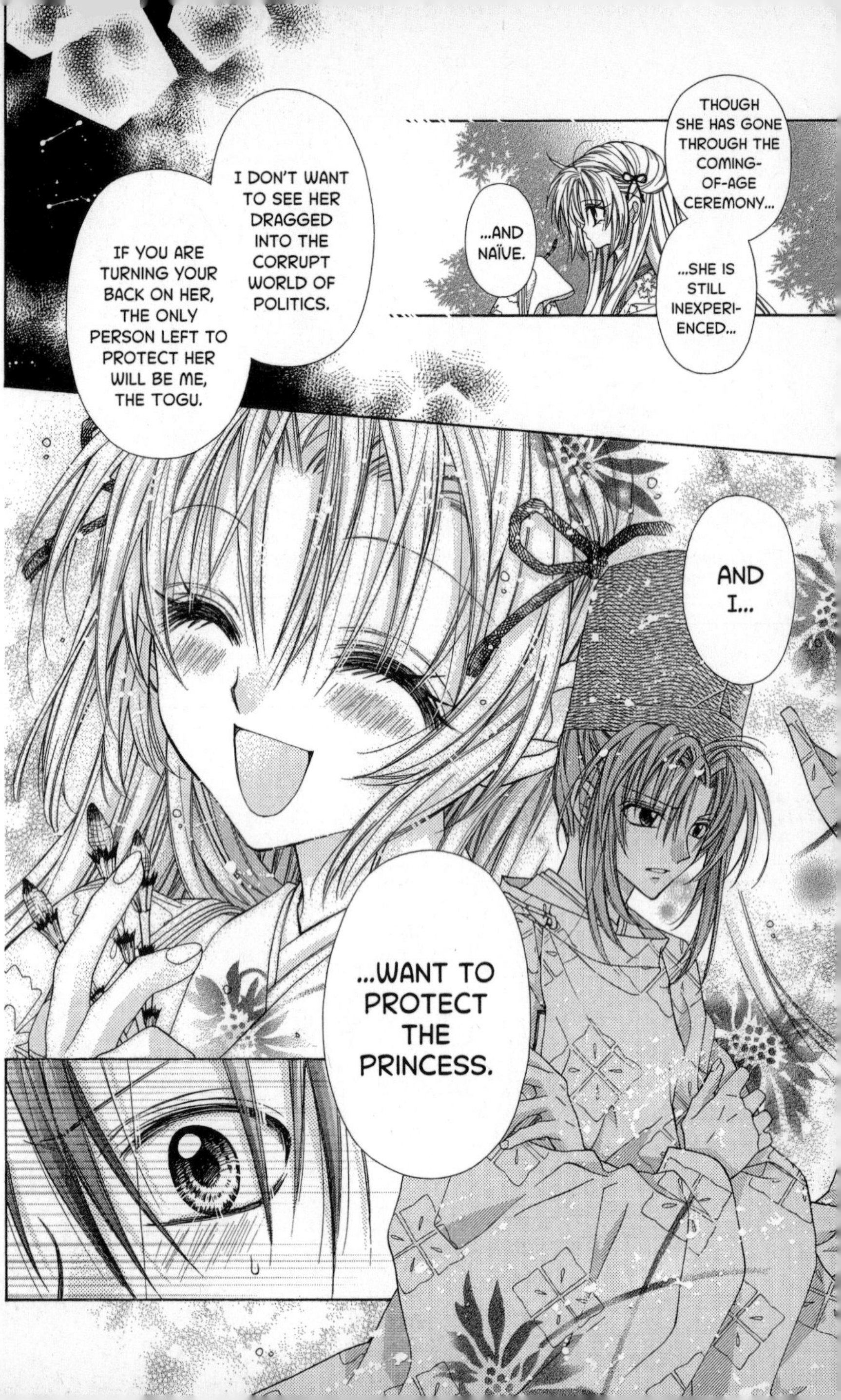
THOUGH SHE HAS GONE THROUGH THE COMING-OF-AGE CEREMONY...
...SHE IS STILL INEXPERIENCED...
...AND NAÏVE.
I DON'T WANT TO SEE HER DRAGGED INTO THE CORRUPT WORLD OF POLITICS.
IF YOU ARE TURNING YOUR BACK ON HER, THE ONLY PERSON LEFT TO PROTECT HER WILL BE ME, THE TOGU.
AND I...
...WANT TO PROTECT THE PRINCESS.

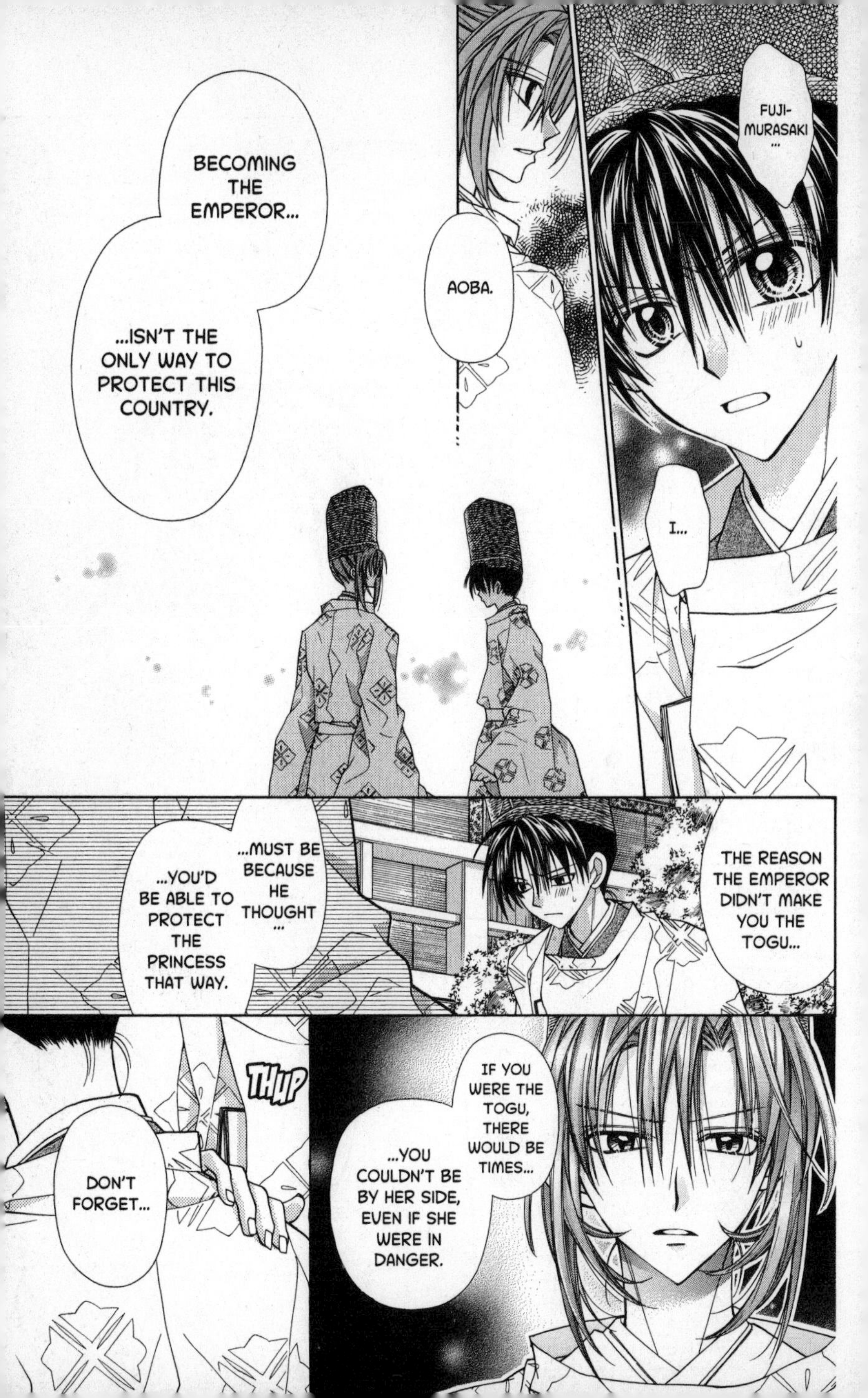
FUJI-MURASAKI...
I...
AOBA.
BECOMING THE EMPEROR...
...ISN'T THE ONLY WAY TO PROTECT THIS COUNTRY.
THE REASON THE EMPEROR DIDN'T MAKE YOU THE TOGU...
...MUST BE BECAUSE HE THOUGHT...
...YOU'D BE ABLE TO PROTECT THE PRINCESS THAT WAY.
IF YOU WERE THE TOGU, THERE WOULD BE TIMES...
...YOU COULDN'T BE BY HER SIDE, EVEN IF SHE WERE IN DANGER.
THWP
DON'T FORGET...

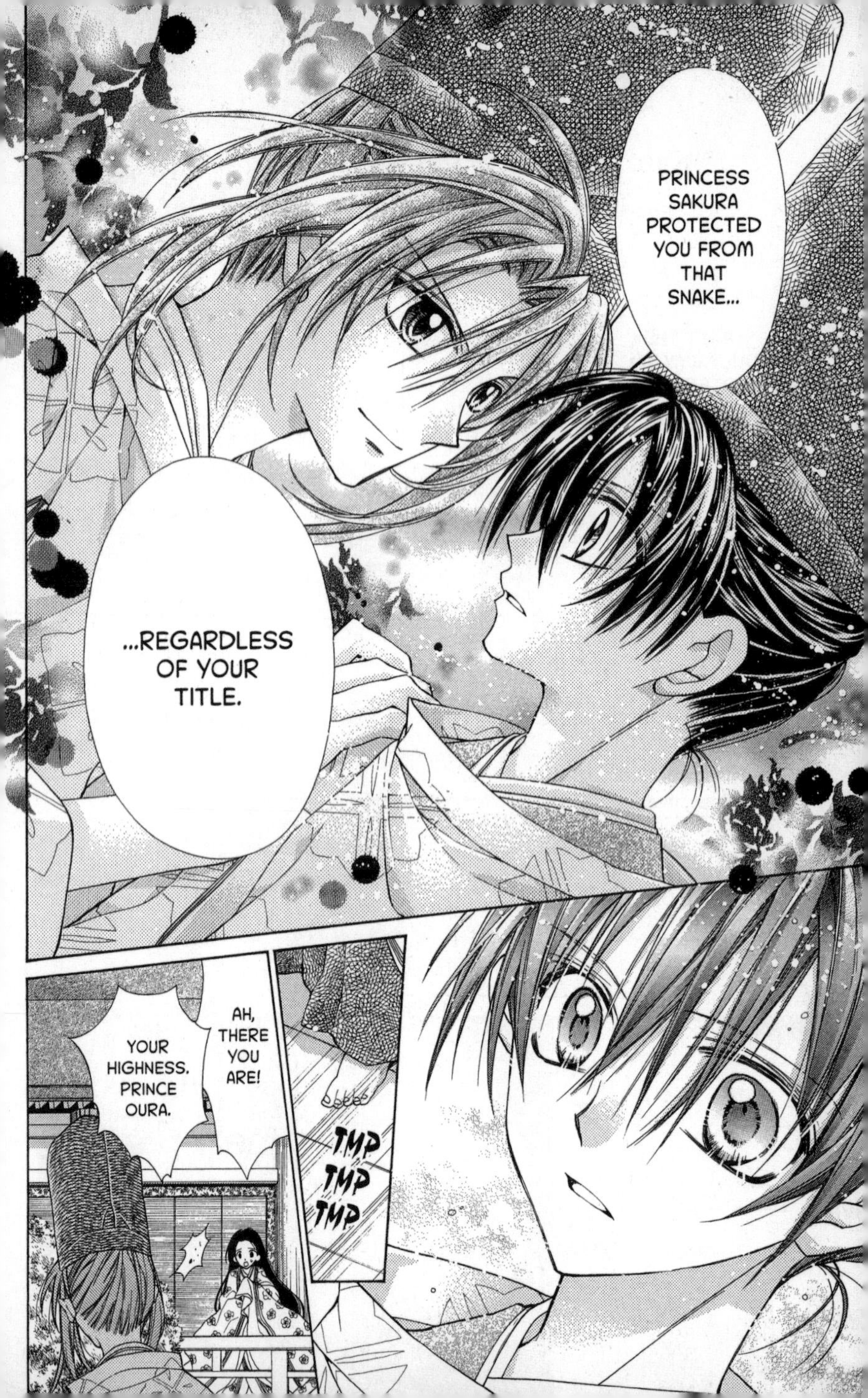
PRINCESS SAKURA PROTECTED YOU FROM THAT SNAKE...
...REGARDLESS OF YOUR TITLE.
AH, THERE YOU ARE!
TMP TMP TMP
YOUR HIGHNESS. PRINCE OURA.

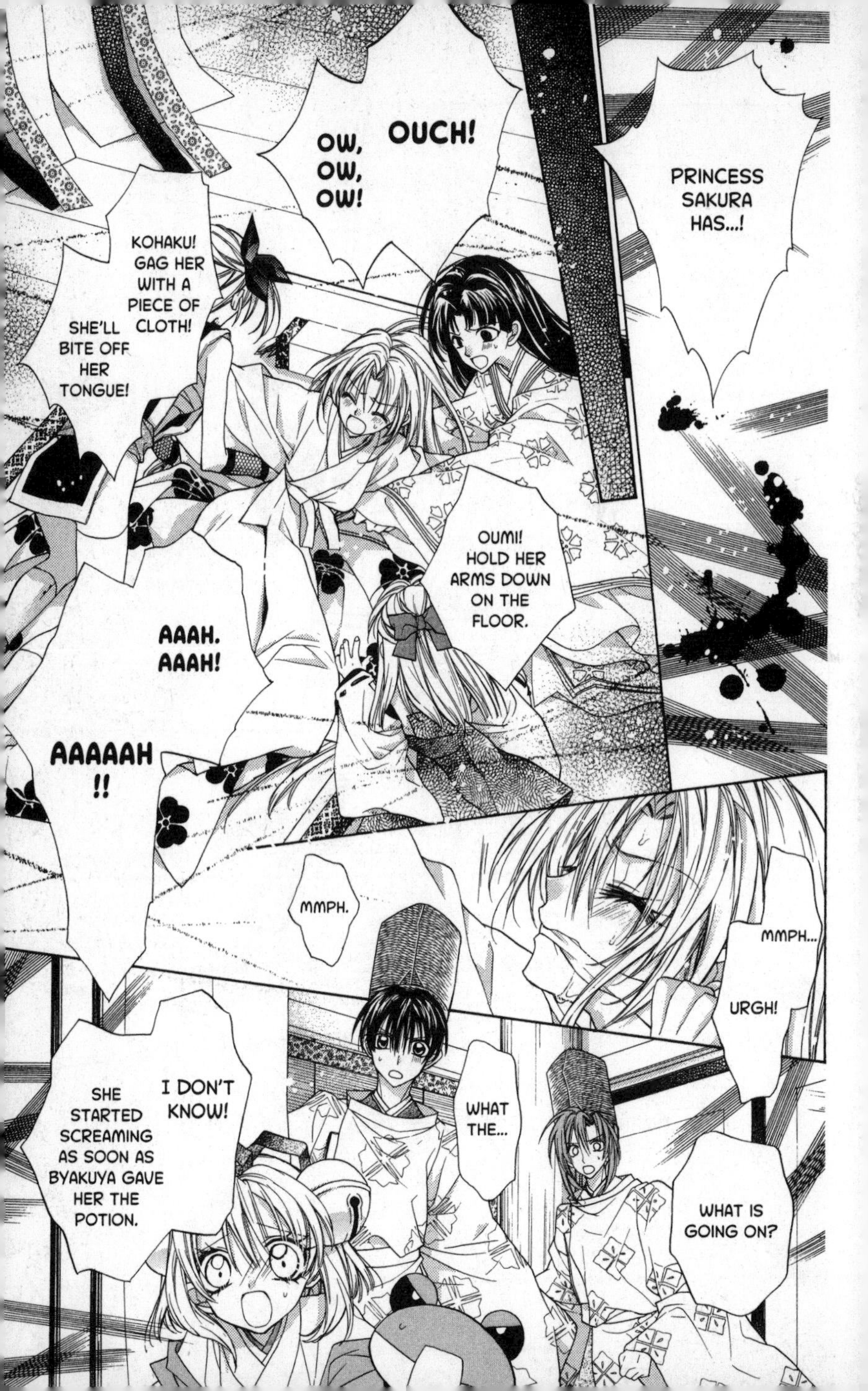
PRINCESS SAKURA HAS...!
OUCH!
OW, OW, OW!
KOHAKU! GAG HER WITH A PIECE OF CLOTH!
SHE'LL BITE OFF HER TONGUE!
OUMI! HOLD HER ARMS DOWN ON THE FLOOR.
AAAH. AAAH!
AAAAAH!!
MMPH...
URGH!
MMPH.
WHAT IS GOING ON?
WHAT THE...
I DON'T KNOW!
SHE STARTED SCREAMING AS SOON AS BYAKUYA GAVE HER THE POTION.

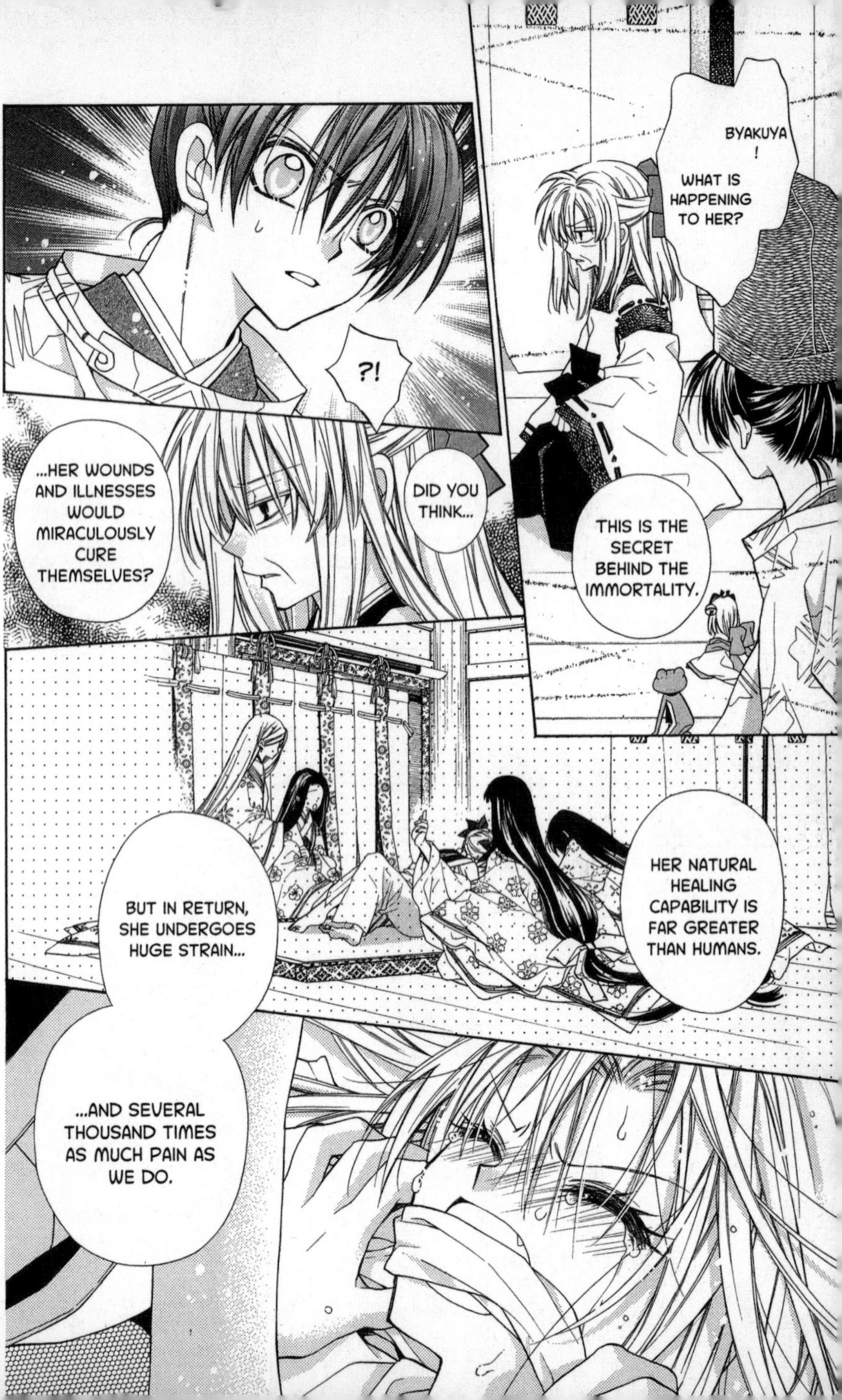
BYAKUYA!
WHAT IS HAPPENING TO HER?
THIS IS THE SECRET BEHIND THE IMMORTALITY.
?!
DID YOU THINK...
...HER WOUNDS AND ILLNESSES WOULD MIRACULOUSLY CURE THEMSELVES?
HER NATURAL HEALING CAPABILITY IS FAR GREATER THAN HUMANS.
BUT IN RETURN, SHE UNDERGOES HUGE STRAIN...
...AND SEVERAL THOUSAND TIMES AS MUCH PAIN AS WE DO.

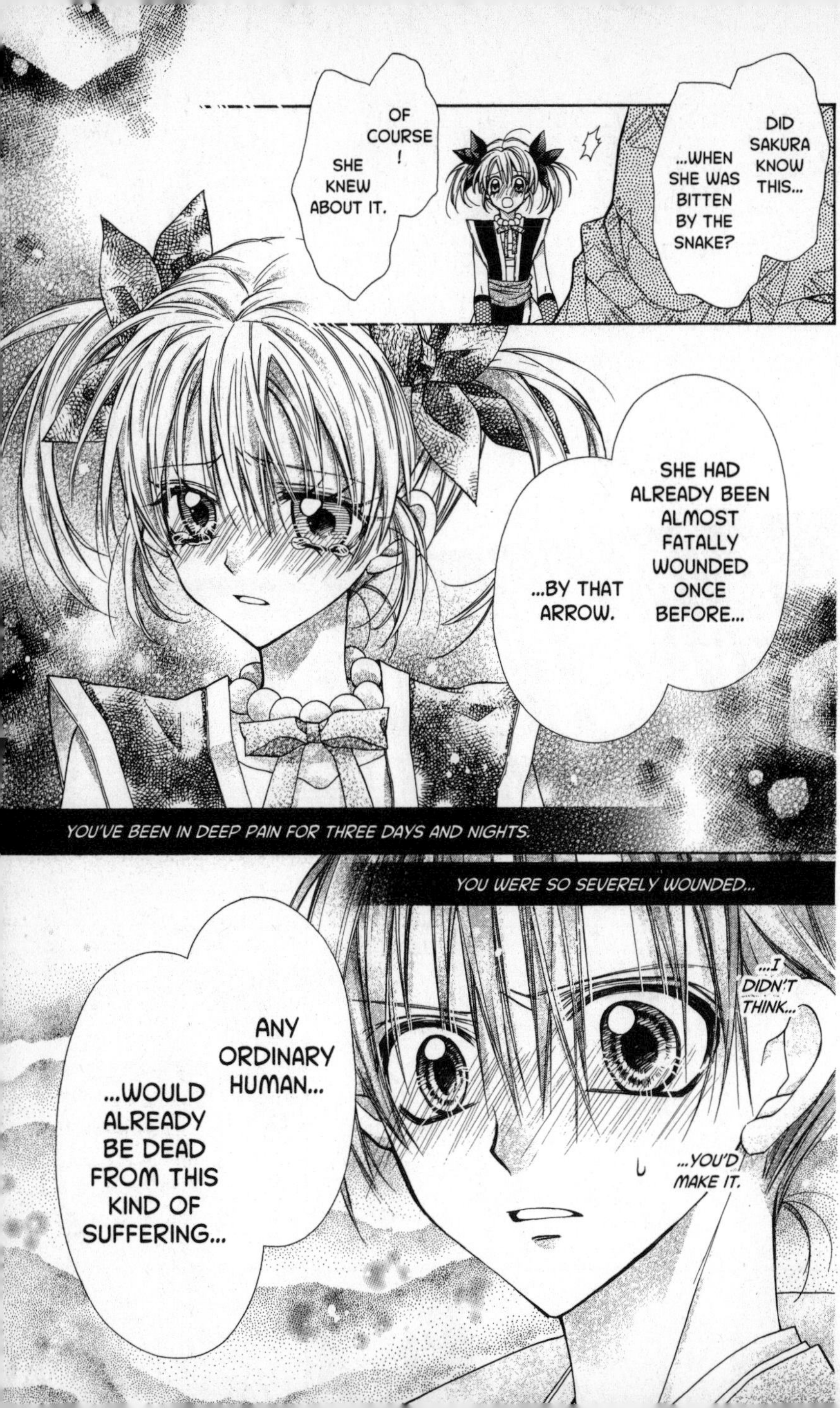
DID SAKURA KNOW THIS...
...WHEN SHE WAS BITTEN BY THE SNAKE?
OF COURSE!
SHE KNEW ABOUT IT.
SHE HAD ALREADY BEEN ALMOST FATALLY WOUNDED ONCE BEFORE...
...BY THAT ARROW.
YOU'VE BEEN IN DEEP PAIN FOR THREE DAYS AND NIGHTS.
YOU WERE SO SEVERELY WOUNDED...
...I DIDN'T THINK...
...YOU'D MAKE IT.
ANY ORDINARY HUMAN...
...WOULD ALREADY BE DEAD FROM THIS KIND OF SUFFERING...

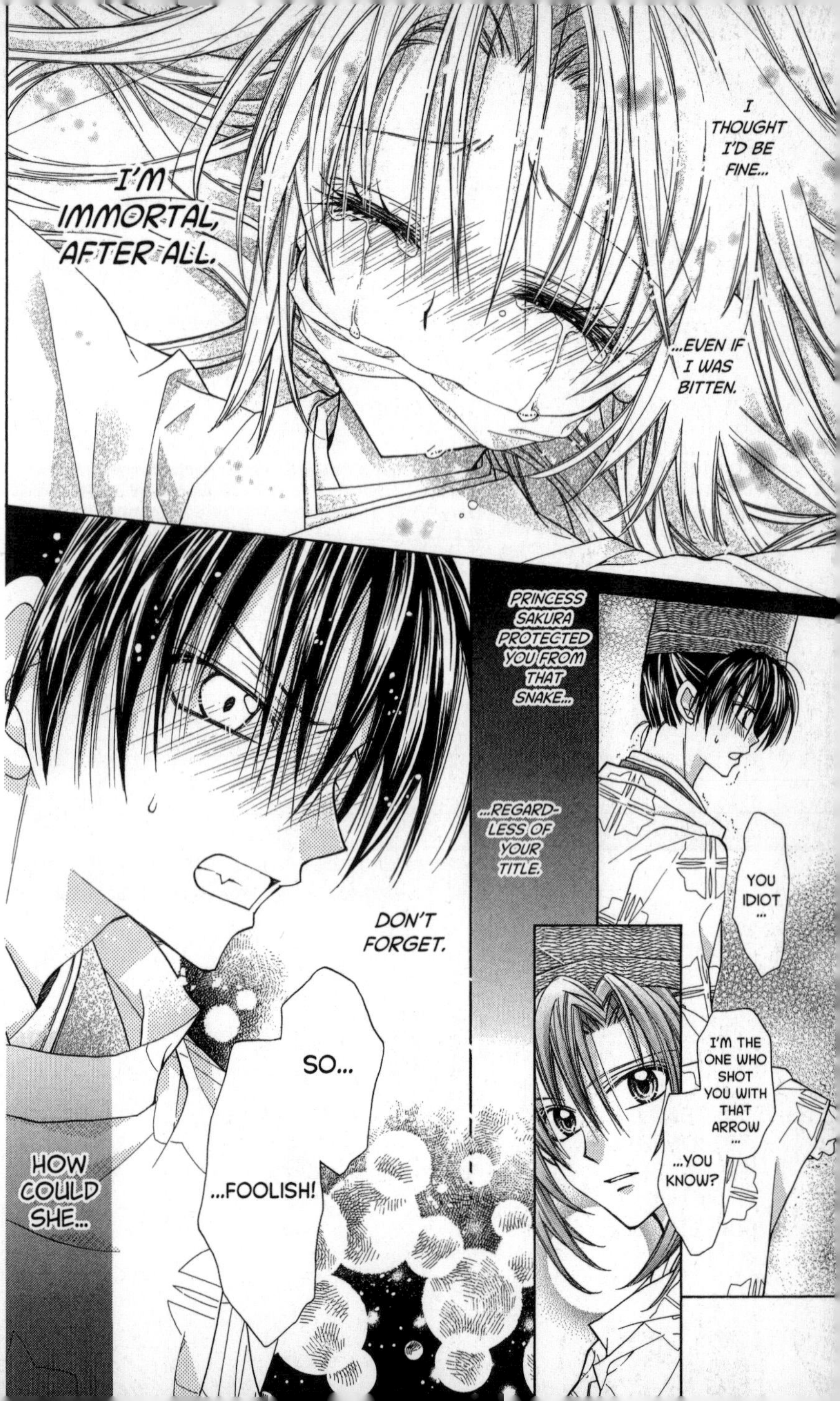
I THOUGHT I'D BE FINE...
...EVEN IF I WAS BITTEN.
I'M IMMORTAL, AFTER ALL.
PRINCESS SAKURA PROTECTED YOU FROM THAT SNAKE...
...REGARDLESS OF YOUR TITLE.
YOU IDIOT...
I'M THE ONE WHO SHOT YOU WITH THAT ARROW...
...YOU KNOW?
DON'T FORGET.
SO...
...FOOLISH!
HOW COULD SHE...

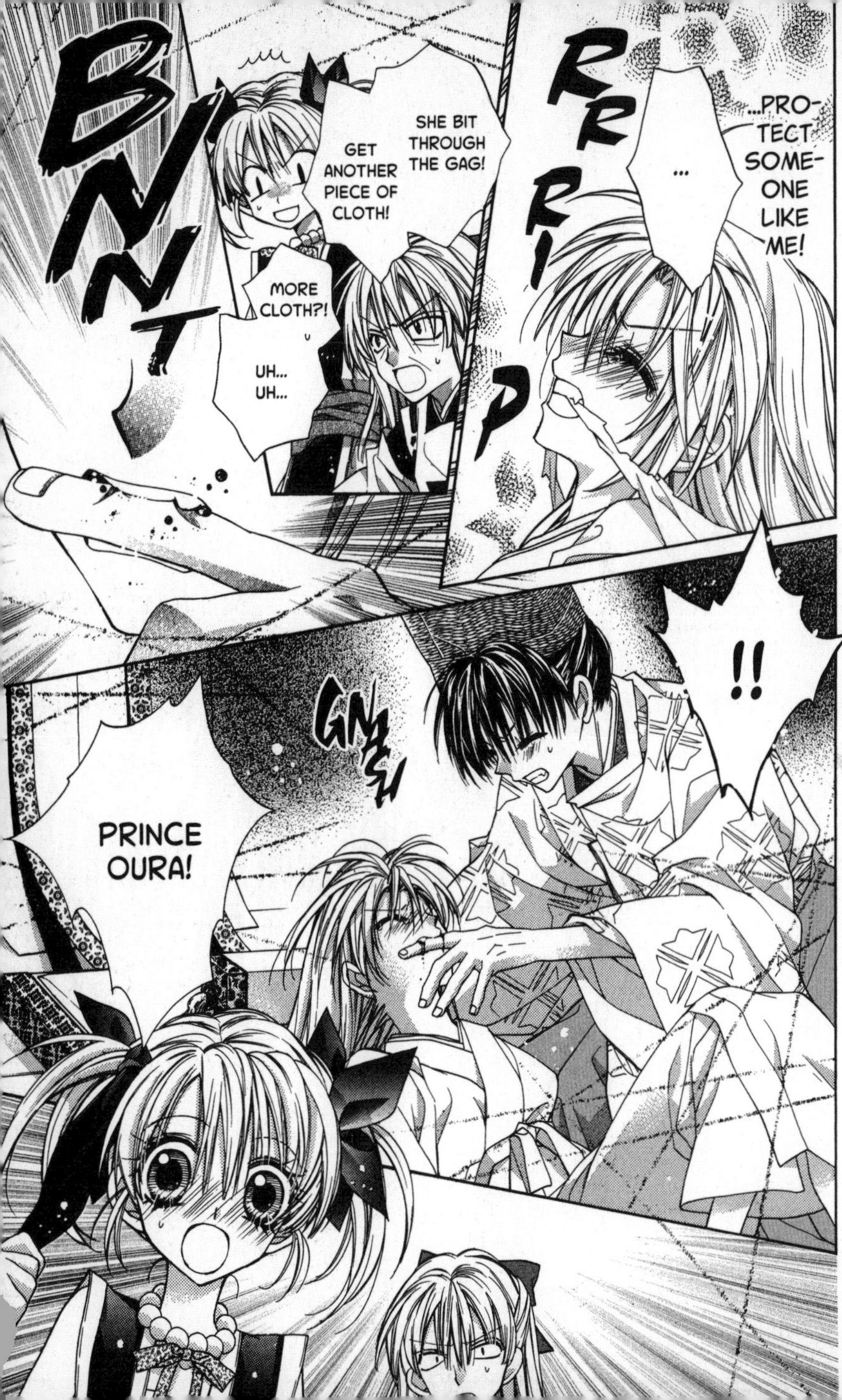
RRRIP
...PROTECT SOMEONE LIKE ME!
...
SHE BIT THROUGH THE GAG!
GET ANOTHER PIECE OF CLOTH!
MORE CLOTH?!
UH... UH...
!!
GNASH
PRINCE OURA!

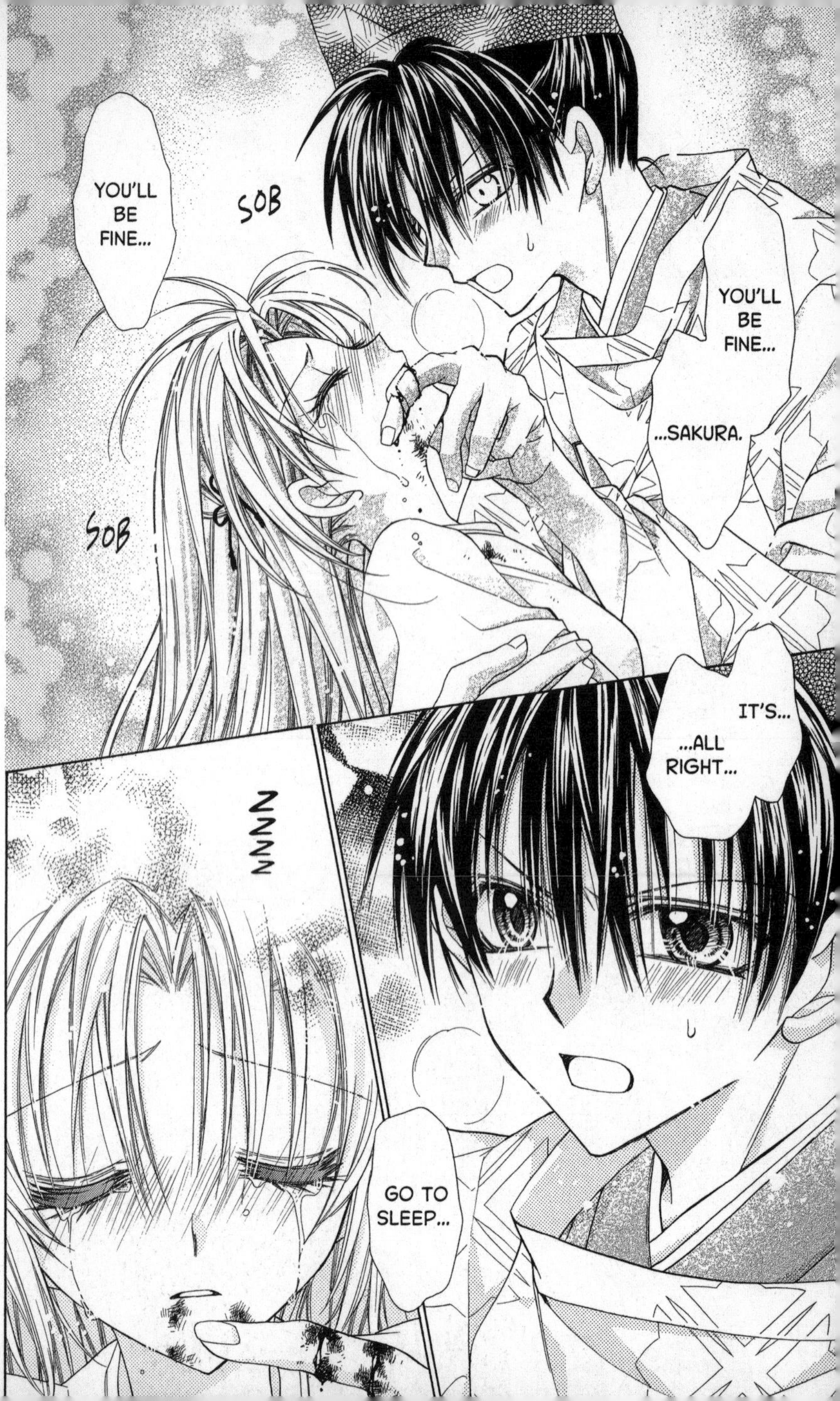
YOU'LL BE FINE... ...SAKURA.
YOU'LL BE FINE...
SOB
SOB
IT'S... ...ALL RIGHT...
GO TO SLEEP...
NNNN

More About *Sakura Hime*

I don't like to read or write the words "death" (死) or "kill" (殺).

As *Sakura Hime* deals with a life-or-death battle, I had some hesitation about making it into a series for *Ribon* magazine. I thought I'd never be able to write this kind of story as long I was with *Ribon*. (In that case, it might be for as long as I live.)

But Kunta-san advised me, saying, "If you really want to create an interesting battle that is as good as the ones in manga for boys, then "death" is something you have to write about." Also, this may sound a little odd to some people, but I have a personal theory that I can draw "anything that my editors tell me I can draw," so I made up my mind to create this story, regardless of running in *Ribon* and whether it would be popular or not.

But I did fit Sakura, the main character, to *Ribon*'s taste. Originally my idea was of a girl who people called "coldhearted" because she never smiled.

But... I don't think the real story has actually started yet. That's because of a certain character—who I think will be my favorite character—has not made an appearance yet... The story won't be complete without that person.

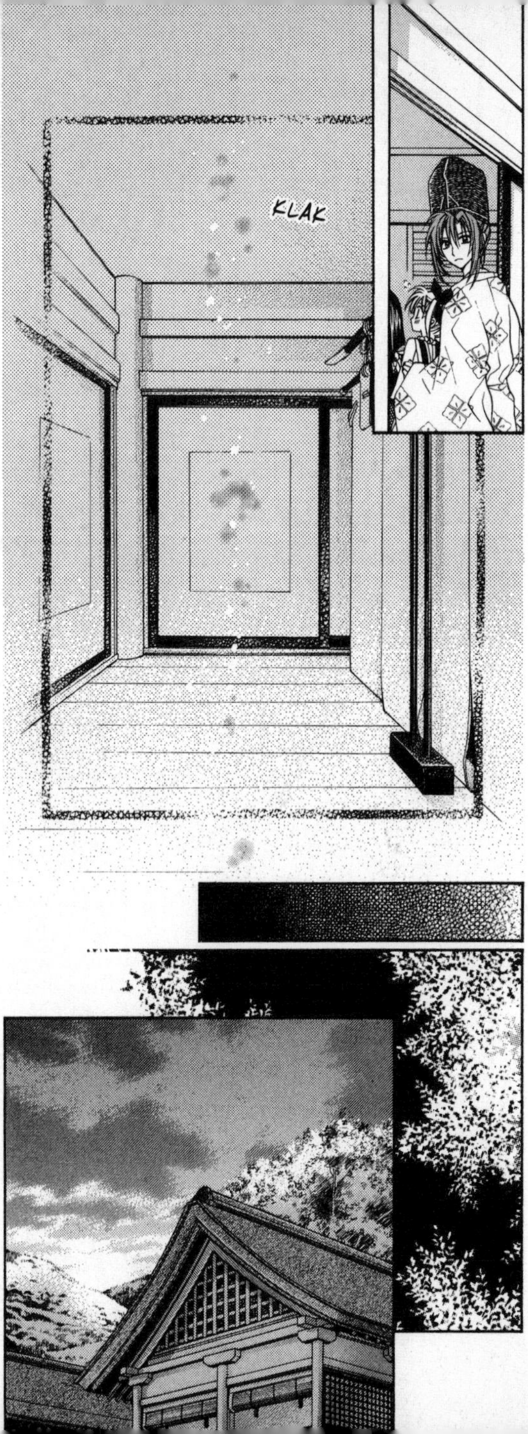
KLAK

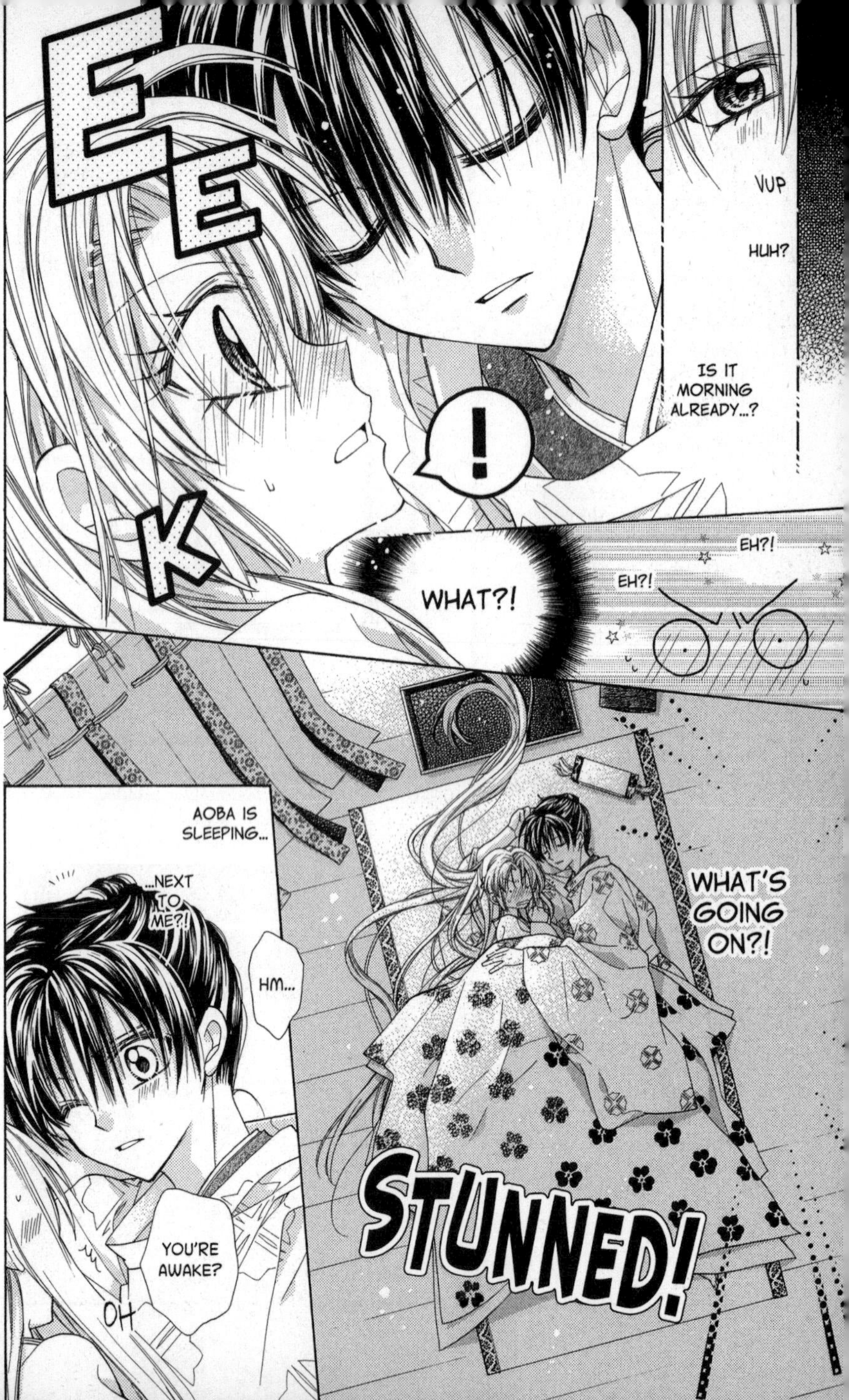
VUP
HUH?
IS IT MORNING ALREADY...?
EEK
!
EH?!
EH?!
WHAT?!
WHAT'S GOING ON?!
STUNNED!
AOBA IS SLEEPING...
...NEXT TO ME?!
HM...
YOU'RE AWAKE?
OH

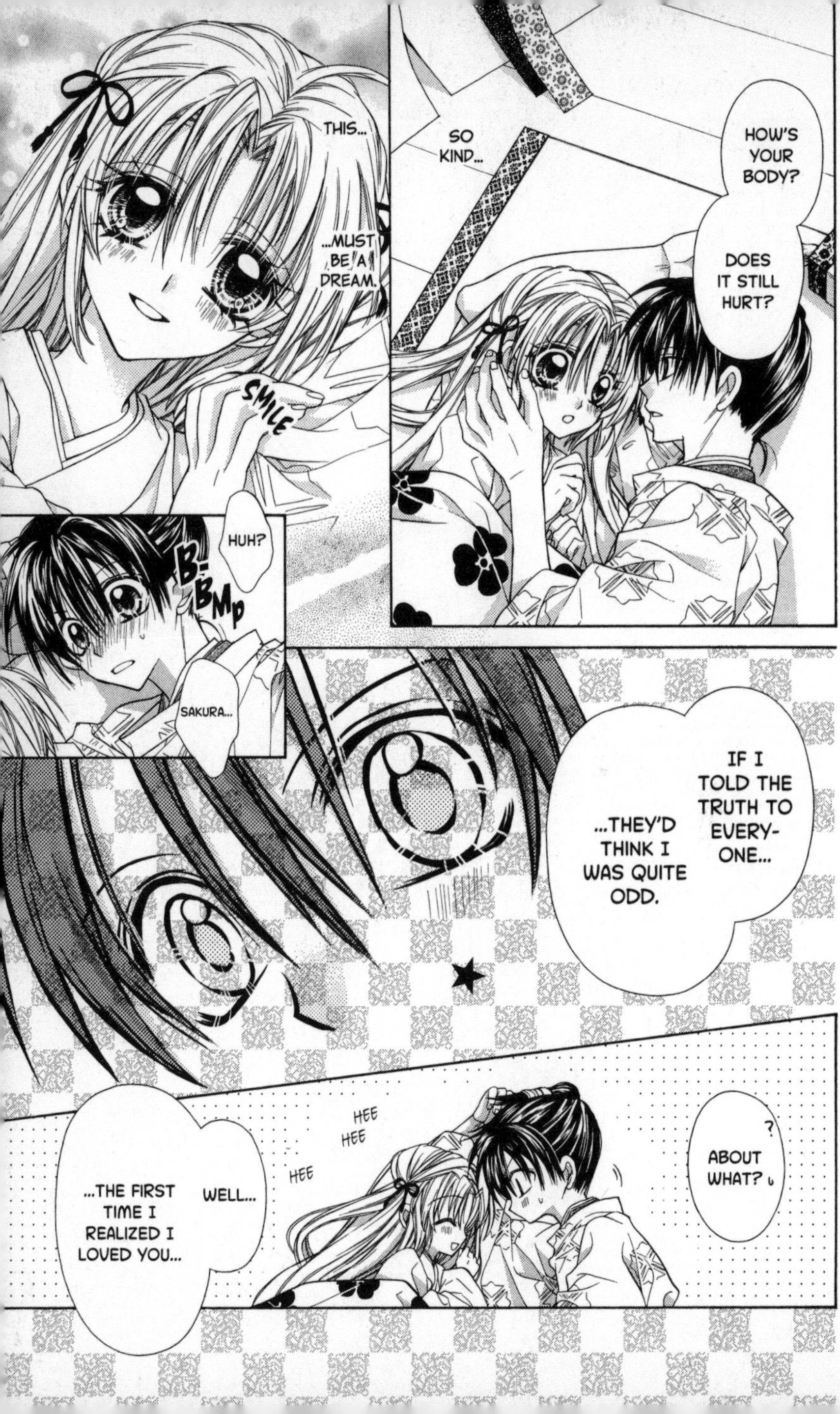
HOW'S YOUR BODY?
DOES IT STILL HURT?
SO KIND...
THIS...
...MUST BE A DREAM.
SMILE
HUH?
B-BMP
SAKURA...
IF I TOLD THE TRUTH TO EVERY-ONE...
...THEY'D THINK I WAS QUITE ODD.
?
ABOUT WHAT?
HEE HEE
HEE
WELL...
...THE FIRST TIME I REALIZED I LOVED YOU...

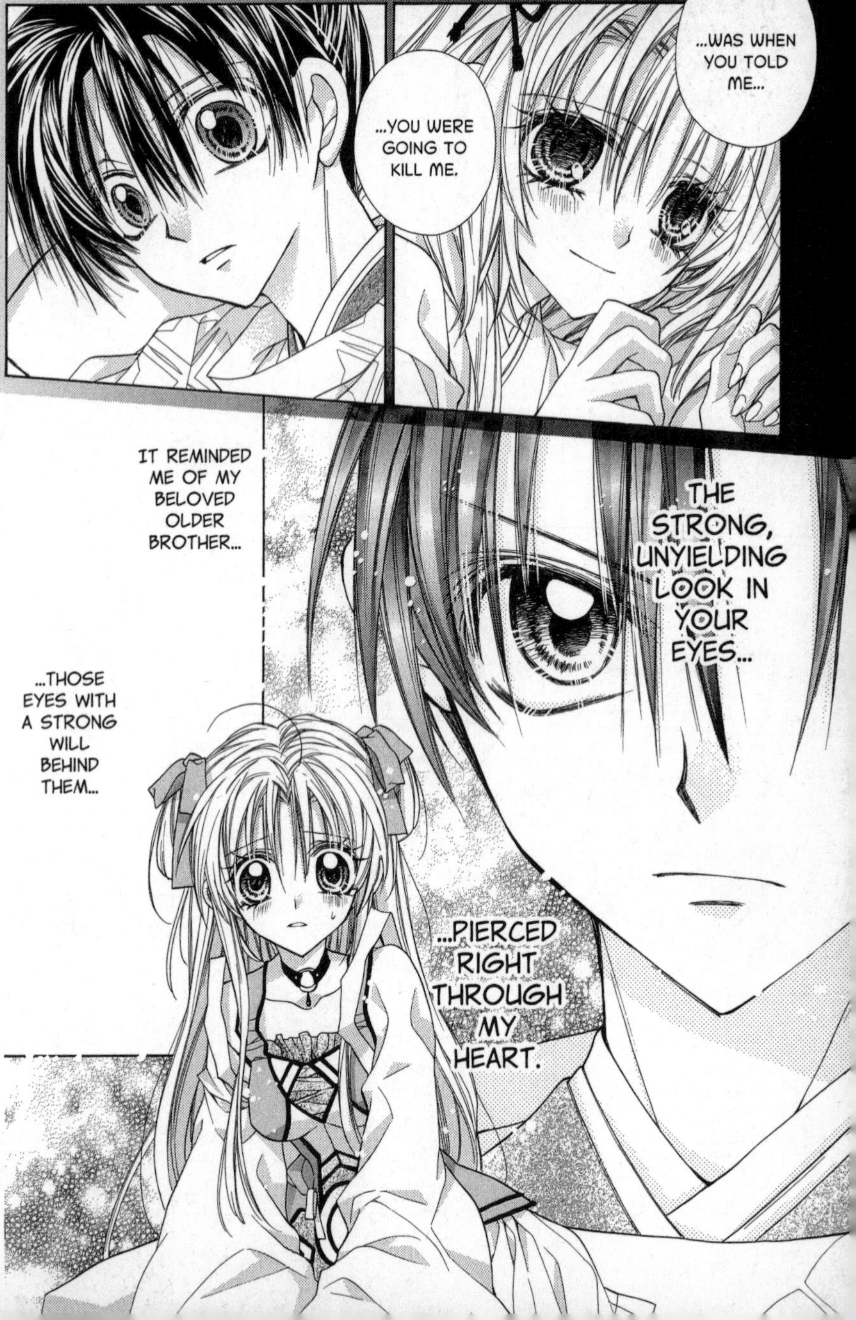
...WAS WHEN YOU TOLD ME...
...YOU WERE GOING TO KILL ME.
THE STRONG, UNYIELDING LOOK IN YOUR EYES...
IT REMINDED ME OF MY BELOVED OLDER BROTHER...
...THOSE EYES WITH A STRONG WILL BEHIND THEM...
...PIERCED RIGHT THROUGH MY HEART.

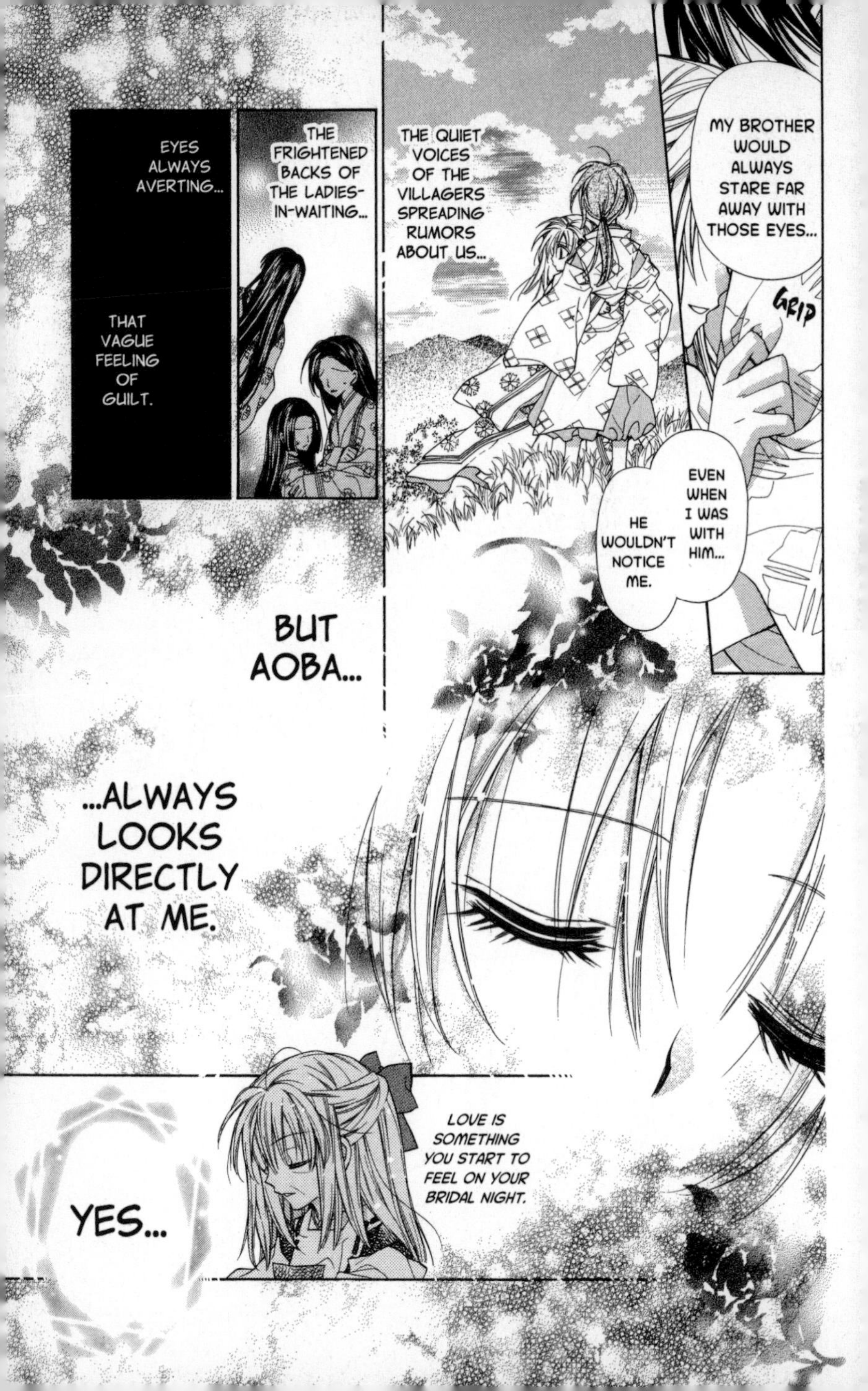
MY BROTHER WOULD ALWAYS STARE FAR AWAY WITH THOSE EYES...
GRIP
EVEN WHEN I WAS WITH HIM...
HE WOULDN'T NOTICE ME.
THE QUIET VOICES OF THE VILLAGERS SPREADING RUMORS ABOUT US...
THE FRIGHTENED BACKS OF THE LADIES-IN-WAITING...
EYES ALWAYS AVERTING...
THAT VAGUE FEELING OF GUILT.
BUT AOBA...
...ALWAYS LOOKS DIRECTLY AT ME.
LOVE IS SOMETHING YOU START TO FEEL ON YOUR BRIDAL NIGHT.
YES...

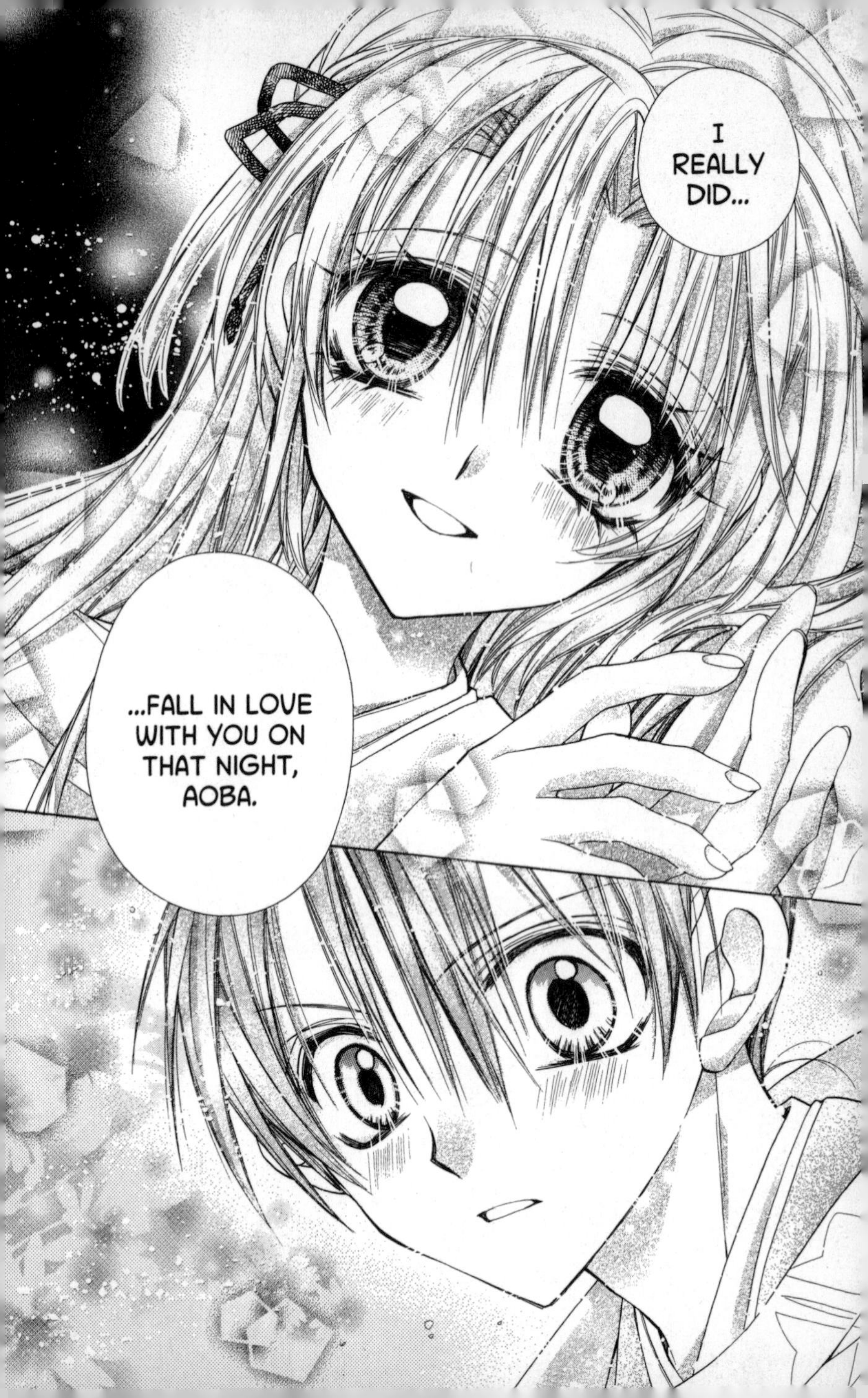
I REALLY DID...
...FALL IN LOVE WITH YOU ON THAT NIGHT, AOBA.

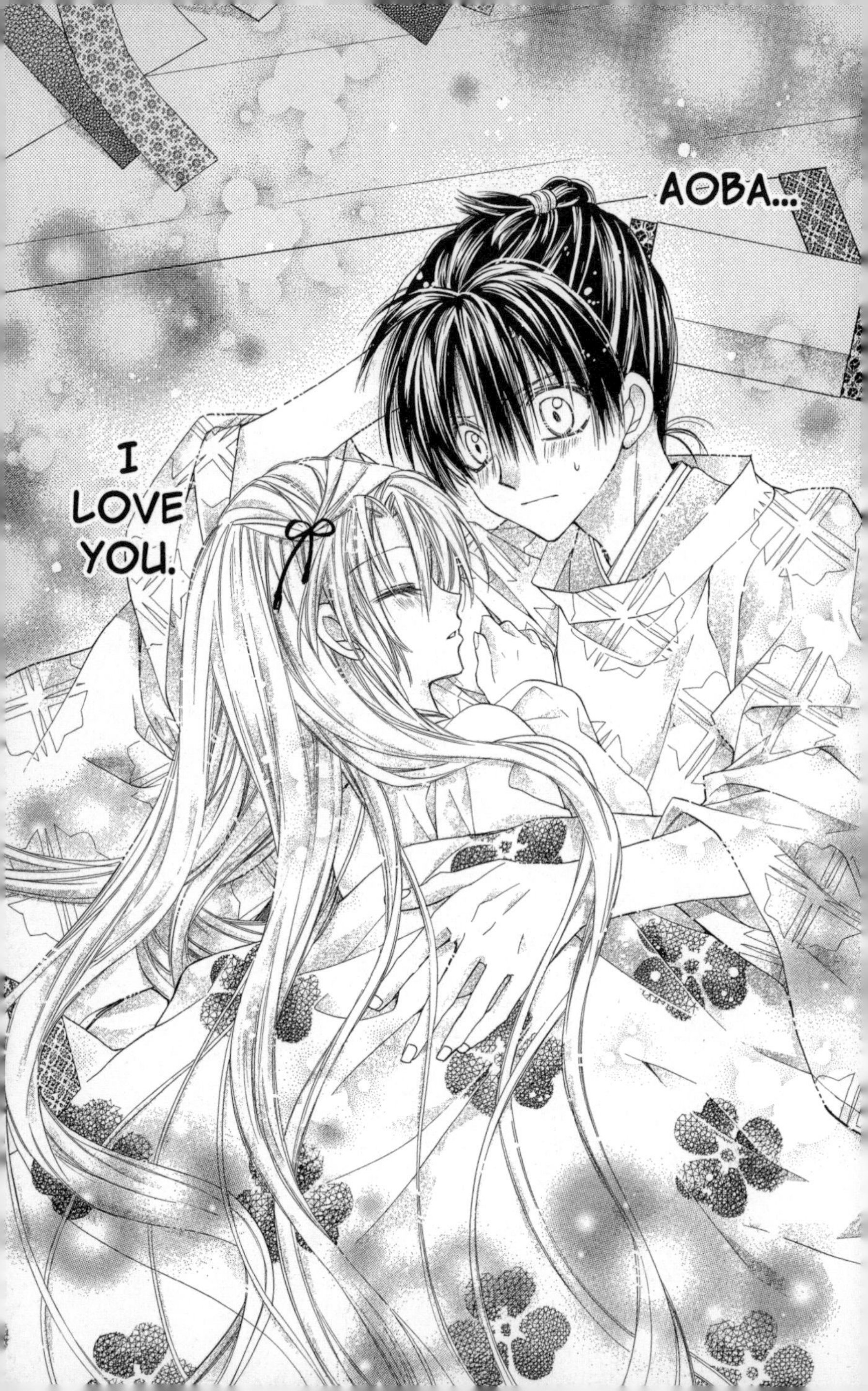
AOBA...
I LOVE YOU.

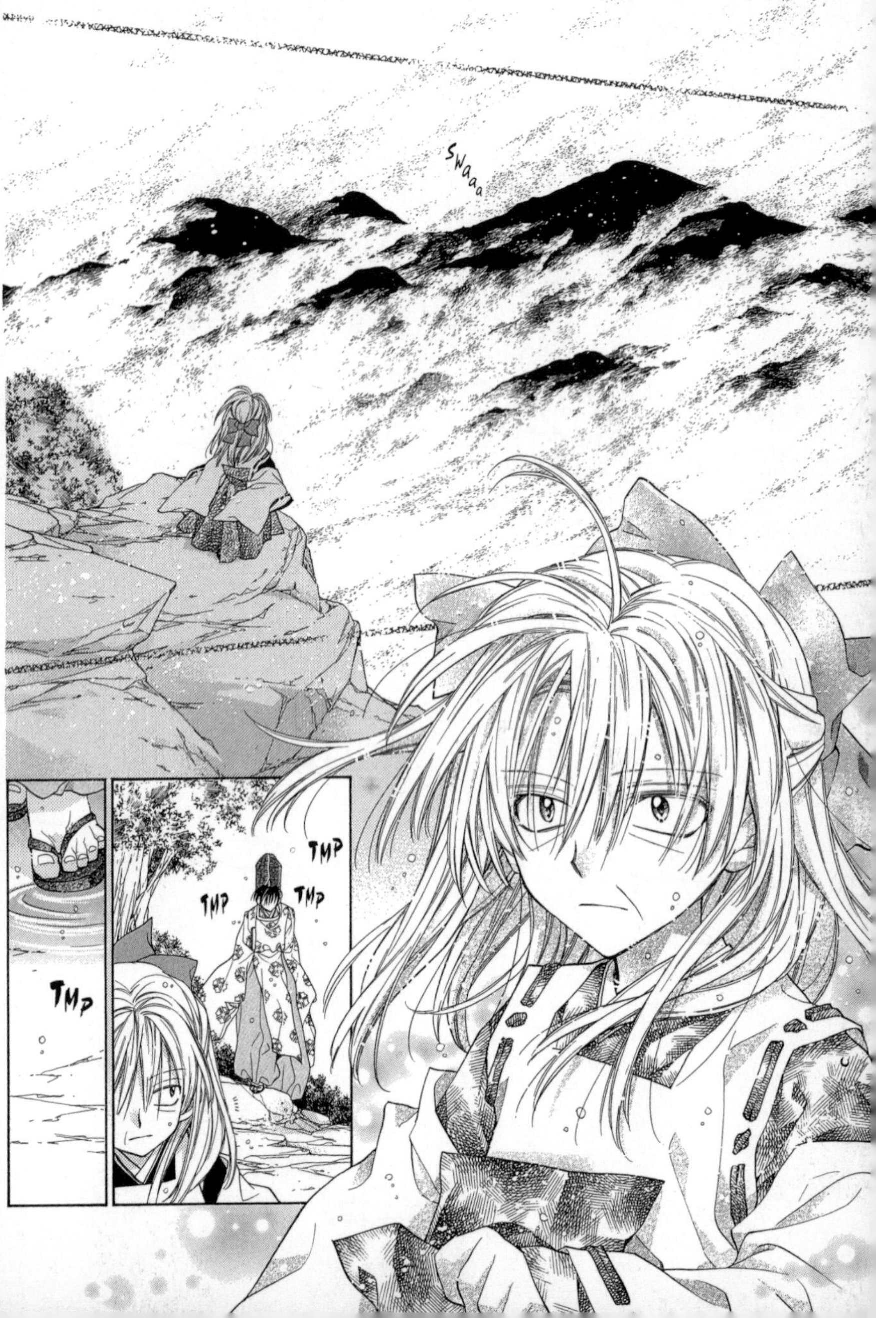
SWAaa
TMP
TMp
TMP
TMp

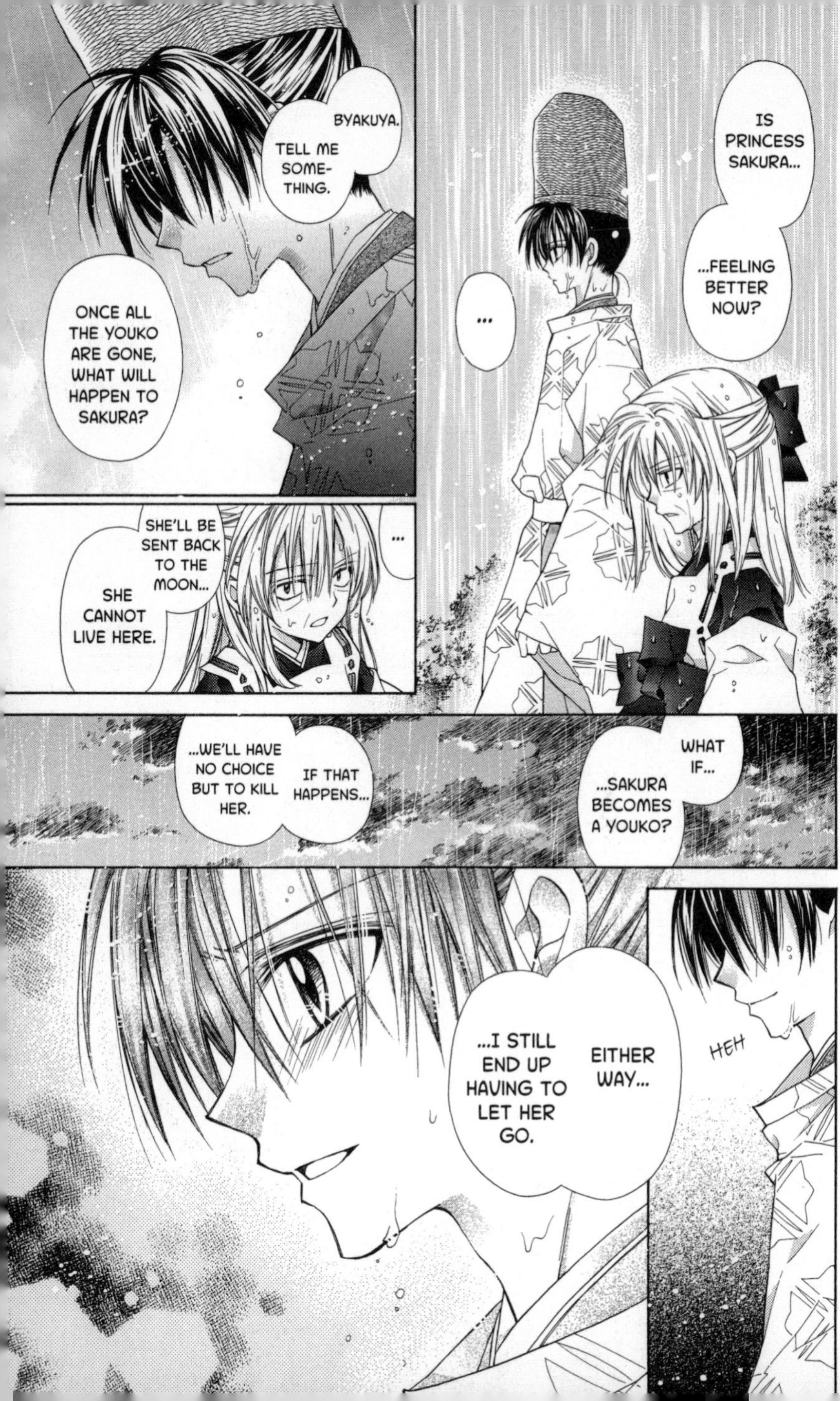
IS PRINCESS SAKURA...
...FEELING BETTER NOW?
...
BYAKUYA.
TELL ME SOME-THING.
ONCE ALL THE YOUKO ARE GONE, WHAT WILL HAPPEN TO SAKURA?
...
SHE'LL BE SENT BACK TO THE MOON...
SHE CANNOT LIVE HERE.
WHAT IF...
...SAKURA BECOMES A YOUKO?
IF THAT HAPPENS...
...WE'LL HAVE NO CHOICE BUT TO KILL HER.
HEH
EITHER WAY...
...I STILL END UP HAVING TO LET HER GO.

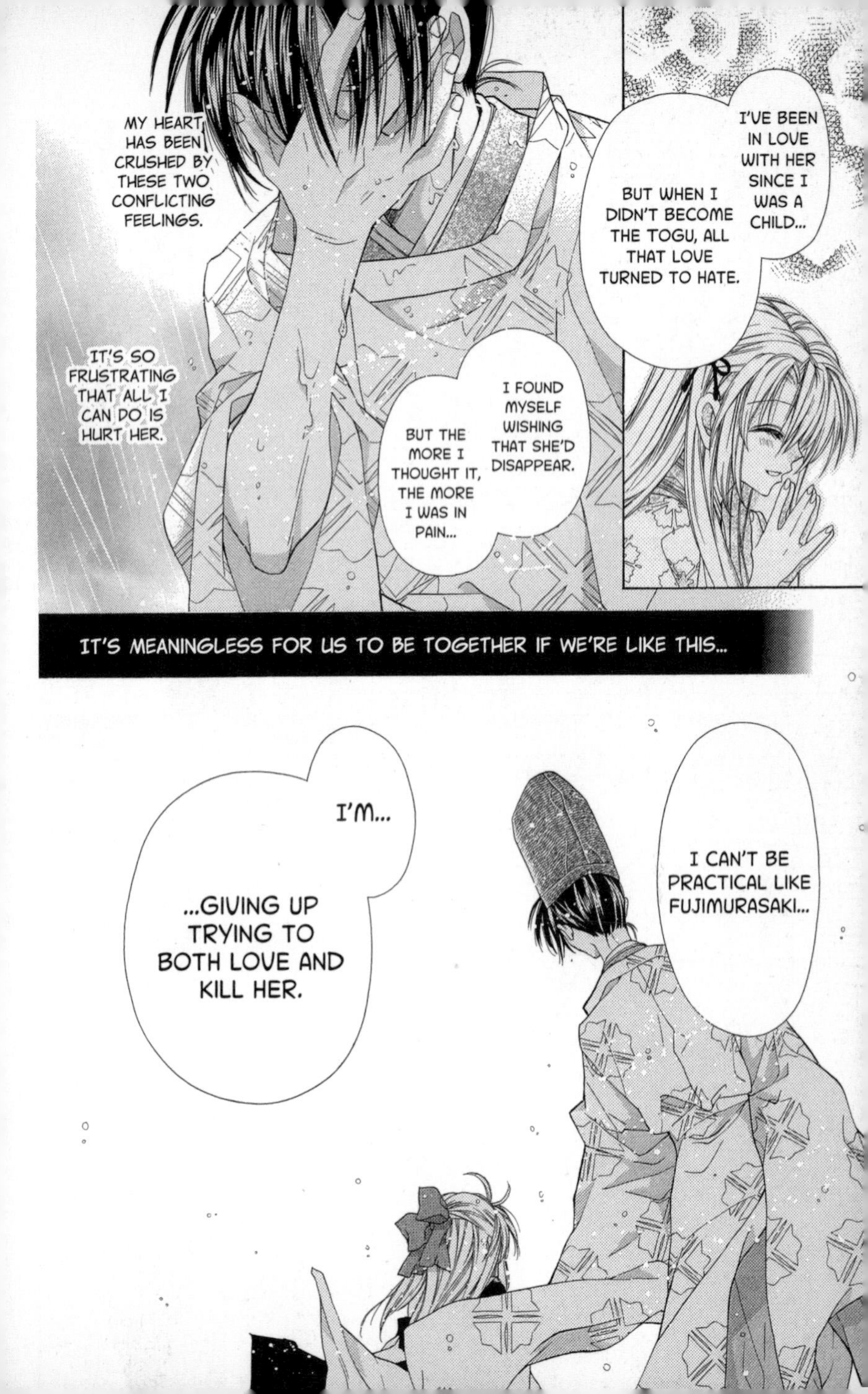

I'VE BEEN IN LOVE WITH HER SINCE I WAS A CHILD...
BUT WHEN I DIDN'T BECOME THE TOGU, ALL THAT LOVE TURNED TO HATE.
I FOUND MYSELF WISHING THAT SHE'D DISAPPEAR.
BUT THE MORE I THOUGHT IT, THE MORE I WAS IN PAIN...
MY HEART HAS BEEN CRUSHED BY THESE TWO CONFLICTING FEELINGS.
IT'S SO FRUSTRATING THAT ALL I CAN DO IS HURT HER.
IT'S MEANINGLESS FOR US TO BE TOGETHER IF WE'RE LIKE THIS...
I CAN'T BE PRACTICAL LIKE FUJIMURASAKI...
I'M...
...GIVING UP TRYING TO BOTH LOVE AND KILL HER.

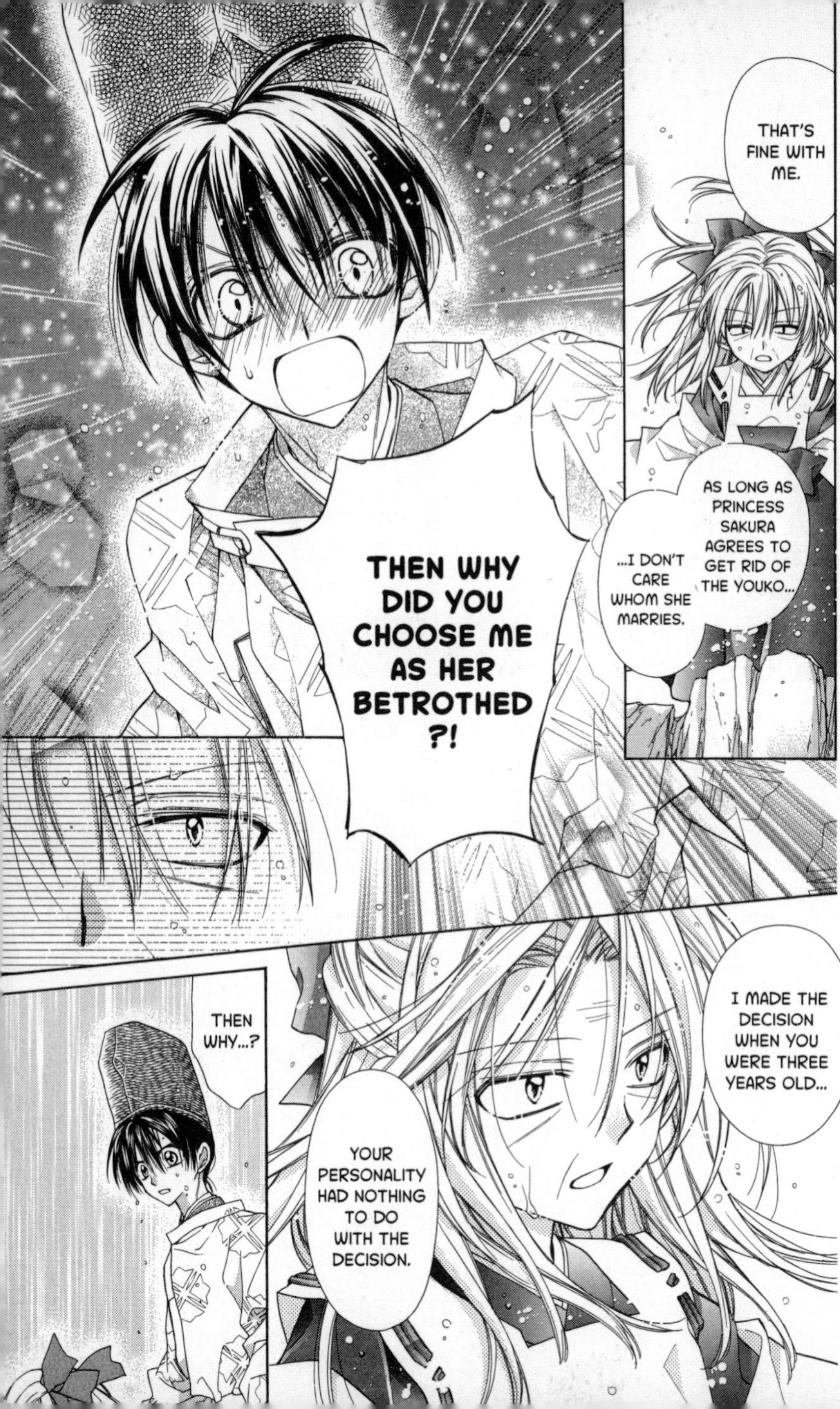
THAT'S FINE WITH ME.
AS LONG AS PRINCESS SAKURA AGREES TO GET RID OF THE YOUKO...
...I DON'T CARE WHOM SHE MARRIES.
THEN WHY DID YOU CHOOSE ME AS HER BETROTHED?!
I MADE THE DECISION WHEN YOU WERE THREE YEARS OLD...
YOUR PERSONALITY HAD NOTHING TO DO WITH THE DECISION.
THEN WHY...?

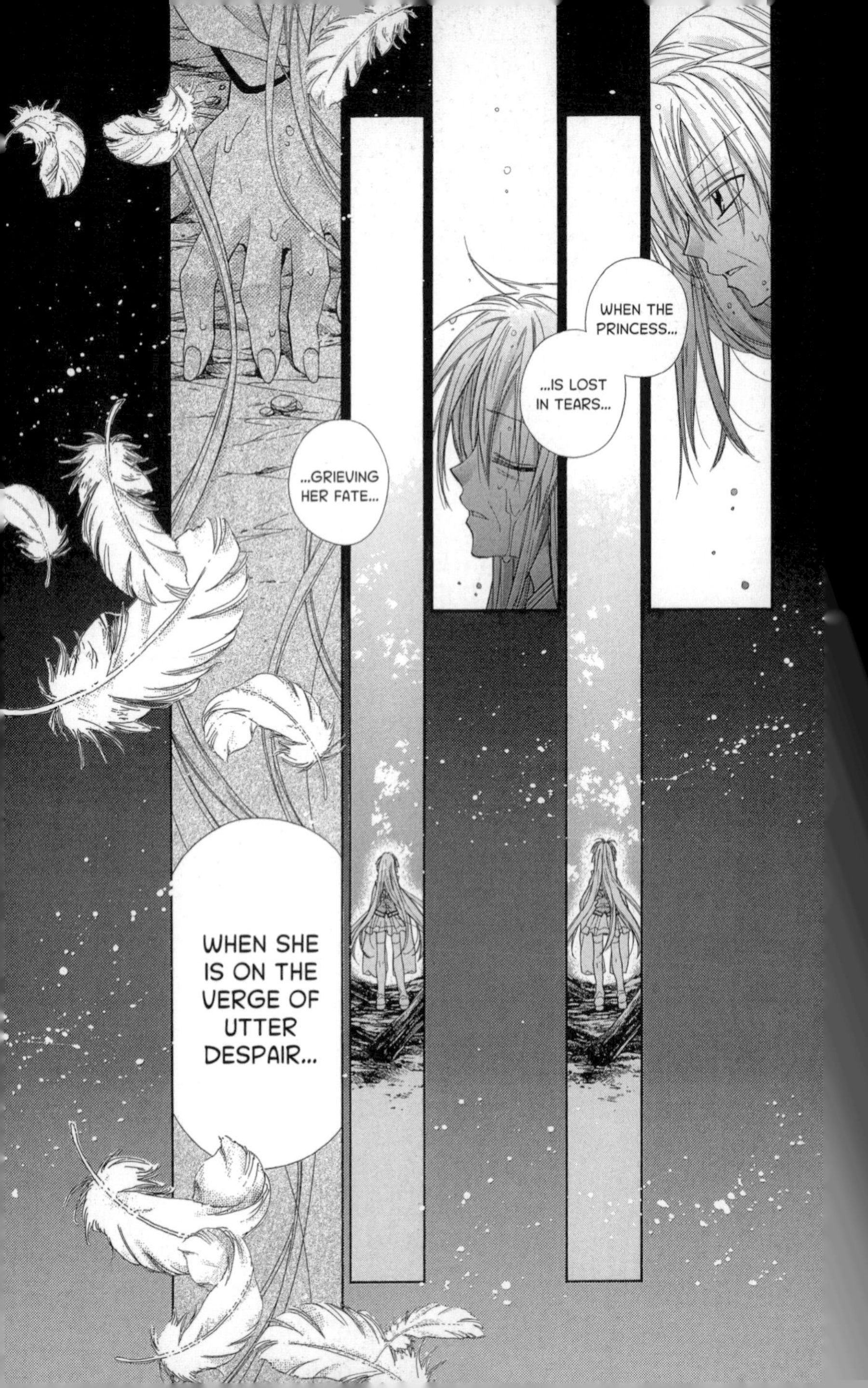
WHEN THE PRINCESS...
...IS LOST IN TEARS...
...GRIEVING HER FATE...
WHEN SHE IS ON THE VERGE OF UTTER DESPAIR...

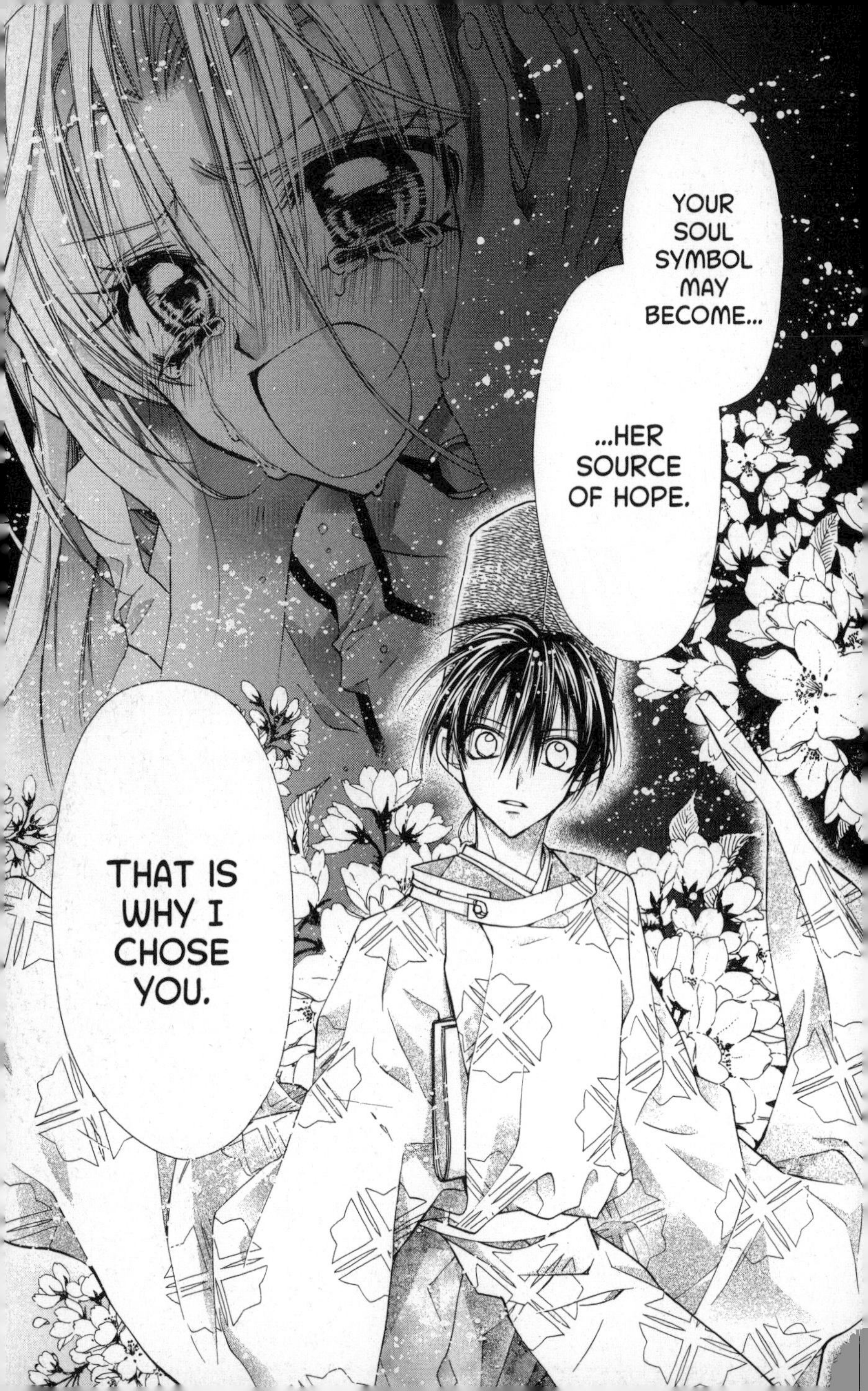
YOUR SOUL SYMBOL MAY BECOME...
...HER SOURCE OF HOPE.
THAT IS WHY I CHOSE YOU.

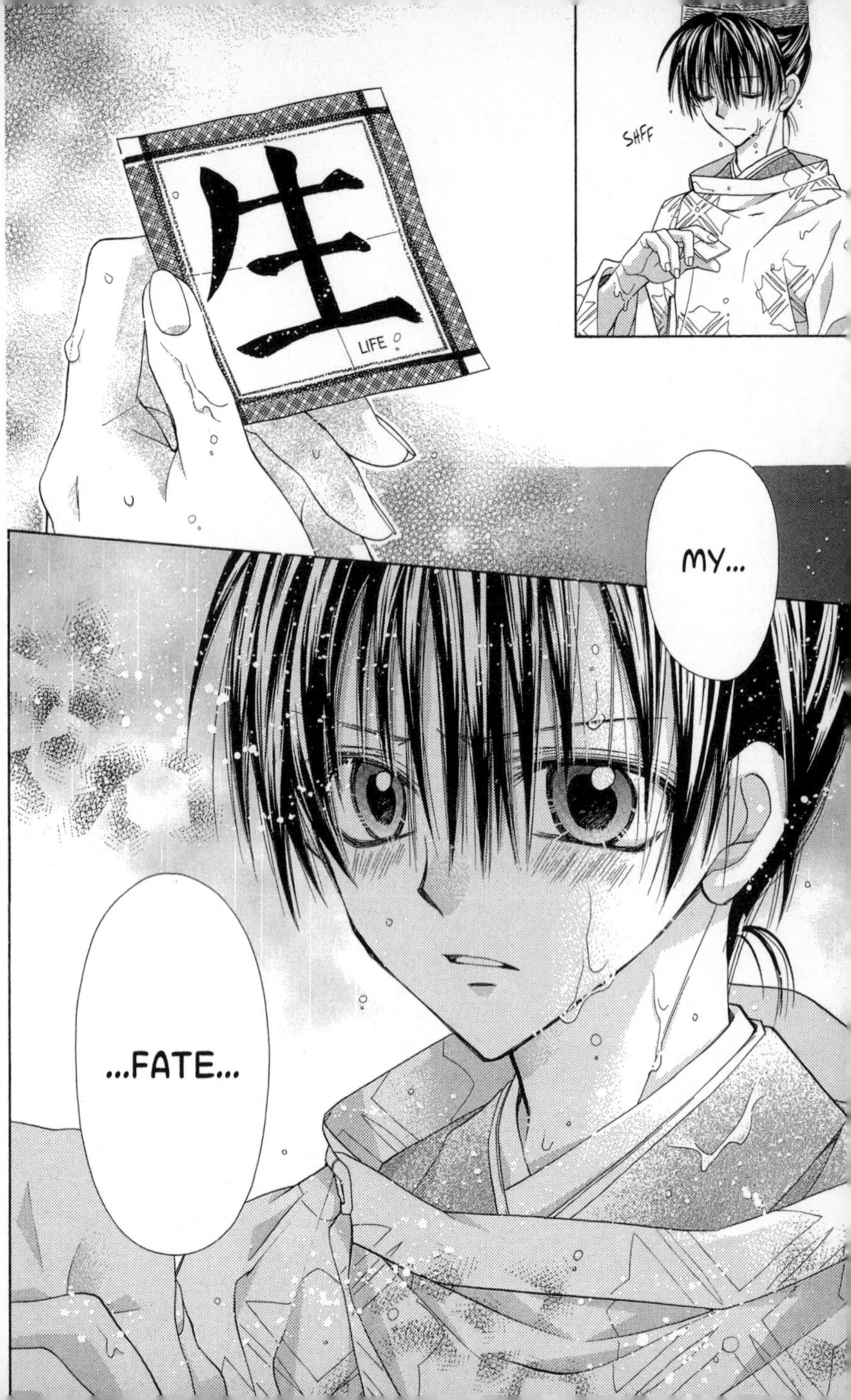
SHFF
生
LIFE
MY...
...FATE...

More About *Sakura Hime*

At the moment, Princess Sakura and Asagiri are by far the most popular. They are so popular that the other characters rank pretty much the same.

As for me... Um... I guess I like Sakura and Asagiri too.
I have a kind of "fondness" for his Highness Fujimurasaki, which is similar to my fondness for Eichi-kun... (But Eichi-kun is still way high up there.)
Aoba's popularity is still very, very low.
(You can do it, Aoba!! I know you're going to rise up!!) I think... I hope...
mumble
mumble

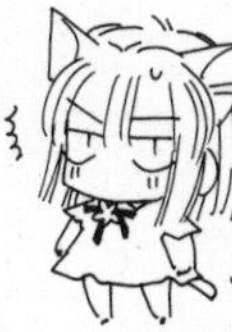
jolt

Kohaku is like a pet to me...

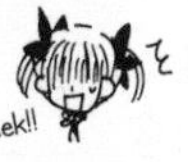
Eeek!!

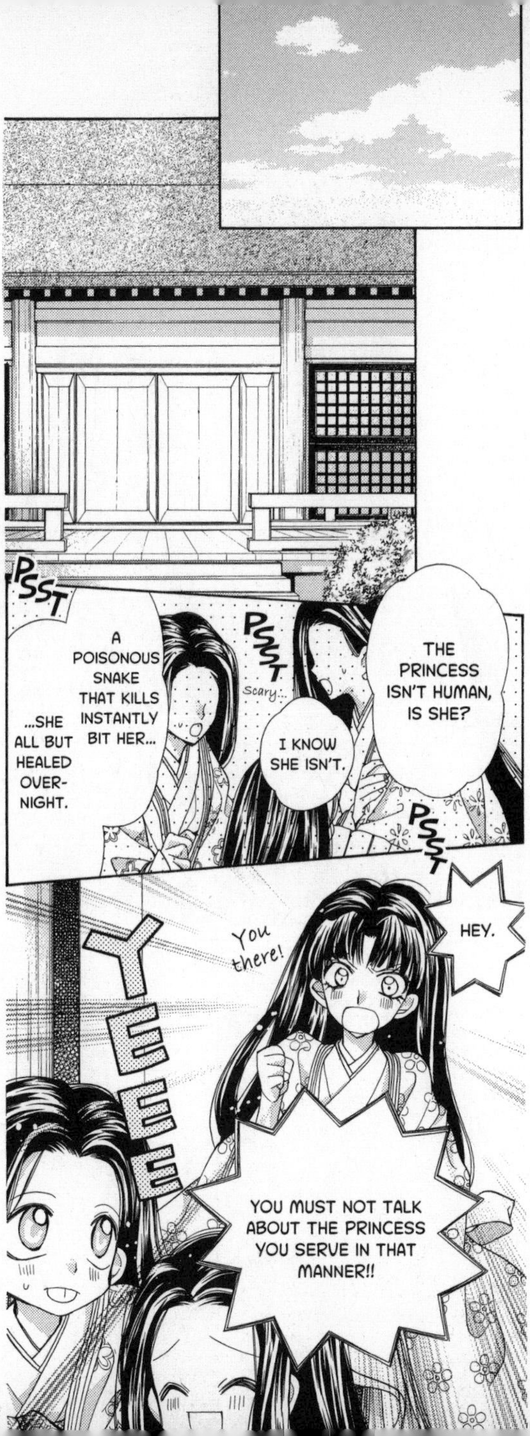
THE PRINCESS ISN'T HUMAN, IS SHE?
PSST
I KNOW SHE ISN'T.
PSST
Scary...
A POISONOUS SNAKE THAT KILLS INSTANTLY BIT HER...
...SHE ALL BUT HEALED OVERNIGHT.
PSST
HEY.
You there!
YEEEE
YOU MUST NOT TALK ABOUT THE PRINCESS YOU SERVE IN THAT MANNER!!

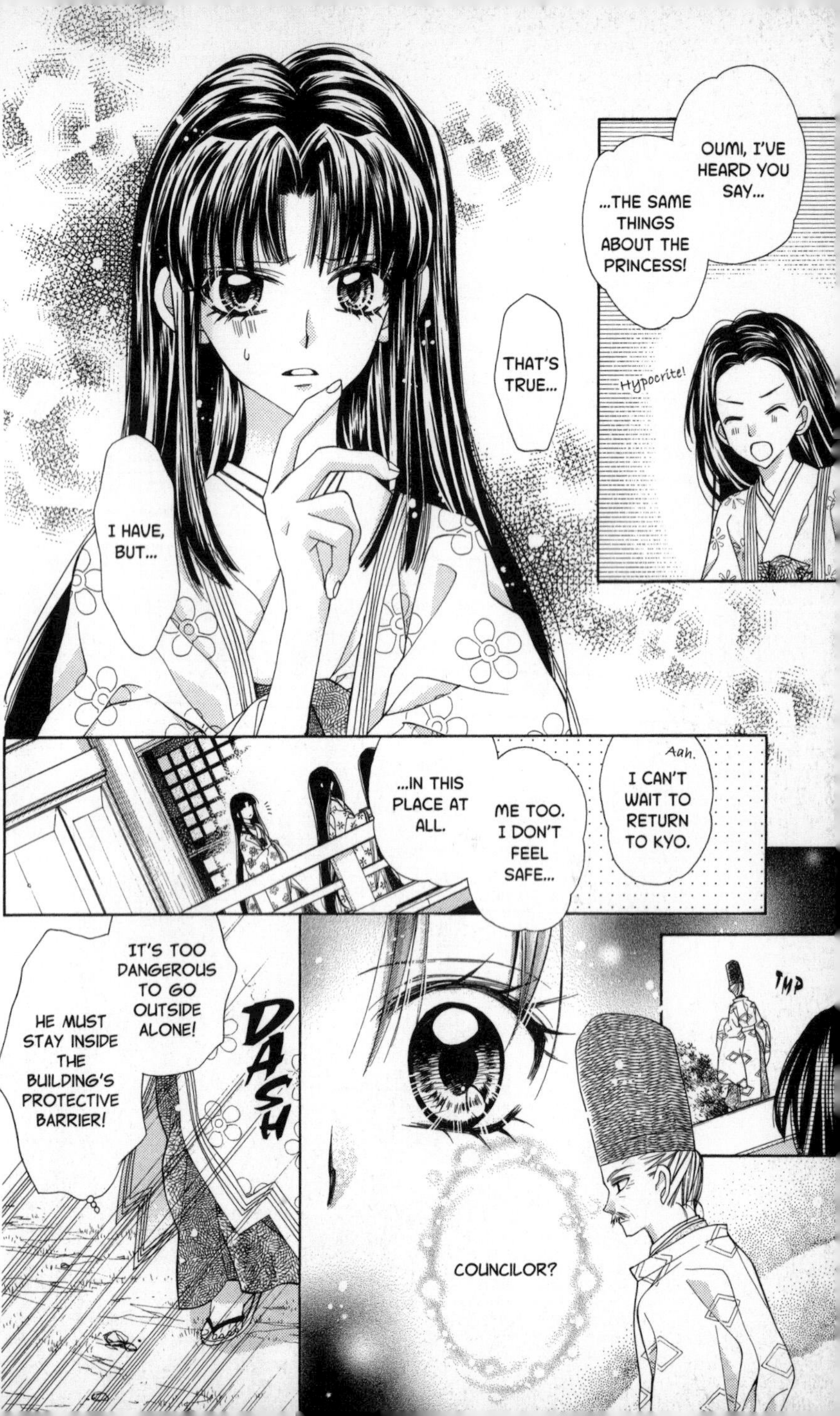
OUMI, I'VE HEARD YOU SAY...
...THE SAME THINGS ABOUT THE PRINCESS!
Hypocrite!
THAT'S TRUE...
I HAVE, BUT...
Aah.
I CAN'T WAIT TO RETURN TO KYO.
ME TOO. I DON'T FEEL SAFE...
...IN THIS PLACE AT ALL.
TMP
COUNCILOR?
DASH
IT'S TOO DANGEROUS TO GO OUTSIDE ALONE!
HE MUST STAY INSIDE THE BUILDING'S PROTECTIVE BARRIER!

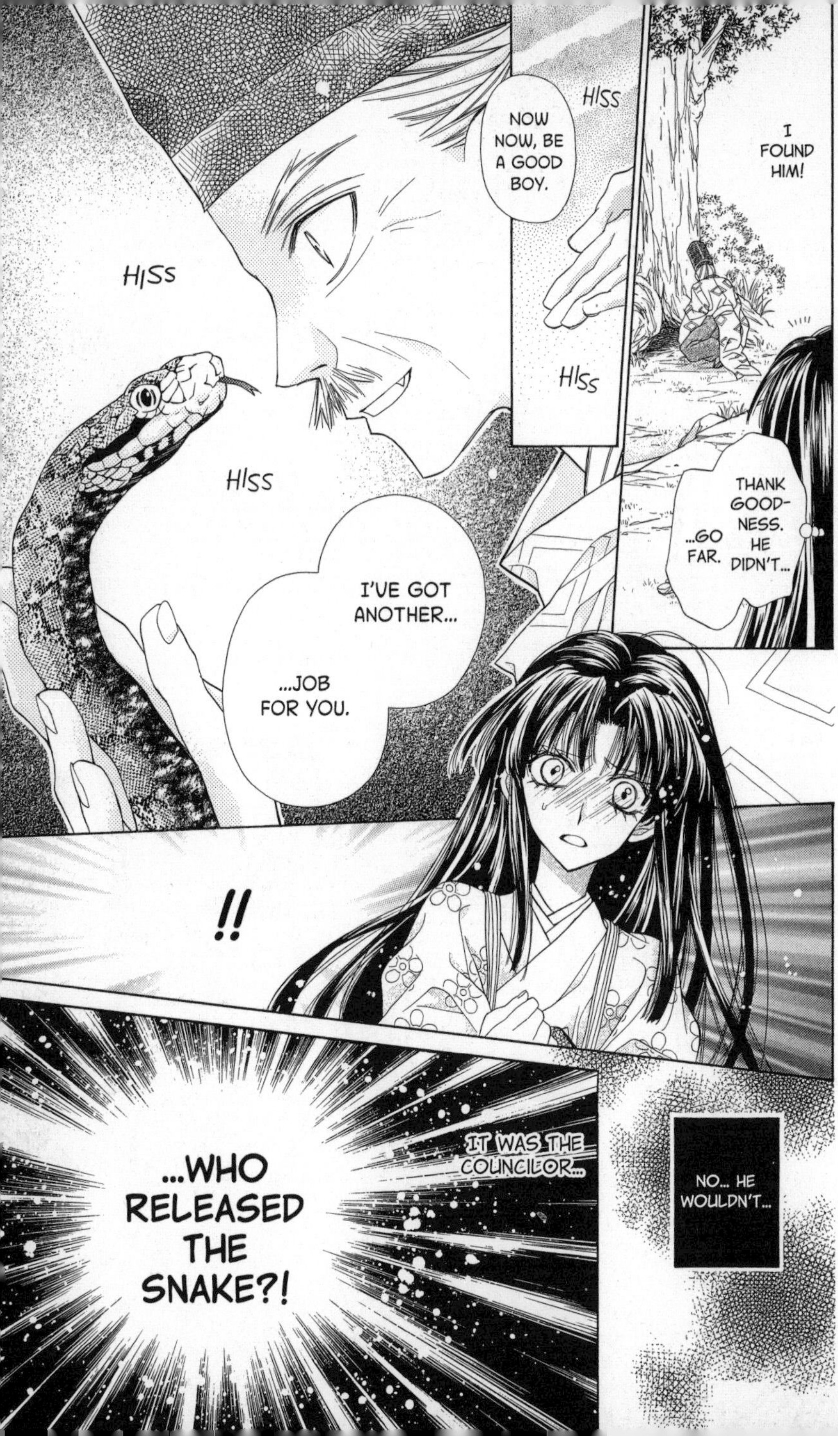
I FOUND HIM!
!!!
THANK GOODNESS. HE DIDN'T...
...GO FAR.
HISS
NOW NOW, BE A GOOD BOY.
HISS
HISS
HISS
I'VE GOT ANOTHER...
...JOB FOR YOU.
!!
NO... HE WOULDN'T...
IT WAS THE COUNCILOR...
...WHO RELEASED THE SNAKE?!

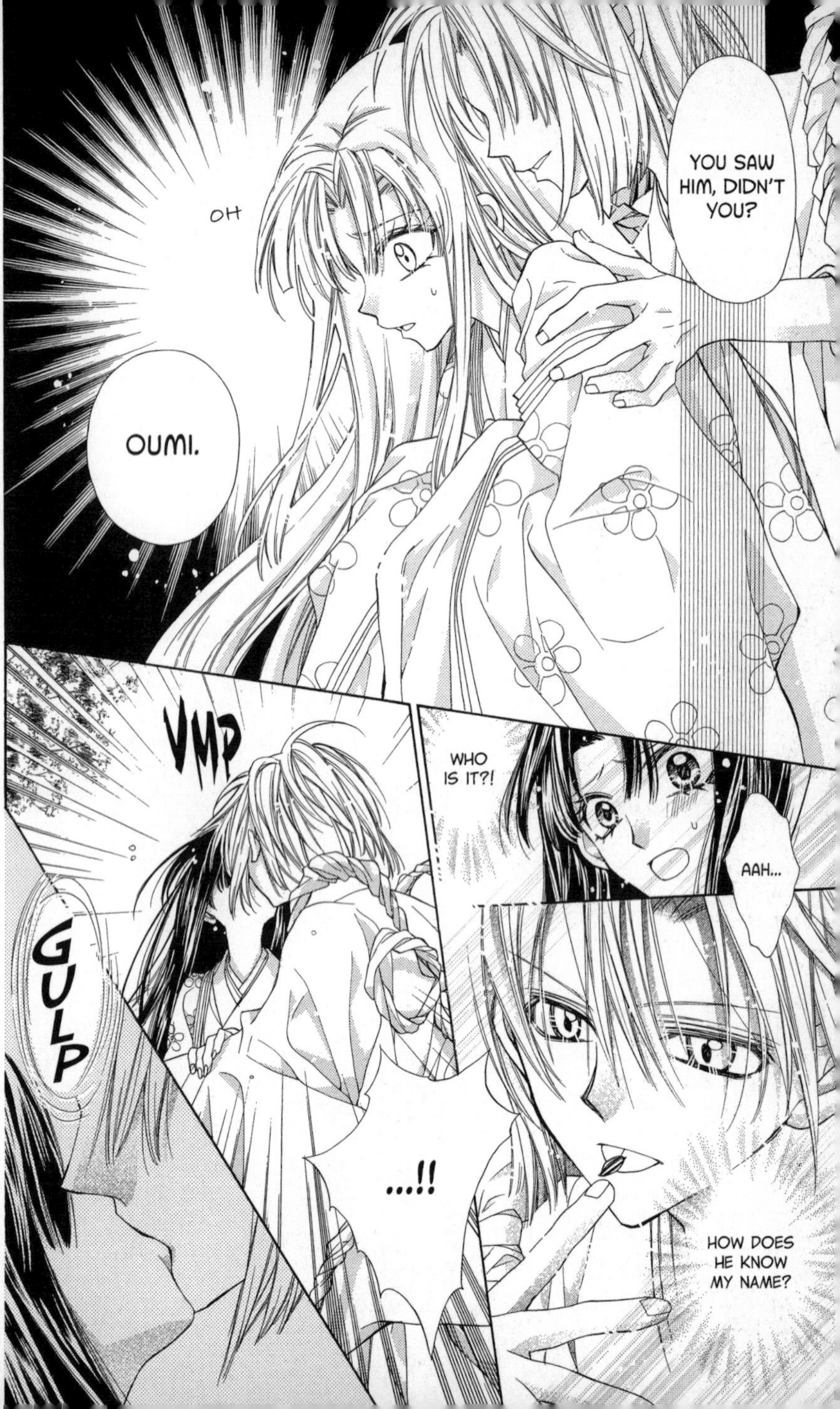
YOU SAW HIM, DIDN'T YOU?
OH
OUMI.
AAH...
WHO IS IT?!
HOW DOES HE KNOW MY NAME?
VMP
GULP
...!!

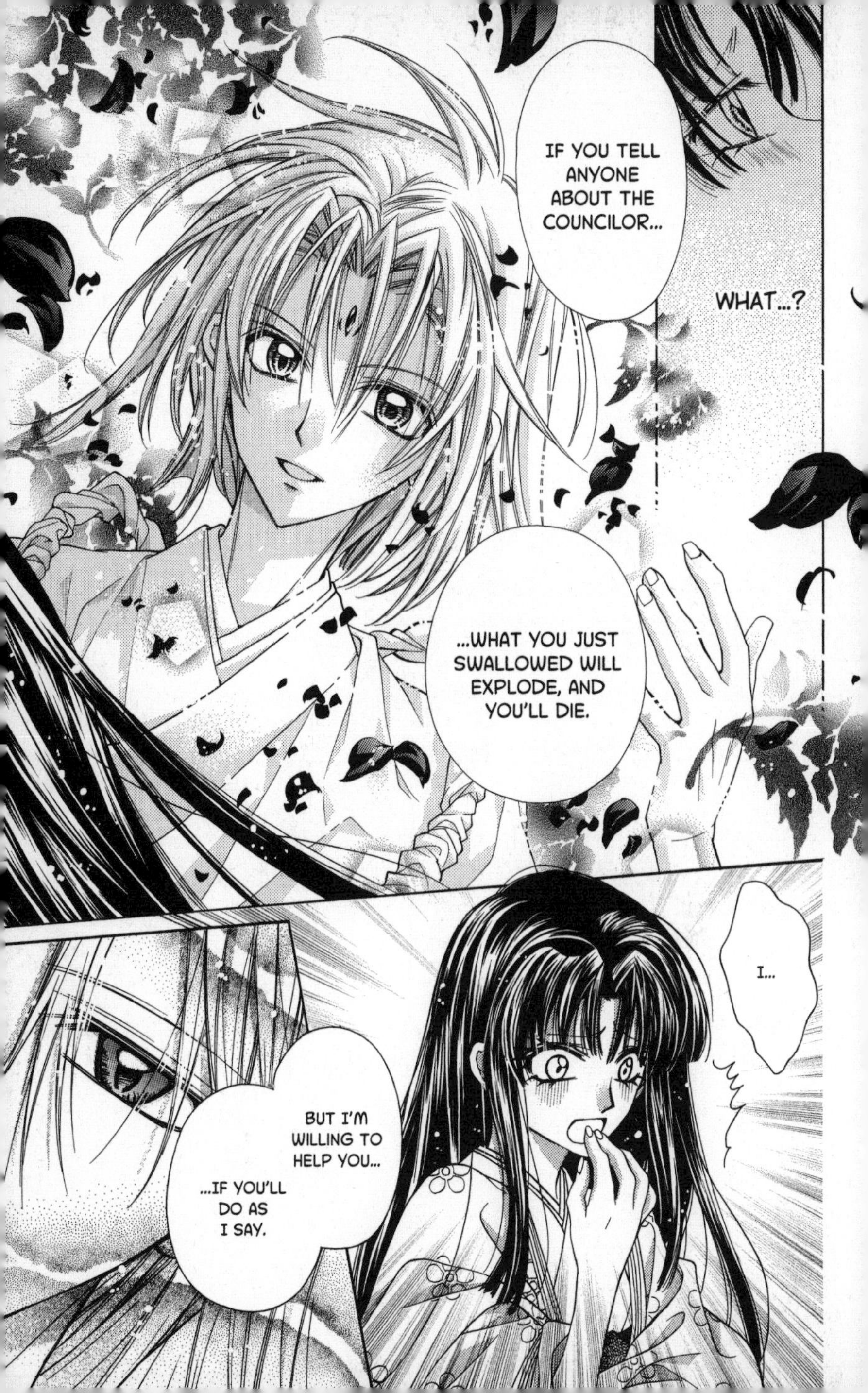
WHAT...?
IF YOU TELL ANYONE ABOUT THE COUNCILOR...
...WHAT YOU JUST SWALLOWED WILL EXPLODE, AND YOU'LL DIE.
I...
BUT I'M WILLING TO HELP YOU...
...IF YOU'LL DO AS I SAY.

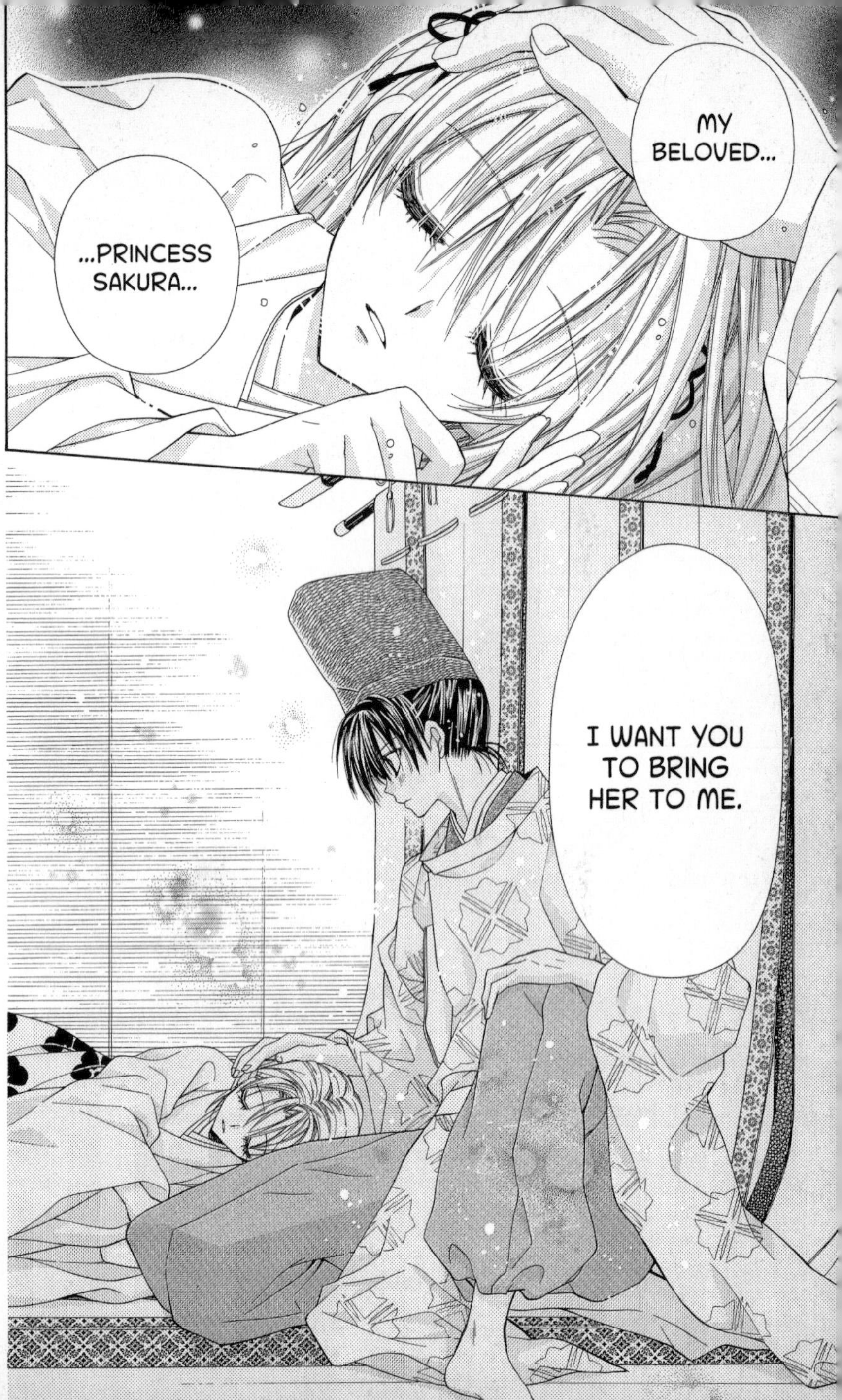
MY BELOVED...
...PRINCESS SAKURA...
I WANT YOU TO BRING HER TO ME.

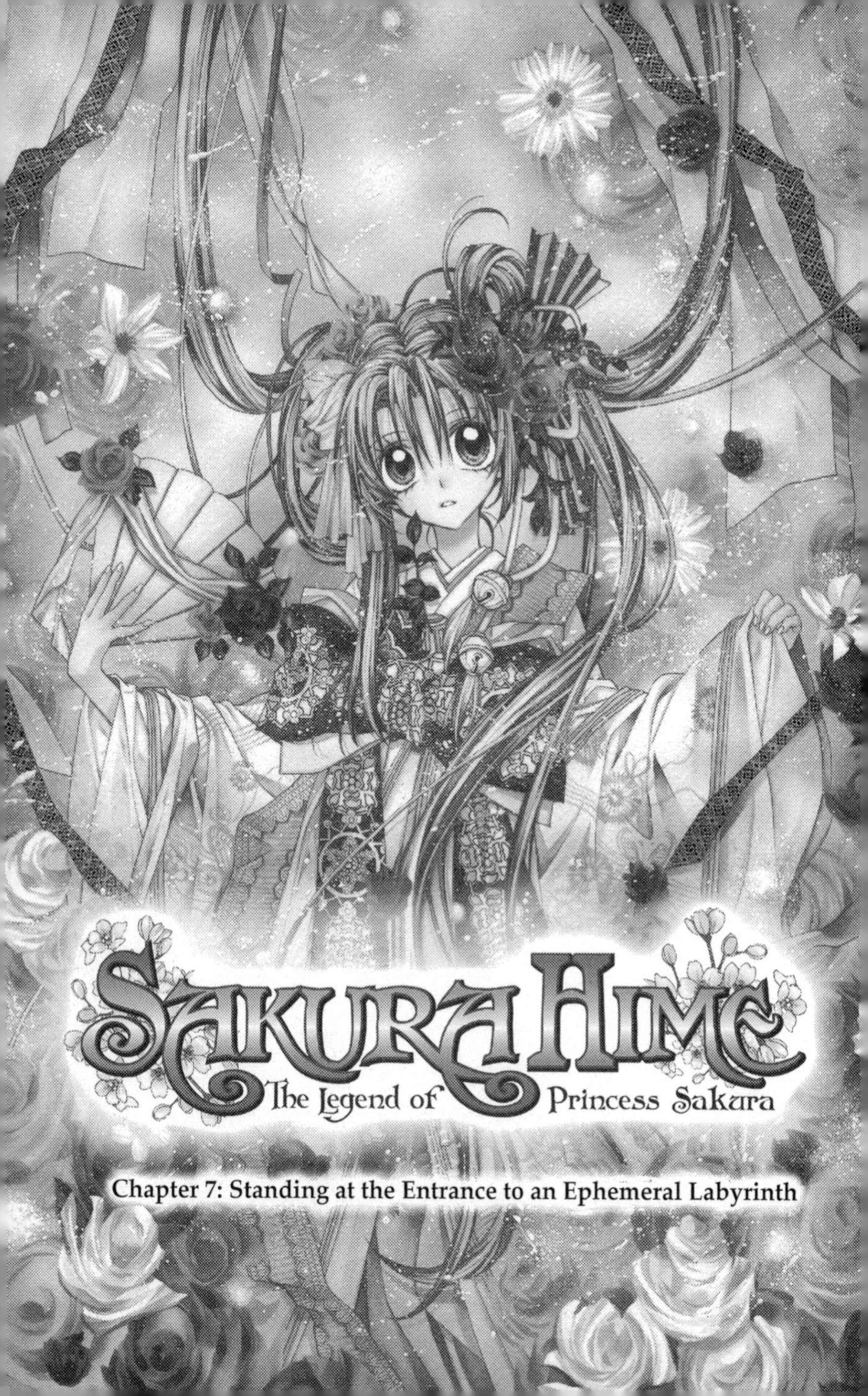
SAKURA HIME
The Legend of Princess Sakura
Chapter 7: Standing at the Entrance to an Ephemeral Labyrinth

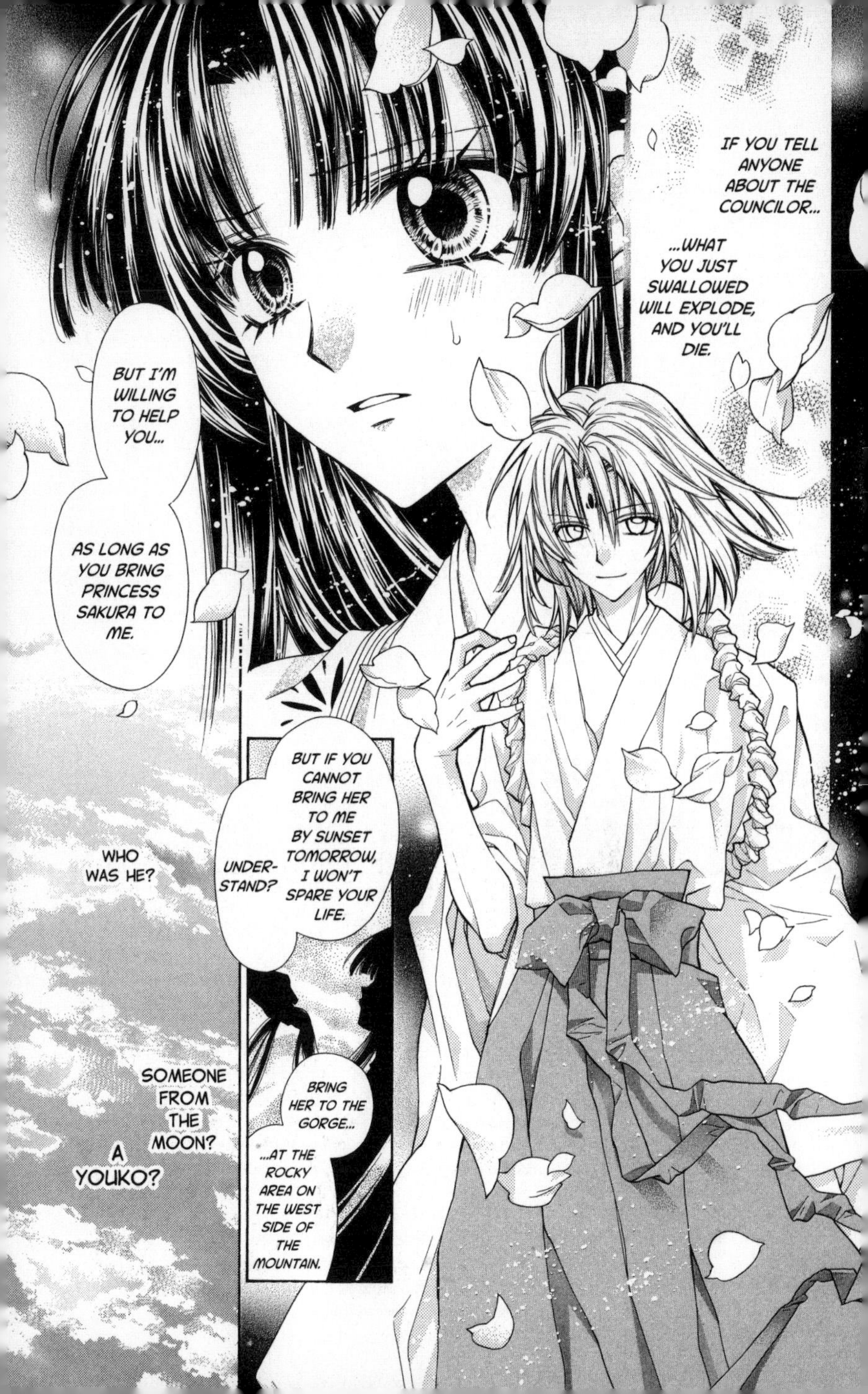
IF YOU TELL ANYONE ABOUT THE COUNCILOR...
...WHAT YOU JUST SWALLOWED WILL EXPLODE, AND YOU'LL DIE.
BUT I'M WILLING TO HELP YOU...
AS LONG AS YOU BRING PRINCESS SAKURA TO ME.
BUT IF YOU CANNOT BRING HER TO ME BY SUNSET TOMORROW, I WON'T SPARE YOUR LIFE.
UNDER-STAND?
BRING HER TO THE GORGE...
...AT THE ROCKY AREA ON THE WEST SIDE OF THE MOUNTAIN.
WHO WAS HE?
SOMEONE FROM THE MOON?
A YOUKO?

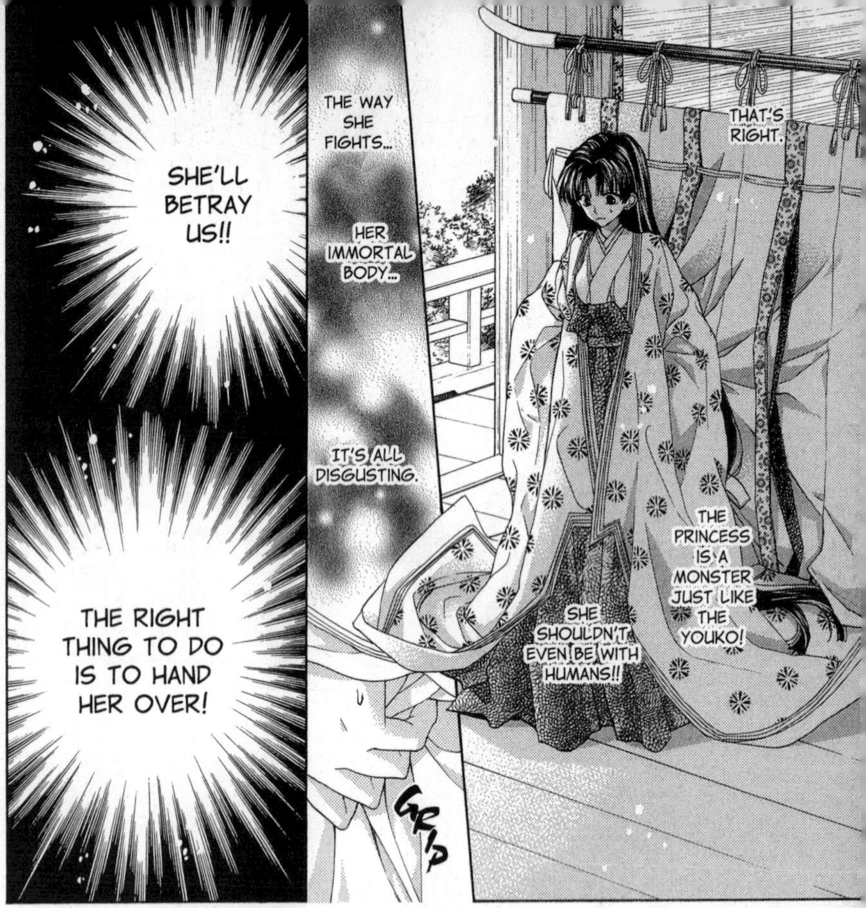
THAT'S RIGHT.
THE PRINCESS IS A MONSTER JUST LIKE THE YOUKO!
SHE SHOULDN'T EVEN BE WITH HUMANS!!
THE WAY SHE FIGHTS...
HER IMMORTAL BODY...
IT'S ALL DISGUSTING.
GRIP
SHE'LL BETRAY US!!
THE RIGHT THING TO DO IS TO HAND HER OVER!

Chapter 7: Standing at the Entrance to an Ephemeral Labyrinth

※ I'm giving away the story.

I asked my editor to write the lead-ins for now.

Aaah, I did it! ↑ This is the same word as the one in the chapter title for chapter 4!! (Word? Phrase?) I'm sorry... I didn't notice it. I'll be more careful next time. >_<; I like this word. I'm sorry.

I handed the storyboard over to my assistant saying, "This chapter isn't that good," (as I had lost confidence in the quality of this chapter) but she said, "The readers are interested in Oumi more than you think"... I see. I'm creating this story because I want to, so... Well... Thank you. And I never expected to receive so many responses about this chapter either, so I guess I really can't be confident about my hunches... Geh.
As for the youko... I'm sorry for Sakura, but I decided to leave some signs of when Oumi was human so that Sakura would have doubts. (Sorry... I've decided to make the walls before Sakura as high as possible.)

By the way, for *Sakura Hime* I've started to hold back on the amount of screentones I use, but what do you think about it? Is it easier to read?? As the creator, I'm a little worried that the pages seem rather empty... Wah. There seems to be the idea that "manga that doesn't make use of screentones are amazing" in this world, but I don't agree with that. Most manga without screentones are hard to read. Using moderate amounts is the best, so I'm trying to aim for that. It's nice to have a little jazziness!

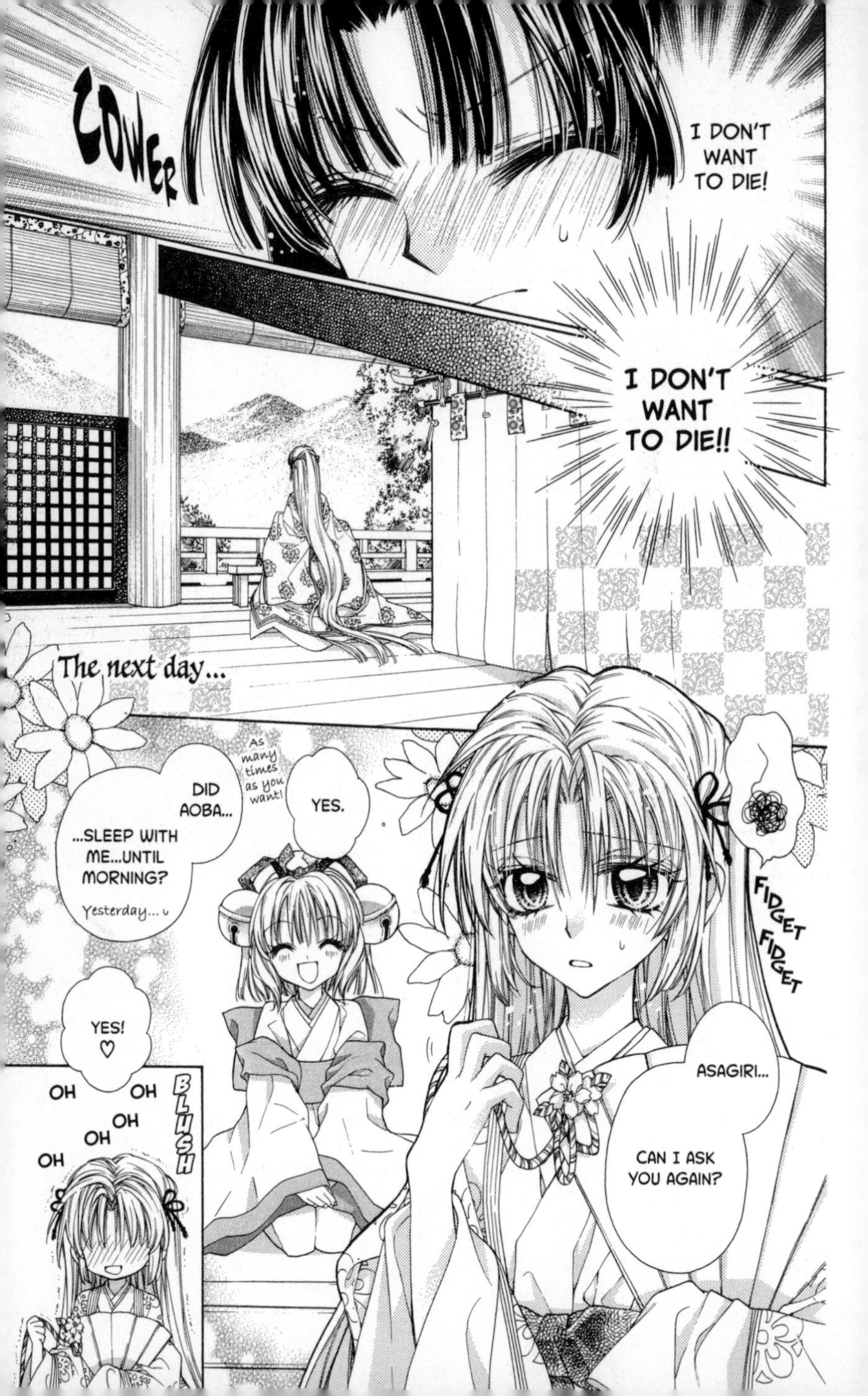
I DON'T WANT TO DIE!
COWER
I DON'T WANT TO DIE!!
The next day...
ASAGIRI...
CAN I ASK YOU AGAIN?
FIDGET FIDGET
YES.
As many times as you want!
DID AOBA...
...SLEEP WITH ME...UNTIL MORNING?
Yesterday...
YES! ♡
BLUSH
OH OH OH OH OH

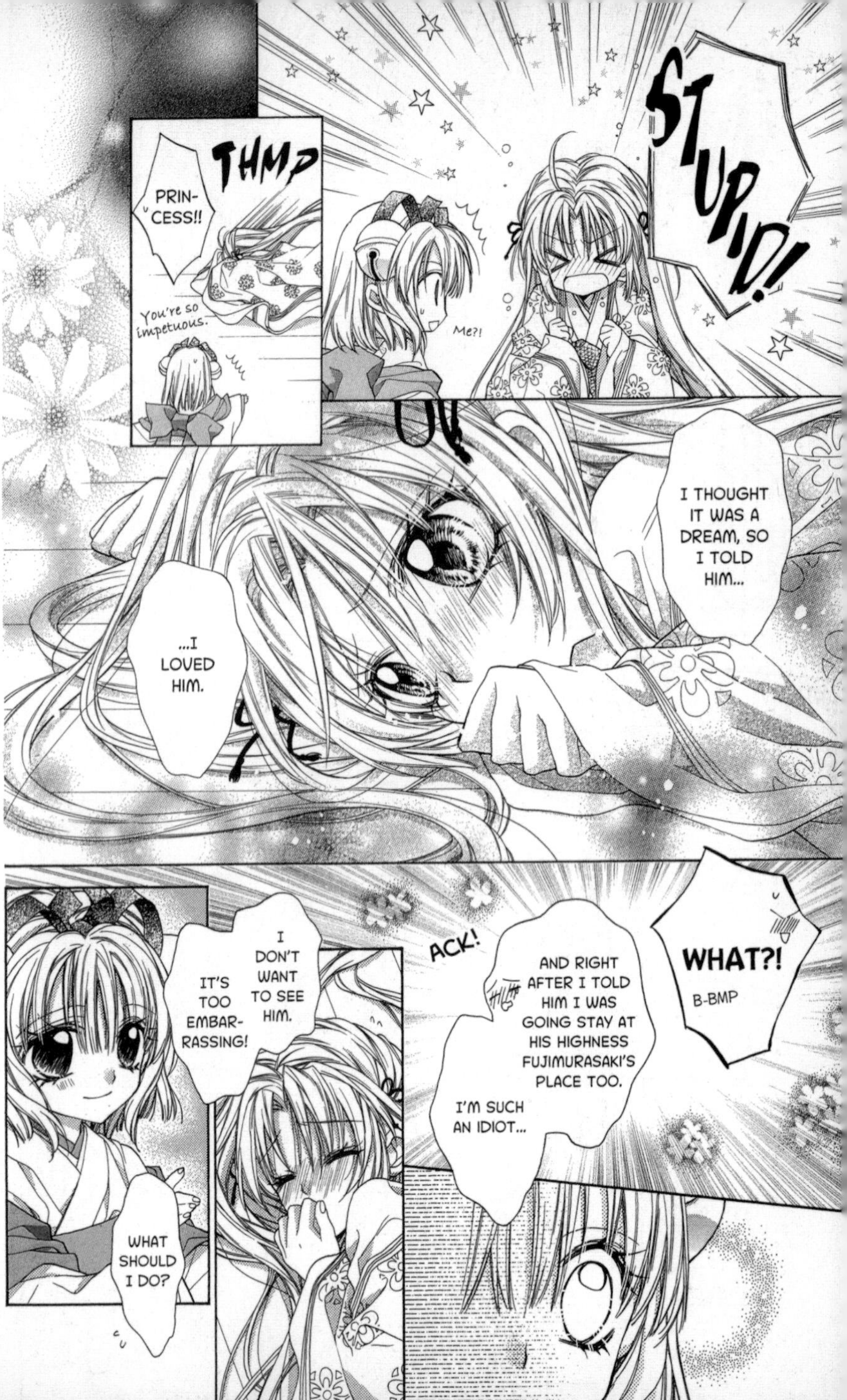
STUPID!!
Me?!
THMP
PRIN-CESS!!
You're so impetuous.
I THOUGHT IT WAS A DREAM, SO I TOLD HIM...
...I LOVED HIM.
WHAT?!
B-BMP
AND RIGHT AFTER I TOLD HIM I WAS GOING STAY AT HIS HIGHNESS FUJIMURASAKI'S PLACE TOO.
I'M SUCH AN IDIOT...
ACK!
I DON'T WANT TO SEE HIM.
IT'S TOO EMBARRASSING!
WHAT SHOULD I DO?

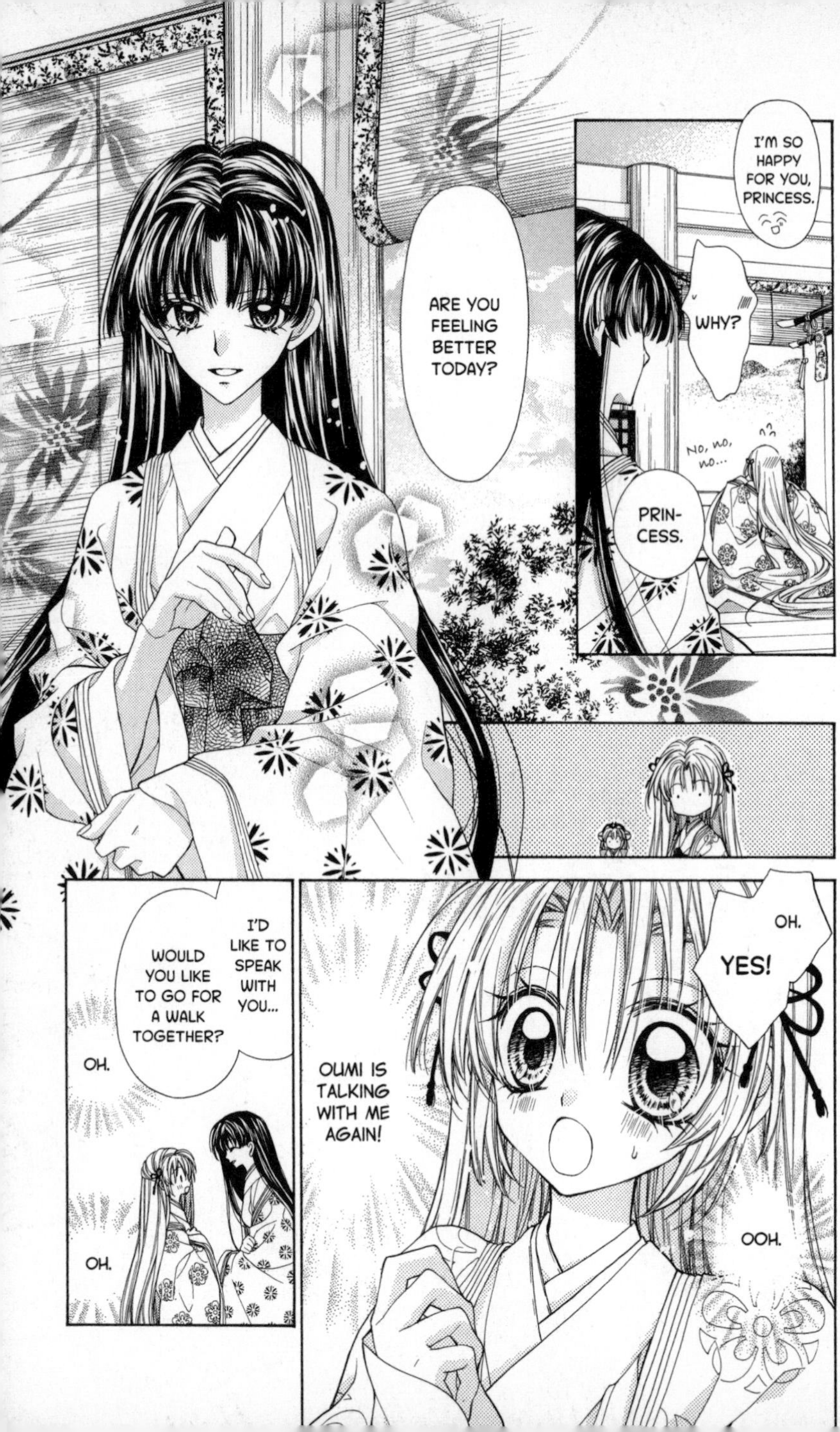
I'M SO HAPPY FOR YOU, PRINCESS.
WHY?
No, no, no...
PRIN-CESS.
ARE YOU FEELING BETTER TODAY?
OH.
YES!
OUMI IS TALKING WITH ME AGAIN!
OOH.
I'D LIKE TO SPEAK WITH YOU...
WOULD YOU LIKE TO GO FOR A WALK TOGETHER?
OH.
OH.

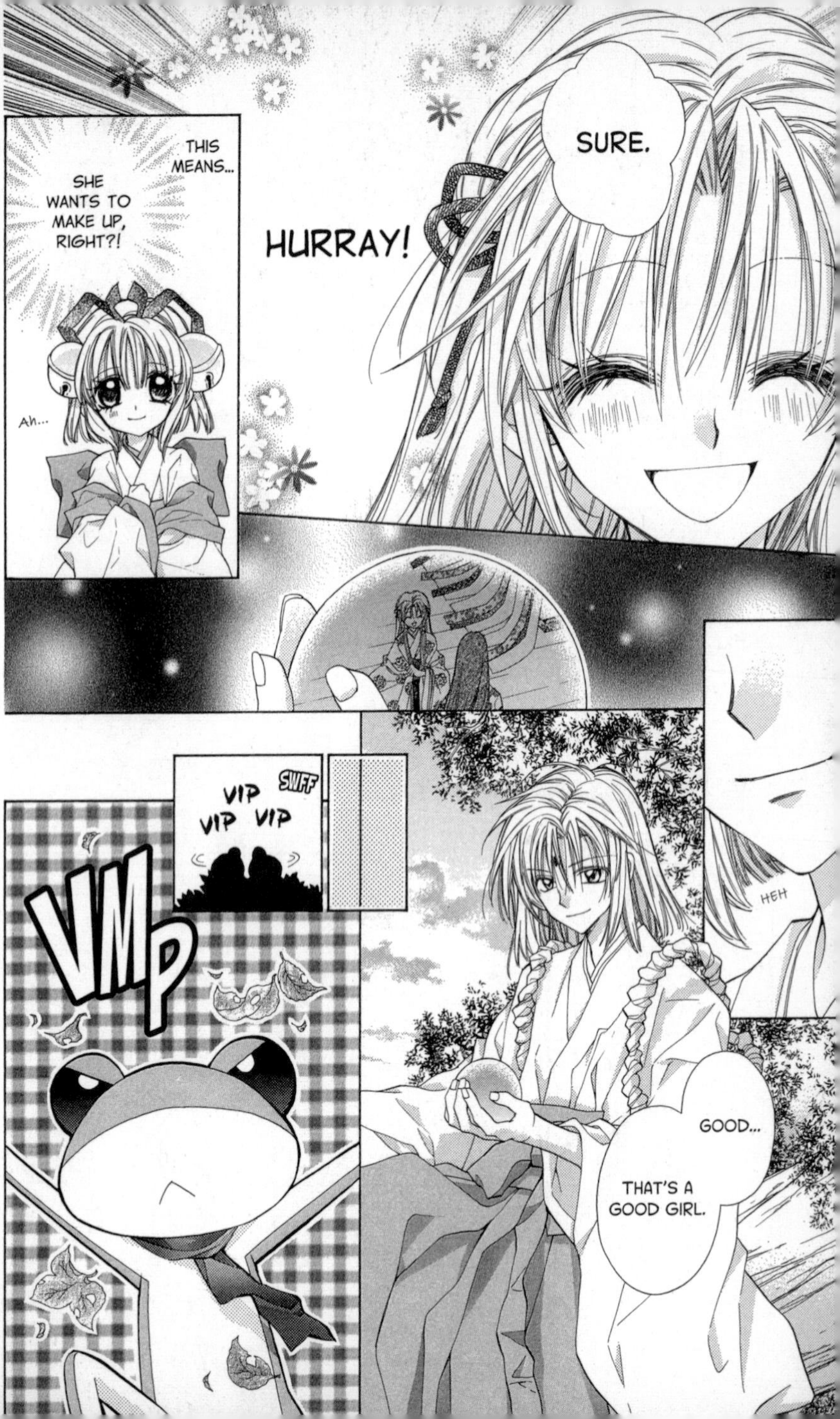
SURE.
HURRAY!
THIS MEANS...
SHE WANTS TO MAKE UP, RIGHT?!
Ah...
HEH
GOOD...
THAT'S A GOOD GIRL.
SWFF
VIP VIP VIP
VMP

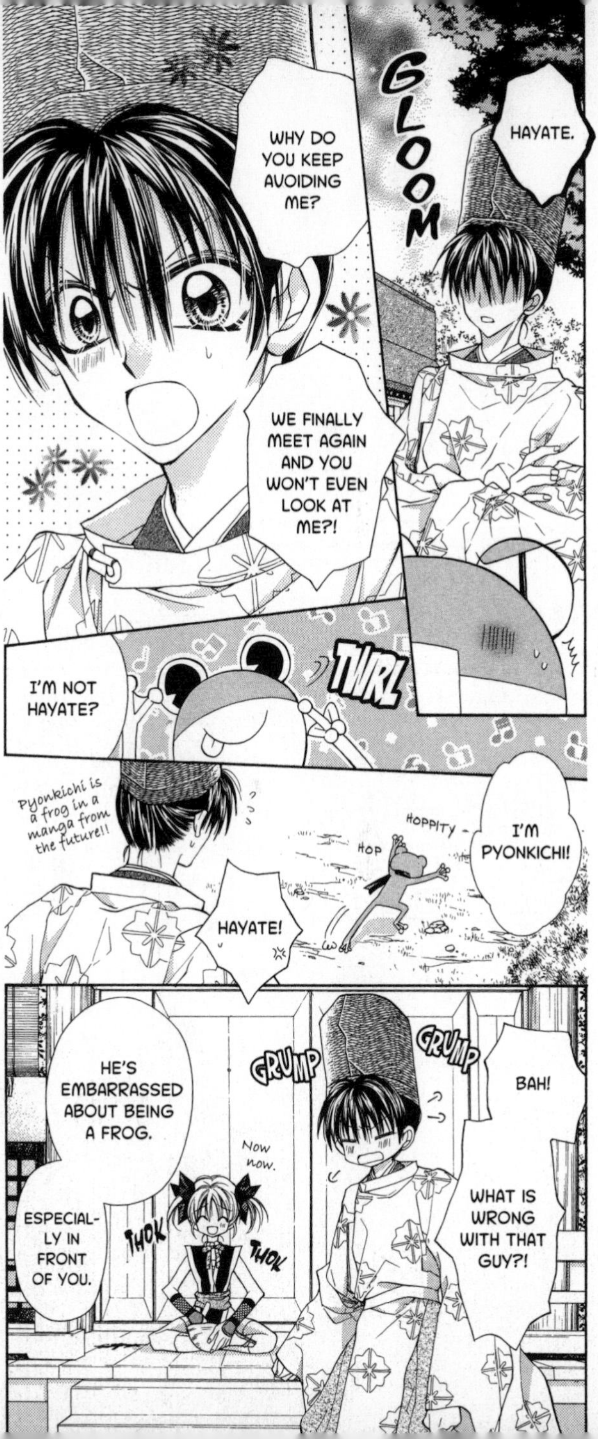
HAYATE.
GLOOM
WHY DO YOU KEEP AVOIDING ME?
WE FINALLY MEET AGAIN AND YOU WON'T EVEN LOOK AT ME?!
TWIRL
I'M NOT HAYATE?
I'M PYONKICHI!
HOPPITY
HOP
HAYATE!
Pyonkichi is a frog in a manga from the future!!
BAH!
GRUMP
WHAT IS WRONG WITH THAT GUY?!
GRUMP
Now now.
HE'S EMBARRASSED ABOUT BEING A FROG.
ESPECIAL-LY IN FRONT OF YOU.
THOK
THOK

OBARA-SAN'S HAIR SALON

The hairdresser Obara-san who has always done my hair is starting his own shop, so I drew the illustration for their business card.

You can have it for free when you go to his shop, so please drop by to get a haircut or perm. ♥
(The first 100 people who have their hair done will get a card with my autograph on it.)

6th Floor, Odawaraya Building
2-25-10 Dogenzaka, Shibuya-ku, Tokyo
150-0043

It's...

R∴EVOL

PC
http://www.revol.hair-dressing.jp

Mobile
http://n.833hd.co.jp/revol/

If you get your hair done there, you'll be able to hear a lot about me. You can also talk about my work with Obara-san.

But I guess that's not important. ♥
Um, he's a skilled hairdresser!

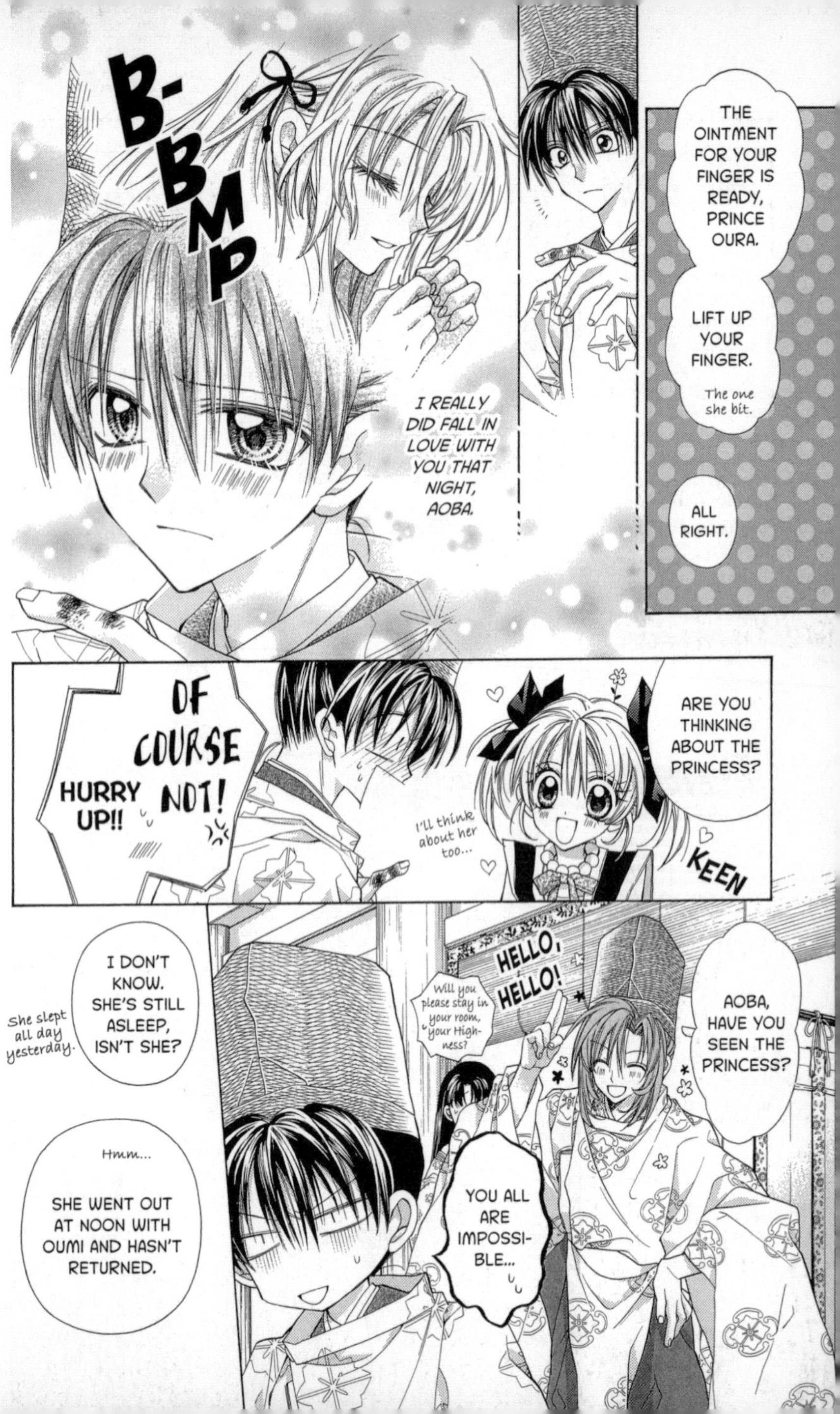
THE OINTMENT FOR YOUR FINGER IS READY, PRINCE OURA.
LIFT UP YOUR FINGER.
The one she bit.
ALL RIGHT.
B-BMP
I REALLY DID FALL IN LOVE WITH YOU THAT NIGHT, AOBA.
ARE YOU THINKING ABOUT THE PRINCESS?
KEEN
I'll think about her too...
OF COURSE NOT!
HURRY UP!!
AOBA, HAVE YOU SEEN THE PRINCESS?
HELLO, HELLO!
Will you please stay in your room, your Highness?
YOU ALL ARE IMPOSSIBLE...
I DON'T KNOW. SHE'S STILL ASLEEP, ISN'T SHE?
She slept all day yesterday.
Hmm...
SHE WENT OUT AT NOON WITH OUMI AND HASN'T RETURNED.

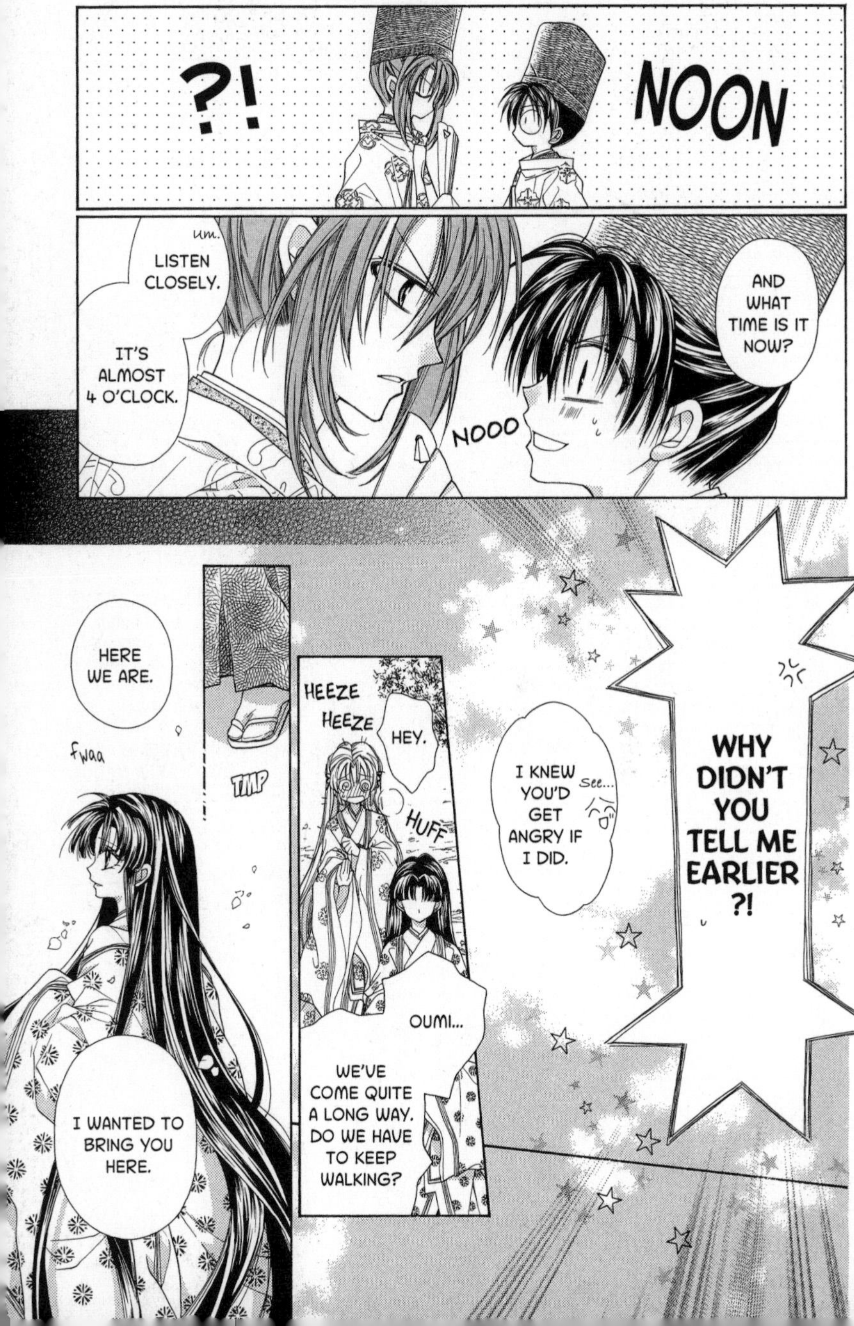
NOON
?!
AND WHAT TIME IS IT NOW?
NOOO
um.
LISTEN CLOSELY.
IT'S ALMOST 4 O'CLOCK.
WHY DIDN'T YOU TELL ME EARLIER?!
See...
I KNEW YOU'D GET ANGRY IF I DID.
HEY.
HEEZE
HEEZE
HUFF
OUMI...
WE'VE COME QUITE A LONG WAY. DO WE HAVE TO KEEP WALKING?
TMP
HERE WE ARE.
fwaa
I WANTED TO BRING YOU HERE.

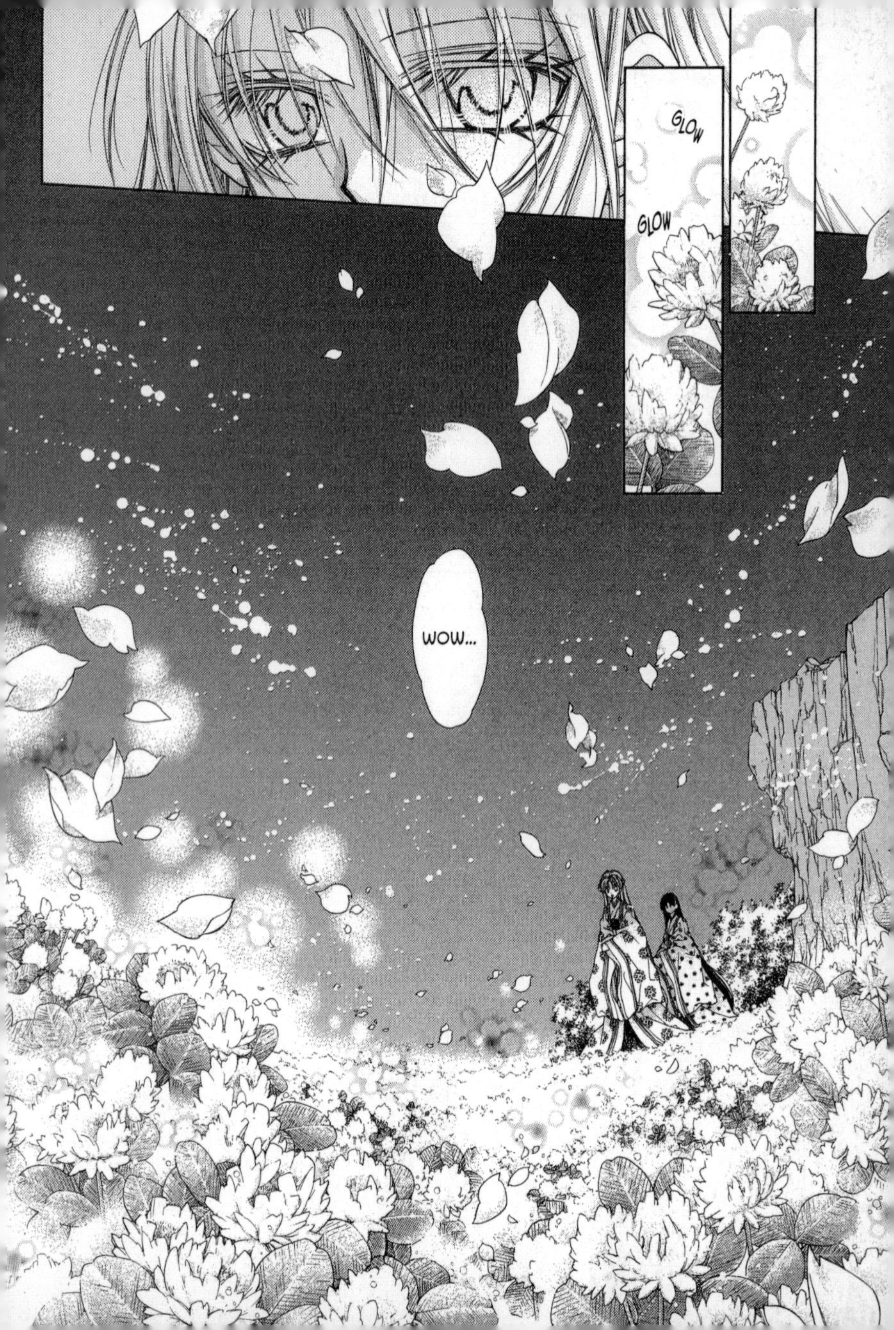
GLOW
GLOW
WOW...

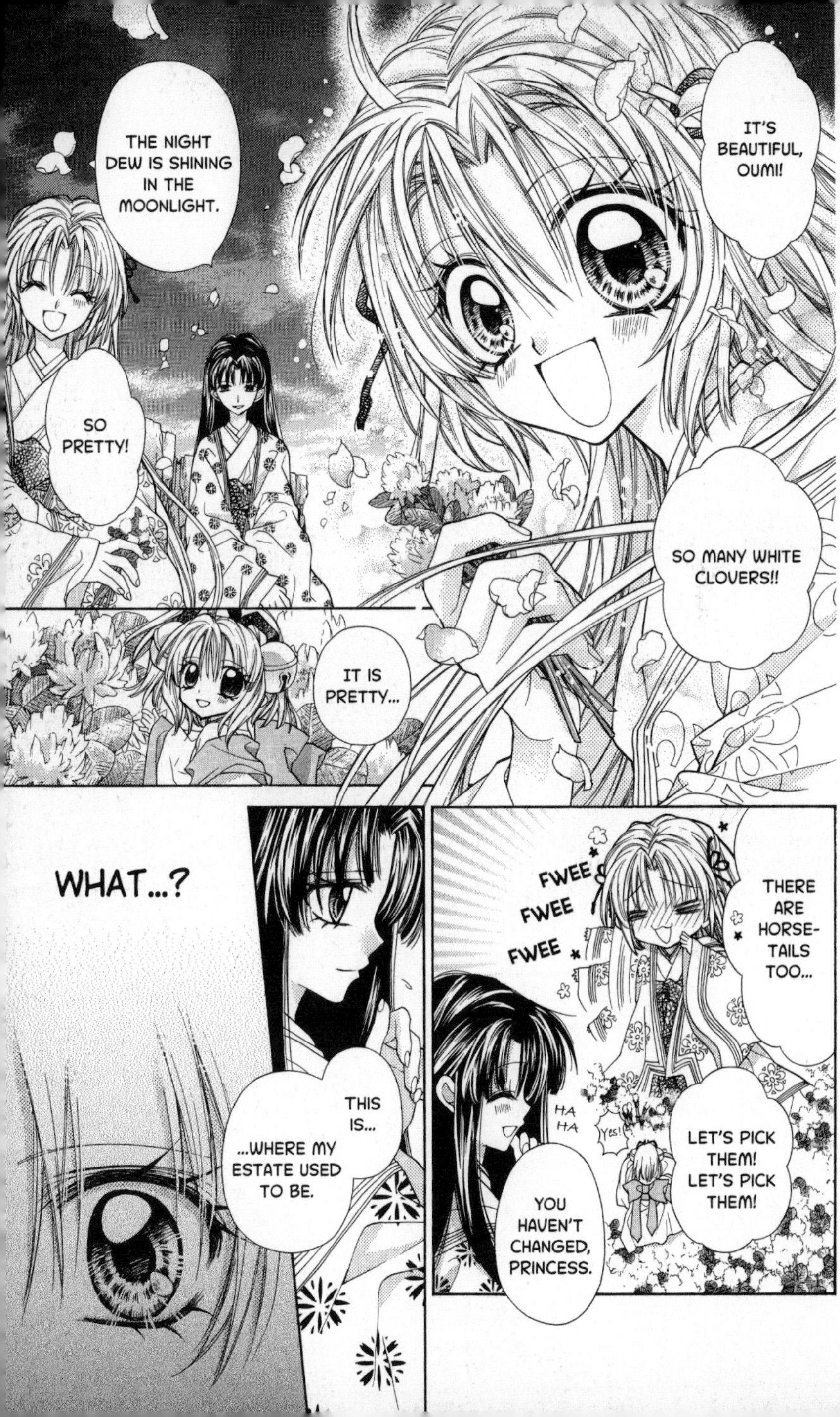

IT'S BEAUTIFUL, OUMI!
SO MANY WHITE CLOVERS!!
THE NIGHT DEW IS SHINING IN THE MOONLIGHT.
SO PRETTY!
IT IS PRETTY...
FWEE FWEE FWEE
THERE ARE HORSE-TAILS TOO...
Yes!
LET'S PICK THEM! LET'S PICK THEM!
HA HA
YOU HAVEN'T CHANGED, PRINCESS.
THIS IS...
...WHERE MY ESTATE USED TO BE.
WHAT...?

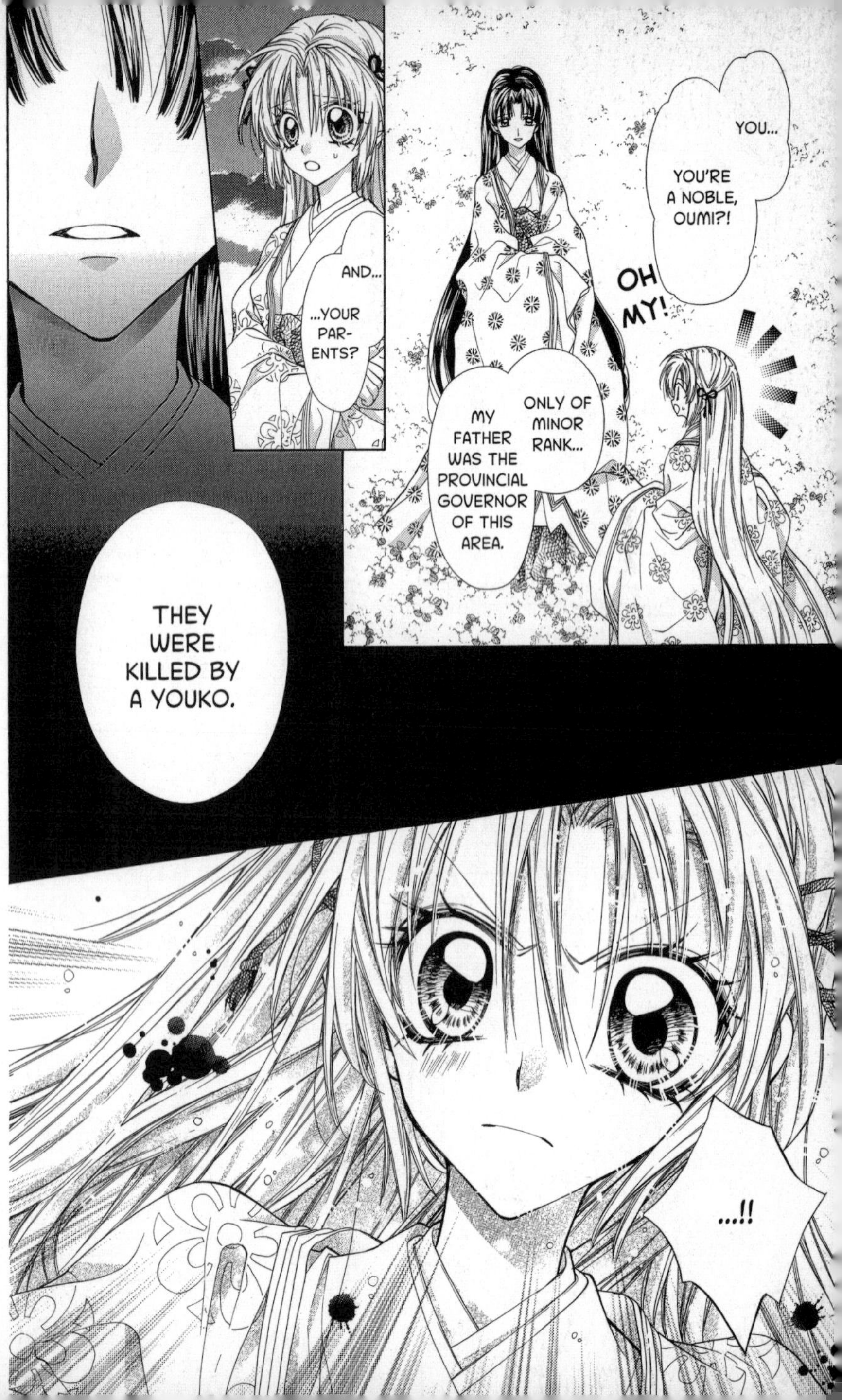
YOU...
YOU'RE A NOBLE, OUMI?!
OH MY!
ONLY OF MINOR RANK...
MY FATHER WAS THE PROVINCIAL GOVERNOR OF THIS AREA.
AND...
...YOUR PARENTS?
THEY WERE KILLED BY A YOUKO.
...!!

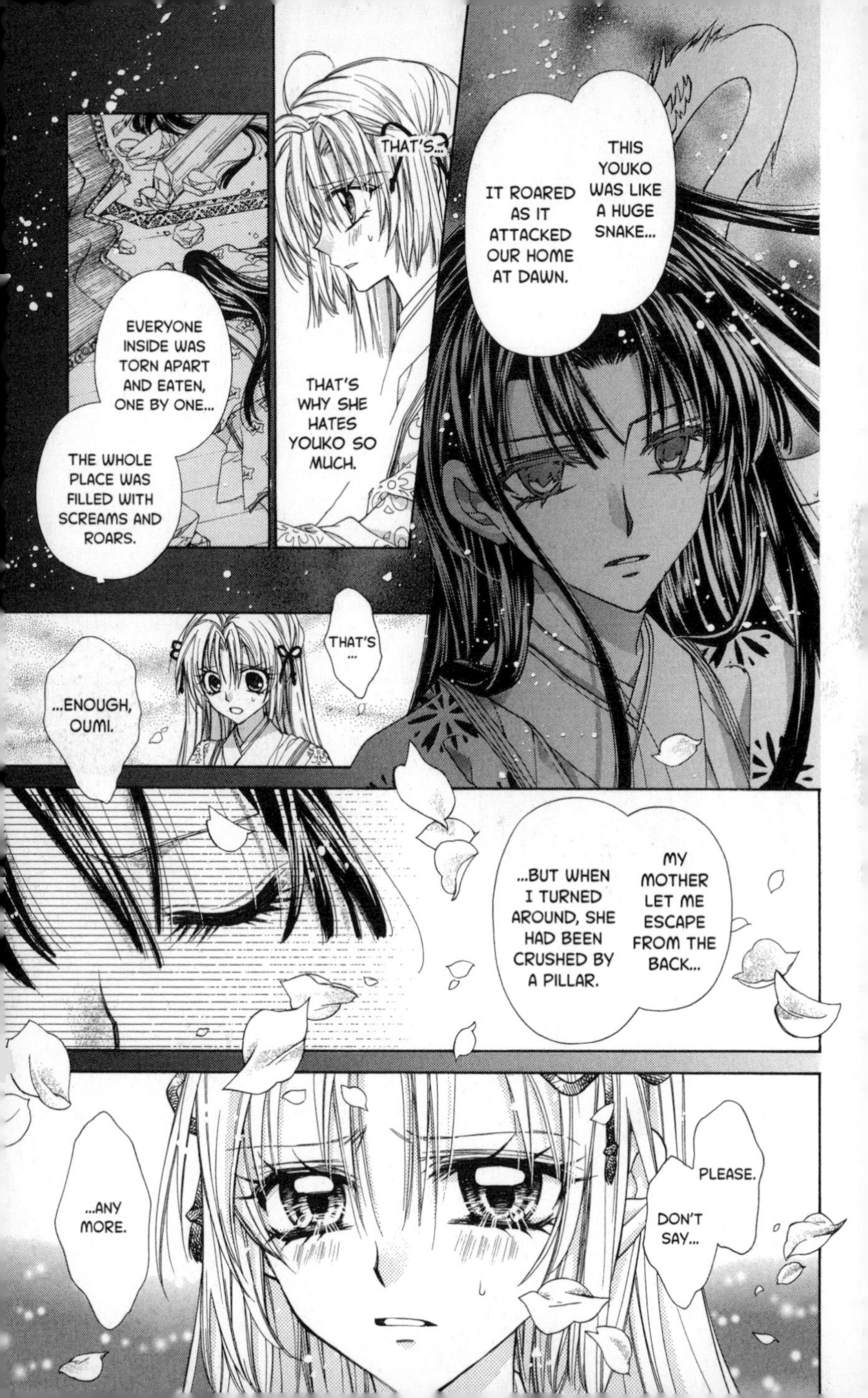
THIS YOUKO WAS LIKE A HUGE SNAKE...
IT ROARED AS IT ATTACKED OUR HOME AT DAWN.
THAT'S...
THAT'S WHY SHE HATES YOUKO SO MUCH.
EVERYONE INSIDE WAS TORN APART AND EATEN, ONE BY ONE...
THE WHOLE PLACE WAS FILLED WITH SCREAMS AND ROARS.
THAT'S...
...ENOUGH, OUMI.
MY MOTHER LET ME ESCAPE FROM THE BACK...
...BUT WHEN I TURNED AROUND, SHE HAD BEEN CRUSHED BY A PILLAR.
PLEASE.
DON'T SAY...
...ANY MORE.

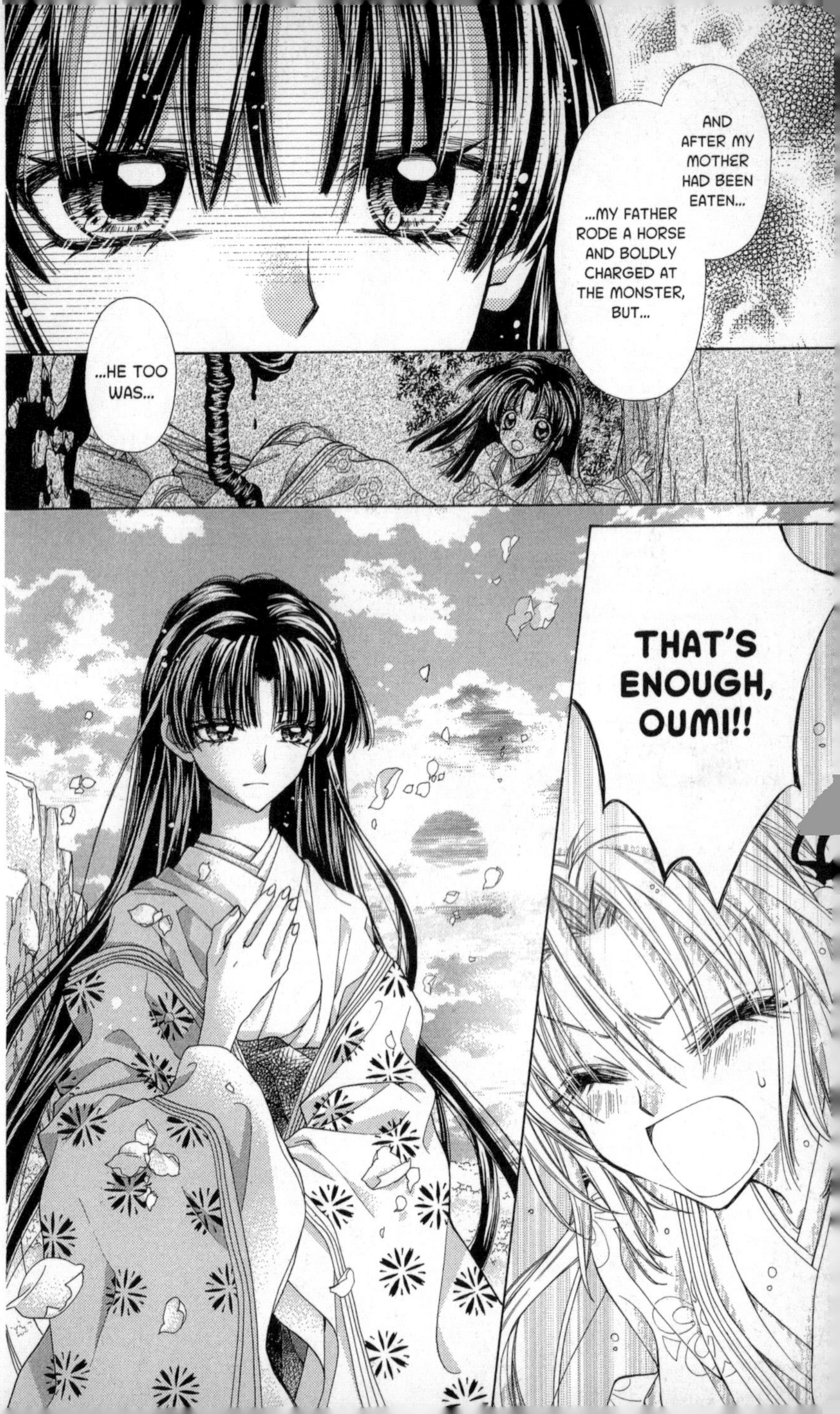
AND AFTER MY MOTHER HAD BEEN EATEN...
...MY FATHER RODE A HORSE AND BOLDLY CHARGED AT THE MONSTER, BUT...
...HE TOO WAS...
THAT'S ENOUGH, OUMI!!

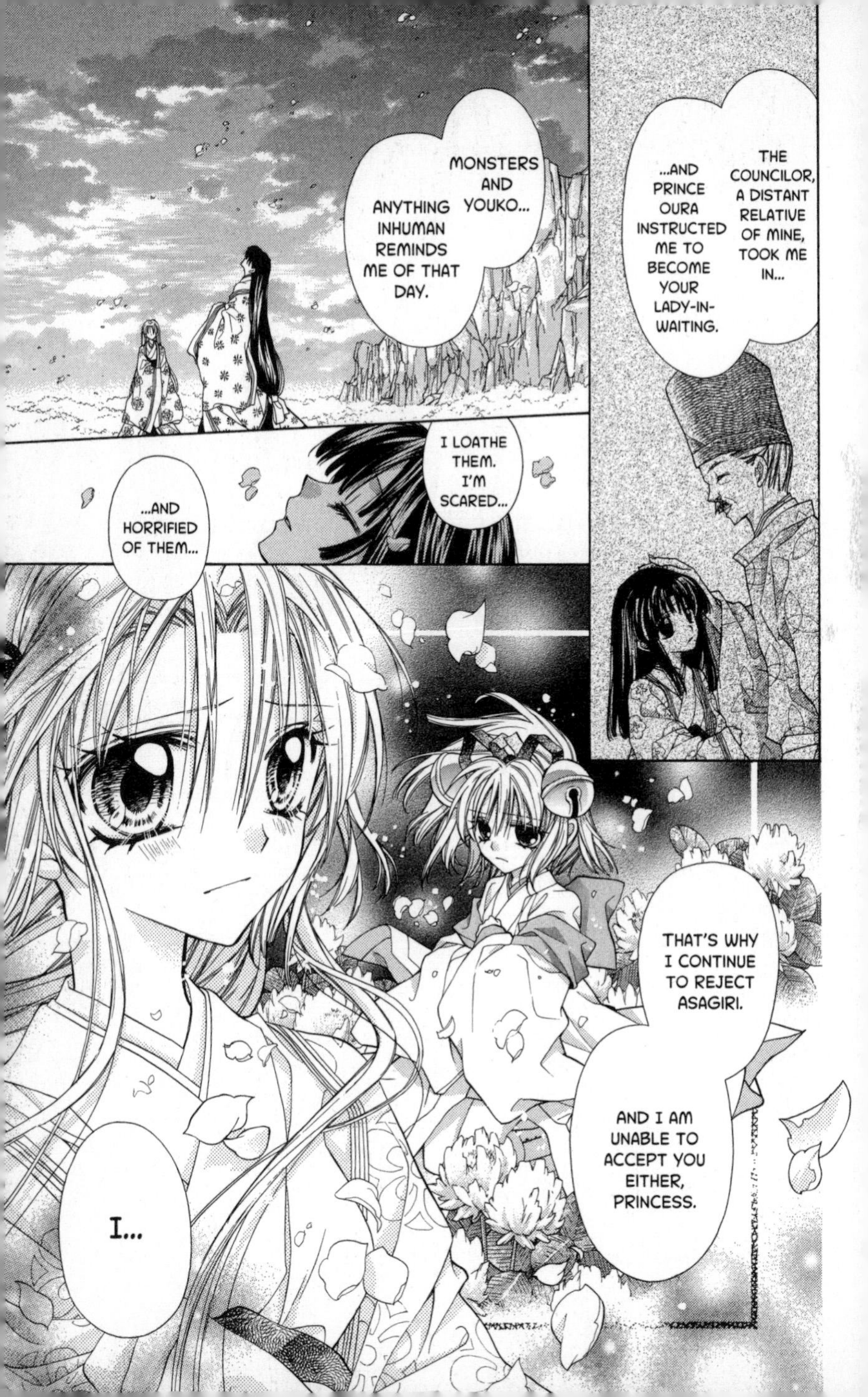
THE COUNCILOR, A DISTANT RELATIVE OF MINE, TOOK ME IN...
...AND PRINCE OURA INSTRUCTED ME TO BECOME YOUR LADY-IN-WAITING.
MONSTERS AND YOUKO...
ANYTHING INHUMAN REMINDS ME OF THAT DAY.
I LOATHE THEM. I'M SCARED...
...AND HORRIFIED OF THEM...
THAT'S WHY I CONTINUE TO REJECT ASAGIRI.
AND I AM UNABLE TO ACCEPT YOU EITHER, PRINCESS.
I...

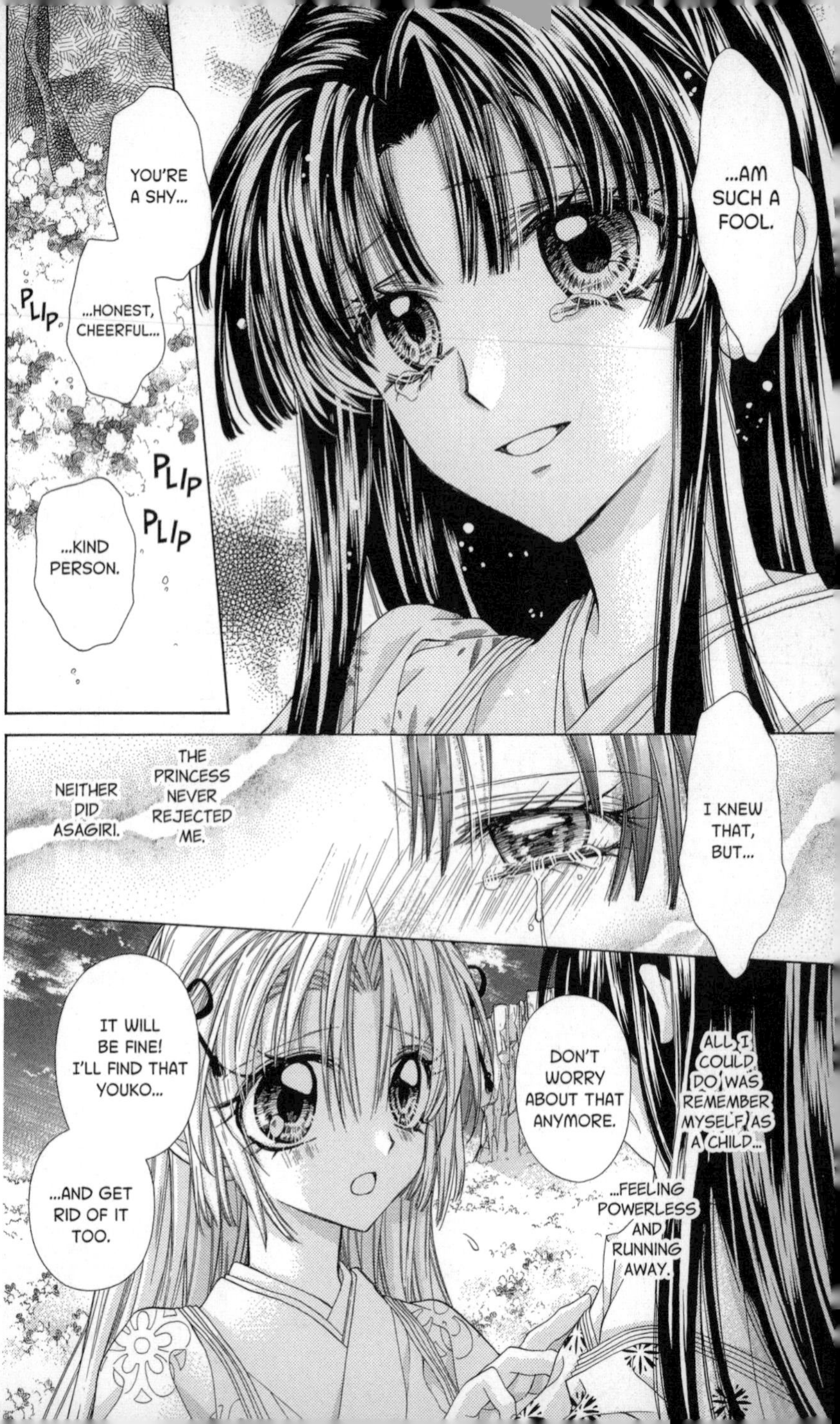
...AM SUCH A FOOL.
YOU'RE A SHY...
...HONEST, CHEERFUL...
PLIP
PLIP
PLIP
...KIND PERSON.
I KNEW THAT, BUT...
THE PRINCESS NEVER REJECTED ME.
NEITHER DID ASAGIRI.
ALL I COULD DO WAS REMEMBER MYSELF AS A CHILD...
...FEELING POWERLESS AND RUNNING AWAY.
DON'T WORRY ABOUT THAT ANYMORE.
IT WILL BE FINE! I'LL FIND THAT YOUKO...
...AND GET RID OF IT TOO.

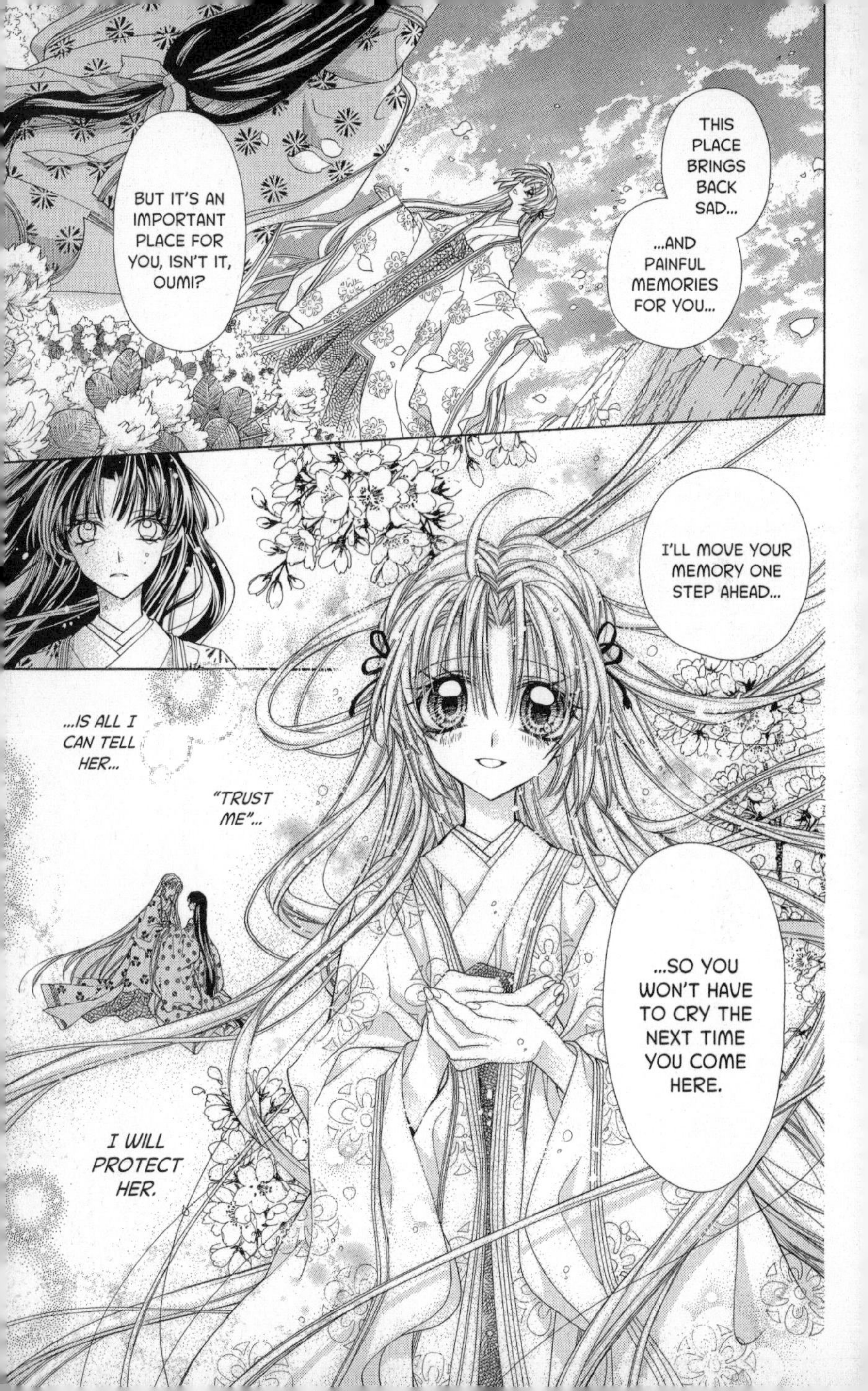
THIS PLACE BRINGS BACK SAD...
...AND PAINFUL MEMORIES FOR YOU...
BUT IT'S AN IMPORTANT PLACE FOR YOU, ISN'T IT, OUMI?
I'LL MOVE YOUR MEMORY ONE STEP AHEAD...
...SO YOU WON'T HAVE TO CRY THE NEXT TIME YOU COME HERE.
"TRUST ME"...
...IS ALL I CAN TELL HER...
I WILL PROTECT HER.

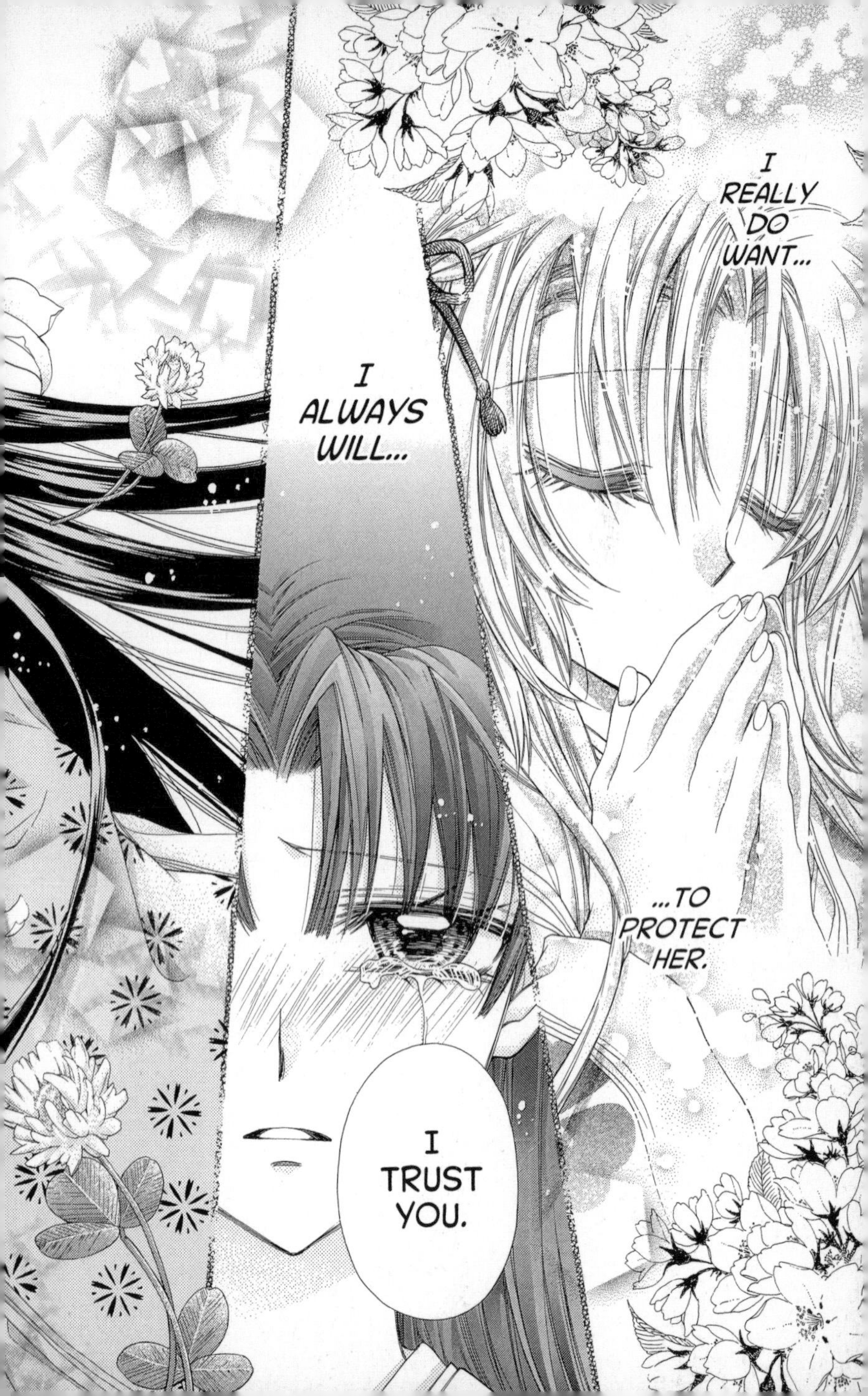
I REALLY DO WANT...
...TO PROTECT HER.
I ALWAYS WILL...
I TRUST YOU.

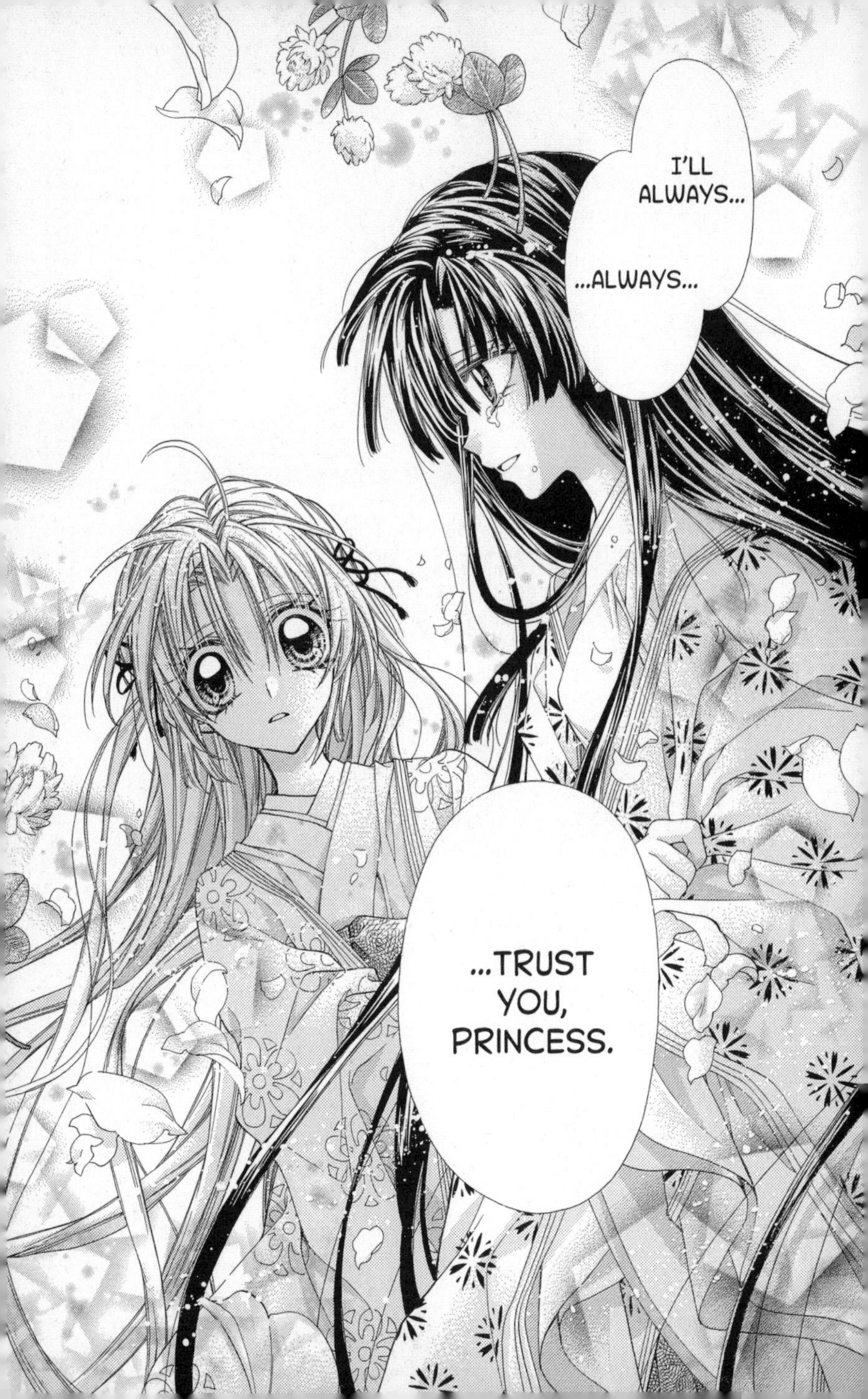
I'LL ALWAYS...
...ALWAYS...
...TRUST YOU, PRINCESS.

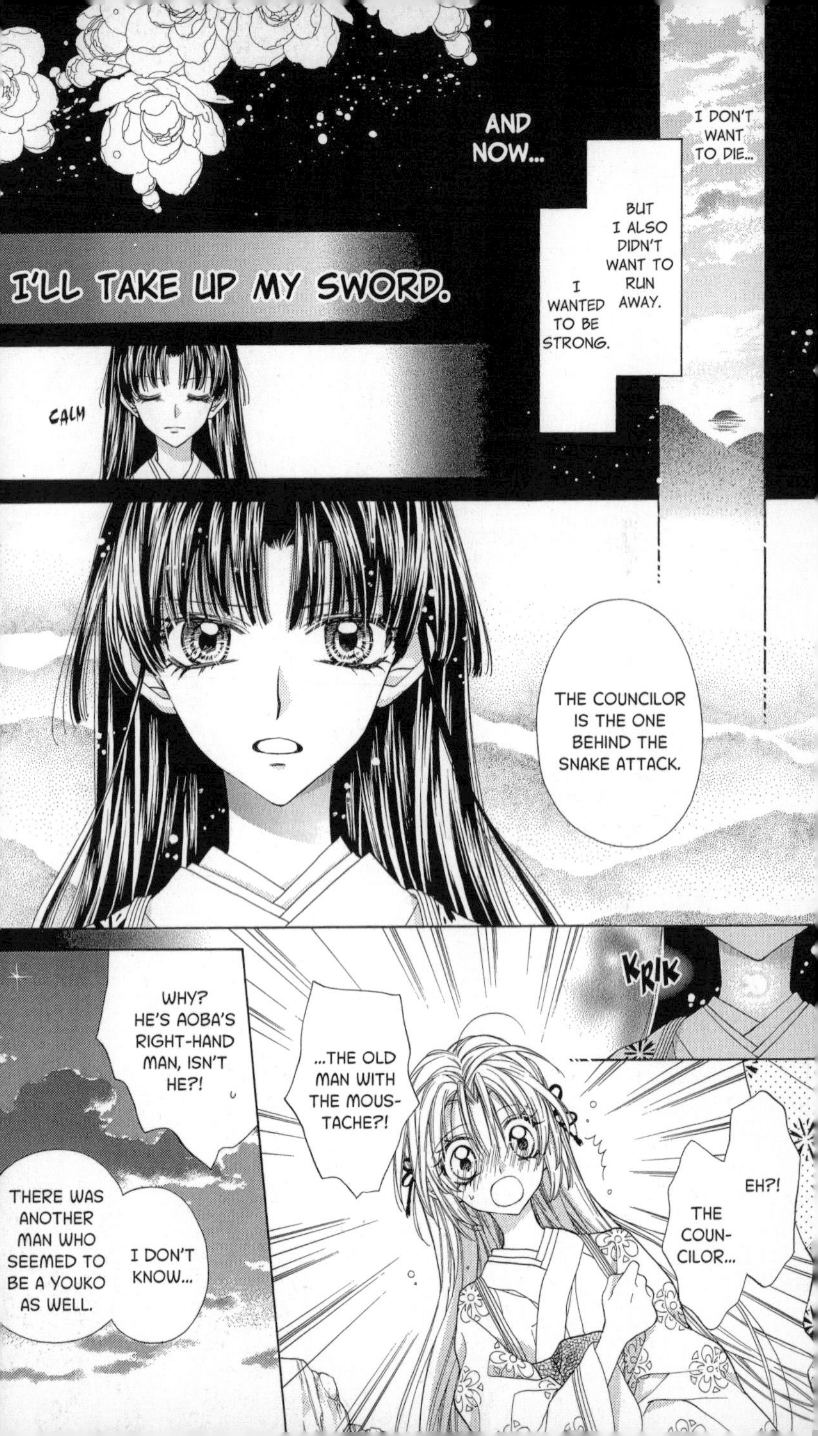
I DON'T WANT TO DIE...
BUT I ALSO DIDN'T WANT TO RUN AWAY.
I WANTED TO BE STRONG.
AND NOW...
I'LL TAKE UP MY SWORD.
CALM
THE COUNCILOR IS THE ONE BEHIND THE SNAKE ATTACK.
KRIK
EH?!
THE COUN-CILOR...
...THE OLD MAN WITH THE MOUS-TACHE?!
WHY? HE'S AOBA'S RIGHT-HAND MAN, ISN'T HE?!
I DON'T KNOW...
THERE WAS ANOTHER MAN WHO SEEMED TO BE A YOUKO AS WELL.

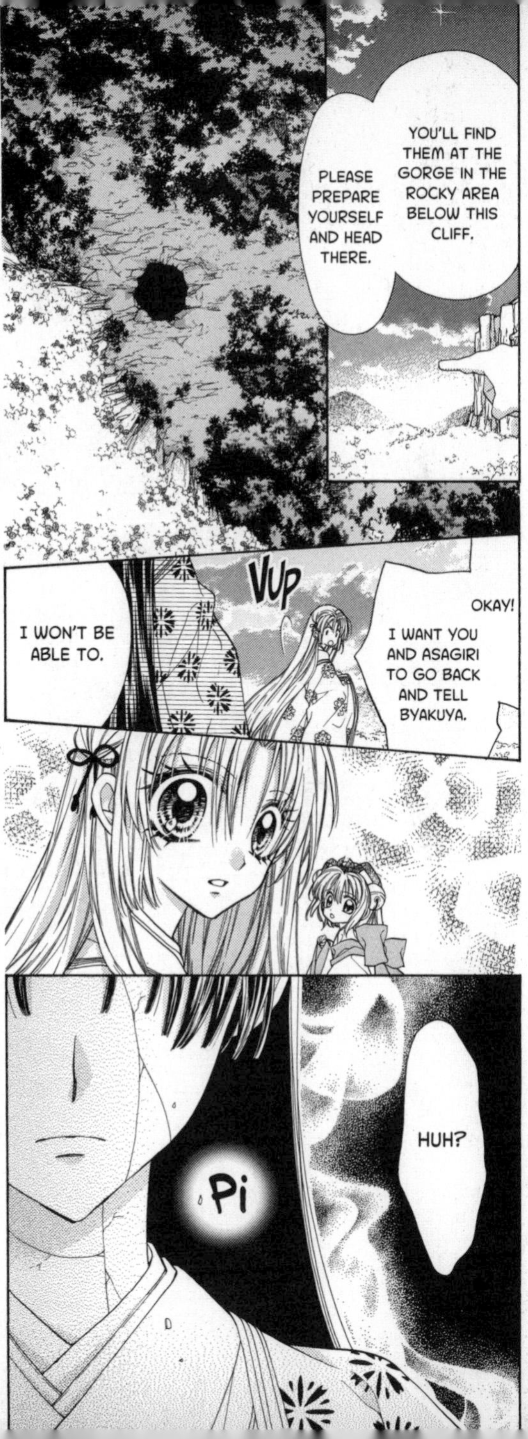
YOU'LL FIND THEM AT THE GORGE IN THE ROCKY AREA BELOW THIS CLIFF.
PLEASE PREPARE YOURSELF AND HEAD THERE.
OKAY!
I WANT YOU AND ASAGIRI TO GO BACK AND TELL BYAKUYA.
VUP
I WON'T BE ABLE TO.
HUH?
Pi

COMEDY

I have always liked comedy (Down Town, to be exact ♥). And the comedians are highly spirited these days as the economy is bad!

So here are the comedians I like:

• Chihara Jr.
I just love him! He's so good at having random conversations, and the show is so great with him in it! That's what I think. I especially like it when he's in *Yarisugi Koji.* ♥

• Savannah
I started to like Takahashi after watching *Ametalk* and *Yarisugi Koji*, but I like Yagi as well. ♥ (He's a natural comedian...)
They're a relaxing pair to watch.

• Rozan
I got hooked on them after watching *Ametalk*'s "Partner-Loving Comedians" ♥ (Comedians who just love their partner so much), and got hooked even more after seeing the DVDs and reading *Kyoto University Comedian*. They're so cute, and it is so adorable to see how well they get along with each other!!

• Audrey
I can't get enough of them! They appear in so many shows right now that I don't have enough space on my hard drive. By the way, I like Wakabayashi. I like how he tends to be harsh to other people in a moderate manner.

And the hall of famers are Imada, Higashino, Summers, and Cream Stew. I'll probably like them forever.

Comedy is great, isn't it?!

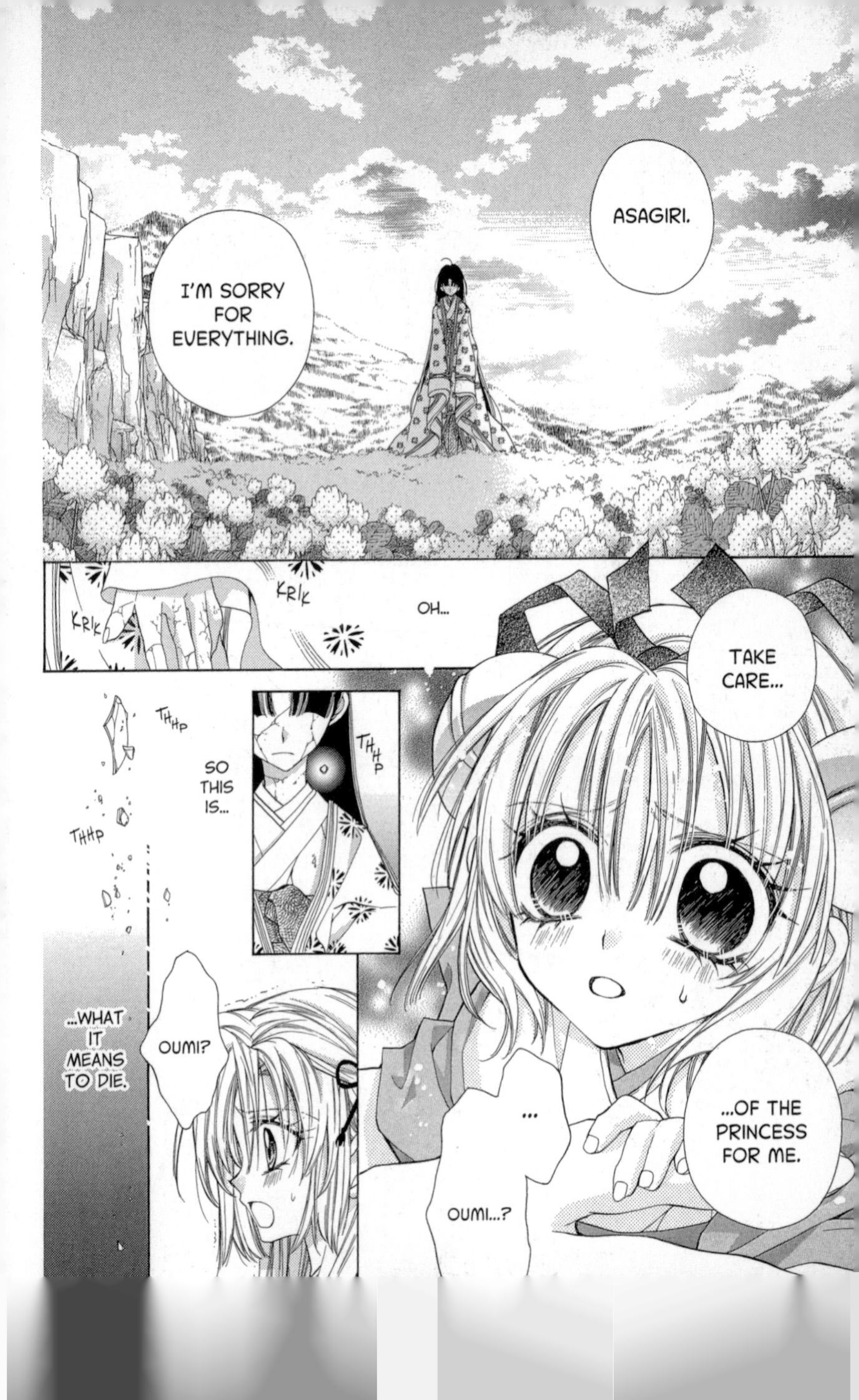
ASAGIRI.
I'M SORRY FOR EVERYTHING.
TAKE CARE...
...OF THE PRINCESS FOR ME.
KRIK
KRIK
OH...
THHP
THHP
SO THIS IS...
THHP
...WHAT IT MEANS TO DIE.
...
OUMI...?
OUMI?

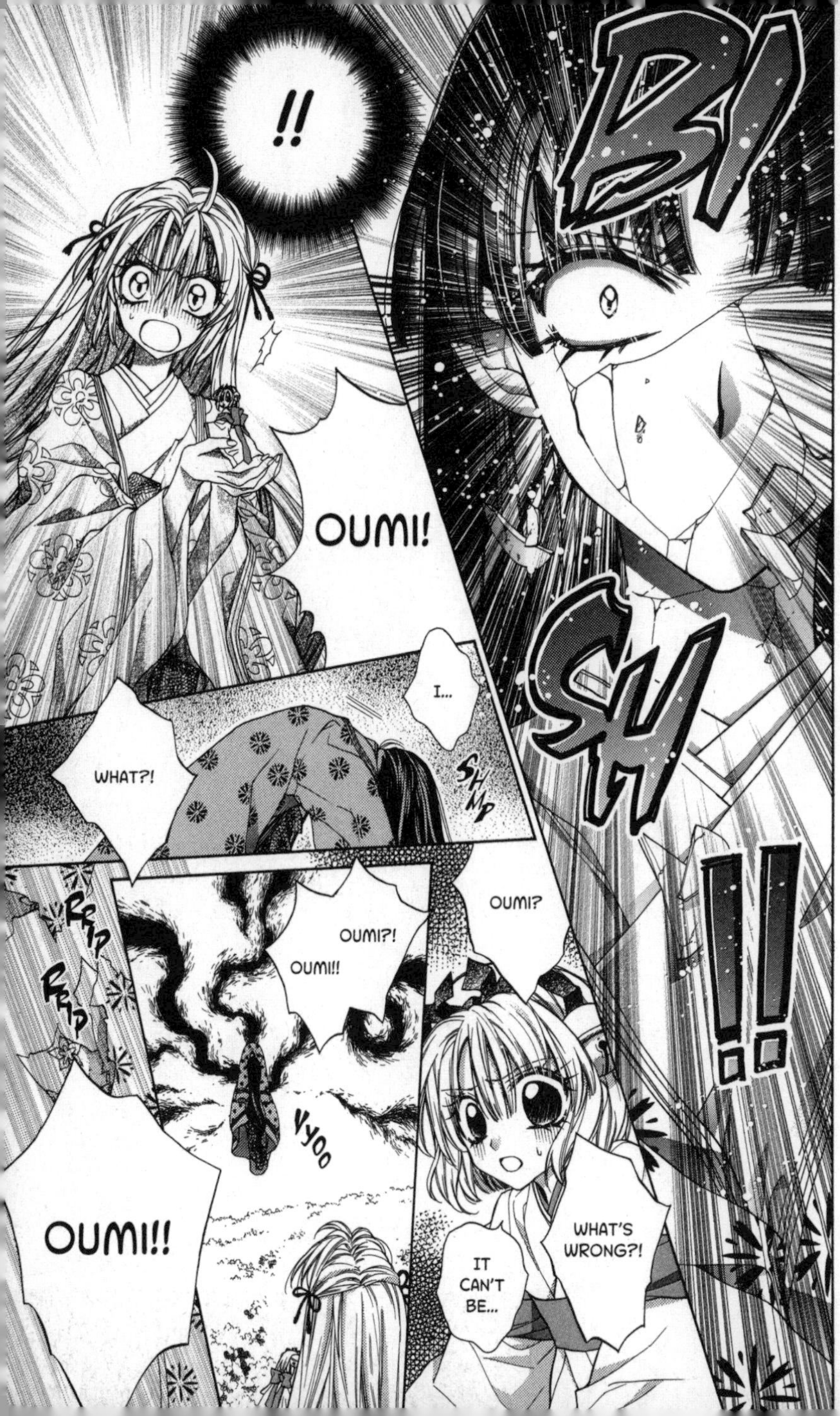
BASH!!
!!
OUMI!
I...
SHMP
WHAT?!
OUMI?
WHAT'S WRONG?!
IT CAN'T BE...
OUMI?!
OUMI!!
VYOO
RRIP
RRIP
OUMI!!

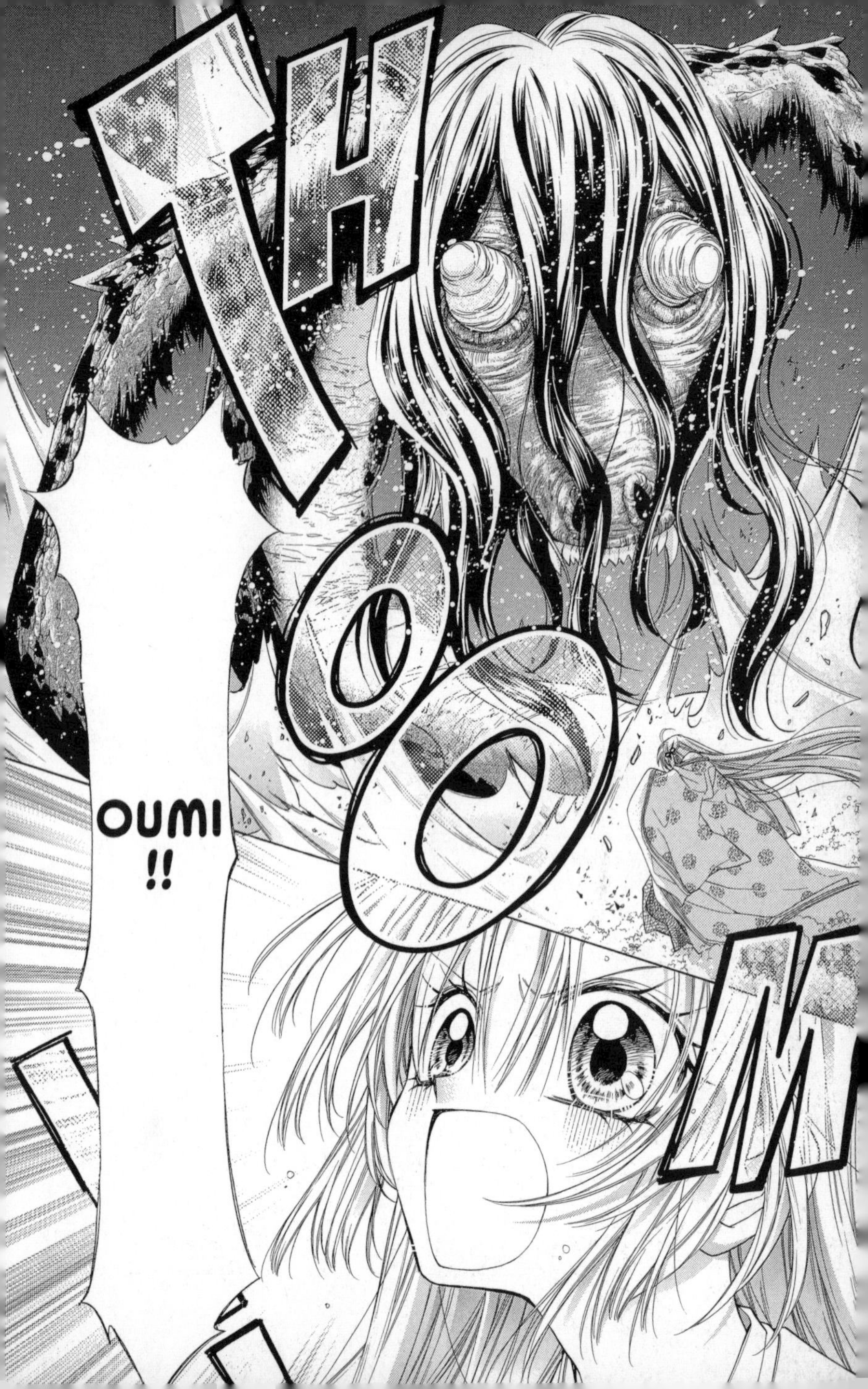
THOOOM
OUMI
!!

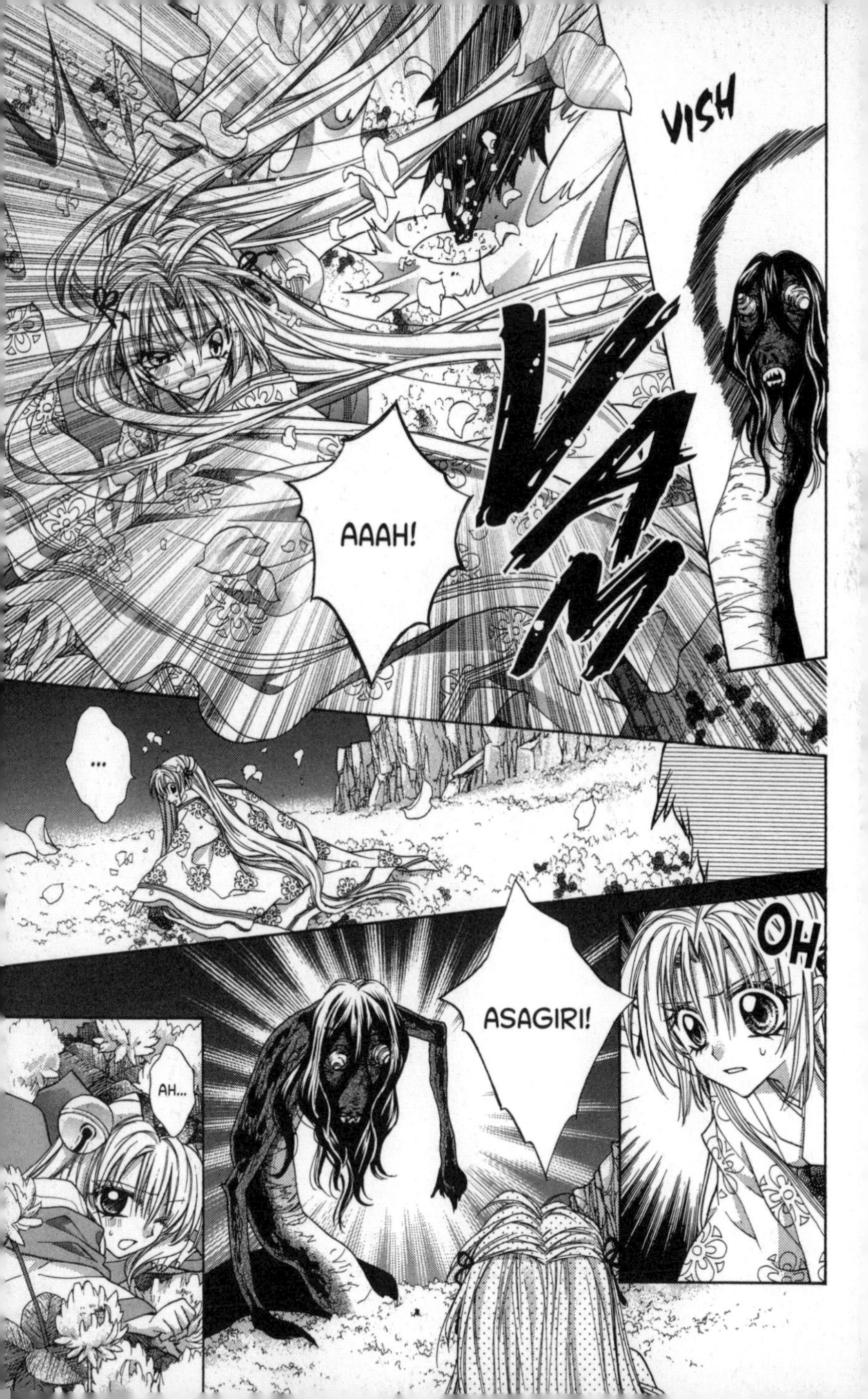
VISH
AAAH!
...
OH
ASAGIRI!
AH...

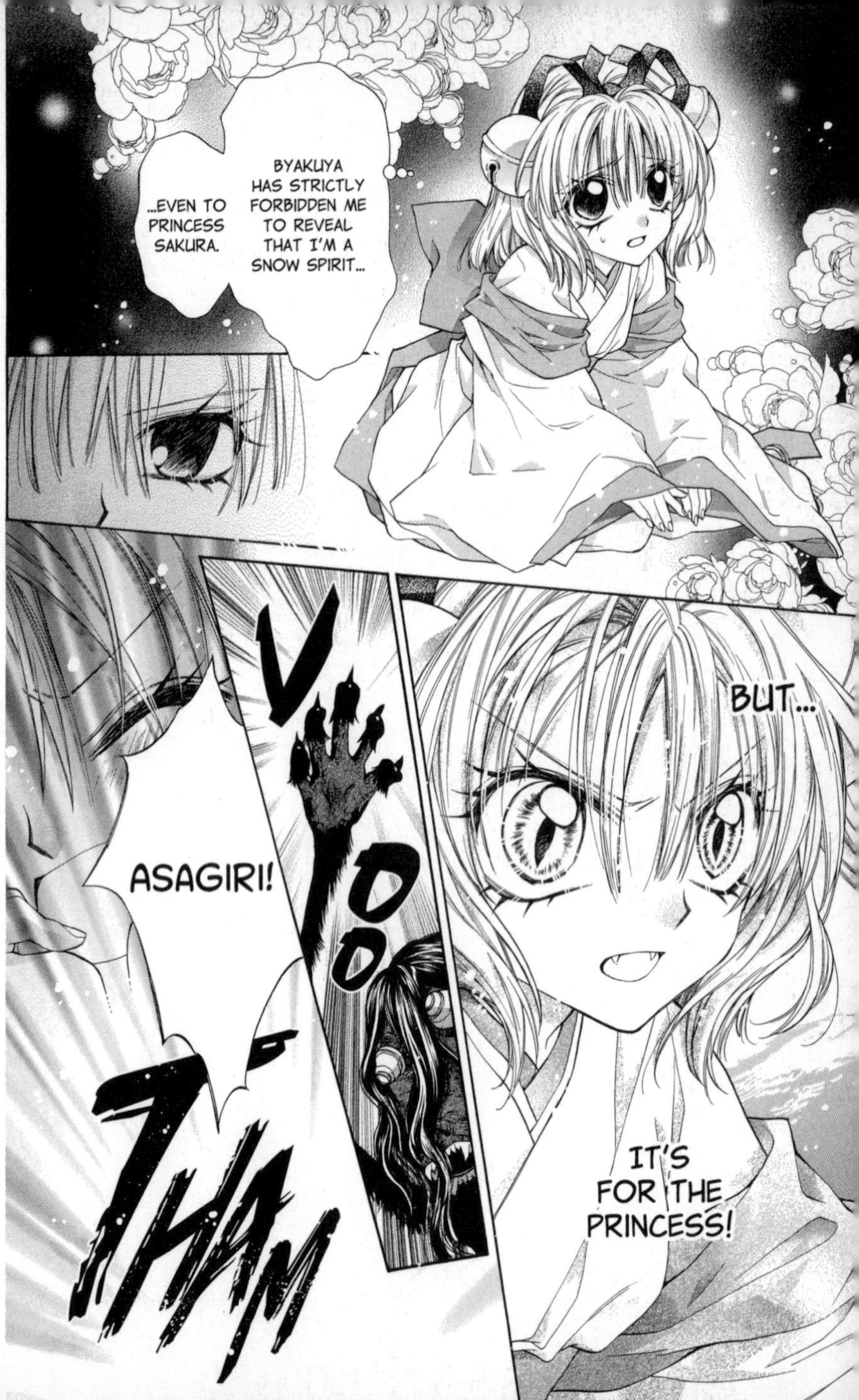
BYAKUYA HAS STRICTLY FORBIDDEN ME TO REVEAL THAT I'M A SNOW SPIRIT...
...EVEN TO PRINCESS SAKURA.
BUT...
IT'S FOR THE PRINCESS!
ASAGIRI!

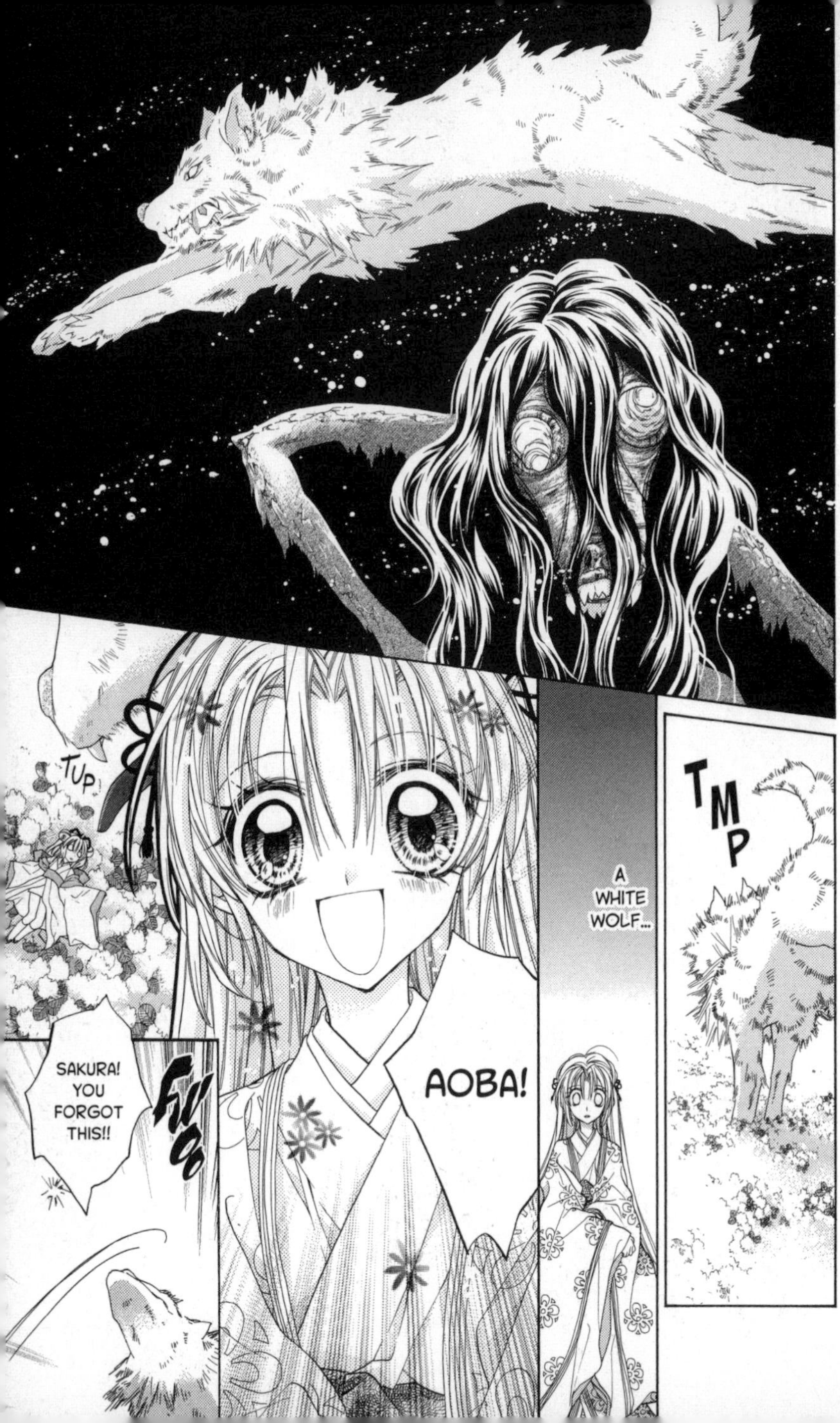
TMP
A WHITE WOLF...
AOBA!
TUP
SAKURA! YOU FORGOT THIS!!

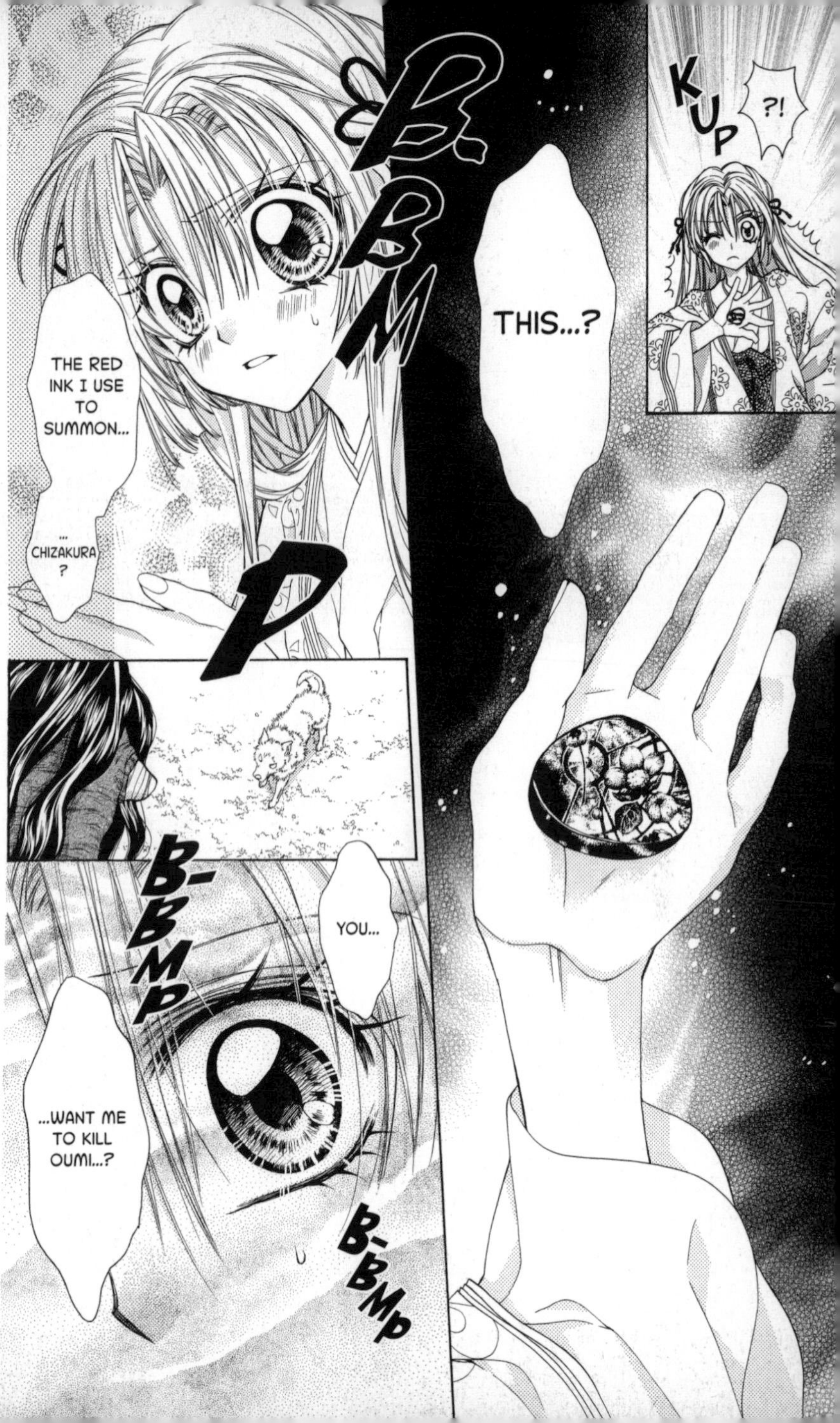
KUP
?!
THIS...?
B-BBMP
THE RED INK I USE TO SUMMON...
...CHIZAKURA?
B-BBMP
YOU...
...WANT ME TO KILL OUMI...?
B-BMP

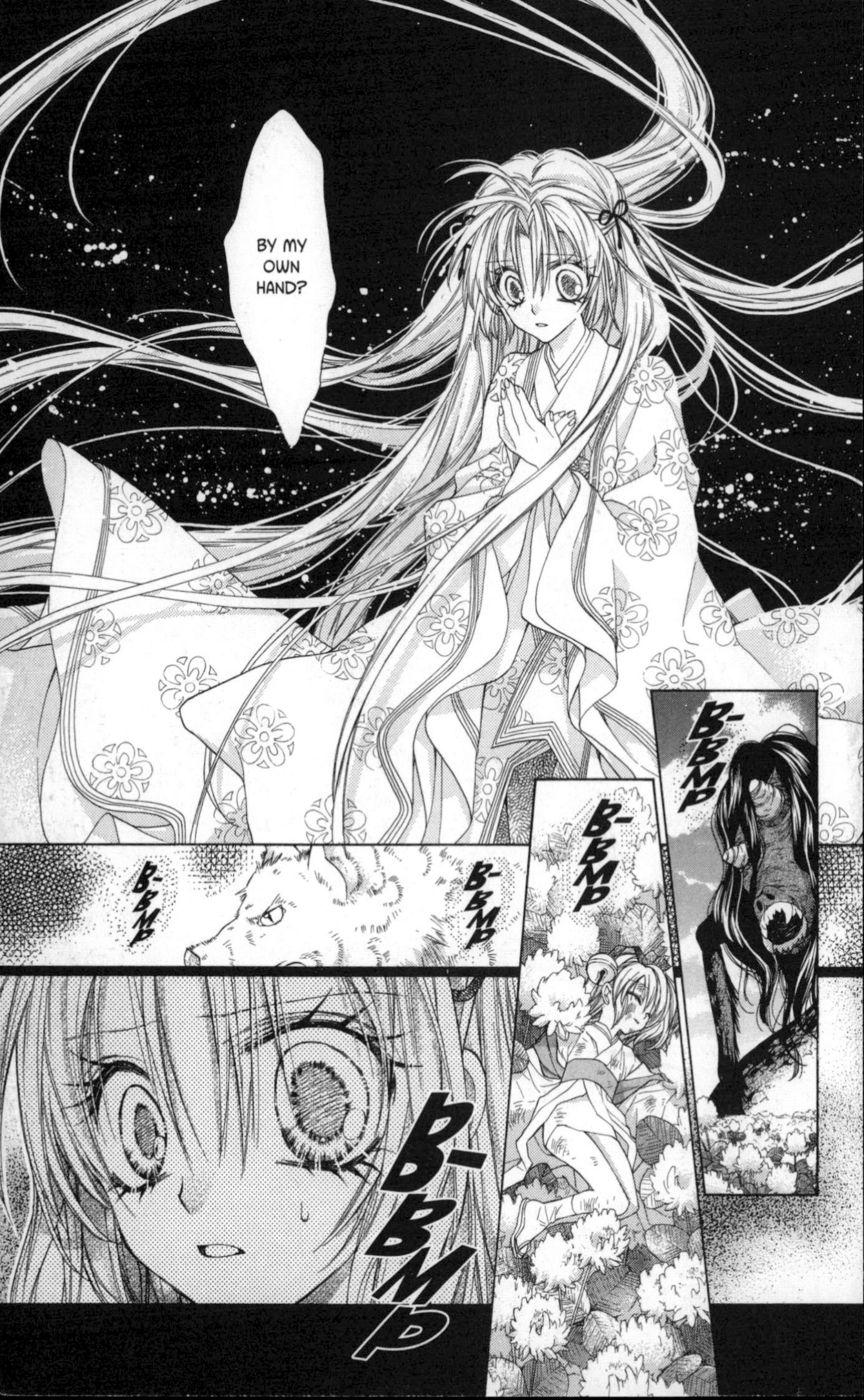

BY MY OWN HAND?
B-BBMP
B-BBMP
B-BMP
B-BMP
B-BBMP

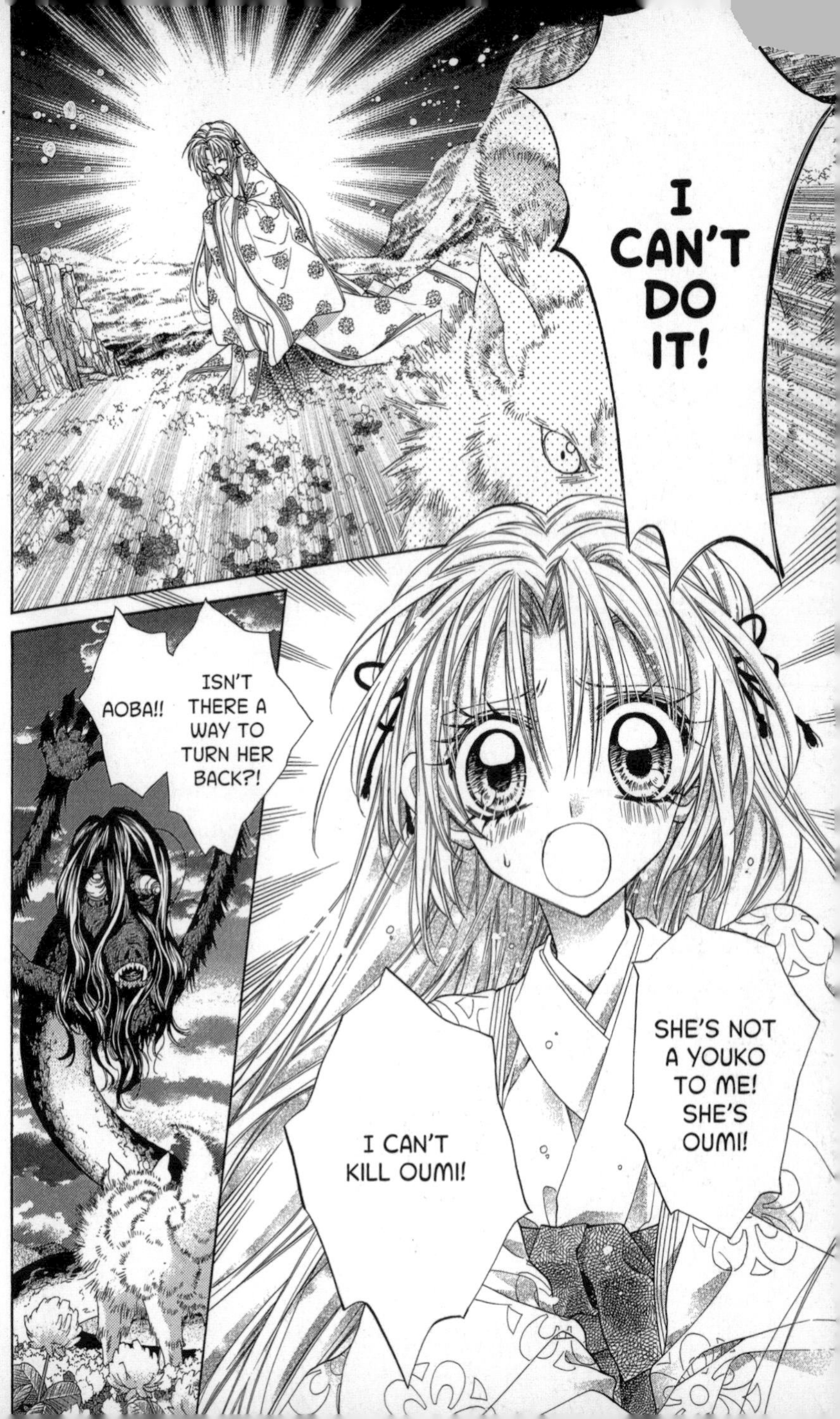
I CAN'T DO IT!
SHE'S NOT A YOUKO TO ME! SHE'S OUMI!
I CAN'T KILL OUMI!
AOBA!! ISN'T THERE A WAY TO TURN HER BACK?!

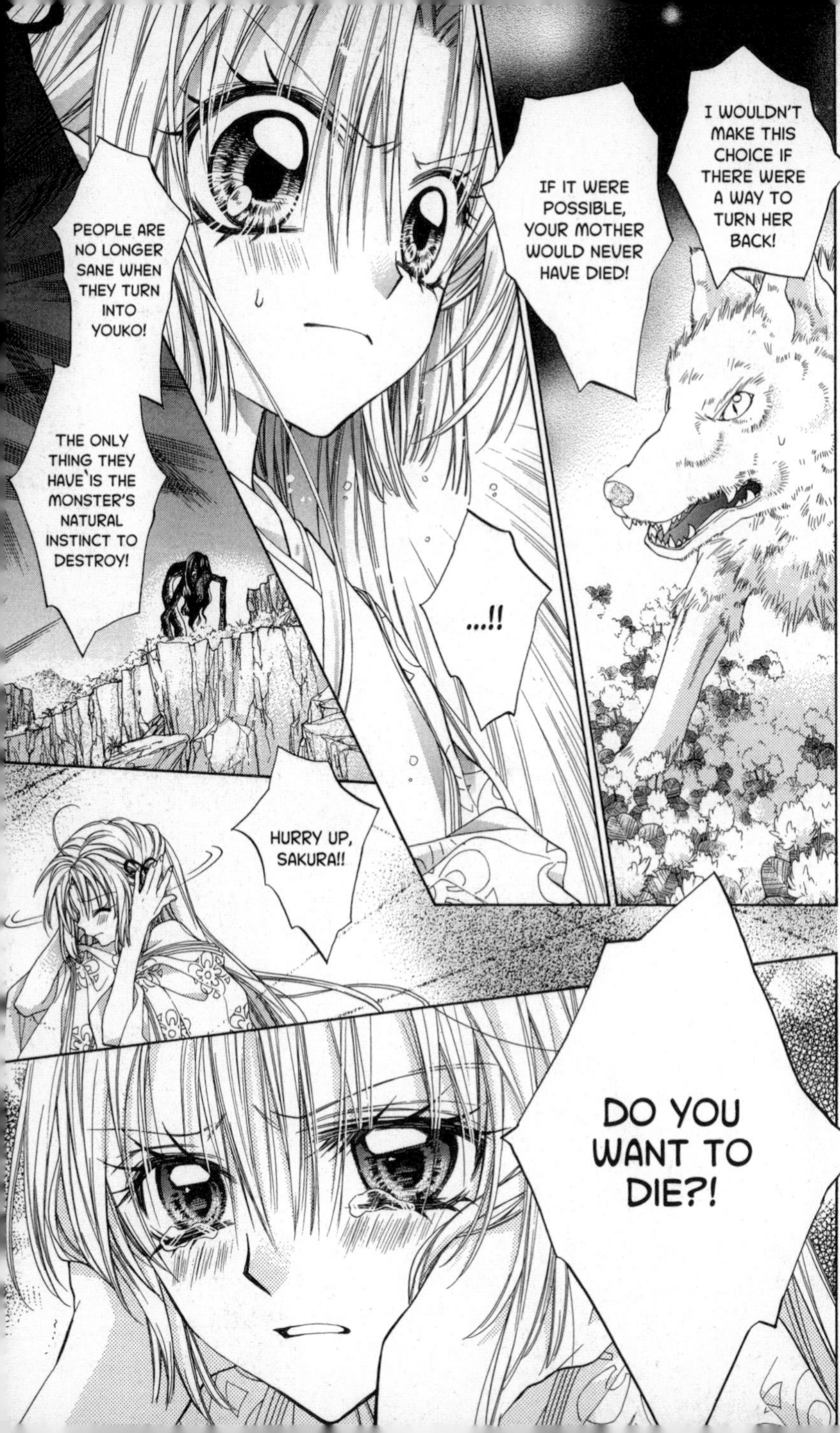
I WOULDN'T MAKE THIS CHOICE IF THERE WERE A WAY TO TURN HER BACK!
IF IT WERE POSSIBLE, YOUR MOTHER WOULD NEVER HAVE DIED!
...!!
PEOPLE ARE NO LONGER SANE WHEN THEY TURN INTO YOUKO!
THE ONLY THING THEY HAVE IS THE MONSTER'S NATURAL INSTINCT TO DESTROY!
HURRY UP, SAKURA!!
DO YOU WANT TO DIE?!

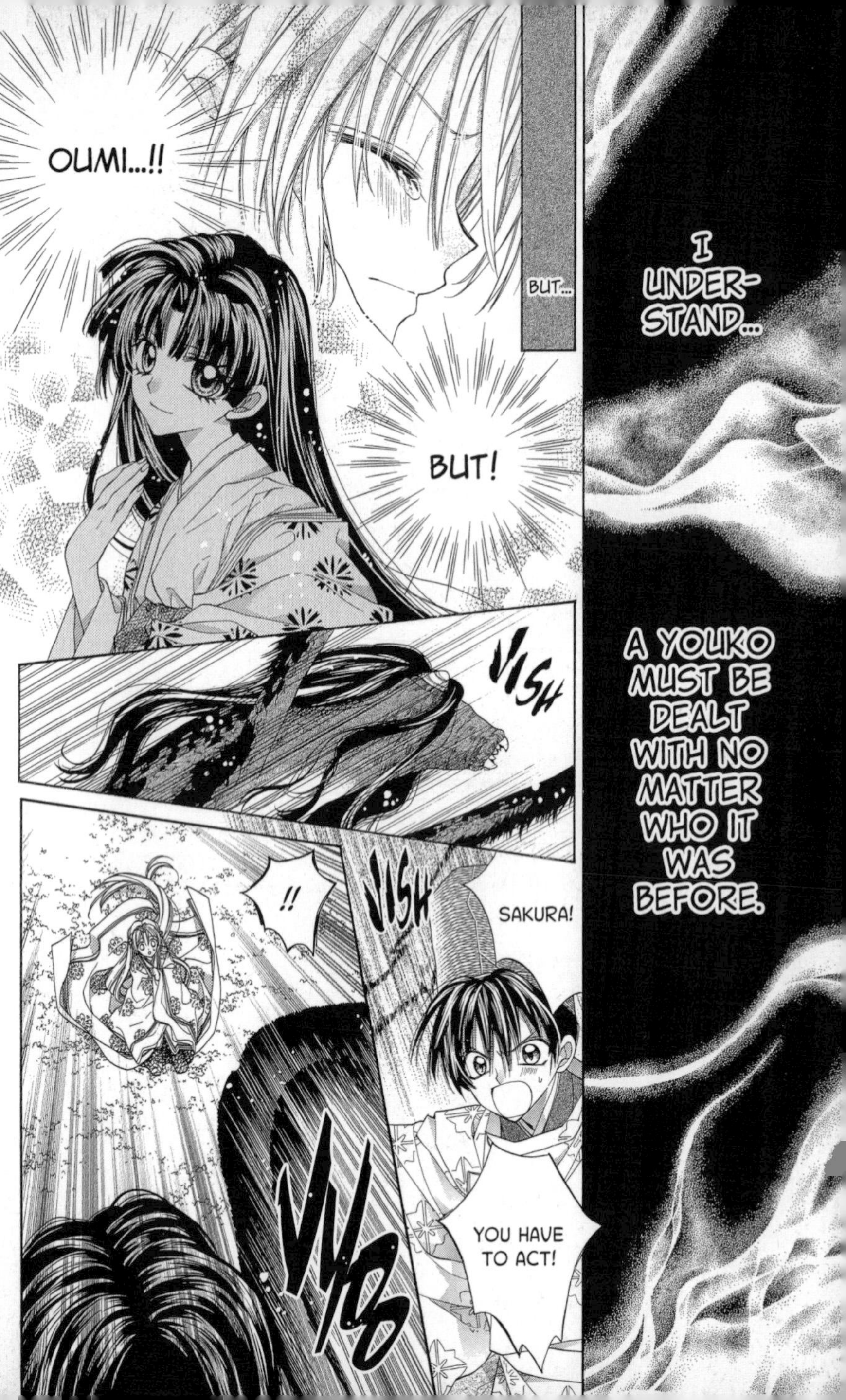
I UNDER-STAND...
A YOUKO MUST BE DEALT WITH NO MATTER WHO IT WAS BEFORE.
BUT...
OUMI...!!
BUT!
VISH
VISH
SAKURA!
YOU HAVE TO ACT!
!!

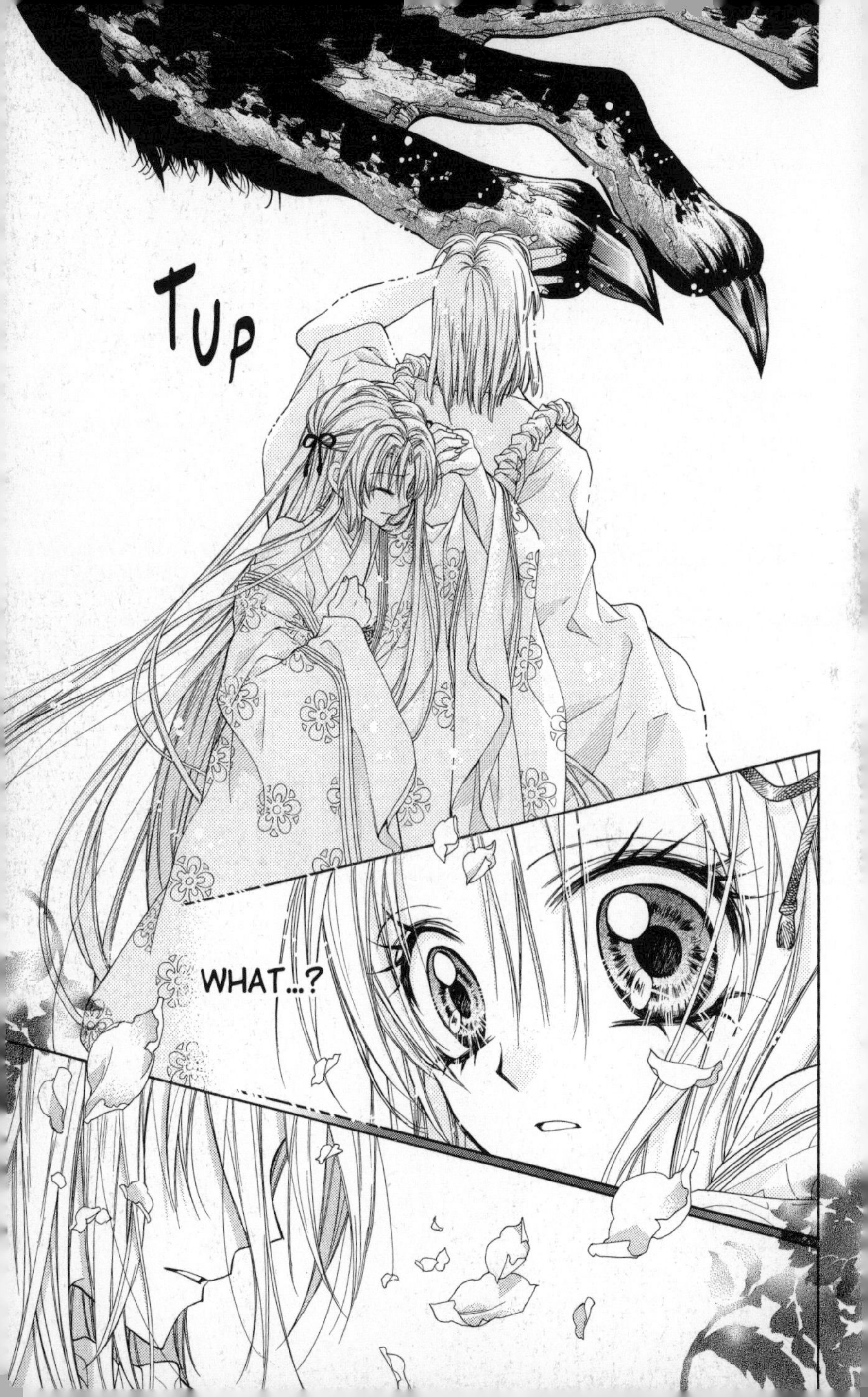
TUP
WHAT...?

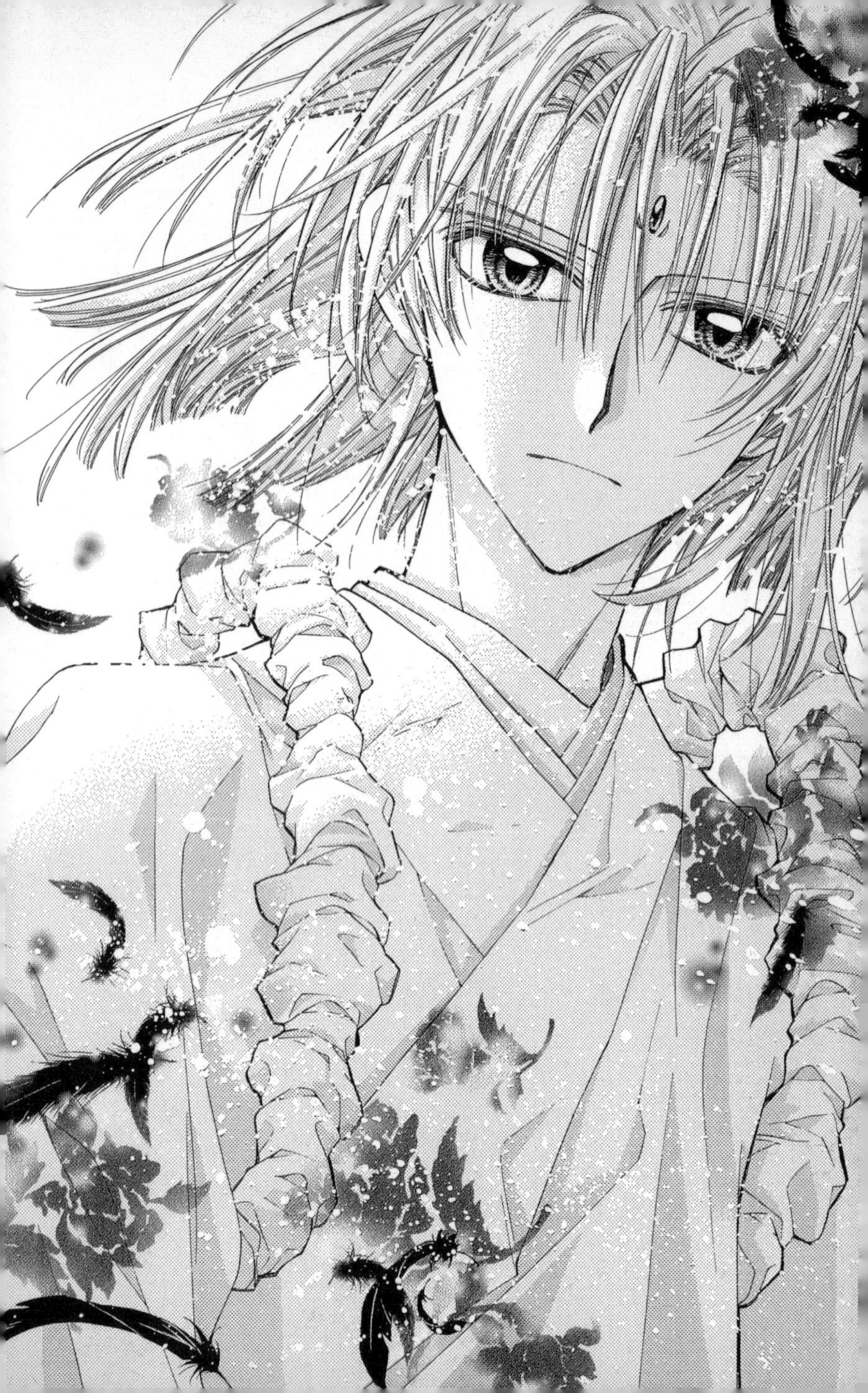

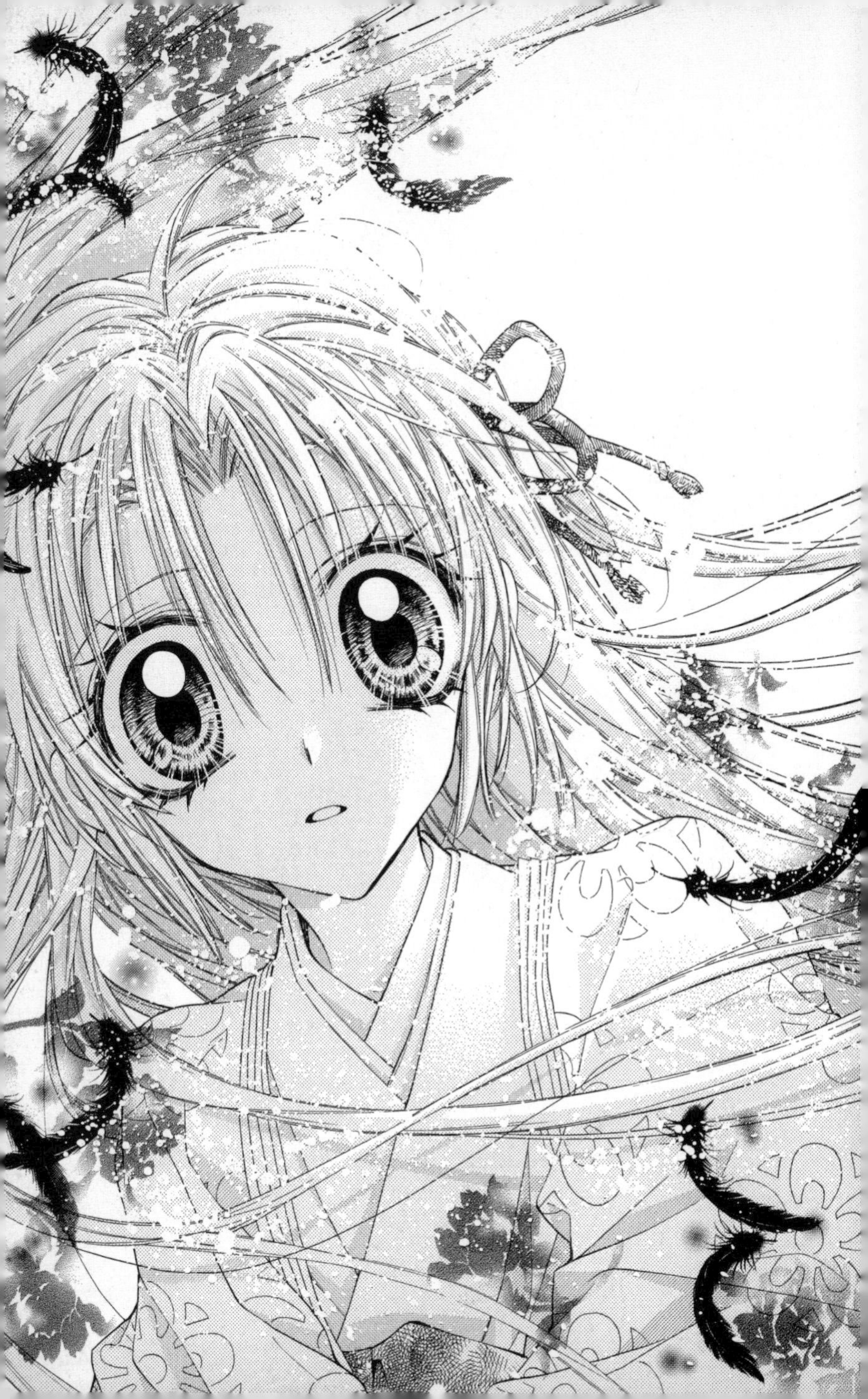

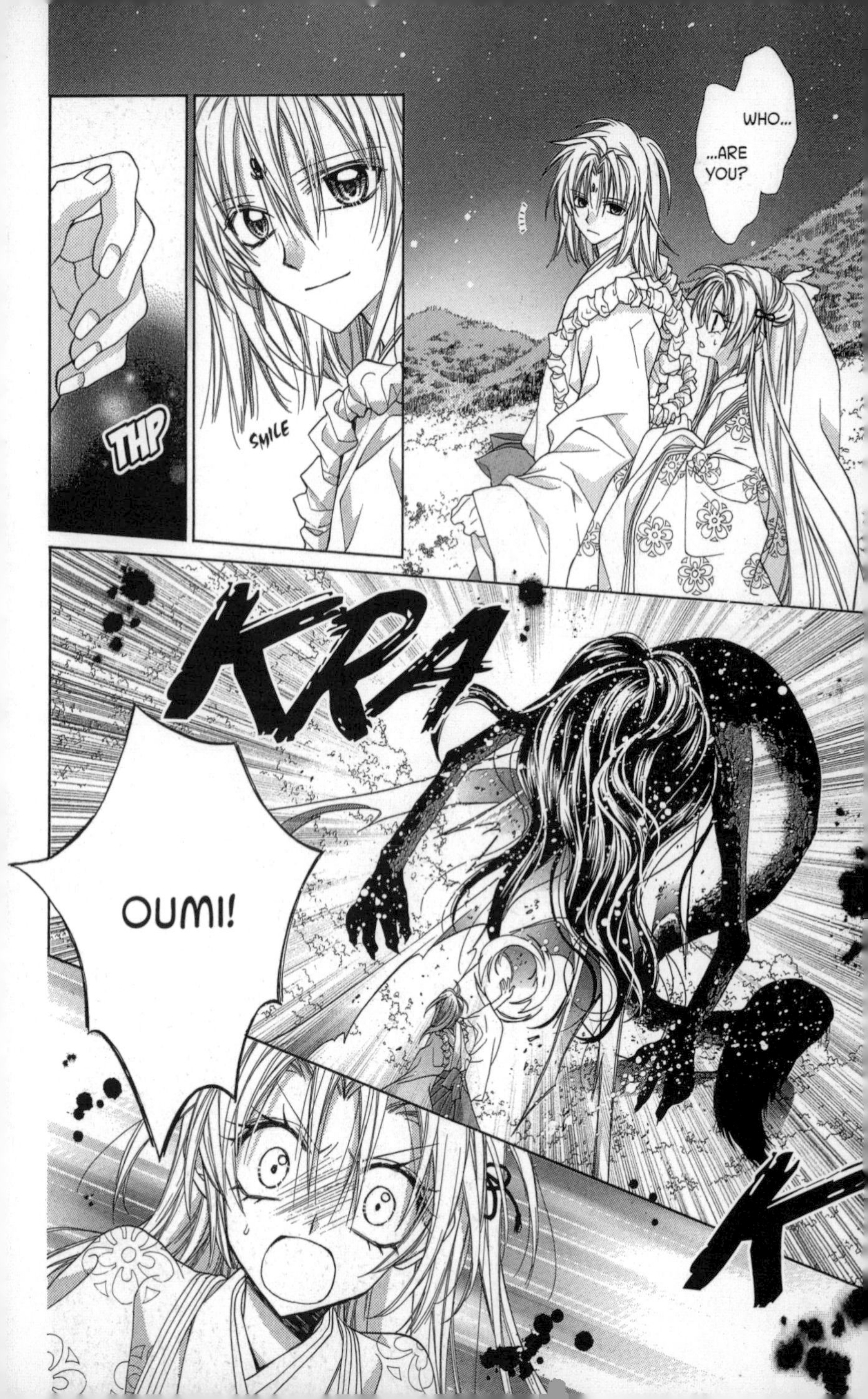
WHO...
...ARE YOU?
SMILE
THP
KRA
OUMI!
K

GOODBYE

I talked about various things in this volume, but how did you like it?! I'm going to attend an autograph session at an event in Germany again in July, so I hope to write about that in volume 3.

Special Thanks

✿ Nakame ✿

Izhizuka-san ✿ Mizuguchi-san
Nakazawa-san ✿ Ueda-san
Kurachi-san ✿ Saori
Yuki-chan ✿ Chihiron
Konako

✿ Ammonite Ltd.
✿ Shueisha, Ribon Editorial Department
Editor O-sama

Designer: Kawatani-san
✿
Soubisha

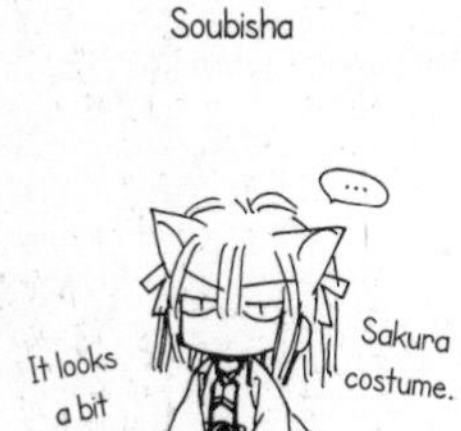

...
Sakura costume.
It looks a bit strange.

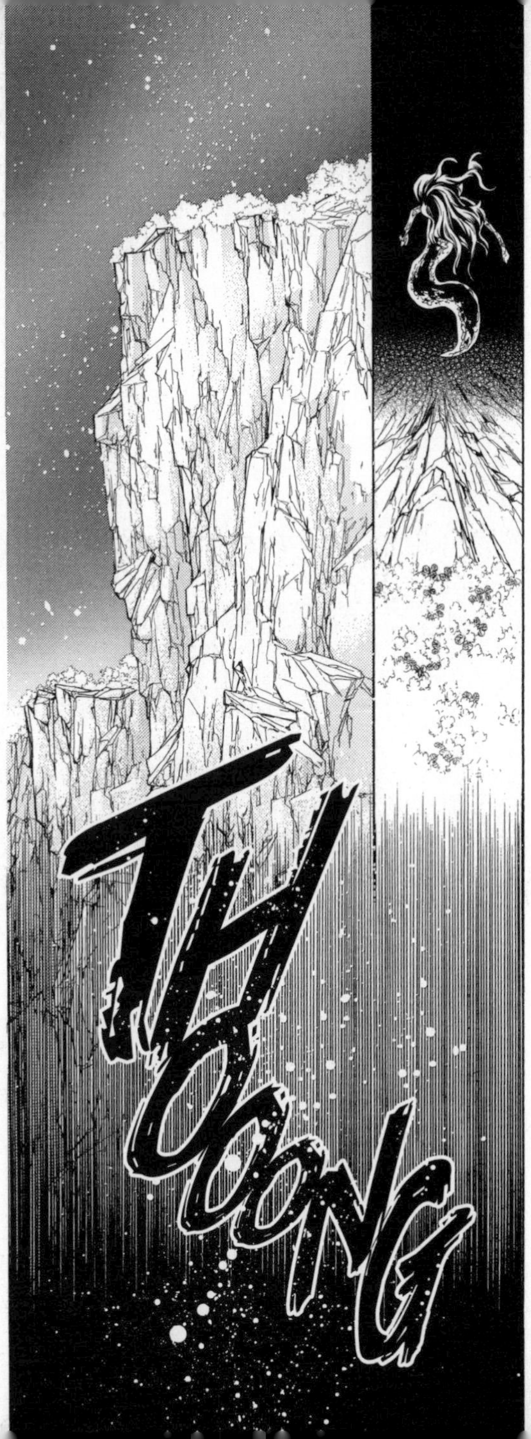

THOOONG

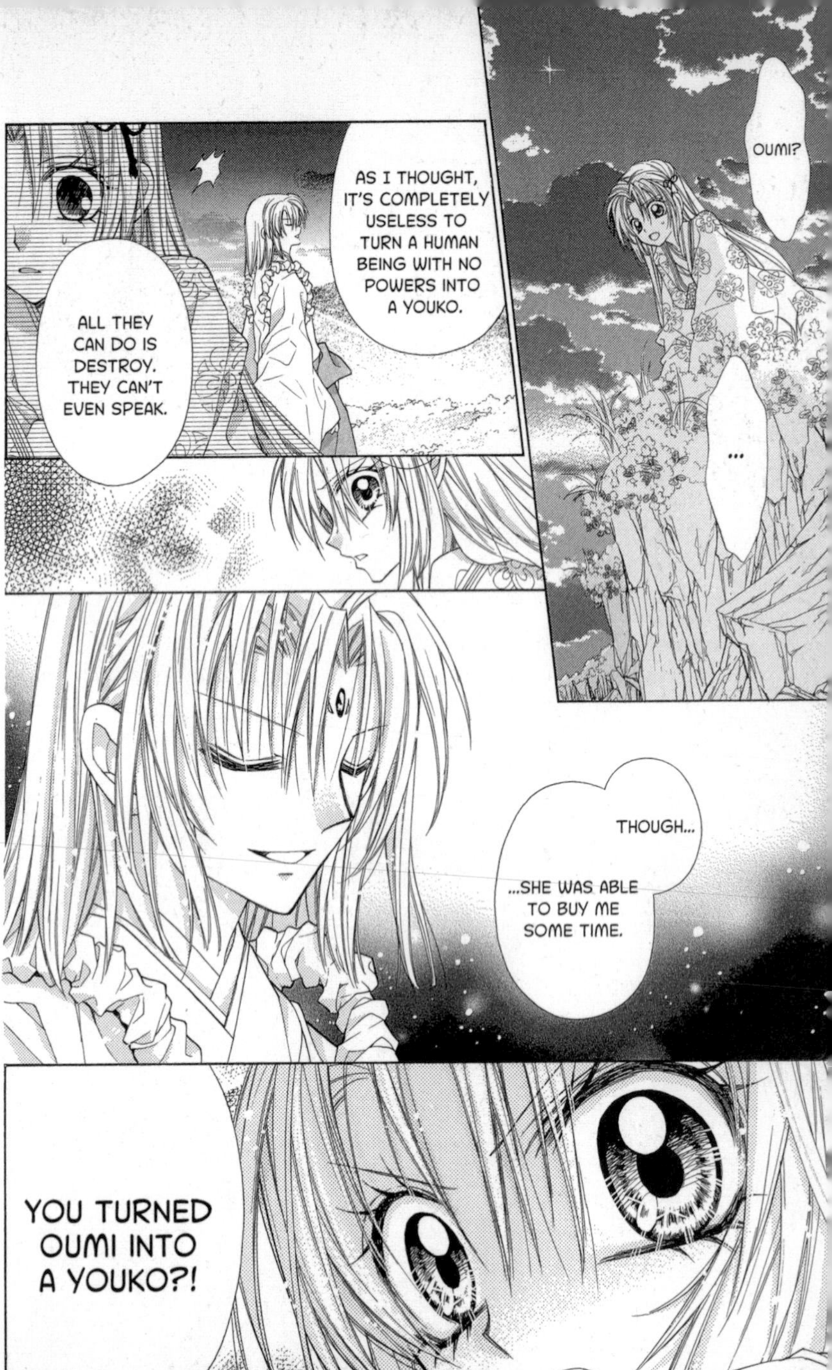
OUMI?
...
AS I THOUGHT, IT'S COMPLETELY USELESS TO TURN A HUMAN BEING WITH NO POWERS INTO A YOUKO.
ALL THEY CAN DO IS DESTROY. THEY CAN'T EVEN SPEAK.
THOUGH...
...SHE WAS ABLE TO BUY ME SOME TIME.
YOU TURNED OUMI INTO A YOUKO?!

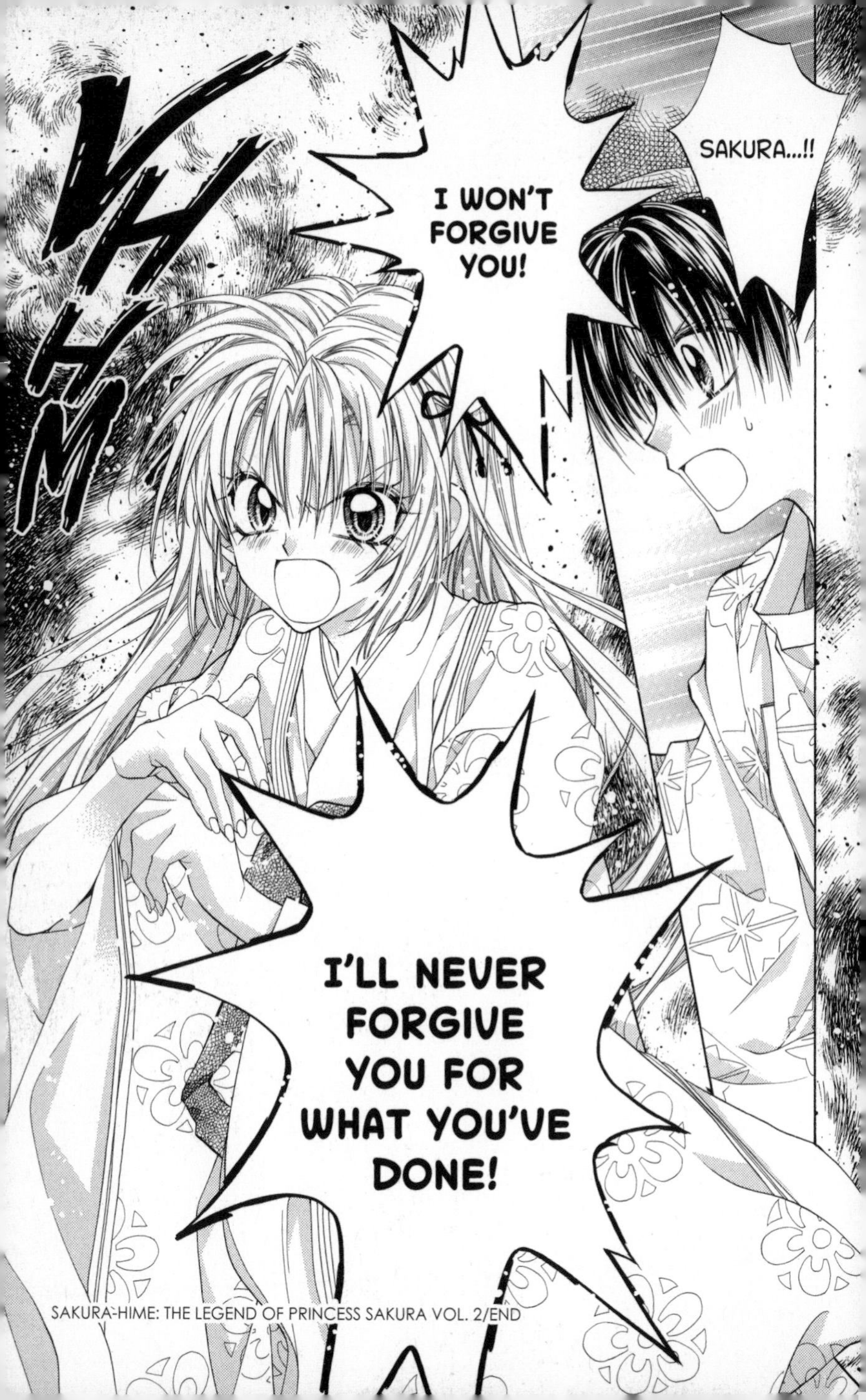
SAKURA...!!
I WON'T FORGIVE YOU!
I'LL NEVER FORGIVE YOU FOR WHAT YOU'VE DONE!

SAKURA-HIME: THE LEGEND OF PRINCESS SAKURA VOL. 2/END

ARINA TANEMURA

This is the Uji story arc (which includes the Aoba arc). There are so many things I have to draw that it's starting to upset my schedule. Also, someone I hadn't planned on is starting to take a very active role in the story. It is His Highness Fujimurasaki, the Togu. Fujimurasaki is a character made up out of the leftovers from my ideas for Aoba and Enju, whom I had to simplify. His soul symbol is something very important to me. I would like to reveal it soon, but I have a feeling that my schedule will continue to be upset...

Arina Tanemura began her manga career in 1996 when her short stories debuted in *Ribon* magazine. She gained fame with the 1997 publication of *I•O•N*, and ever since her debut Tanemura has been a major force in shojo manga with popular series *Kamikaze Kaito Jeanne*, *Time Stranger Kyoko*, *Full Moon*, and *The Gentlemen's Alliance †*. Both *Kamikaze Kaito Jeanne* and *Full Moon* have been adapted into animated TV series.

Sakura Hime: The Legend of Princess Sakura
Volume 2
Shojo Beat Edition

STORY AND ART BY
Arina Tanemura

Translation & Adaptation/Tetsuichiro Miyaki
Touch-up Art & Lettering/Inori Fukuda Trant
Design/Sam Elzway
Editor/Nancy Thistlethwaite

SAKURA-HIME KADEN © 2008 by Arina Tanemura
All rights reserved.
First published in Japan in 2008 by SHUEISHA Inc., Tokyo.
English translation rights arranged by SHUEISHA Inc.

The rights of the author(s) of the work(s) in this publication
to be so identified have been asserted in accordance with the
Copyright, Designs and Patents Act 1988. A CIP catalogue
record for this book is available from the British Library.

Printed in the U.S.A.

Published by VIZ Media, LLC
P.O. Box 77010
San Francisco, CA 94107

10 9 8 7 6 5 4 3
First printing, June 2011
Third printing, October 2012

www.shojobeat.com   www.viz.com

kimi ni todoke
From Me to You
Karuho Shiina

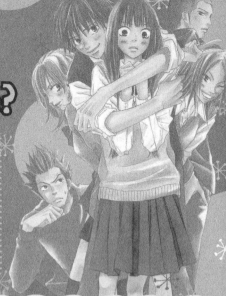

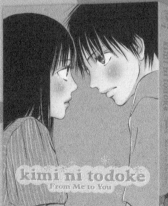

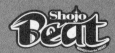

WELCOME to Imperial Academy: a private school where trying to become SUPERIOR can make you feel INFERIOR!

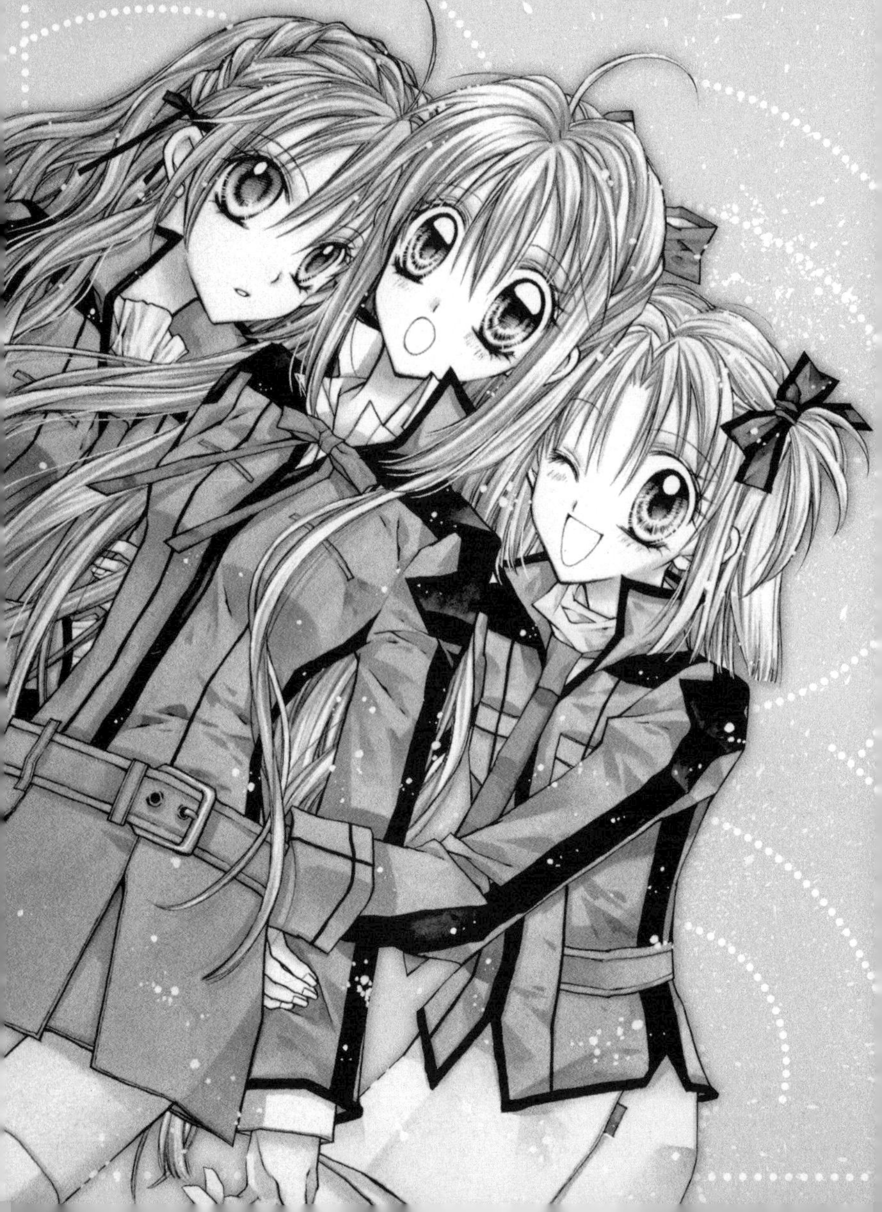

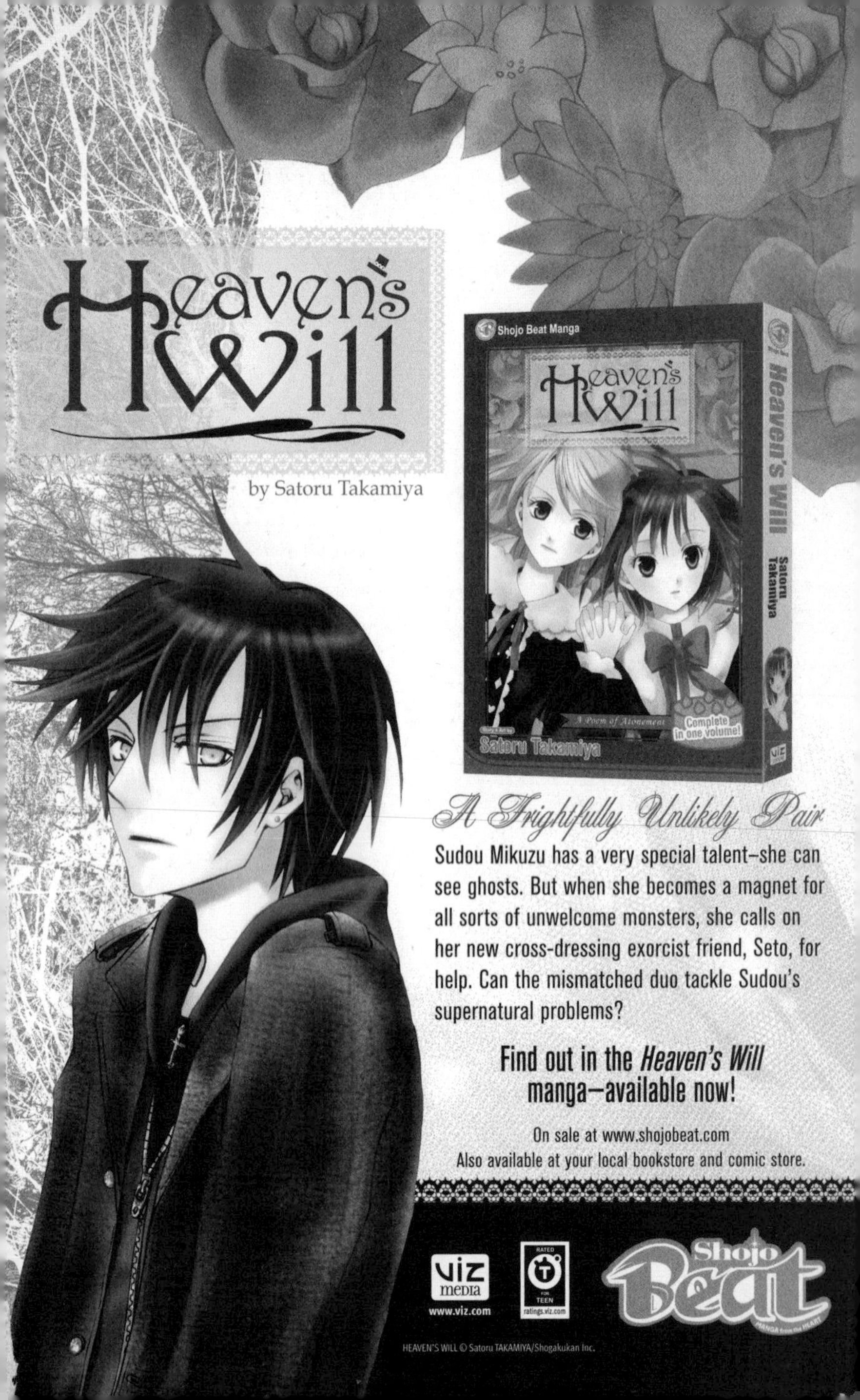
Heaven's Will
by Satoru Takamiya
Shojo Beat Manga
Heaven's Will
Heaven's Will
Satoru Takamiya
A Poem of Atonement
Complete in one volume!
Satoru Takamiya
A Frightfully Unlikely Pair
Sudou Mikuzu has a very special talent–she can see ghosts. But when she becomes a magnet for all sorts of unwelcome monsters, she calls on her new cross-dressing exorcist friend, Seto, for help. Can the mismatched duo tackle Sudou's supernatural problems?
Find out in the *Heaven's Will* manga—available now!
On sale at www.shojobeat.com
Also available at your local bookstore and comic store.
viz media
www.viz.com
RATED T FOR TEEN
ratings.viz.com
Shojo Beat
HEAVEN'S WILL © Satoru TAKAMIYA/Shogakukan Inc.

SURPRISE!

You may be reading the wrong way!

It's true: In keeping with the original Japanese comic format, this book reads from right to left—so action, sound effects, and word balloons are completely reversed. This preserves the orientation of the original artwork—plus, it's fun! Check out the diagram shown here to get the hang of things, and then turn to the other side of the book to get started!

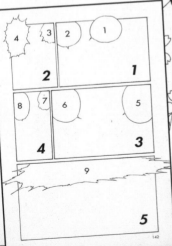

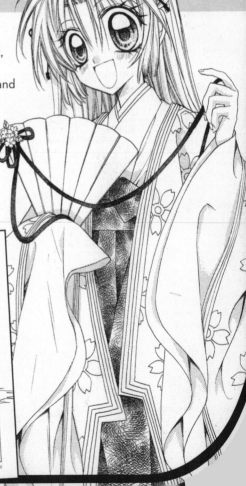